Knowledge

The theory of knowledge, or epistemology, is often regarded as a dry topic that bears little relation to actual knowledge practices. This book aims to correct this by showing the roots, developments and prospects of modern epistemology from its beginnings in the nineteenth century to the present day.

Contemporary epistemology is shown to draw on the insights of a wide range of disciplines. Philosophy has always been concerned with how we balance aspiration, belief, experience and knowledge. Science has come to represent a very highly privileged knowledge, whilst recent insights from psychology and sociology have questioned how knowledge is acquired and structured. Meanwhile, theology has shaped the quest for knowledge in ways which have only relatively recently become separate from more secular knowledge systems.

The book offers readers a very broad, cross-disciplinary, and historically-informed assessment of the ways in which humanity has, and continues to, pursue, question, contest, expand and shape knowledge.

Steve Fuller is Auguste Comte Professor of Social Epistemology at the University of Warwick. He is the author of twenty books, including *The Knowledge Book* and *Science*.

Knowledge

The philosophical quest in history

Steve Fuller

LONDON AND NEW YORK

First published 2015
by Routledge
2 Park Square, Milton Park, Abingdon, Oxon OX14 4RN

and by Routledge
711 Third Avenue, New York, NY 10017

Routledge is an imprint of the Taylor & Francis Group, an informa business

© 2015 Steve Fuller

The right of Steve Fuller to be identified as the author of this work has been asserted in accordance with sections 77 and 78 of the Copyright, Designs and Patents Act 1988.

All rights reserved. No part of this book may be reprinted or reproduced or utilized in any form or by any electronic, mechanical, or other means, now known or hereafter invented, including photocopying and recording, or in any information storage or retrieval system, without permission in writing from the publishers.

Trademark notice: Product or corporate names may be trademarks or registered trademarks, and are used only for identification and explanation without intent to infringe.

British Library Cataloguing in Publication Data
A catalogue record for this book is available from the British Library.

Library of Congress Cataloging-in-Publication Data
A catalog record has been applied for.

ISBN: 978-1-84465-817-6 (hbk)
ISBN: 978-1-84465-818-3 (pbk)

Typeset in Gill Sans
by Cenveo Publisher Services

Printed and bound in the United States of America by Edwards Brothers Malloy
on sustainably sourced paper.

Contents

List of tables	*vii*
Acknowledgements	*viii*

Introduction: is there a problem *of* or *with* knowledge?   1

1   Epistemology as cognitive economics   19

Social epistemology as the art of cognitive management, 19 ·
Two kinds of cognitive economy for social epistemology, 22 ·
The history of epistemology as a struggle over cognitive
economy, 25 · The problem of the economic use of knowledge
already produced, 29 · Why did our ancestors seem to know
so much more than we know now?, 34 · Projecting the future
of social epistemology: the proactionary imperative, 38

2   Epistemology as divine psychology   41

The divine origins of intellectual life, 41 · Secularizing the
sacred mind: the centrality of theodicy, 46 · Theism by other
means: sociology's secular problematic, 54 · Why naturalism
is too conservative to explain science, 59 · David Hume:
naturalist philosopher of diminished expectations, 63 · The
need for theism to explain science, 69 · The awkwardness of
natural theology in the secular world, 74 · Intelligent design: a
"Left Creationist" affirmation of science, 86 · Darwinism's
own anti-humanist theodicy, 90 · Recap: the Creationist
Left's challenge to the science–religion nexus, 96

3   Epistemology as psychology of science   102

In the beginning the psychologist was the self-conscious
scientist, 102 · The genealogy of validity: from the bank to

vi *Contents*

the lab bench, 106 · The need for psychology of science to
improve the conduct of science, 117 · Conclusion: how
scientific creativity went from being abundant to scarce, 121

4   Epistemology as philosophy of science   130

By misunderstanding Kuhn, we misunderstand our own
times, 130 · Kuhn's legacy of prescriptive/descriptive
confusion, 134 · Popper's (pre-)challenge to Kuhn and Kuhn's
anti-rationalist response, 141 · Kuhn's contemporary legacy:
the naturalization of consensus in science, 149 · The problem
of positioning Popper on his own terms, 154 · The key to
Popper: the psychologist who never really left the lab, 161 ·
The problem of assessing Popper's philosophical fortunes, 166

5   Epistemology as sociology of science   169

In search of the "will to science": from religious inspiration
to remunerated research, 169 · Science and expertise:
natural bedfellows or mortal enemies?, 177 · Expertise as site
for normative recession in analytic social epistemology, 181 ·
Expertise as site for normative recession in science and
technology studies, 187 · Learning from the past to redeem a
normatively "fuller" social epistemology, 192 · The challenge
ahead: the legacies of Kuhn and Latour as obstacles, 202

6   Epistemology as counterfactual historiography   210

The complementarity of freedom and determinism in the
modern world-view, 210 · Freedom and determinism as a
problem of historical perspective, 220 · Possible worlds as the
micro-structure of freedom and determinism, 232 · The
normative stakes of a flexibly revisable history, 242 · Giving
the past back its future: the ultimate test of "giving voice", 250

Conclusion: redeeming epistemology from the postmodern
condition   262

Bibliography   *280*
Index   *301*

Tables

1	Social epistemology as (1) epistemology and (2) sociology.	6
2	The existential horizons of social epistemology.	15
3	The two philosophical traditions before cognitive economics.	26
4	The two philosophical traditions after cognitive economics.	29
5	The realm of the knowable.	35
6	Philosophy of science or for science?	145
7	The two modern world-views.	211
8	The two modal logics of history.	225
9	The epistemic rudiments of time travel.	228

Acknowledgements

I must acknowledge the support of those who over the past fifteen years have provided the conditions and criticism necessary to develop the arguments in these pages: Elisabeth Arweck, Babette Babich, Jesus Zamora Bonilla, James Robert Brown, Jim Collier, Manuel Crespo, Jean-Pierre Dupuy, Mark Erickson, Greg Feist, Bob Frodeman, Tom Glick, Jim Good, Michael Gorman, Mathew Guest, Morteza Hashemi Madani, Ian Jarvie, Byron Kaldis, Ilya Kasavin, Noretta Koertge, Veronika Lipinska, Juan Vicente Mayoral, Martin Medhurst, Jaume Navarro, Greg Radick, Paul Roth, Raphael Sassower, Sergio Sismondo, Nick Turnbull, Stephen Turner, Immanuel Wallerstein. I must also thank my long-suffering editor Tristan Palmer at Acumen. This book is dedicated to Emilie Whitaker, someone whose generosity of mind and spirit can merely be gestured at in a work such as this.

I would like to acknowledge the Institute of Philosophy (Department of Social Epistemology) of the Russian Academy of Sciences and the Russian Science Foundation for funding the project on "Social Philosophy of Science" (grant #14-18-02227) which was made in support of some of this work.

Introduction

Is there a problem *of* or *with* knowledge?

Humans are gods in the making. An actual deity may be guiding or otherwise enabling the process, but even if that turns out to be false, *Homo sapiens* has distinguished itself from other animals most remarkably by acting as if having been touched by the divine. As a result, *we live in the future perfect* – that is, the time when our ideas will have come to be realized. In this respect, it is telling that induction becomes a significant "problem of knowledge" only in the final quarter of the nineteenth century, once Thomas Henry Huxley popularizes David Hume as a precursor of Charles Darwin's view that we are animals conditioned by experience to believe that the future will be like the past. Before that time, only self-avowed "traditionalists", such as Bishop Richard Whately, would have accorded the past such strictly epistemic weight. And notwithstanding the continued popularity of the "problem of induction" in analytic philosophical circles, we have come to value the future over the past in quite radical ways – albeit resulting in enormous distress, including incredible violence to various groups of people at various times, as well as the rest of the natural world. And even if postmodernism has made it no longer fashionable to believe in the idea of progress, we still hold personal sacrifice in high esteem while pathologizing those who "discount the future too heavily", as the economists gingerly say. Compared with other animals, we seem to take our imaginative projections much more seriously than the evidence of experience would require – or even advise. Only an Abrahamic God could be sanguine about humanity's track record based on its having adopted such a mind-centred, future-oriented view of the world. Of course, theologians may be correct that this is simply because we are so much like the deity that "People of the Book" have envisaged – one in whose "image and likeness" we were created. After all, the Abrahamic deity creates through dictation, something to which humans aspire, be it understood as the imposition of will, delivery on a promise or, more recently, the execution of a programme.

Against this backdrop, "knowledge" is a troublesome concept: It draws attention to just how far short we still fall from divine perfection, even assuming that it is a reasonable aspiration. Thus, philosophers – in the

2   Introduction

modern period under the guise of *epistemology* – have dealt with knowledge forensically to distribute responsibility across a variety of agents for who said or did what when and where, not only to settle scores that might inform judicial verdicts but also to get everyone focused on the larger project of indefinitely expanding the sphere of human autonomy and thereby rendering humanity – either individually or collectively – more godlike.

Clearly, then, epistemology is not a branch of philosophy whose legitimacy should be taken for granted. Indeed, there are probably fewer problems *of* knowledge than *with* it. No sooner had the "theory of knowledge" become independent of general metaphysics in the second half of the nineteenth century than Marxists began to suspect the field of being the subtlest form of false consciousness. If classical political economy was the means by which the capitalist class disguised its collective will behind "laws of nature", classical epistemology was the means by which everyone else came to be convinced that "truth" was conformity to laws of nature beyond their control rather than something to be achieved through their own collective will. The few remaining Marxists – typically travelling under the banner of "critical theory" – would probably be even less impressed with the state of epistemology today, given its preoccupation with aligning our minds with some pre-existent reality, as if thinking were no more than that elaborate form of template matching that is grandiosely called the "correspondence theory of truth". In the "analytic" school of philosophy – whose prominence tracks the ascent of English as the world-historic language in the twentieth century – this intuition is enshrined in the definition of knowledge still taught in introductory epistemology classes: "Knowledge = Justified True Belief" (plus some magic X Factor that overcomes counterexamples to the definition). I have been contesting this definition throughout my career (Fuller and Collier 2004: ch. 3).

In the last fifty years, largely under the influence of the US logician W. V. O. Quine (1969), a "naturalistic" version of this sort of epistemology has flourished that increasingly nods in the direction of Darwin. That should come as little surprise, since Darwin's main evolutionary process of natural selection is also something to which organisms need to conform in order to ensure their species survival. Naturalistic epistemology is distinctive in that, *à la* natural selection, it does not require that knowers even know why their beliefs are true (when they are), just as long as those beliefs have been the result of reliable processes, as judged by, say, a cognitive scientist, neuroscientist or behavioural geneticist. Thus, conformity to reality is operationalized as propensity to survival, in which the knower's understanding – let alone consent – is an optional extra. Daniel Dennett (1995) may be counted as a contemporary champion of this view. Some have argued that this version of "epistemology naturalized", which removes any sense of subjectivity from the process of knowing, is better suited for androids than human beings (Alston 2005).

The previous two paragraphs suggest that the most irksome feature of "epistemology" as it exists today is its tendency to reduce the possession of knowledge to the capacity for deference to a rather anonymous but ultimate authority called "reality" – or reality's authorized mouthpieces, whom we shall periodically encounter in this book under the rubric of "experts". Such a deferential attitude towards knowledge may explain why analytic philosophers have been drawn to the idea that inferences need to be "licensed", as if reality were some early modern European absolute monarch who dispensed trading rights to worthy merchants. Thus, notwithstanding the lip service that professional epistemologists continue to pay Kant, knowing appears to be less about the "anticipation of experience" than playing catch-up with that overbearing "reality". The difference is subtle but significant. For all his caution and caveats, Kant saw knowledge as a constructive process that can be best understood – albeit not justified – in terms of humanity's partaking in the creative capacity of God, in whose image and likeness the Judaeo-Christian tradition says we are made.

The depth of impression that this Biblical idea has left in the modern era is easily underestimated because of the secular guises in which it normally appears: *the social contract, the method of hypothesis, the cult of artistic genius*. In all these cases, one literally knows by doing, more specifically by creating worlds in one's mind to which one's actions are then normatively bound, for better or worse, perhaps to the point of self-identification, if not self-destruction: I become the citizen who is willing to die for my country, I become the scientist who stakes my reputation on a theory, I become the artist who deposits all that I value into the production of an artefact. In each case, I come to know who I am by doing as I do. St Augustine, following St Paul's and St John's example of assimilating Stoic ideas into the Christian message, invented a mental power to account for humanity's experience of these godlike moments: *the will*.

On the basis of this Christian heritage, as filtered by Kant, it is easy to see how the general field of metaphysics came to be subdivided into fields called "ontology" and "epistemology", the former concerned with the order of being and the latter the order of knowing. The fundamental metaphysical question then became whether being is already fixed before it comes to be known ("realism") or it is, in some sense, "constituted" in the process of being known ("antirealism", or "constructivism"). In terms of this question, which I believe is perspicuously posed, "epistemology" is better seen as a style of doing metaphysics as a whole, rather than a proper part of the metaphysical field. The epistemologist is compelled to consider the human as the creator of the reality that he or she experiences

4 Introduction

in a way that the self-avowed "metaphysician" is not. To be sure, this experienced reality may not be the "real reality", which in a world where rational human judgement lacks a divine signature (*pace* Descartes) opens the door to the sort of scepticism over which professional epistemologists lose sleep. But of course, even a metaphysician who is not prima facie disposed to the divinity of humanity can simulate the epistemologist's horizon by envisaging an entity – call it "human" – that not only conforms to reality but also somehow manages to understand reality as a whole and uses that as a basis for enhancing the world's overall value. Indeed, the twenty-first century's most persuasively progressive philosophy, transhumanism, originated in just this way (Fuller and Lipinska 2014: ch. 3).

The epistemologist's way of doing metaphysics, whereby knowledge lays down the tracks of our collective self-discovery (or self-invention), is of course familiar from Kant's most radical follower, Hegel – whose ideas of *praxis* were then concentrated by Marxism in the nineteenth century and then diluted by pragmatism in the twentieth. But as we shall see below, the idea of collective self-discovery also featured prominently in the context in which epistemology first emerged in the mid-nineteenth-century English-speaking world, namely, as the quest for "absolute knowledge". It anticipates the *social epistemology* perspective that has characterized my own work for the past quarter-century. Before resuming with the emergence of epistemology in the history of philosophy, I should say a bit about social epistemology and, more specifically, my belief that *all epistemology is always already social epistemology* – and that provides the *via regia* to metaphysics.

In simplest terms, social epistemology is the normative study of knowledge as a product of social organization. It is a cross-disciplinary nomad, equally at home in philosophy and policy (Fuller 1988). There is disagreement over whether it is meant to be a branch of epistemology or sociology, or something that transcends both of these disciplines. Consider three types of social epistemology that canvass these possibilities, followed by an extended discussion of the most ambitious form of social epistemology, which attempts to bridge the analytic-continental divide within contemporary philosophy, while providing an account of the social construction of intellectual progress. Thus, social epistemology may be regarded in one of three ways: (1) as a branch of epistemology; (2) a branch of sociology; or (3) a field that transcends the difference between (1) and (2). Let us take each in turn.

1 As a branch of epistemology, social epistemology asserts that an adequate grasp of the state of knowledge in society requires more than generalizing from what a single ideal (Cartesian) or average (Humean)

mind knows. It requires recognizing the distributed nature of knowledge, either emergent on specific forms of life (i.e. folkways) or divided according to some overarching rational plan (i.e. science). But in both cases, the whole knowledge system is very much more – and even other – than the sum of what individuals know. On the one hand, theories of rationality and the scientific method – perhaps most strikingly Karl Popper's falsificationism – operate as a corrective social norm to the cognitive liabilities of individuals; on the other, no collectively agreed scientific theory of the sort that might govern a Kuhnian paradigm is likely to be known entirely by anyone or equally well-known to everyone who claims adherence (Fuller 1993). In this respect, the fallacies of composition and division – two ways of confusing properties of a whole and its parts – mark the boundary of social epistemology (Fuller 1988: intro.).

2 As a branch of sociology, social epistemology asserts that social relations can be organized in terms of the differential, often hierarchical, access that a society's members have to a common reality (Durkheim 1961). Plato originally advanced a static version of this thesis in the *Republic*. There each level of human understanding – from the ideal to the base – corresponded to a stratum in a myth-based caste system. A more dynamic version, based on the stages of human intellectual progress, was advanced over 2000 years later by Auguste Comte in his positivist polity. In this context, earlier religious and metaphysical forms of epistemic authority served atavistic class-like functions in a science-led social order (Fuller 2006a: ch. 2). The general idea continues to fascinate philosophers, as it raises the prospect of non-violent, large-scale social control by deference to expertise, aka "division of cognitive labour" (Kitcher 1993). Indeed, such knowledge-based politics is arguably the most Machiavellian of all, as it delegates the application of force to individuals whose willed compliance is socially rewarded with their being assigned the title of "rational". The history of medicine probably provides the clearest trace through this issue (Latour 1988; cf. Fuller 2007b: ch. 3).

3 Finally, "social epistemology" may simply be a good contemporary name (another might be "cognitive science", especially in the broad sense of, say, Jerry Fodor) for epistemology's original project – put in Hegelian terms, to render knowledge "self-conscious". This point pertains to the English coinage of "epistemology" as a distinct branch of philosophy in the mid-nineteenth century concerned with the conditions under which things may be known, where the very idea of the "unknowable" was treated as an oxymoron symptomatic of a (presumably defunct) metaphysics in which humanity remained permanently alienated from the divine source of reality's intelligibility.

6 Introduction

To be sure, many – perhaps even most – things remained unknown but nothing was unknowable. Thus, alongside "epistemology" was christened "agnoiology", the field that was supposed to capture the sphere of remaining ignorance in the spirit of an achievable research programme (Ferrier 1875: sec. 2; cf. Rescher 1999). The main secular descendant was the logical positivist aspiration for a unified scientific language in which anything worth saying could be said. By the 1960s, courtesy of Thomas Kuhn (1970) and Michel Foucault (1970), this aspiration had become relativized to successive phases (paradigms or *epistemes*) in the history of science (Fuller 2007b: ch. 2).

The difference between the first and second types of social epistemology is encapsulated in Table 1. The chart highlights the extent to which knowledge can be seen as either a (1) *dynamizing* or a (2) *stabilizing* force in society (cf. Fuller 2000b: conclusion). The third type is the one that serves as a regulative ideal for my own social epistemology.

Moreover, an argument can be made that something that might be reasonably called "social epistemology" has been always central to both analytic and continental traditions in modern European philosophy, despite their strikingly opposed ways of characterizing the overall social dynamic of knowledge. This contrast is epitomized in their respective signature phrases for embodied social knowledge: Analytic philosophers stress *common sense*, continental philosophers *collective memory* (Fuller 2007a: 6–9). The difference between the two can be explained in terms of their default theological starting points. Common sense theorists take the reliability of our mental faculties to be underwritten by our divinely

Table 1 Social epistemology as (1) epistemology and (2) sociology.

Social organization of knowledge	(1) Epistemology – Collectively produced and individually redistributed	(2) Sociology – Individually distributed and collectively reproduced
Symbol of social epistemology	Encyclopedia (esp. cross-cutting referencing)	Evolution (esp. irreversible specialization)
Knowledge as a principle of social order	Research and education	Expertise and stratification
Exemplar	Dynamic university	Stable ecology
Division of labour	Temporary and exploitative	Fixed and interdependent
Discovery vis-à-vis justification	Discovery is of biased origins and justification redistributes the privilege contained in that bias to all (delta)	Discovery is of disparate origins and justification channels it into the mainstream (tributaries)
Knowledge vis-à-vis power	Disintegrative ("creative destruction")	Integrative ("social equilibrium")

created souls, the repository of *a priori* knowledge, whereas collective memory theorists take those faculties to be born contaminated by our animal bodies, perhaps as living reminders of Original Sin.

To be sure, both positions have been secularized over the past 200 years: On the one hand, the seat of common sense migrated from a specifically Christian (Thomas Reid) to a more generically Platonic (G. E. Moore) sense of the soul that by the 1950s had left its trace on "ordinary language" (Peter Strawson). On the other hand, collective memory has lost its original associations with *theodicy*, the project of justifying God's ways to humanity (Hegel), to embrace more explicitly materialist conceptions of progress (Marx), which in the twentieth century became increasingly demystified and deconstructed (Freud, Heidegger, Foucault, Derrida). The social epistemology of science can be more specifically understood as variants of both traditions. So-called naturalists and evolutionary epistemologists, exemplified by John Dewey, treat science rather sanguinely as an extension of common sense, whereas self-styled critical rationalists such as Karl Popper see science in constant struggle with its own collective memory, which is presumed to be riddled with errors, the discovery of which then constitutes progress, understood as a clarification of the original vision.

Whereas the common sense theorist values knowledge that enables one to come closer ("correspond") to the world as it naturally is, the collective memory theorist values knowledge that enables one to stand apart ("self-differentiate") from the world as a second-order entity – ideally to remake the world in one's own image. The one privileges conformity, the other autonomy as an epistemic virtue: that is, *getting it right* versus *thinking for oneself*. The two social epistemologies differ interestingly on induction as a source of knowledge. For the common sense theorist, induction is a positive mental tendency that reflects accumulated experience, whose sheer survival provides forward momentum for future epistemic judgements. In theological terms, it constitutes a *gift* from God that we should always acknowledge. In contrast, the collective memory theorist regards induction more negatively as the path-dependent drag of the past that fails to distinguish what is truly needed for effective future action. In the theological terms, it signifies a *test* from God that calls for a decision on our own part. What the former regards as *wisdom*, the latter treats as *prejudice*. In both cases, it is called "induction".

When James Ferrier (1875), a Scottish importer of German idealism, coined "epistemology" in 1854, he was operating from a collective memory perspective in explicit contrast to the common sense tradition dominant in his homeland (Broadie 2010: ch. 10). Ferrier defined knowledge as a second-order awareness of our mental states, a conscious organization of experience into a systematic whole. Recall that the Cambridge

8   *Introduction*

Christian Platonist Ralph Cudworth had introduced "consciousness" into English in 1678 as the seat of personal identity (aka soul), on the basis of which we judge in this life and are judged in the next one (Passmore 1951). In other words, the mind always already contains a representation of reality's validation mechanism that enables the mind to recognize the truth even when it goes against what is expected or desired, a capacity familiar in ethical contexts as "conscience" and in psychoanalytic ones as "superego". In the three centuries after Cudworth, this idea was divested first of its theological baggage and then, in the twentieth century, even of its psychological baggage. Thus, with the advent of logical positivism, Alfred Tarski secularized this second-order awareness as a "metalanguage" (or "semantics") that provides the truth conditions for our beliefs, now understood as first-order statements. By the 1970s, thanks largely to Saul Kripke, this idea became the cornerstone of the theory of reference, specifically the concept of "semantic reference" (Schwartz 1977).

In terms of this overall trajectory, Ferrier is a transitional figure, whose nod to theology remains in his definition of the goal of knowledge as the "absolute", which alludes to the Christian idea of *absolution from sin*. Political theorists will have come across this idea in modernity's "pre-democratic" era, when the "absolute monarch", typically with church backing, was capable of cancelling all previously incurred injustices, including crimes and debts, as if he or she were God's representative on Earth. More directly relevant here is Hegel's background in theology, especially his modelling the progress of the world-historic spirit as theodicy played out on a temporal stage: that is, it is only in the fullness of time that we come to terms with evils that are always already justified from God's eternal standpoint as necessary means to the ultimate good. The corresponding vision of the human knower is as an agent who proceeds through the world with, so to speak, "dirty minds" just as, morally speaking, we proceed with "dirty hands", both of which have the capacity to become "cleaner" over time. On this view, then, human epistemic progress consists in getting better at telling the difference between God's dirty means and his clean ends. In this context, the relevant complement to "absolute" is "pristine", that is, a world in which dirt has yet to be introduced – such as the Biblical Garden of Eden. The latter is the source of ideas of *prisca sapientia* that at first motivated Renaissance scholars to study the languages in which the original sacred works were written in order to fathom the mind of God, but under the influence of Jean-Jacques Rousseau morphed into a pre-linguistic state of "noble savagery" that began to associate the "pure" or "unfallen" human condition with that of pre-human primates (Corbey 2005).

Stripped of all this Judaeo-Christian baggage, epistemology turns out to be about separating the wheat from the chaff of our beliefs and integrating the wheat to enable the emergence of a larger truth that gives direction to our inquiries and provides meaning to our lives. It is what Marxists call the "dialectical method". Just as sin is inevitable in a world where fallible beings are called to act, so too error is inevitable in a world where we cannot learn anything at all without relying on our fallible faculties. In this respect, the Popperian imperative to test our spontaneously formed beliefs is the epistemic equivalent of a conscience in morality.

Left hanging in the balance, even in these post-theological times, is the legacy of Hegel's treatment of absolution as a self-reflexively applied process – that is, humanity's collective capacity to absolve itself of sin/ error without explicit divine guidance. This idea has proved a source of hope for ambitious politicians over the past two centuries, most notably Marxists, who have desired to build a "Heaven on Earth" (Passmore 1970: ch. 11). But the view has also had its admirers among those more clearly associated with the canon of scientific epistemology, such as Charles Sanders Peirce's self-correcting version of scientific inquiry, understood as a collective process that over time "converges" on the ultimate representation of reality – aka absolute truth (Laudan 1981: ch. 14). To be sure, Peirce's conception is ambiguous with regard to the nature of validation: Does a maximally comprehensive scientific consensus emerge from common recognition of the truth or is the truth itself the product of such a consensus? Put theologically, are we ultimately validated *by* or *as* God? The logic of this idea was explored by perhaps the most interesting social epistemologist in the analytic tradition, Fredcrick Will (1988), albeit largely to the deaf ears of his colleagues. Today Will is known mainly as the father of the noted US conservative pundit, George F. Will.

Perhaps the issue on which analytic social epistemology comes closest to a continental philosophical sensibility is the distinction in science's contexts of *discovery* and *justification*, according to which germs of truth (i.e. discoveries) are extracted from history and then justified as part of an ongoing collective inquiry towards the ultimate truth (Fuller 2000b: ch. 1). Despite various criticisms, the distinction remains a commonplace in philosophy of science courses. Nevertheless, from a continental standpoint, analytic philosophers show remarkably little concern for how the passage from discovery to justification occurs. Indeed, as if to formally end his early years as a psychologist, Popper (1959) casts the contexts of discovery and justification as a strict division of labour between psychology and philosophy, respectively, thereby absolving philosophers of any need to worry about the process of transitioning between the two states. Thus analytic philosophers have focused overwhelmingly on the canonical representation of a new discovery's place within a justified theoretical framework (Fuller 2003: ch. 12). The rhetorical effect has been to suggest that any given discovery could have been made by other inquirers by

10 *Introduction*

other means – such that, say, the fact that Isaac Newton discovered the laws of motion or Charles Darwin the theory of natural selection is incidental to the validity of what they discovered – and that others with rather different training and interests may extend or apply these discoveries in the future. Thus, science becomes "universal knowledge" in a sense that Hegel would have recognized. Nevertheless, continental philosophers linger over the costs of what Gilles Deleuze and Felix Guattari (1977) would call the "de-territorialization" of locally embodied discoveries in the name of more abstract and global epistemic ends. Already, in the early twentieth century, the Neo-Kantian philosopher Ernst Cassirer (1923) had cast this process as the conversion of substantive insights about earthbound nature into a more universal scheme of possible experience closed under mathematical functions – in the case of Galileo, a fairly explicit turn away from Aristotle and back to Plato.

But as suggested in the "sociology" column of Table 1, analytic social epistemologists such as Goldman (1999) and Kitcher (2001) have resorted to disciplinary cross-dressing, tarting up their epistemologically threadbare wares in a vulgar sociologism, as if once people come to realize that they know more and more about less and less, they would cede more of their epistemic authority to others whom they (implicitly, via "trust") empower to do research and pass judgements on their behalf. Perhaps Auguste Comte would approve of this trajectory but the resulting epistemic ecology is not sustainable in the long term. Even if people are naturally inclined to defer to authority, the funding costs of indulging this inclination in the case of knowledge production are likely to become prohibitive (Frodeman 2013). Put bluntly, for policy purposes, it may be more rational to rely on a sophisticated search engine than to commission new research, especially if "research" is scrupulously distinguished from "policy", as the normative conventions of our time would seem to require.

Indeed, if, as bibliometric evidence suggests, the vast majority of research is never read, even if worth reading, time might be better spent catching up with that backlog than commissioning new projects (Swanson 1986). We have arguably already produced more than enough knowledge to make perfectly decent policy decisions – provided that institutional safeguards are in place to enable those decisions to be reversed if they result in more harm than good. (This is what Popper famously called "piecemeal social engineering".) Nevertheless, it is easy to see the opposing pull: Scientists can enhance their employment prospects by playing themselves against the perceived self-interestedness of politicians who claim that "more research" may not be best use of public money.

However, as Randall Collins (1998) has demonstrated in an exhaustive cross-cultural history of institutionalized intellectual life, this strategy does not always work. The levels of conceptual sophistication and empirical breadth demanded of philosophical and scientific inquiry have been subject to ebbs and flows, depending on the ambient political economy. There is no unequivocal measure – other than sheer quantity of output – in terms of which it can be said that humanity, or even just the West over the past 250 years, has made progress. However, what is clear is that *any* expansion or contraction of the discursive space for knowledge production can be – and has been – justified as progressive. Thus, a growing research environment tends to be seen more in terms of opening up new horizons than exhibiting a dispersion of effort, whereas a shrinking environment gets interpreted as consolidating and focusing effort instead of arresting development. Here social epistemology could make greater use of Leon Festinger's (1957) cognitive dissonance theory of social psychology, especially its core concept of "adaptive preference formation", whereby thwarted expectations provide an opportunity for people to re-think their priorities, in the course of which they re-organize their relationship to the past so as to provide the legitimatory grounds for embarking on a fundamentally different future. Indeed, as Kuhn (1970) originally observed, this is one of the most important yet still least remarked achievements of scientific textbooks in the aftermath of a scientific revolution.

An interesting story yet to be told is how epistemology – a field originally conceived as a vehicle for achieving "absolute knowledge" – acquired a renewed taste for the problem of scepticism, once it fell into the hands of the post-positivist "analytic" philosophers who have dominated the discipline in the Anglophone world since the end of the Second World War. These philosophers have resorted to various "foundational" projects, ranging from introspectively based indubitable intuitions, as in the case of Roderick Chisholm (1977), to more objectively determined reliable processes, as in the case of Alvin Goldman (1999). A curiosity of analytic epistemology's self-understanding is its collapse of Kant's strong distinction between "rationalist" and "empiricist" traditions in the history of philosophy (something to which I shall return in Chapter 1), such that, say, the Cartesian self-certifying assertion of *"cogito ergo sum"* is treated as simply trying to authorize knowledge in the same sense as David Hume's failed attempt to find a purely rational basis for generalizing from sense experience. This overlooks the rather different starting points of the two thinkers: Descartes already believed that he knew the truth but wanted to justify it, whereas Hume could not already justify an allegedly true belief and so he doubted the belief's truth (cf. Burge 1993).

In practice, the foundationalist project of epistemology championed by analytic philosophy has amounted to reducing rationalism to an over-confident form of empiricism, in which Hume's sceptical conclusion is

12 Introduction

taken as the starting point for any future theory of knowledge. The most obvious source for this perspective is Bertrand Russell's (1912) explicit definition of knowledge as "justified true belief". However, it is equally clear that Russell's default epistemic position was more positive than that of any of his analytic offspring. Russell defines knowledge in a way that is designed to remove *a priori* restrictions (i.e. biases, prejudices, superstitions, blind spots) on our understanding of reality, as he believed the early twentieth-century revolutions in mathematical logic and relativity physics had already begun to do. A latter-day concept that approximates Russell's original spirit is "epistemic injustice", which aims to reduce the power-effects of knowledge claims by proportioning their credibility to the weight of evidence in their favour (McConkey 2004). Regardless of what one makes of proposals along these lines, they clearly differ in spirit from what is on offer from Chisholm and Goldman, who are much more concerned with protecting whatever we might know from contamination by error.

One explanation for the risk-averse character of analytic philosophy is that the twentieth century's two science-led world wars have shifted the discipline's default epistemic starting point from "how to go forward" to "how not to slip backward". The fear of backslide began in the aftermath of the First World War, the so-called Great War in which for the first time scientists very publicly supported national military objectives, only to result in unprecedented levels of disaster. By 1920, a year after the Treaty of Versailles, a learned obituary on the idea of progress (J. B. Bury's *The Idea of Progress*) and an ominous prophecy about the future of the Western Civilization itself (Oswald Spengler's *The Decline of the West*) had been published. Against this backdrop, the logical positivists sought epistemic foundations based not on natural induction, common sense or collective memory, but on an agreed observation language through which knowledge claims could be verified. Their main concern was to penetrate disciplinary jargons that overstated ("totalized") the jurisdiction of their knowledge claims, reaching into areas of life where individuals were entitled to a free choice. In this respect, the great American project of the positivists, the International Encyclopedia of Unified Science, provided, albeit without the original's literary flare, a two-century update of the original *L'Encyclopédie* of Diderot and d'Alembert as a provocation to bourgeois academic sensibilities. Although the positivists often used the word "convention" to characterize the sort of foundational decisions they encouraged their scientifically minded readers to take, the connotations of this term perhaps focus too much on the arbitrariness of the specific agreement (i.e. the fact that it could have been otherwise) rather than its binding character, which is more in the spirit of a social contract – and the sense of social epistemology promoted in these pages.

An alternative, broadly "Neo-Kantian" strategy for dispelling the anti-progressive gloom after the First World War was inspired by Max Weber and promoted by Karl Jaspers. It aimed to instil rhetorical self-restraint on academic experts by teaching them how their field's specific history has conditioned their world-view, a point that should be transmitted to a field's new recruits (Ringer 1969: ch. 2). Nowadays this approach, especially popular in the social sciences, is called "reflexive", a word that Alvin Gouldner (1970) introduced to radicalize American sociology's self-understanding, where the generality of the discipline's discourse had masked the specificity of its own history and that of the society that had shaped it. (Gouldner's own hobbyhorse was the elective affinity between the dominance of Talcott Parsons's structural-functionalism in sociology and the "welfare-warfare state" mentality of the US Cold War consensus.) By learning the path-dependent way in which sociology – or any other discipline – has acquired its specific technical character, students will learn of abandoned alternatives, from which much may still be learned. Indeed, these counterfactuals may even serve as new foundations for a radically new conception of the discipline. In Chapter 6 of this book, I take the transformative power of counterfactuals seriously, even though this general approach to the problem of epistemic legitimacy is actively discouraged in the natural sciences (Brush 1975).

Still more drastic solutions to the post-First World War crisis of epistemic legitimacy in the sciences were proposed by two other philosophers who first came to prominence in the 1920s, but whose influence would peak only after the Second World War, Martin Heidegger and Theodor Adorno. Whereas Adorno proposed endless self-criticism of the power-relations that normally legitimize knowledge claims, Heidegger advanced a philologically inspired strategy to recover the ground of ultimate being in its original Greek manifestation (Fuller 2003: chs 13, 16). Between them the "made for export" market for "continental" European philosophy was defined in the postwar period. This "crisis" mentality reflected a lost sense of organized inquiry as integral to humanity's collective self-realization as a species. What before the First World War had been celebrated as an increasingly rationalized division of cognitive labour by the end of the Second World War had come to be diagnosed as a debilitating fragmentation of inquiry.

Concern about the alienating if not outright de-humanizing tendencies of the advancement of science was given its most mature and articulate expression in a series of public lectures in the 1930s by transcendental phenomenology's founder, Edmund Husserl (1954), who canonized the distinction between, on the one hand, the sciences' explicitly rival "systematic" visions of the world and, on the other hand, a tacit yet presumptively coherent human "life-world". The reconciliation of these

14 Introduction

two visions captured the imaginations of postwar philosophers on both sides of the analytic-continental divide, most notably Wilfrid Sellars (1963) and Jürgen Habermas (1981).

Husserl's call for a return to epistemic foundations was predicated on science's self-destructive tendencies, its Babel-like proliferation of cross-cutting discourses, each claiming the entire universe as its purview, and the separation of those discourses from the overriding quest for meaning in life, especially in a secular age where neither science (*à la* Comte) nor the state (*à la* Hegel) nor some global revolutionary movement (*à la* Marx) had successfully replaced Christendom's normative unity of knowledge and power. In this respect, Husserl, writing in the twilight of his career, may be seen as the original postmodern Cassandra, a point not lost on the master deconstructionist, Jacques Derrida, whose first published work was a translation and commentary of a speculative essay on the origin of geometry that formed the appendix of Husserl (1954). For Husserl, Euclid is to be credited – or blamed – for having first abstracted a systematic vision of reality from life-world practices that could be then used as a normative rubric for evaluating and directing those practices. Indeed, Euclid arguably invented normativity.

My own project of social epistemology has been dedicated to the recovery of this lost sense of unity that Husserl bemoaned. I have struggled with two competing visions of that unity: One vision identifies the individual as the principle of unity who integrates the different forms of knowledge into a unique, personal world-view, as in the medieval master of liberal arts or, in a more modern vein, a Romantic genius such as Goethe. The other vision locates unity in the social integration of the different forms of knowledge in the spirit of a free trade zone between experts, or "doctors", each of whom professes over a discrete domain of reality (Fuller 2013a). In terms of Table 1, these two visions correspond to the "epistemological" and the "sociological" way of understanding "social epistemology". A more exact formulation of the distinction is presented in Table 2 below, which contrasts an *agent-* and *object*-oriented social epistemology, adumbrating some of the themes raised in the rest of this book (cf. Fuller 2006a: ch. 3).

In the following chapters, readers will see that my sympathies lie with agent-oriented social epistemology, though Fuller (1988) began from a much more ambivalent standpoint. What has been clear throughout – and is made evident in Chapter 1 – is that trade-offs have been necessary to arrive at a credible theory of knowledge. This is because our normal theorizing and planning face exactly the same problem of the Abrahamic deity, namely, how to realize a design in a medium that is inherently resistant to any such designs. Even those who do not wish to carry the theological baggage of this line of thought will be forced to think about

Table 2 The existential horizons of social epistemology.

Version of social epistemology	Agent-oriented social epistemology	Object-oriented social epistemology
Nature of knowledge	Knowledge is unified according to our subjective interests	Knowledge is divided according to the nature of its objects
Underlying metaphysics	Epistemology "artificially" constructs ontology	Epistemology "naturally" mirrors ontology
Status of humans	Humans are aspiring deities	Humans are receptive animals
Structure of mind	Will extends the intellect: "anticipation of experience"	Will is subordinated to the intellect: "reflection of reality"
Christian precedent	The dissenting tradition: Franciscans, Protestants	The establishment tradition: Dominicans, Catholics
Locus of academic authority	Masters of liberal arts	Doctors of professions
Temporal authority	The future (unless checked otherwise)	The past (unless checked otherwise)

the constitution of reality in economistic terms, specifically in terms of costs and benefits. Put in the very stark terms that theodicy invites – but many tender secular souls would not permit: *Ours being the best of all possible worlds is compatible with its being radically suboptimal in many if not all of its parts.* Thus, the world's surface imperfection and even evil may end up serving a higher good, in which case the benefit will have been worth the cost. What analytic philosophers have sometimes ridiculed as their own discipline's historic preoccupation with the "meaning of life" is no more and no less than this sort of metaphysical bookkeeping. Towards this end, I have advocated a social epistemology that is equally concerned with the *ethics* and the *engineering* of reality construction, a vision rather close to the "sciences of the artificial" envisioned by Herbert Simon (1977), the inspiration of my doctoral dissertation (Fuller 1985).

I say the above by way of explaining the structure of this book, which begins with an explicit reading of the history of epistemology as being about "cognitive economics". In Chapter 2, the theological provenance of this orientation is discussed, focusing on theodicy as the sacred precursor of secular political economy and natural ecology. Although "theodicy" exists today as a boutique topic within theology, its spirit is present whenever science touches on matters of world-view. This is most evident in the debates surrounding Darwinism, the least theologically friendly of evolutionary theories, which over the past half-century has become the dominant biological world-view. Against this backdrop I defend a "Left Creationist" standpoint, which aims to resituate biology in an explanatory framework that reasserts the centrality of human agency, without denying the empirical findings of the disciplines that are seen as contributing to the "Neo-Darwinian synthesis". Those who have followed my

16   *Introduction*

interventions in the intelligent design controversy – more to the point, those who have followed my own statements on the matter – will see that for me Left Creationism provides the prehistory to contemporary trans-humanism, which has gradually emerged in my previous work (see Fuller 2007b: ch. 6; 2007c: chs 2–5, conclusion; 2008a; 2010; 2011; 2012; and, most explicitly, Fuller and Lipinska 2014).

Chapters 3–5 are arranged in an order that successively descends from the idea that epistemology is "divine psychology", an exercise in getting into the "Mind of God" and, wherever possible, re-thinking God's thoughts. Psychology is placed first because that science originated as the study of the minds of scientists, who were seen as having the best – albeit fallible – access to the Mind of God. Philosophy and sociology are then discussed from a more contemporary perspective, with most of the theological baggage dropped, though the connections to psychology remain in full view. For the most part, these two chapters extend and update perspectives that will be familiar to followers of my earlier work in social epistemology, which conjoins a belief in long-term epistemic progress and a critical attitude towards short-term expertise. Chapter 6 deals with epistemology as "counterfactual historiography", by which I mean the form of intellectual intuition that enables us to imagine how things could have been otherwise – and might be otherwise. Here revisionist history meets time travel as instruments for expanding our epistemic horizons. Both require a godlike detachment to challenge the ordinary significance of events. In effect, theodicy is re-inscribed, but this time at a much more empirical level. I believe that the more seriously we take counterfactual historiography, the more godlike we become, which brings us to the Conclusion. The postmodern condition is the great foil to the spirit of this book's argument, especially with its sceptical attitude to the very idea of human progress. Yet, at the same time, postmodernism has encouraged counterfactual speculation, largely to undermine attempts to grant legitimacy to any particular narrative of progress. While postmodernists themselves tend to regard this exercise as a *reductio* to all such narratives, I regard it as a largely salutary second moment of an ongoing dialectic that serves to hone humanity's epistemic capacities.

Finally, readers of my work often ask two questions:

1   *Why do I write in a way that provides a direction but without a clear destination?* An author's primary obligation should be to answer readers' "why" and "how" questions about what is worth thinking about. However, whatever conclusions that the author him- or herself reaches on these worthwhile issues should be understood as artefacts of the contexts that call for conclusions, which may involve completing a book, speaking to a journalist or deciding on the fates of millions. In

other words, the biases and tendencies that readers detect in the author may well be correct *for now* but not the end of the story. While I never wish to provide a text that is merely "useful" for my readers, as if it were a pre-fitted tool to their pre-existing aims, I do hope that readers find in these pages *capital* that is available for a variety of purposes, but in each case more work by the reader is required. The most productive response to my text is: "OK, I follow the argument, and it seems important, but what do I do with it?" The follow-up actions may include open endorsement and extension, open opposition and contention, polite acknowledgement or polite neglect (the final two not so easy to distinguish).

2 *Why do I insist on proceeding by means of normatively charged polarities that "on the ground" are much more messy, blurry, uncertain, etc., than I make them out to be?* I take seriously that philosophy is something other than proto- or (more likely) bad sociology. To be sure, this is a lesson that analytic social epistemologists have yet to learn, though the intellectually barren character of their pursuits has already persuaded some of their smarter students to leave the field. In any case, philosophy, true to its theological roots, places enormous – albeit often implicit – normative weight on what might be realized in the future, even if there is little evidence in the present. Were philosophers to deviate significantly from that metaphysical orientation, they would indeed merge with sociologists and the practitioners of the empirical disciplines – a point that in recent memory Richard Rorty perhaps understood most clearly, albeit with a disconcerting indifference as to how philosophers should respond – that is, become general sociologists or secular theologians? All things considered, I prefer the latter option. In any case, those who see Rorty's vision as edifying need to figure out how to pursue it vigorously without corrupting the academic brand in the process. Contrary to what the philosophy establishment supposes, lack of vigour, not threat of corruption, poses the greater problem here.

1 Epistemology as cognitive economics

Social epistemology as the art of cognitive management

More than twenty-five years ago, the first edition of *Social Epistemology* (Fuller 1988) began as follows:

> The fundamental question of the field of study I call "social epistemology" is: *How should the pursuit of knowledge be organized, given that under normal circumstances knowledge is pursued by many human beings, each working on a more or less well-defined body of knowledge and each equipped with roughly the same imperfect cognitive capacities, albeit with varying degrees of access to one another's activities?*

This form of words, which now serves as the epigraph for social epistemology's online presence (www.social-epistemology.com), clearly suggests a vision of social epistemology as a kind of "cognitive management". An appendix of the book spoke about a curriculum for "knowledge policy", based on the full range of resources offered by the field of science and technology studies (STS). Some of my later books, such as *The Governance of Science* (Fuller 2000a) and *Knowledge Management Foundations* (Fuller 2002), are also contributions to cognitive management. However, the spirit of this enterprise differs from that of what is normally called "cognitive science", which, as Jerry Fodor (1981) shrewdly observed, assumes a Cartesian starting point (aka "methodological solipsism") that would have us understand the mind in its own terms before trying to figure out its relationship to the non-mental world. Thus, "artificial intelligence" has been more concerned with specifying the conditions that would qualify an entity as "intelligent" than with whether such an entity must be an animal operating in a physical environment or can be simply an avatar in cyberspace.

In contrast, without denying the potential multiple embodiments of intelligence, my version of social epistemology considers, so to speak, the "formal" and "material" elements of cognition *at the same time*. In that respect, it is closer to *economics* in its conception. Thus, whatever cognitive goals we may wish to pursue, we need to consider the costs, how those costs would be borne and, as a consequence, whether the goals are really worth their cost. While this economic specification gives social epistemology a concreteness that has been often lacking in contemporary theories of knowledge, it by no means involves a downsizing of our epistemic ambitions. It is simply a call for those engaged in "knowledge policy" to provide an open balance sheet that reveals the costs and benefits behind particular strategies of cognitive re-organization. We may indeed be willing to suffer radical changes to our lifestyles and work habits, if we think a particular set of goals are worth pursuing. But wherever there is a gap, the social epistemologist has her work cut out.

In the back of my mind when I wrote those opening words in 1988 was Adam Smith's argument for the rationalization of the division of labour in the economy as a means to increasing society's overall wealth. Smith observed that individuals doing everything for themselves were less efficient than each person specializing in what they do best and then engaging in exchange with others to obtain what they need. My point here is not to endorse any specific policies inspired by Smith but to acknowledge that he thought about the matter the right way in the following two senses:

1 People are capable of changing even their fundamental habits if provided with sufficient reason (or "incentive").
2 People are a source of untapped potential that may be released by altering ("liberalizing") the conditions under which they are allowed to express themselves.

Many things are implied here, perhaps most importantly the plasticity of human beings and hence the openness to social experimentation. Human history has only revealed a fraction of what we are capable of. This is a faith that united both capitalism and socialism in the modern era – and one that my version of social epistemology carries forward.

Perhaps in these "times of austerity", the drive to "economize" is understood as a counsel to "do more with less" in a way that presupposes that we have fewer resources than we first thought. On the contrary, when Smith and the original political economists in Britain and France – most notably the Marquis de Condorcet – promoted "economizing" in the eighteenth century, they had in mind working more efficiently so as to conserve effort so that more can be done. This is the context in which greater productivity was seen as a natural consequence of the rational organization of human activity (Rothschild 2001). We are held back not by the finitude of matter but the finitude of our minds to manage matter. The benchmark for this entire line of thought was the Augustinian doctrine of *creatio ex nihilo*: The ultimate rationality of divine creation is that

God creates everything out of nothing – that is, no effort is wasted whatsoever. And if we are created "in the image and likeness" of this deity, which Augustine emphasized as a lesson of Genesis, then we are tasked with achieving this divine level of performance.

It is also worth distinguishing my version of cognitive management from the appeal to economics made by analytic social epistemologists, such as Alvin Goldman (1999) and Philip Kitcher (1993), who for the past twenty years have gravitated to aspects of economics that play to their default methodological individualism, whereby knowledge is sought or possessed in the first instance by individuals and then aggregated into "social knowledge" in a literal "marketplace of ideas" (Fuller 1996). Thus, analytic social epistemologists have fancied microeconomic models that propose the optimal flow of information, division of cognitive labour, etc. In contrast, my own sense of cognitive management concerns the *macro*economics of knowledge, which is concerned with the overall efficiency of the epistemic enterprise, what Nicholas Rescher (1978), with a nod to the US pragmatist philosopher Charles Sanders Peirce, properly called "cognitive economy".

The idea of "cognitive economy" was a product of the so-called "marginalist revolution" in the final quarter of the nineteenth century, when the study of political economy came to acquire the shape of the discipline that today we call "economics" (Proctor 1991: ch. 13). Peirce extended what had been the key conceptual innovation of that revolution: namely, the principle of diminishing marginal utility. Applied to knowledge production, this principle implies that the indefinite pursuit of a particular intellectual trajectory is justifiable not as an end in itself but only on a benefit-to-cost basis. Our best epistemic enterprises provide the most cognitive benefit at the lowest cost. This principle was explicitly proposed for science policy by the "finalization" movement associated with Jürgen Habermas when he directed a Max Planck Institute dedicated to the "techno-scientific life-world" in the 1970s (Schaefer 1984). Their idea was that puzzle solving in "normal science" as described by Kuhn (1970) eventually suffers from diminishing marginal returns on further investment. Thus, rather than following the Kuhnian strategy of running paradigms into the ground by deploying enormous effort to make relatively little technical progress (which finally forces even the most dogmatic scientist to realize that a radical change in perspective is needed), the finalizationists after a certain point would shift resources to fields with better epistemic yields or these mature fields would be drawn together to solve standing social problems – such as cancer or environmental degradation – that escape the expertise of any particular discipline.

However, ideas surrounding cognitive economy may be deployed in other ways, such as a principle for the critical evaluation of existing

22 *Epistemology as cognitive economics*

knowledge systems. Across the range of national and corporate research systems, the rate of return on investment varies significantly. For example, the US may by far produce the most science, but the UK is much more productive relative to resource allocation. A comparable point may be made about educational systems. Harvard and Oxford may produce the most impressive roster of graduates, but they also have the most impressive intake of students. The "added value", cognitively speaking, of attending these institutions is probably much less than universities operating with much fewer resources that nevertheless produce distinguished graduates out of students of humbler origins. Worth stressing is that the main value associated with cognitive economy in keeping with the Augustinian point about *creatio ex nihilo* is best measured in terms of the opportunity costs that can be minimized or avoided, as efficiency savings make more resources available for other projects. The underlying intuition is that one acts now so as to maximize the degree of freedom that is later at one's disposal. I have been toying with this idea for a while, originally as "epistemic fungibility" (Fuller 2000a: ch. 8).

Two kinds of cognitive economy for social epistemology

To understand the dynamic of the history of epistemology as a species of cognitive economy, we need to start by distinguishing *demand-* and *supply-*side epistemic attitudes. Demand-siders proportion their belief to the need served by the belief. In other words, the more necessary the belief is to one's sense of self, the more it will be actively pursued. In contrast, supply-siders believe in proportion to the available evidence for the belief, even if that leads to a more diminished sense of self. Demand-siders characteristically hold that knowing is not complete without doing (i.e. generating the knowledge products that satisfy our cognitive needs), whereas supply-siders typically put in less effort in the cognitive process and expect less in return (i.e. conserving what is already known and ensuring that it does not deteriorate or become contaminated). As a first approximation, the demand-sider might be regarded as holding an "industrial" model of cognitive economy that is focused on increased productivity, whereas the supply-sider holds a more "agricultural" model that is more concerned with a steady yield in balance with the environment.

To make this distinction still more vivid, consider the demand-sider as someone who treats his ideas as opportunities to formulate hypotheses that then lead him to conduct experiments to discover something about the world that he had not previously known, which then forces him to redefine his objectives. Such a person is clearly in the business of self-transcendence. Whether his experiments have turned out to be true or false, he has acquired a power that he previously lacked. The only question is whether he has budgeted properly to reap the full benefits of that potential. This "budgeting" should be understood in both cognitive and material terms. In particular, the demand-sider needs to be flexibly minded to see the intellectual possibilities that are opened up by being forced to give up old epistemic assumptions as a result of an unexpected research outcome. To the supply-sider, this requires the remarkable capacity to remain mentally invested in an array of possible futures, including ones that go against most of one's own previous cognitive and material investments. Only a deity could be so capable of such equanimity in the face of what are bound to be many thwarted expectations. In humans such an attitude can easily look like that of Dr Pangloss, Voltaire's satirical portrayal of Leibniz in *Candide*. Worse still perhaps, the supply-sider might wonder whether the demand-sider has not succumbed to what social psychologists call "adaptive preference formation", specifically the kind that Jon Elster (1983) dubbed "sweet lemons". This is the inverse of "sour grapes", whereby one becomes incapable of facing failure on its own terms, always seeing the silver lining in every cloud. In the course of this self-delusion, so the supply-sider worries, the demand-sider detaches himself from any sense of security and becomes reckless with his own life – and perhaps the lives of others.

At this point, it is worth remarking that what in a comic frame might appear panglossian, in a tragic frame might come to be seen in Nietzsche's Zarathustrian terms: "What doesn't kill me makes me stronger." (Stanley Kubrick's Dr Strangelove may be seen as someone whose identity shuttles between these two frames.) One contemporary context for understanding these two attitudes is former market trader's Nicholas Taleb's (2012) distinction between "fragile" and "antifragile" approaches to life, which correspond, respectively, to the world-views of the supply- and demand-side epistemologists. Taleb generalizes the lesson that he first taught concerning "black swans", namely, those highly improbable events that when they happen end up producing a step change in the course of history (Taleb 2007). His starting point is a dismissal of those who claim in retrospect that they nearly predicted such events and think they "learn" by improving their capacity to predict "similar events" in the future. Such people, who constitute an unhealthy proportion of pundits in the financial sector (but also a large part of the social science community), are captive to a hindsight illusion that leads them to confuse explanation with prediction. The lesson they should learn is that prediction of extreme events is always a mug's game. Rather, what matters is coming out stronger regardless of how one's future predictions turn out.

In Taleb's presentation, antifragility belongs to a tripartite distinction in world-views, roughly defined in terms of how one deals with error or unwanted situations more generally. The "fragile" agent is one who needs to control the environment in order to maintain its normal condition. A slight shift in the environment can result in devastating consequences. In supply-side epistemology terms, this is the problem of scepticism. In contrast, the "robust" agent maintains its normal condition in response to changes in the environment. But an "antifragile" agent always maintains or improves its current condition as the environment changes, without any preordained sense of normality. A sense of the difference between a "robust" and an "antifragile" agent is captured by, on the one hand, a gambler who is simply concerned with always being able to return to the casino no matter how his bets turn out and, on the other, a gambler who always bets so that his losses can never outpace his wins, which generally means placing a somewhat larger than expected bet on improbable events and a somewhat smaller than expected bet on probable ones. The robust gambler does it as a hobby; the antifragile one does it to make a living.

The key to the antifragile mentality is what Taleb calls "optionality", namely, the use of degrees of freedom as a proxy for knowledge. In other words, if you do not know what will happen, make sure you have most options covered. In gambling circles, it is called "spread betting", and there is an art to exactly how much one should underestimate continuity and overestimate rupture with the past in order to profit significantly in the long term. Interestingly, some computer scientists hypothesize that intelligence dawns in physical systems that conserve their potential, neither by responding similarly to all contingencies nor by trying to limit the contingencies to which they are exposed. Rather, intelligence emerges from keeping as many options open as possible so that the agent flourishes regardless of the contingency encountered (Wissner-Gross and Freer 2013). In practice, this implies a regular process of sorting the wheat and chaff in one's cognitive horizons – that is, distinguishing the features that need to be preserved in any possible future from those that may be abandoned once they appear to be a liability, thereby resulting in a sense of "sustainable error".

In any case, this process is psychologically much more difficult than it seems for two reasons, one obvious and the other subtle. Obviously, as the supply-side epistemologist would stress, much of our sense of reality's stability rests on the future continuing the past being a "sure bet". Why then waste time and money on outliers? Nevertheless, Taleb counsels that it is better to run slightly behind the pack most of the time by devoting a small but significant portion of your resources to outliers, because when one of them hits, the rewards will more than make up for the lower return that you had been receiving to date. This raises a subtler psychological difficulty with antifragility: Once you decide that your bets require redistribution – say, in light of failed outcomes – how do you preserve the information that you learned from your failed bets in your next portfolio of investments? Rarely is the matter as straightforward as simply shifting out of the failed bets to the ones that did best, since the latter may be only temporarily protected from the same fundamental problems that led your other bets to fail. In other words, every failure provides an opportunity for a fundamental re-think about all your bets, including the successful ones. This is how "learning", properly speaking, is distinguished from mere "surviving" over time. In that sense, you really never reduce uncertainty but you learn to game it better.

Taleb's (2012) main piece of advice here is that one's epistemological insight is sharpened by having "skin in the game", to use the gangster argot for having a material investment in the outcomes. Scornful of academic and other professional pundits, who are paid to issue predictions but are not seriously judged on their accuracy, Taleb dubs them the "fragilista" because they are insulated from the environments to which they speak. Thus, they have the luxury of behaving either like "foxes" or "hedgehogs" in the political psychologist Philip Tetlock's (2005) sense: that is, they can simply mimic the trends or stick with the same position until it is borne out by events. They have no incentive to think more deeply about the nature of the reality that they are trying to predict.

The history of epistemology as a struggle over cognitive economy

Immanuel Kant originally glimpsed the demand- and supply-side epistemic attitudes towards the management of knowledge production at the end of modern epistemology's cornerstone work, *Critique of Pure Reason* (1781). In that work, demand- and supply-side epistemology are famously canonized as representing two traditions with deep historical roots. They continued to be enshrined in the curriculum as the foundations of what is still called "modern philosophy". The demand- and supply-side attitudes are known, respectively, as *rationalism* and *empiricism*. Kant suggested that this distinction had been played out across the entire history of philosophy, moving roughly from one of general metaphysics to a more narrowly epistemological horizon, as the distinctness of "the human" itself came more clearly into view. In Table 3, I have elaborated the historical trajectory that Kant leaves implicit, by tracing the path of these parallel legacies from their classical expression in Plato and Aristotle through the alternative Hellenistic life-philosophies of the Stoics and Epicureans, the high medieval definitions of the human in the Franciscans and Dominicans – the two mendicant Christian orders that staffed the first universities – to the early modern form in which Kant inherited the legacies. (A more elaborate discussion of these parallel streams of thought may be found in Fuller 2011: ch. 2, though they are first introduced in Fuller 2008a: ch. 2.)

26 *Epistemology as cognitive economics*

Table 3 The two philosophical traditions before cognitive economics.

Era	Key philosophical problem	Rationalism (legislation)	Empiricism (medication)
Greek	Form–matter relation	Divided (Plato)	Merged (Aristotle)
Roman	Nature of life	Outworking of spirit (Stoic)	Coalescence of matter (Epicurean)
Medieval	Definition of the human	Apprentice deity (Franciscan)	Enhanced animal (Dominican)
Early Modern	Function of mind	Expression of reason (Descartes, Leibniz)	Reception of experience (Locke, Hume)
High Modern	Post-Kantian division of metaphysics	Germany (will as realization of idea in the world): Fichte	Austria (intellect as adequacy to objects in the world): Brentano

The pedagogical import of these two legacies should not be underestimated. Historically important philosophers can be deemed significant for radically different reasons, which have profound downstream consequences for what is seen as significant in contemporary philosophy. A case in point is René Descartes. To a supply-sider (typically influenced by Anglophone trends), Descartes is someone whose scepticism was born of the potential unreliability of his senses and intellect. In contrast, to a demand-sider (typically influenced by Franco-German trends), Descartes tried to make explicit the special relationship that we have with God that underwrites the general reliability of our senses and intellect. One consequence of this difference in emphasis is that in the English-speaking world "epistemology" is naturally aligned with the *philosophy of mind*, which focuses on what happens inside individual heads as we try to secure what little we can know, while in the French- and German-speaking worlds epistemology is more naturally aligned with the *philosophy of science*, which focuses on what happens when the structured interactions of individuals produce epistemic wholes, such as a Kuhnian paradigm, that exceed what any of the constitutive individuals could grasp or pursue by themselves.

A good way to think of the overall development of this two-tracked trajectory is in terms of humanity pulled in two directions, up and down – towards the heavens (demand-side, where we re-enact divine creativity) and towards the earth (supply-side, where we re-embed into the natural world). I first pursued this contrast in Fuller (2007c: ch. 2), but it is most fully developed in Fuller (2011: ch. 2). But before Kant's two traditions began to be treated in more explicitly economic terms in the late nineteenth century, the most natural way to think about their contrasting normative orientations to philosophy had been in terms of the secular professions of law and medicine, specifically *legislation* versus *medication*: On the one hand, the imposition of reason on the world by sovereign will; on the other, the adjustment of the soul to the world by

Epistemology as cognitive economics   27

the rationalization of sentiment. Often this captures the actual pre-occupations of the relevant parties (e.g. Plato and Leibniz in law, Aristotle and Locke in medicine).

However, as philosophy came to acquire a distinctly academic cast in the generations after Kant's death, this distinction in life orientations was domesticated as a division within the ancient discipline of metaphysics into the modern ones of epistemology and ontology. They reflect nineteenth-century developments in Germany (led by Prussia) and Austria, two nations with radically different political outlooks. Whereas Germany aspired to unify modern Europe, Austria struggled to cope with its decline as the seat of Christendom from its days as the centre of the Holy Roman Empire. Translated into philosophy, the German side fully autonomizes epistemology from ontology, arguably rendering ontology a second-order effect of epistemology (i.e. knowledge is *constructive* of being). In terms of medieval theology, the intellect is imposed on the world through the will, as if the human were a deity in the making. In contrast, the Austrian side makes epistemology dependent on, if not a second-order effect of, ontology (i.e. knowledge is *representative* of being). The theological analogue here is that the intellect disciplines the appetites in one's own being, which suggests that humans are the species that is most adept at self-mastery. If the German world-view moves seamlessly from science to technology as "the extensions of man" (Brey 2000), the Austrian world-view aims to return thought to the ground of being, which may be defined as "nature", the "given", the "unconscious" – or simply what Freud's and Husserl's philosophy teacher, Franz Brentano, called *Evidenz*, which captures the experience of our pre-mediated attachment to reality (Turner 2010: ch. 6).

While the German and Austrian sides of the divide are both secular, they are secularizing opposing strands of Christianity. The German version secularizes from Protestantism and culminates in the collectivization and centralization of knowledge and power, *à la* socialism, while the Austrian view descends from an anti-Enlightenment Catholic backlash that is sceptical of human attempts to approximate divine omniscience and omnipotence; hence, the rise of so-called Austrian economics in the late nineteenth century. (Joseph de Maistre is an important transitional figure, as noted by Hirschman 1991.) It should come as no surprise that these radically contrasting visions are rooted in strikingly polarized attitudes to David Hume, the philosopher with whom Kant struggled the most during his most creative period. On the one hand, the German idealists saw Humean scepticism as the enemy that had to be overcome through a strongly proactive conception of the mind that distanced the intellect from sensation to impose order on an otherwise indeterminate material world (Beiser 2000), whereas on the other hand the Austrian realists saw in Hume's

28 Epistemology as cognitive economics

scepticism a precautionary check on our intellectual ambitions in terms of what may be adequately justified by experience (B. Smith 1994).

In the late nineteenth century, the "economic" character of this distinction explicitly came to the fore, with Ernst Mach and Charles Sanders Peirce arriving at some of the most memorable formulations. However, the clearest trace of this transition to "cognitive economy" transpired in two public talks: W. K. Clifford's "The Ethics of Belief" in 1877 (Clifford 1999) and William James's "The Will to Believe" in 1896 (James 1960), the latter delivered in explicit response to the former. Both cast against type, Clifford the mathematician defended a "supply-side" empiricist epistemology, whereas James the physician backed a "demand-side" rationalist epistemology. (If "rationalist" seems like a strange way to cast James, recall the Enlightenment sense of "Reason = Intellect + Will".) For the Jamesian voluntary believer, epistemology is about leveraging what we know now into a future we would like to see. In contrast, for the Cliffordian ethical believer, epistemology is about shoring up what we know so that it remains secure as we move into an uncertain future. The former seeks risks and hence errs on the side of overestimating our knowledge, while the latter avoids risk and hence errs on the side of underestimating our knowledge.

In Table 4, I have marked this version of demand- versus supply-side epistemology in terms of a distinction that emerged in the early modern period of Western philosophy between, respectively, *belief by decision* and *belief by evidence* (Fuller 2003: ch. 11). In colloquial terms, this is the distinction between providing a "reason" in terms of the end you are striving to achieve and in terms of the evidence that licenses your claim. In most general philosophical terms, it also captures deduction vis-à-vis induction, as science's *modus operandi*. In the former, one decides upon a hypothesis and submits it to testing; in the latter, one allows the evidence speak for itself without prejudice of prior hypotheses. In the case of "belief by decision", a decision projects a future from an otherwise indeterminate evidence base through an act of will. Very much like Pascal's "wager" for the existence of God, to assume an option as one's own is to confirm additional support for its truth. A technological innovation of probability theory was to reduce this process to the assignment of numerical weightings ("degrees of belief") in which the mathematics revealed the commitments one had effectively made. In contrast, "belief by evidence" envisages evidence as a constraint on an otherwise indeterminate decision procedure by offering the record of experience as the path to follow of least resistance to what lies beyond one's will. An updated version of this mentality from the economics of technology is the idea of "path-dependency" (Arthur 1994).

In its day, the distinction between belief by decision and by evidence was seen as a less metaphysically freighted and more psychologically

Epistemology as cognitive economics 29

Table 4 The two philosophical traditions after cognitive economics.

	Belief by decision (James)	Belief by evidence (Clifford)
Metaphysics	Transcendentalism	Naturalism
Truth goal	The whole truth (plus some false?)	Only the truth (minus some half-truth?)
Likely error	Overestimation	Underestimation
The nature of experience	Test of ignorance to be met and overcome	Ground on which knowledge is built
Epistemic value	Profit (i.e. added value from an investment)	Rent (i.e. derived value from an asset)
The role of evidence	Costs (i.e. falsification)	Interest (i.e. confirmation)
Attitude to risk	Proactionary (risk seeking)	Precautionary (risk averse)
Psychopathology	Adaptive preference (too eager to embrace the new)	Confirmation bias (too reluctant to reject the old)
Motto	"What doesn't kill me makes me stronger"	"If it ain't broke, don't fix it"

dynamic version of the rationalist's "innate ideas" and the empiricist's *"tabula rasa"*, respectively. However, probably the most direct historical source for the distinction in the early modern period was the search for a perspicuous way to interpret probability – or, put more poetically, to "tame chance" (Hacking 1975, 1990). Should we deal with chance by placing bets with an eye to maximizing personal advantage (the standpoint of subjectivist approaches to probability, such as Bayes's theorem) or by registering and adapting to spontaneous emerging tendencies in nature (the standpoint of objectivist approaches to probability, as in normal distribution curves)?

While my own version of social epistemology aims to update James over Clifford, a normally functioning cognitive economy tries to strike a balance between the two positions. For example, in Table 4, consider countervailing forces of the two "psychopathologies", adaptive preference formation and confirmation bias. If you are too attracted to novelty, then the weight of the past acts as ballast; whereas if you are instinctively attracted to the familiar, then a mind-set that allows you to see opportunity in novelty is welcomed. The founding sociologist of scientific knowledge David Bloor tapped into this intuition, borrowing (without citation) from Vilfredo Pareto's "parallelogram of forces" account of ideological formation (Bloor 1976: ch. 2).

The problem of the economic use of knowledge already produced

Questions remain regarding not only whether resources are used efficiently in the production of knowledge, but also whether the knowledge

30   *Epistemology as cognitive economics*

so produced is used efficiently. More than a quarter of a century ago, the University of Chicago library and information scientist Don Swanson (1986), himself originally trained in physics, managed to understand the aetiology of a medical condition simply by reading across literatures in various fields (which the specialists themselves had not done) and piecing together a hypothesis that was then empirically vindicated by a targeted experiment, facilitating the development of an effective treatment. Swanson had been motivated by various bibliometric facts of the sort originally highlighted by the science historian Derek de Solla Price in the 1960s; namely, that an exaggerated version of the Pareto 80/20 statistical principle of elite formation operates in science such that 90 per cent of the citations accrue to 10 per cent of the authors (Price 1986).

Sociologists have tended to conclude with Robert Merton (1977) that the uncited articles are either truly worthless or their content is eventually incorporated into the cited articles. This has led to institutional incentives for scientists to publish in "high impact" journals or team up with people whose work is already well cited. Information economists, perhaps drawing on Leibniz's explanation for the presence of evil in (this) the best of all possible worlds, creatively suggest that the mass of relatively uncited work serves to draw attention to the relatively few pieces of work that are well cited – the signal that penetrates the noise, as it were (Dietz and Rogers 2012). Truth may be known as a whole for all eternity in the divine mind, but time is required for humans to detect it in our necessarily piecemeal fashion; hence the need for the accumulation of experience as registered in the Science Citation Index (SCI). Theologically speaking, a mark of our fallen state is that much effort needs to be exerted in trial and error in order for truth to emerge – but eventually it does for all to see.

Don Swanson thought of the matter much more straightforwardly. Given the lack of evidence that the uncited articles were actually read, he concluded that they were simply neglected and may well contain valuable knowledge. But this result would require a change in scientific reading habits. Scientists would need to not so strongly focus on the dominant research tendencies in the specific fields where the research was published – in terms of which the uncited pieces no doubt seem irrelevant. Rather, scientists would have to learn to read across fields to make the connections where the uncited pieces appear as relevant to some other set of problems. An ambitious follow-up to the Swanson result would involve re-deploying research agencies so that they allocate funds to academics who try to solve standing intellectual and social problems by combing and combining the existing literature. These agencies would then commission targeted first-order research aimed at testing knowledge claims the validity of which cannot be agreed simply from a comprehensive and measured reading of that literature. Already "knowledge managers" outside of academia have developed "data mining" procedures for accessing knowledge that, for the most part, academia has failed to exploit but could inspire industrial applications and patents (Fuller 2002). However, there is no reason why such discovery procedures (or "retrieval strategies") should remain solely in the private sector and oriented solely towards commercial interests.

One cost-effective policy that library and information professionals could ensure in the name of social epistemology is that, in preparing grant proposals, researchers have identified the full range of precedents for the proposed work, in relation to which the research project would then be formulated. Such a policy would revive the original SCI concern to avoid the duplication of effort in an expanding knowledge system. Given the increasing specialization of today's researchers, research topics that potentially traverse several disciplinary boundaries may require library and information professionals as co-principals to grant proposals to ensure not only the efficient utilization of the already available knowledge but also the comprehensive dissemination of the resulting research to relevant academic and non-academic constituencies. This value-added character to the conduct of research is discussed below in terms of *epistemic justice*.

Were library and information professionals in charge of the knowledge system, no new research into a topic would be commissioned unless the already existing knowledge base had been exploited to its full extent. Thus, resource-intensive methods of original data generation and collection could be replaced, or at least deferred and attenuated, by the development of clever automated search engines ("knowbots") with access to multiple disciplinary literatures. This policy would be very much in the spirit of another University of Chicago librarian, Jesse Shera (1983), who had coined the phrase "social epistemology" in the 1960s to keep advances in information technology firmly under the control of the field's original humanist animus. Translated into practice, what Don Swanson (1986) called "undiscovered public knowledge" supports the maintenance and use of institutional archives, in the face of increasing budgetary pressures to discard rarely consulted old books, serials and other documents. The general failure of universities and other knowledge-based institutions to follow Swanson's precedent has resulted in an epidemic of "corporate amnesia", aka "mad archive disease" (King 2002).

But it would be a mistake to conclude that corporate amnesia is merely the by-product of financially motivated negligence. It is also a design feature of science, akin to "planned obsolescence", whereby sciences with more clearly defined and rapidly advancing research frontiers have shorter citation half-lives. In other words, the relevance of each new

32 Epistemology as cognitive economics

text to the discipline's current state of play is evaluated quickly, clearly, and irreversibly. This implies a sharpening of the distinction between, so to speak, the discipline's "short term" and "long term" memory, corresponding to a division of labour between a practitioner and a historian of a discipline (Fuller 2007a: 6–9). Thomas Kuhn (1970) went so far as to argue that the functional differentiation of practitioners and historians of science is itself constitutive of scientific progress, as it operationalizes the idea that science moves forward by leaving its past behind. The aforementioned Derek Price, a contemporary of Kuhn's, demonstrated that the harder the science, the sooner most of its literature is consigned to history. "Price's Index" implies that a sense of historicity is automatically generated by new literature falling, as David Hume said of his own first book, "still born from the presses" into oblivion (De Mey 1982: 120).

Against this backdrop, library and information science stands virtually alone among academic disciplines in its presumption of what might be called a "strong universalism" with regard to knowledge. The field aims to produce knowledge that is "universal" not only in terms of validity but also availability, such that knowledge functions simultaneously as a source of authority and a mode of empowerment. This prospect animates what social epistemologists call "epistemic justice" (Fuller 2007a: 24–29). Key to the administration of epistemic justice is a reduction in the gap between historian and practitioner knowledge, so as to minimize the power that expertise can exert over lay knowledge. After all, the faster the research frontier recedes from the view, the easier it is for one to be left behind; hence, the familiar phenomenon of a once active researcher who, after a few years in university administration, finds it impossible to return to her original field. This epistemic distance often appears as a layer of new jargon (expressed in both words and symbols) that functions as a barrier to latecomers, while allowing work to be redescribed as failed, primitive or incomplete, but, in any case, superseded by the new.

Philosophically speaking, a repository for all knowledge would entail access to, as courts demand of witnesses, "the whole truth and nothing but the truth". From the standpoint of social epistemology, the field of library and information science exists in the tension between the "whole" and the "nothing but" in the slogan, which in Table 4 we captured in terms of James's and Clifford's views. An expert-driven, discipline-based epistemic culture would have the field focus on nothing but the truth, while a more consumer-driven, democratized epistemic culture would have the field cover truth as a whole. The former strategy is clearly more conservative than the latter, as a focus on nothing but the truth would allow, in statistical jargon, "false negatives", while a concern for the whole truth would allow "false positives". Hanging in the balance is whether library and information science should reproduce the default search patterns of established disciplines. This would run the risk of peremptorily ignoring relevant work, or offer an independent and possibly more adventurous set of recommendations that itself would run the risk of throwing up a lot of false leads but may end up, *à la* Swanson, reorienting more discipline-bound inquirers.

The two main philosophical approaches to social epistemology divide precisely on this point. On the one hand, some see the differentiation of knowledge into distinct expertises as a normal feature of the growth of knowledge. Often this process is depicted in terms of exfoliation or evolution, in both cases implying that expertise is an entitlement earned by those who have trained in and contributed to the discipline historically recognized as authorized to pronounce on a knowledge domain. From this standpoint, library and information professionals identify and police the boundaries separating these knowledge domains, directing users to the expert sources most relevant to their needs. Goldman (1999) revealingly calls this position "epistemic paternalism", implying that an increasingly complex knowledge system requires that users be given increasing guidance on appropriate sources of knowledge. However, it takes for granted that the current division of cognitive labour is itself appropriate and necessary. On the other hand, my own version of social epistemology urges library and information professionals to adopt a more critical stance towards the historically contingent and institutionally entrenched character of existing disciplinary boundaries (Fuller 1998, 2002, 2008b).

From this standpoint, Swanson's "undiscovered public knowledge" draws attention to the increasing gaps between domains of knowledge that result from the tunnel vision induced by disciplinary specialization. However, this must be distinguished from what the great social science methodologist Donald Campbell (1988) originally called the "fishscale model of omniscience", which implies that personal expertises overlap so much that, taken together, there are no epistemic gaps in the community of inquirers. While Campbell's point may describe the aggregate of people's actual knowledge bases, Swanson nevertheless captures people's tendency to interpret what they know of neighbouring fields by the standards of their own fields, thereby limiting the prospects for those fields altering their own frame of reference. Here library and information professionals can facilitate the shifting between disciplinary frames, say, by the design of search engines that cross-classify cognate material so that users are forced to confront items they would not have otherwise deemed relevant to their inquiries. The result would be to shift users into a broader-gauged "browsing" mode, albeit within the general parameters of their original search. It would strike a small but reliable blow for epistemic justice.

Why did our ancestors seem to know so much more than we know now?

To understand the full import of Swanson's achievement, we need to start by recalling that when the Scottish metaphysician James Ferrier introduced "epistemology" into the English language in the mid-nineteenth century, it was under the influence of German idealism. In particular, he was persuaded by a certain metaphysical interpretation of logic that was originally used to overcome the cognitive impenetrability of Kant's "noumenon", the realm of things as they are "in themselves". The idealists interpreted the "known" and the "unknown" as proper subsets of the "knowable". In that case, the "unknowable" makes sense only as a relative concept. In other words, something is unknowable only relative to the specific terms that are used to define what is knowable (Fuller 2007b: 32–33). William James turned this idealist move into a cornerstone of pragmatism, arguing that certain things are unknowable only because we lack the appropriate "conceptual scheme" for detecting them. It follows that we should remain open to the prospect of discovering just such a scheme, which would effectively serve as a key that unlocks a previously hidden aspect of reality. James clearly had in mind here psychic phenomena, the detection of which he took seriously as a scientific project (Fuller 2014). However, perhaps a more persuasive example was set by James's older contemporary, the chemist Louis Pasteur, a non-conformist Christian who provided a secular update for Augustine's instructions on how to seek God, namely, "discovery favours the prepared mind". In Pasteur's case, this amounted to remaining open to the prospect that a solution to a practical problem – namely, spoilage in wine and beer – might require a radical reconceptualization of the nature of life itself (Stokes 1997).

Nevertheless, James's insight and Pasteur's example still leave unanswered the exact sense of psychological openness needed for acquiring a new conceptual scheme capable of rendering certain currently unknowable things knowable. But in principle at least, James was suggesting that such things – indeed, any such unknowable things – could be known under the right circumstances. For example, the speed at which Earth orbits the Sun was knowable only once Earth was assumed to move, after which Earth's speed became a matter of routine calculation. Kuhn's (1970) theory of scientific revolutions, in which paradigm shifts are likened to the Gestalt switches involved in religious conversions, may be seen as a legitimate heir to this perspective, which Kuhn may have picked up on as a Harvard undergraduate from James's student, C. I. Lewis (Fuller 2000b: ch. 6). However, the key Kuhnian insight relevant to social epistemology as cognitive economy is that these paradigm shifts may incur transaction costs, as the conceptual scheme of the new paradigm both renders knowable what had been previously unknowable and, more subtly, renders unknowable what had been previously knowable. (This is sometimes called "Kuhn Loss".) Thus, when Max Weber spoke of the "disenchantment" of the world entailed by modern science, he meant *inter alia* that conceptions of purpose in nature that had been so clear to the medieval scholastics became very difficult, if not impossible, to express coherently in the language of pure mechanism (Proctor 1991: ch. 3). An exemplar of this point is Kant's *Critique of Judgement*, which is best read as just such an act of recovery of a lost sensibility, but in purely modern terms.

An efficient if perhaps surprising way of encapsulating this general idealist-pragmatist construal of epistemology is through the infamous quote about "known unknowns" and "unknown unknowns" uttered by US Defence Secretary Donald Rumsfeld during the Iraq War when explaining issues surrounding military strategy. His source for these turns of phrase appears to have been Taleb (2007), who had been recently consulted by the Pentagon (Evans 2012: ch. 9). The implied logic of this way of understanding cognitive economy defines the realm of the "knowable" in terms of the matrix presented in Table 5, which I have adapted to account for the issues of most concern to social epistemology. In what follows, I discuss how a paradigm shift in the knowable in the aftermath of the First World War led people to conclude that, while we have undoubtedly produced more knowledge since the eighteenth century, we know less of what is knowable than those living, say, a century or more earlier.

One of the most curious features of modern intellectual history is that educated people today feel that they know much less of all that there is to know than their counterparts did, say, 100 or perhaps even 200 years ago. Clearly the boundaries of the knowable changed dramatically in this period, especially with regard to our framing of the very old, the very large, the very small and the very fast. In addition, humanity's own status as a being uniquely well-positioned to master the knowable has been challenged – especially by Charles Darwin – in the name of the very "science" that in the eighteenth century had been the source of our epistemic empowerment. Nevertheless, from roughly the mid-eighteenth to the early twentieth century, people thought that they understood – or were on the verge of understanding – the fundamental principles governing natural and

Table 5 The realm of the knowable.

	Known	Unknown
Knowns	What is published and used	Swanson's "undiscovered public knowledge"
Unknowns	Experiments where risk is calculable (i.e. social engineering)	Experiments where risk is not calculable (i.e. entrepreneurship)

human reality, most likely under a unified set of laws. This expectation cut across most scientific, religious, philosophical and political differences. Indeed, one could easily find both "idealist" and "materialist" expressions of this faith. This confident organizational approach to inquiry, which in the early nineteenth century had come to be called "consilience", was modelled on Newton's grand mathematical physical synthesis of the motions of the heavens and the earth. Indeed, given that mathematics and physics ended up uncovering the Achilles Heel of such confidence, in the form of Einstein and Gödel, it is worth recalling that one of the eighteenth century's notable mathematicians, Jean d'Alembert, who co-edited the Enlightenment's most influential publishing project, *L'Encyclopédie*, thought of his own field as no more than an adjunct to engineering, dedicated to calculating and measuring entities whose reality had been already vouchsafed by Newton (R. Collins 1998: ch. 11). In terms of Table 5, d'Alembert and his contemporaries clearly thought science dwelled firmly in the realm of "known unknowns".

In this context, the main point of empirical research was not to solve ever more specialized academic puzzles but to extend and apply known general principles to contexts where a deep understanding of the case at hand was necessary for the principles to do some palpable good. This point applied no less to social engineering than civil engineering. We would now call it "policy-based research", and it helps to explain the epistemic orientations of figures as otherwise different in political and moral outlook as G. W. F. Hegel, Auguste Comte, John Stuart Mill, Karl Marx and Herbert Spencer. None of these people founded academic disciplines because they believed that disciplines were remnant of medieval scholasticism. This was true even of the one academic in the bunch, Hegel. For him the various disciplines were simply the concrete outworkings of "consciousness", a secular sense of "spirit" that Hegel held to be the proper subject matter of philosophy, a "meta-discipline" that students acquired as the final stage of their self-development, during which they integrated the knowledge they had acquired from the particular disciplines in a personal synthesis that would provide direction for their lives.

All of the above nineteenth-century thinkers are now seen as having underestimated the significance of the new round of disciplinary specialization that by the end of that century became the hallmark of the modern research university, producing the great mass of "undiscovered public knowledge", called "unknown knowns" in Table 5. Two other nineteenth-century developments stand out here. One is the division of German theology faculties into pastoral and scholarly sides, the latter driven by an indefinite freedom of inquiry, regardless of its implications for matters of faith. To be sure, this *wissenschaftlich* theology had its own radical political consequences, especially in the hands of Ludwig Feuer-bach and the "Young Hegelians". However, its *modus operandi* was the popularization of current esoteric research, not the application of established universal principles (R. Collins 1998: ch. 12).

A second development, closely associated with William Whewell's coinage of "scientist" as the name of a specific profession, was the full incorporation of the natural sciences into the university curriculum. These disciplines differed from those of the medieval university in that their knowledge production required mastery of technical skills traditionally associated with the manual arts and where the primary knowledge output was not a text but an artefact. Despite Whewell's own emphasis on the need for overarching explanations in science, the radical diversification of epistemic practices effectively undermined the drive to integration at the core of the Enlightenment project. This loss of the unifying spirit became self-conscious with the rise of modern library and information science, as discussed in the previous section. It is traceable to the Belgian lawyer Paul Otlet, an inspiration for the logical positivists, who in the early twentieth century proposed a universal classification scheme for "docu-ments" (a broader category than academic writings) to improve the com-munication of scientific knowledge, even within science itself (Fuller 2007a: 69–73).

So far all of the above developments in managing the cognitive econ-omy of science were executed in the spirit of the Enlightenment, even in the cases – as we have just seen – where the letter undermined the spirit. The only clear sources of dissent from this general progressive sentiment were the ultra-conservatives (e.g. Joseph de Maistre) who glossed the faith in progress as modernist hubris, presaging a second coming of Adam's Fall. They saw their fears vindicated with the bloody 1789 French Revolution and copycat attempts at violent organized resistance against established authority that punctuated nineteenth-century politics and culminated in the events of the First World War and the Bolshevik Revolution. All of these events appeared to be inspired by humanity's godlike self-belief that it could create anew from first principles societies superior to the ones that they had inherited. These ultra-conservatives accepted the name "reactionaries" to emphasize that their principled opposition to the progressive tendencies resembled Newton's third law of motion. The reactionaries longed for a return to the Holy Roman Empire, in which an infallible (and inscrutable) Pope, understood as God's emissary on Earth, presides over a heterogeneous domain in which direct control is devolved "naturally" to the level at which those with the most first-hand knowledge (based on long-standing experience) enjoy the most authority. In today's European Union, this sentiment is codified as the principle of "subsidiarity" (Siedentop 2000).

38 *Epistemology as cognitive economics*

After 1917, former devotees of the Enlightenment themselves began to adopt a secular version of this reactionary perspective in the great march towards today's neo-liberalism. Here the invisible hand of self-organizing markets functioned as the inscrutable deity whose *modus operandi* was channelled by the state bureaucracy operating under the principle of subsidiarity (Plehwe and Mirowski 2009). The *locus classicus* for this metamorphosis is Hayek (1952). Although the position arose as an explicit response to the violence that had been done against humans in the name of things written in books, its own stance allowed for the violent replacement of books – say, of Marxist or, later, Keynesian macroeconomics – by the personal experience of humans, especially when engaged in free exchange. At this point, it becomes easy to see how the microeconomic interests of shopkeeper capitalism – *la petite bourgeoisie* – might find common cause with the studied irrationalism of *Heimat* ("homeland") thinking promoted by Martin Heidegger (Fuller 2003: ch. 15ff.).

Moreover, we can put a face on this "missing link" between Austrian free market economics and Heidegger's fundamental ontology, namely, Friedrich von Hayek's PhD supervisor, Othmar Spann, who also served as Max Weber's *bête noire* in his final years (Ringer 1969: ch. 4). An interesting point of convergence between neo-liberalism's anti-intellectualism towards the economy (i.e. macro-theories are no substitute for micro-experience) and James's voluntarist approach to conceptual schemes is a valorization of the "unknown unknowns" quadrant of Table 5, understood as a sphere of bold social experimentation that I have discussed in terms of *moral entrepreneurship* (Fuller 2011: ch. 5; Fuller 2012: ch. 4). This attitude is core to what in the concluding section I call the "proactionary" approach to risk (Fuller and Lipinska 2014).

Projecting the future of social epistemology: the proactionary imperative

Perhaps the most important overarching problem for social epistemology is the relationship between so-called *moral* and *epistemic* values. Although several different characterizations have been given of this relationship, generally speaking either (1) epistemic values are cast as a special case of moral values or (2) moral values are portrayed as placing constraints on the realization of epistemic values. In the case of (1), epistemic values are envisaged as a kind of "ethics of belief", again recalling Clifford, which famously defined intellectual discipline as "belief proportional to evidence". To be sure, in recent times, a broadened conception of "epistemic virtue" that harks back to Aristotle and Aquinas rather than Bacon and Mach has taken root in social epistemology, which is more focused on character-based values of the epistemic agent, such as honesty, humility, open-mindedness, tolerance, etc. (Zagzebski 1996). In the case of (2), epistemic values are portrayed as potentially undermining of the human condition if they are not pursued within a certain ethical horizon. This orientation conjures up the spectre of the morally indifferent if not inhuman scientist, who in turn requires the oversight of institutional review boards, if not natural law-based restrictions on scientific experiments on humans and animals.

As opposed to both of these, my own preferred view involves taking Ockham's razor to the distinction between moral and epistemic value by arguing that their real difference lies in the time horizon within which a more generic sense of "value" is expected to be fully realized (Fuller 2009a: ch. 4). Specifically, so-called "epistemic value" operates with a much longer time horizon for realizing the same sense of "value" as that of so-called "moral value". Here I am identifying "epistemic value" with the pursuit of truth as an end in itself regardless of the means pursued to achieve it (which in practice amounts to an ethic of efficiency). Given my associating social epistemology both with the original collective tele-ological project of "epistemology", and the more recent development of "post-" and "trans-"human normative horizons – whereby the values that humans have traditionally tried to achieve come to be realized in some successor "species" – I have come to believe that we should take seriously the claim of extreme scientists – including Nazi ones – that their research aims to benefit the human condition despite possibly harming many humans in the short to medium term.

While we should not give a free pass to scientists who engage in research that places human beings in extreme situations, we also should not pre-emptively invalidate their claims by demonizing them as "pathological", "inhumane", etc. After all, precedent for the long-termist, "end justifies the means" ethic of extreme scientists may be found in utilitarian arguments for the welfare of future generations. These arguments would have people discount or deny the value of their own current pleasures in favour of imagined future ones that may well be experienced by others rather than by oneself. Moreover, these arguments may be deployed to justify the systematic redistribution of various resources away from their default users and uses. Thus, one may feel morally obliged to curb one's personal expenditure of money, carbon, etc. The salient differ-ence between this case and the epistemic value case, I believe, is that the latter is effectively a second-order version of the former. In other words, sacrificing part of the current population to benefit some indefinitely extended future population is like sacrificing a part of one's current self to benefit either a future version of oneself or some future being whose values are sufficiently similar to one's own.

It is only for historical reasons that the relationship between moral and epistemic value has not been seen in this way. In particular, past cases of

40 *Epistemology as cognitive economics*

the dominance of "epistemic value" (e.g. eugenics) have been coerced rather than freely chosen by those who would be most likely to suffer the immediate consequences. In the emerging world of "Humanity 2.0" political ideologies, I have characterized the second-order, epistemic value-led option as *proactionary* (suggesting a risk-seeking mentality) and the first-order, moral value-led option as *precautionary* (suggesting a risk-averse mentality). This characterization might be understood as my twenty-first-century way of casting the difference between the demand- and supply-driven epistemologies that has framed the argument of this chapter (cf. Fuller and Lipinska 2014: ch. 1). Both sides require a substantial re-distribution of personal sentiment and material resources. However, the social-epistemic standpoint of the precautionary ideology is that of those living now who then imagine others who would wish to live like them in the future, as opposed to the proactionary ideology, which envisages future life as involving roughly the same degree of dismissal, incorporation and extension of the past as previous generations have done to their predecessors.

2 Epistemology as divine psychology

The divine origins of intellectual life

An intellectual is someone who lives by exemplifying "ideas", in the sense of adopting specific attitudes towards specific propositions, which are then used to justify action. When intellectuals are seen as "demystifiers", it is because they bring to light taken-for-granted ideas that, once revealed, no longer seem to justify action. In turn, intellectuals can be themselves "demystified" by revealing that their ideas merely "rationalize" actions that were taken for other, typically self-interested reasons. In practice, intellectuals have been effective when they can exemplify ideas in multiple media to different audiences in various contexts (Fuller 2005). The above definition is especially relevant to the great proselytizing religions, Christianity and Islam, which aspire to universal membership yet require that each potential member find their own way to God (Fuller 2010: ch. 2). While the following discussion is confined to the Christian intellectual tradition, similar developments – albeit operating under rather different political arrangements – can be found in Islam (Brague 2007).

In the history of Christianity, the independence of intellectual life explicitly becomes an issue in debates over what it means to live "in imitation of Christ". In the thirteenth century, the Minister General of the Franciscan Order, St Bonaventure, notably argued that to imitate Christ is to live in the spirit of Jesus, not to copy his exact acts, which may be inappropriate in one's own life-context (Passmore 1970: 73). This careful appeal to "the spirit" versus "the letter" of Jesus's teaching became a time-honoured strategy by which intellectuals have revealed a more unified sense of truth from what can be gleaned from seemingly disparate phenomena (Fuller 2005: 51ff.). Of special concern to this chapter, however, is that the distinction also echoes the Janus-faced character of Christendom, which carried over into secular modernity. The "letter" side derived from St Peter, the source of a "papal" (i.e. paternal) church structure modelled on clear dynastic lines of descent, while the "spirit" side followed from St Paul, the source of an evangelizing approach that sells the case for Jesus anew to each audience on their own terms. The former presumed an authority in

42 Epistemology as divine psychology

time immemorial that the latter always felt had to be earned from moment to moment.

The trajectory from Jesus to modern secular intellectual life flows most directly through the Pauline tradition, which always appealed to those on the outer reaches of clerical control. Consider the two Christian heresies of greatest longevity, Arianism and Pelagianism, which were among St Augustine's original fifth-century foes in his efforts to consolidate a religious orthodoxy. Their namesakes, Arius and Pelagius, were among Christendom's most learned and charismatic outliers, the one from Libya and the other from Ireland. Together they supply many, if not most, of the distinctive attitudes associated with modern secular intellectual life. Arius and Pelagius attempted to minimize both the metaphysical and ecclesiastical distance between ordinary humans and God by offering radical interpretations of our having been created "in the image and likeness of God", which after Augustine's own commentary on Genesis has come to be known as the *imago dei* doctrine.

In the first instance, the impact was grammatical, whereby the implied right to self-assertion has left a lasting linguistic trace in the normalization of the voice of the first person ("I", "we") in European speech. For example, such explicit self-assertion – an innovation in Latin – features in Pelagius's private correspondence, the philosophical legacy of which is most easily recognized as Descartes's *cogito ergo sum* (Borkenau 1981). In the long term, Arianism provided the basis for scientific progress as the project of self-transcendence, the quest to enter the "mind of God", while Pelagianism underwrote technological progress as the project of building a "heaven on earth" (Fuller and Lipinska 2014: ch. 2).

Intellectual self-assertion was expedited during the Middle Ages by an increasingly secular treatment of sacred texts, which stressed the role of human reason in resolving inconsistencies and providing closure and unity. Consider three influential examples from the twelfth and thirteenth centuries:

1 Peter Abelard, whose famed dialectical method was honed in the early days of what became the University of Paris, juxtaposed contradictory texts from and about the Bible as a rite of passage for his students to come to terms with the exact nature of their faith.
2 Joachim of Fiore, an abbot in papal favour, attempted to harmonize the Old and New Testaments, resulting in a proto-Hegelian dialectical plot structure to human history corresponding to the manifestation of each of God's three persons, which in turn would enable us to prepare for the Final Judgement, the ultimate synthetic moment.
3 Robert Grosseteste, Oxford University's first chancellor, took the Biblical account of creation sufficiently literally to infer that we might

understand the principles governing physical creation by decoding its repeated appeal to the language of light and reconstructing its underlying metaphysics. Grosseteste's fellow Oxford Franciscan Roger Bacon took up this challenge with the most gusto.

Common to these secularizing tendencies is a "univocal" approach to sacred language that would receive its most sophisticated articulation in the fourteenth century by another Oxford Franciscan, John Duns Scotus, to be then popularized by his student, John Wycliffe. In a nutshell, the language with which God communicates in the Bible is not some unfathomable tongue referring to a reality other than the one that humans normally inhabit. On the contrary, human language is itself an imperfect version of the divine *logos*, which is precisely about everything that is possible, including the actual world. The mark of our "fallen" state is that we literally do not know what we are talking about until we have made the sort of intellectual journey that Abelard, Joachim and Grosseteste advised. The dawn of what we now regard as "modernity" involved using such a "literal" understanding of the Bible as a springboard for regaining our capacity to communicate effectively with God (Fuller 2010: ch. 5).

This trajectory bore enduring intellectual fruit in that aspect of the seventeenth century that we now call the "Scientific Revolution", when experimentation – rather than prayer – began to serve as our fallible channel for "talking back" to God about what is possible (Harrison 2007). In effect, the *imago dei* doctrine morphed into the concept of the *intelligibility* of the universe, which implied a potential meeting of minds between humans and God through the progress of science (Fuller 2007c: ch. 1). After having been given an increasingly activist interpretation during the Protestant Reformation, the *imago dei* doctrine was explicitly secularized as Unitarianism and Deism in the eighteenth century and by the nineteenth century came to be aligned with various forms of Humanism, including Idealism, Positivism and even Marxism, movements that generally defined themselves in opposition to established religion. A proper history of this large movement in thought would show how the theology of divine providence morphed into a theory of scientific progress, with Joseph Priestley – the Unitarian preacher, experimental chemist and confidant of the US Founding Fathers – serving as the key transitional figure (Passmore 1970: ch. 10; Fuller 2011: ch. 4).

However, we also need to give the Petrine tradition its due. In the High Middle Ages, roughly 1250 to 1350, the Peter–Paul division reached a watershed formulation in the mendicant orders who supplied most of the intellectual leaders of the first European universities: the Petrine Dominicans and the Pauline Franciscans. In the next section, I shall explore the economic significance of the common "mendicant" (i.e. begging) nature of these religious orders. But we shall now focus on the epistemological roots of their palpable political differences. On the one hand, the Dominican Thomas Aquinas served as papal emissary and others of his order served as papal inquisitors. On the other, the Franciscan William of Ockham conspired to have the Pope replaced by a secular emperor strong enough to prevent corruption in the clergy, while others of his order encouraged personal forms of spirituality that often put them at odds with papal authority (Sullivan 2011). Indeed, the Franciscans inspired waves of heretical movements against the authority of the Church of Rome, culminating in the Protestant Reformation (Leff 1967).

Behind these politically salient divisions lay a profound epistemological disagreement about the sort of access that Biblical language allows humans to have to the workings of the divine intellect. The disagreement turned on the nature of "divine predication", that is, whether the same thing is meant when the Bible says that God and humans are "good", "powerful", "intelligent", and so forth. On the one hand, the Dominicans, championed by Aquinas at the University of Paris, believed that such terms could be applied only analogically (or perhaps even "equivocally", as critics claimed) to God; on the other, the Franciscans, championed by Scotus at the University of Oxford, held that the terms mean the same in both cases but that God's capacity for, say, good is infinitely greater than our own. While the Dominican view became the Catholic orthodoxy by the fourteenth century, the Franciscan view was effectively taken up by the Protestant reformers, the Scientific Revolutionaries and later thinkers concerned with a "universal language of thought", the secular descendant of the divine *logos*, as logic was increasingly portrayed in the modern period through its closer association with mathematics (Fuller 2011: ch. 2).

It is not hard to see how the Dominican view of predication has served to insulate the claims of theology from those of science. For example, self-styled "theistic evolutionists" today are comfortable with the idea that divine creativity is so radically different from human creativity that it is reasonable to suppose that it might appear to us in the guise of Darwin's theory of evolution by natural selection, even given the high degree of contingency and apparent purposelessness that the theory attributes to nature. This would not deny God's creative power at all but only the appropriateness of thinking about it in terms that would be normally associated with human creation. Atheists have provided helpful guidance on this conceptualization via what Stephen Jay Gould (1999) canonized as the "non-overlapping magisteria" (NOMA) stance to the science–religion relationship. NOMA's segregationism ensures science a free rein in the understanding of nature (i.e. the "how" questions), while preserving a qualitatively different "supernatural" sphere for devotion to God (i.e. the "why" questions). Under this regime, our relationship to God tends to be defined in *permanently* paternalistic terms. We are children who never seem to reach adulthood, contrary to Kant's Enlightenment promise that we will be released from our "nonage" if we follow the call of *aude sapere*, "Dare to think for yourself" (Schmidt 1996).

In contrast, from St Bonaventure (1993) onward, the Franciscans have plotted trajectories – "courses of study" at university – to enter into the divine mindset. By the time of the Scientific Revolution, this rather literal understanding of the natural path of human inquiry resulted in epoch-making explorations of the idea that the universe itself might be a divine artefact, one that may be modelled, however imperfectly, by human artefacts. The ideal generated by this turn of mind, the so-called "mechanical world-system", encouraged people to take seriously the idea that our distance from God simply lay in our failure to distinguish short-term from long-term benefit. By the late seventeenth century, this became the cognitive problem posed by *theodicy*, the branch of modern theology concerned with "divine justice", understood in terms of justifying creation as an optimally designed machine, in which it is presumed that compromises must be reached between the parts, such that one requires explanations for why, say, particular individuals appear to have their lives "cut short". Contemporary intelligent design theory should be understood as the latest phase of this trajectory, which I argue can provide the basis for a *Creationist Left*.

In this context, the long-term significance of the Protestant emphasis on Bible-reading to elicit the spirit of Jesus should not be under-estimated. This practice re-established the Judaic centrality of literacy to intellectual life that had been consistently supported only by the Platonic tradition in the Greek and Roman Catholic cultures, but proved a harbinger of modern secular intellectual life. Here the Protestant stress on what is sometimes called a "literal" interpretation of the Bible refers mainly to the process of reading its words for oneself, through which one then directly encounters the "spirit", evidence for which is provided by a distinctive performance in the world, as if one had authored the words oneself – a practice akin to "method acting" (Fuller 2008a: ch. 7). This practice contrasts with one in which the words are read by an authorized interpreter (e.g. a Catholic priest) that are then used to evaluate and prescribe the activities of the faithful. The former practice aims at self-empowerment, the latter submission to authority.

Christianity's Peter–Paul division started to be secularized in the aftermath of the English Civil War of the mid-seventeenth century. On the secularized Petrine side, the social contract laid down in Thomas Hobbes's *Leviathan* should makes sense as a post-Biblical covenant prescribing the descent of dynastic authority in a world where the state has replaced the church. On the secularized Pauline side, John Milton's

46   *Epistemology as divine psychology*

Areopagitica offered a defence of creative self-assertion in a republican polity, but now understood more in terms of innate "freedom of expression" than the calling forth of the divine within ourselves, as the Franciscans had urged. By the late eighteenth century these two sides would be synthesized in a political statement that for more than two centuries now has functioned as a secular Bible for hopeful people throughout the world – the Constitution of the United States of America.

We shall see in what follows that secularization turns out to be less a rejection than a purification and amplification of the Biblical roots of intellectual life. In this respect, *outworking*, with its dual meaning of "working out in concrete terms an initial conception" and "working more efficiently than before", better captures the overall significance of secularization. Against this backdrop, *naturalism* appears as a conservative, earthbound position that fails to take seriously the feats of outworking – what spiritual people call "self-transcendence" – that humanity has achieved through that greatest of secularizers, science.

Secularizing the sacred mind: the centrality of theodicy

The intellectual bases of secularization have been most cogently and exhaustively elaborated in Hans Blumenberg's *The Legitimacy of the Modern Age* (1986), which traces science's divestiture of theology to the removal of God as a necessary motive force in the physical universe in the seventeenth century. The focal concept here is *inertia*, which Newton defined as intrinsic to bodies for purposes of mathematical calculation. This enabled him to determine the state and motion of physical objects without reference to some higher-order entity that guided their passage (unlike the rival concept, *conatus*). To be sure, Newton did not make a clean break with theism, since his mathematics required periodic divine intervention to inject new energy into the universe. This is the source of the "god of the gaps" epithet that continues to dog those who would see the cosmos as the product of intentional agency, or "intelligent design" (ID). Nevertheless, Newton's very light-touch deity was a striking advance over his rival Descartes, whose physics required that God recreate the universe on a moment-to-moment basis. Moreover, Newton's less mathematically exact contemporaries helped the secular revolution along. In particular, Leibniz held that God could have only created the best of all possible worlds, which implies that any difficulties in calculation simply reflect our own failure to have fathomed God's equations – not, as Newton had thought, God's periodic need to compensate for an original inadequacy (Funkenstein 1986: chs 2–3).

It was a tricky choice theologically: On the one hand, Newton presented the known universe in calculable form, but at the cost of God

Epistemology as divine psychology 47

having periodically to reset its parameters. On the other, Leibniz refused to believe that Newton had the final word, even though Leibniz himself lacked a comparably articulated alternative account of the cosmos. The history of physics over the past 300+ years is best understood as recognizing Newton's achievement but treating it from a Leibnizian point of view. Thus, even atheist physicists (e.g. Hawking 1988) continue to profess their desire to enter "the mind of God", which assumes the existence of what Leibniz called "sufficient reason" for the idiosyncrasies that mark our universe. For his part, Newton thought that he had already done the deed, given his Unitarian view of the deity as an indefinitely greater version of our individual selves. But that meant that God's hand could not be completely hidden. Even the deity's best laid plans face a recalcitrant, if not ill-disposed, material medium in need of continual monitoring and periodic adjustment. Here Newton appeared to be closer to Descartes than Leibniz in proposing an irreducible dualism of mind and matter, whereby the deity demonstrates its transcendence of material reality by periodically intervening in its operations.

For his part, Leibniz argued that matter is literally mind without sensory transparency, and hence – as Hegel would later put it – exists "in itself". This view proved influential in the nineteenth century as the basis for using physical probes to explore mental reality, the basis of experimental psychology (Heidelberger 2004). An intuitive way to think about this line of thought is that non-human matter suffers from an extreme version of the "locked-in syndrome": It resembles a brain-functioning human who lacks the capacity to express her thoughts, which means that others need to intervene to release her cognitive potential. In that case, we differ from rocks simply in terms of our much greater capacity – and hence responsibility – to release that divinely implanted potential in ourselves and in those creatures that cannot do so for themselves. This is a classic Christian argument in support of the arts and industry that goes back to medieval monasticism, which in the modern period was captured by *vis viva*, or "living force", the prototype of the concept of energy (Noble 1997).

Leibniz's perspective truly came into its own in the early twentieth century with Einstein's confirmation of matter's atomic structure and its convertibility to energy. This was less about the existence of material atoms *per se* (which Leibniz had formally opposed) than their character when taken collectively: Supposedly "dumb" and "inert" matter was revealed to contain a hidden logic, knowledge of which would allow us to unleash entirely new forms of being, most notably nuclear power. By the mid-twentieth century, something similar happened to the nature of life itself, especially in the wake of Erwin Schrödinger's 1943 Dublin lectures "What Is Life?", where he famously cast the molecular constitution of the gene as a code, whose cracking would unleash godlike creative powers as we learn to

48   Epistemology as divine psychology

recombine life's elements in novel ways (Schrödinger 1955; Fuller 2008a: ch. 6). Nowadays Schrödinger is regarded as a John the Baptist figure in the DNA revolution that marks the turn away from Darwin's own rather bleak Malthusian outlook on life's prospects towards the more optimistic visions projected by both biotechnology and intelligent design theory, the version of scientific creationism that treats genetic information as just as much an expression of divine *logos* as the Bible (Meyer 2009).

But even at their best humans are only gods in the making. Thus, the sort of self-conscious knowledge that Leibniz and his intellectual offspring allowed is prone to both epistemic and moral error in ways that can lead to second thoughts about whether our godlike capacities are worth cultivating in the first place. (Think nuclear weapons and eugenics.) Leibniz tried to make sense of such "dirty hands" as the cost of spiritual progress by inventing a discipline, *theodicy*, dedicated to understanding nature's prima facie radical imperfections, ranging from natural catastrophes and evil acts to casual suffering, not as signs of divine weakness but hidden strengths that can be fathomed in the fullness of time. Two of the most influential sociologists of religion in the twentieth century, Max Weber (1963) and Peter Berger (1967), identified theodicy as fundamental to religion's continuing legitimacy, since it promises answers to questions of cosmic justice. However, Weber and Berger defined the force of that legitimacy in opposing terms, each of which has clear secular descendants.

Weber, focusing mainly on medieval monasticism and early modern Puritanism, stressed suffering as an experience less to be tolerated or avoided than to be learned from, so as to continually improve the human condition, if not to recover fully our divine entitlement. From this came the modern scientific world-view that we progress by active learning through trial and error – by experimenting not only on our theories but also our environment and even our own bodies. This has opened the way to religious treatments of contemporary "transhumanism", with its exploration of extending our bodies beyond their natural biological limits and even the transfer of mentality from carbon- to silicon-based vehicles (Amarasingam 2008). It is probably no accident that leaders of three successive generations of the most ambitious project to extend distinctly human traits beyond our carbon-based heritage – the artificial intelligence gurus Norbert Wiener (1950), Herbert Simon (1977) and Ray Kurzweil (1999) – have been drawn from Unitarianism, the modern expression of the Arian heresy that associates the human condition with the imperfect recognition of our intrinsic divinity (Davis 1998; Fuller 2011: intro.).

But, as Weber fully realized, theodicy's didactic character is not limited to ontological suffering but applies equally to occurrent experiences of pleasure and pain. In other words, the rewards reaped by a virtuous life should not be seen as exclusively, or even primarily, the product of one's own efforts. They too are indicative of the disproportionate means by which divine ends are realized in the long term. We may experience the outworking of the divine plan as either misfortune or good fortune, but the aspect of "fortune" – that is, its contingent relationship of our fates to our own plans – needs to be kept firmly in mind to instil the requisite sense of humility and focus. The variation in individual fortunes may be explained as the over- and undershooting of the divine plan vis-à-vis recalcitrant matter, not least our own bodies. Not surprisingly the concept of statistical norm as fluctuation around a central tendency originated as a Newton-inspired attempt to capture divine agency in mathematical terms (Hacking 1975).

Indeed, theodicy arose during the formalization of probability theory in the seventeenth and eighteenth centuries, much of which was accomplished by mathematically adept theologians, most famously the Reverend Thomas Bayes, who wished to accommodate the uncertainty of human judgement and the waywardness of human flesh into a rational account of nature's intelligent design. In other words, the laws of probability were most naturally seen as a divine instrument for harnessing the unruliness of matter in aid of intelligent design (Hacking 1975: ch. 18). Thus, the guiding dichotomy here was not as Darwinists put it today, *design versus not-design*, but rather *good design versus bad design*. In this respect, theodicy simply took for granted our divine entitlement and the findings of science, and then sought to infer an action plan. It was less about justifying God's existence than justifying our own existence as creatures in *imago dei*.

The answers originally proposed had implications that bore on fields now as disparate as ecology, economics and engineering: the so-called systems sciences. The great eighteenth-century naturalist Carolus Linnaeus, whom we now remember for his binomial classification of the species, saw his "economy of nature" as just such an exercise in empirical theodicy (Koerner 1999). Were we to pose the original big question of theodicy today, it would look something like this: *How does the deity optimize, given its ends and the means within which it must realize them?* To be sure, such a question courts blasphemy, as it suggests that God must struggle against matter to get his way, which in turn suggests a certain limitation to his powers *that we are in a position to know*. Moreover, the more we think we know the divine *modus operandi*, the more God's allowance of suffering and evil looks deliberate, albeit not desired. This would seem to put divine action at odds with our own presumably divinely inspired moral scruples that put a premium on the avoidance – if not the elimination – of suffering from the world (Southgate 2008).

But as a matter of fact, our own moral scruples – at least as understood in modern ethics – are due precisely to the sort of knowledge originally

50 *Epistemology as divine psychology*

promised by theodicy but from which theologians now shy away (Schneewind 1997). At the outset, we need to take seriously that humans might learn how to act from what they take to be the example set by God in nature's intelligent design. For example, theodicy originally entertained the prospect that to think like God is to see evil and suffering as serving a higher good, as the deity's primary concern is with the large scale and the long term. Christians may nowadays quibble about whether creation took six days or six billion years, but from the standpoint of theodicy what mattered was that it took any time at all. Thus, "divine omnipotence" was understood as God ultimately getting his way – in the fullness of time – but by means that may not be obvious to the naked eye and hence require scientific study, the fruits of which would provide guidance in our own efforts to realize God's plan. In this respect, the theodicists took the "artificing" of God very literally: God's craft lies in making any matter that he is given conform to his idea.

None of this perhaps makes God very lovable, as he would appear quite willing to sacrifice his creatures for some higher design principle. While theodicy has continued to fascinate politicians who think in world-historic terms and hold other people's lives in their hands, its detached speculations have been widely shunned by clerics who see them as corrosive of the pastoral mission of churches (e.g. Milbank 1990). Nevertheless, Christian theology has long disputed the extent to which emotional attachment is either a sufficient or a necessary condition for moral action (Fuller 2012: ch. 4). Generally speaking, the original theodicists associated the emotions with the animal side of humanity that, to at least some degree, needs to be relinquished in order to live by an ethic fit for creatures in *imago dei*.

The main secular legacy of this theological hard line has been the two main schools of modern ethics – *utilitarianism* and *deontology*. They descend from two kinds of explanations/justifications that theodicists offered to the presence of radical imperfection in nature: The utilitarians secularize the Leibnizian deity's tolerance of suffering and even death in some of his creatures as a learning experience for the rest of us, thereby resulting in "the greatest good for the greatest number". In contrast, the deontologists, who associate ethics with principled action, regardless of consequence, derive from Leibniz correspondent, the great Cartesian theologian Nicolas Malebranche, to Kant a conception of God as the autonomous source of law within which the divine plan must be realized, whatever hardship that causes for humans along the way (Schneewind 1997). Perhaps unsurprisingly, the turn against both positions following Alasdair MacIntyre (1981, 1999) has been to reacquaint those who pass ethical judgement with their (allegedly) irreducibly situated and animal roots.

Epistemology as divine psychology 51

Whether the apparent erratic relationship between events and desert was attributed to a deity blind to detail or to humans blind to the deity's plan, a recipient of good fortune was incentivized to try still harder. It was this mentality, which came into its own with the rise of Calvinism, that enabled the "Protestant Ethic" to evolve into the "Spirit of Capitalism", as successful businesspeople came to value re-investment over personal consumption as the appropriate attitude to profit in a world where one's current state is at best an indirect indicator of future success (Weber 1958a). Here Marx provides the missing link to transhumanism, as the technological principle of efficiency – that is, maximum production from minimum consumption – becomes a materialist version of what Weber (1963) suggestively called "asceticism", recalling the Greek term for an athletic form of self-discipline. Here humanly embodied labour itself comes to be seen as so disposable that we should welcome any opportunity to offload centuries of drudgery to machines and transfer our self-identities to whatever tasks in which our bodies can outperform machines.

In contrast to all this, Berger (1967) provides a more generic treatment of religion which gives greater weight to Buddhism and other Eastern theodicies. He argues that simply to recognize the compatibility of God's best efforts and recurrent suffering provides both consolation and exoneration whenever our own hopes are dashed and our best laid plans go awry. The Western version of this attitude is most pronounced in the classical "pagan" philosophies of Epicureanism and Scepticism, the modern descendant of which is the laissez-faire attitude associated with the Reverend Thomas Malthus's population pressure model of human survival, which Darwin subsequently generalized across all species under the rubric of "natural selection". Malthus argued that statistically regular mortality rates, according to which the poor die more often and more quickly than the rich, belong to some inscrutable divine optimization strategy – not a humanly manageable problem for which poor laws, and later the welfare state, might provide a solution (Fuller 2006b: ch. 13). In effect, God works not *with* us but only *through* us: Our lives are literally the deity's experiments, an understanding of which (so Malthus believed) would allow us to abandon the delusions of grandeur that often pass for a sense of moral obligation towards the poor. Here we should not underestimate the dampening effect that the appearance of statistical data on the relentlessness of, say, infant mortality had on Enlightenment-style optimism. Perhaps the most notable long-term defensive response to such Malthusian pessimism has been the adoption of the same statistical methods to track the efficacy of medical treatments (Wootton 2006: ch. 8).

A striking feature of Weber's and Berger's takes on theodicy is that they both point to the emergence of the secular science of political economy in the late eighteenth century. This "overdetermination" of

52 Epistemology as divine psychology

theodicy's historical trajectory may be understood by considering the legal foundations of the medieval university as one of the original "corporations" (*universitates*) – indeed, that the first university, Bologna, was dominated by a law faculty dedicated to translating Christian theological conceptions of our relationship with God into the precursors of modern economic concepts, especially those taken to be indicative of the capitalist system. Prior to the innovation of the "corporation" as a legal category, an individual's legal status was determined in one of two ways: by birth (*gens*), which was the default position, or by temporary association (*socius*), the exceptional position. Corresponding to this distinction was, on the one hand, ordinary economic activity – the maintenance of the family household – and, on the other, the occasional buying and selling of goods in the market to make up for what one cannot produce in one's own home. Lacking was the third category of a perpetually self-sustaining market for goods regardless of their capacity to satisfy household needs: in other words, the production and distribution of goods for their own sake, the essence of capitalism – but also, of course, the pursuit of science (Fuller 2006b: ch. 4).

An important linguistic innovation of the twelfth century associated with the great Bolognese glossator Azzone Soldanus was the reification of "what is between" – *quod inter est* in Latin (aka *interest*) – to refer literally to the additional value accrued by money in the time spent between the provision of a loan and its repayment (Langholm 1998). Before the coinage of "interest", the idea that one should charge for lending money was seen as taking advantage of another person's misery. However, Soldanus turned the old concept on its head, focusing on the opportunity that the loan provides the poor person to improve himself. After all, if the borrower can repay the loan with interest in the allotted time, then he will probably have generated a profit in the interim, which having raised his standard of living, would demonstrate his worthiness to have received the loan. In short, interest turns the loan into a moral test of the borrower that is made possible through temporary self-restraint on the part of the lender. As Weber (1958a) observed, this moralistic slant on the loan, which ideally eventuates in the improvement of both parties, came to be especially emphasized in Calvinist theology, in which the charging of interest functioned as a vehicle of moral instruction. A secular descendant of this strategy of binding two parties together so that they mutually benefit by cancelling out each other's excesses was used in the eighteenth century to justify the virtue of markets, which were envisaged as forcing producers to be more practical and consumers more discriminating than each might be otherwise (Rothschild 2001; Fuller 2006c).

Two points stand out in this history. First, the general idea that more can be made of less – or even that virtue can be made of vice – reflects our ontological distance from God. God does not require any incentives, nudges or psychological tricks to do what is right: The deity does it spontaneously and without solicitation, let alone at the "right price"; hence, the stark contrast drawn by Calvinists between the Grace by which God saves people without requiring anything in return and the Roman Catholic doctrine of salvation by good works, which was held in contempt for insinuating that the deity would engage in exchange relations, as if God needs or desires something that only we can provide. Second, the implicit valorization of poverty, Weber's "asceticism", pertains to the path we need to undertake to become more "godlike", which again is understood as something radically different from simply trying to please or appease God. One cannot stress too much that the progressive strain in the history of Abrahamic theism takes seriously *both* the blasphemy of our supposing that God wants something that we are uniquely capable of providing and the virtue of aspiring to adopt God's standpoint as our own.

An important benchmark here is the incorporation of the "mendicant" (or begging) Christian orders, the Dominicans and Franciscans, into the Roman Catholic fold in the thirteenth century, mainly to staff the early universities. These orders had arisen to protest the Church of Rome's increasing preoccupation with secular affairs, especially property ownership. By personal example, they demonstrated how one could survive by a sophisticated form of begging that involved earning the respect of multiple benefactors by showing that one could always yield a profit from whatever one was given. At the same time, this "diversity of income streams", as we would now put it, provided a material basis for autonomy that was lacking in the patronage-based political economy of spirituality that characterized most of Christendom and Islam. As a result, these friars persuasively presented themselves as no mere stewards but outright creators of value – and thus not members of a servile species but exemplars of God's offspring. The mendicants' devaluation of steady-state ownership in favour of self-transcending productivity would re-emerge in secular garb as the liberal ideological front of the Industrial Revolution (K. Polanyi 1944).

The mendicants stressed the value added by a "spiritual" life in the material world. It was in this context that "vows of poverty" acquired world-historic significance. "Poverty" (*povertas*) clearly did not have today's negative connotations (Langholm 1998). Indeed, it was most naturally understood as humanity's attempt to approximate divine creation *ex nihilo* by "doing the most with the least". In that sense, poverty was the prototype for the modern concept of *efficiency*. Mendicant poverty may be contrasted with, on the one hand, the *miserable* who are inefficient because their labour is underemployed, and on the other, the *miserly* who are inefficient because they hoard their wealth rather than invest

54   *Epistemology as divine psychology*

it productively. The progress of modern capitalism has heightened the experience of this contrast. On the one hand, the surplus of workers in an increasingly automated workplace drives wages down, resulting in the poor having to struggle more to make ends meet; on the other hand, the rich are caught in an endlessly ephemeral consumer culture, as they need to acquire more goods to maintain the same level of satisfaction. In both cases, diminishing returns on investment is the ultimate secular sin.

The dominant *universitas* of the modern era – the state (first as city-state and then nation-state) – has tried to resolve these countervailing excesses of the human condition through welfare policies, in which redistributive taxation has increasingly figured. It is often overlooked that this development has always had strong cross-ideological (Christian Democrat and Social Democrat) and cross-denominational (Catholic and Protestant) Christian backing on both sides of the Atlantic (Daly 2006). But arguably, from their inception, universities have been in the business of redistributing specifically *epistemic* advantage – in the medieval context, by commenting on canonical sacred and pagan texts, so as to make it easier for students to acquire the scholar's knowledge. On the one hand, this process ensured that scholars did not succumb to the version of sloth that Thomas Aquinas called *acedia*, a souring of the soul that resulted from knowing too much to act decisively. On the other hand, slowly but surely, knowledge that might have otherwise remained esoteric and authoritarian became part of an ideational commons, on which various disenfranchised groups down through the centuries have drawn to free themselves from conditions that inhibited the fulfilment of their divine potential.

Theism by other means: sociology's secular problematic

The very idea of "sociology" has a deep but vexed relationship with theism. I say "the very idea" rather than "the discipline" because Auguste Comte's original coinage of "sociology" in the 1830s referred more to a political ideology than an academic discipline. Indeed, he advocated a "positive religion", or "positivism" (Wernick 2001). Under the circumstances, only the advent of the Third Republic in France in 1870, with its removal of church oversight for public education, made it possible for "sociology" to be incorporated into the school system; hence, the six-decade time lag between Comte's original proposals and Emile Durkheim's establishment of the first sociology department in 1895. In Comte's hands, sociology was designed to mark the culmination of a certain sense of "secularization", whereby religion does not disappear from social life but the basis of worship is shifted from a transcendent deity to "humanity". This ideal had already taken concrete form in the great architectural legacy of the French Revolution, Le Panthéon, the mausoleum to the illustrious dead of France that still overlooks the Sorbonne in the Latin Quarter of Paris.

In its original aspiration to replace – not simply eliminate – theology, Comtean sociology was comparable to the contemporaneous post-Kantian revival of "philosophy" in Germany in the first quarter of the nineteenth century as the pedagogical site for integrating all forms of knowledge into a form of human empowerment that would render obsolete the need for supernatural authority figures (Fuller 2009a: chs 1–2). Powers previously reserved for God would now be placed squarely in the hands of the humans who are their ultimate source. In this respect, the key difference between Fichte, Schelling and Hegel, on the one hand, and Comte, on the other, as agents of "Enlightenment" is that the former promoted their post-theological epistemology from within the institutional protection of a state-backed university system, whereas Comte always remained the outsider in search of an organizational vehicle. This sociological difference may also account for the manner in which the transition from, so to speak, clerical to civic religion was to occur. Whereas the German idealists continued to speak seamlessly in terms of the "spirit" moving various forms of knowledge that are intentionally integrated in the person, Comte spoke much more openly of the replacement of spiritualist by mechanistic explanations, in particular dismissing "psychology" as pseudo-theology whose scientific aspirations would be properly realized by a sociologized version of physiology.

Comte's original alienation from France's Roman Catholic academic establishment enabled him and his followers to develop their intellectual differences from religious dogma more explicitly than their German counterparts. This difference is clearly felt in Durkheim's sociology of religion, which is fixated on the function – rather than the content – of religious concepts. Thus, whereas most of Max Weber's sociology of religion is devoted to how various senses of one's relationship to God and the cosmos have determined specific social relations, Durkheim's is more concerned with the role that religious concepts have played in defining the outer limits of permissible human activity, a sociologized version of Kant's "regulative ideal of reason" (Weber 1963; Durkheim 1961). This difference in emphasis may help to explain why Durkheim appears to have been more optimistic than Weber about humanity's prospects in the face of "secularization". Durkheim fought for a welfare state based on the mutual solidarity of social classes, in which sociology would be taught as "moral education" in lieu of pastoral theology, while Weber remained throughout his life a liberal nationalist who envisaged that the gradual weakening (aka "disenchantment") of the original Christian impulse in modern society might well eventuate in charismatic rule by naked force. Where Durkheim saw in secularization the purification of society's

56 *Epistemology as divine psychology*

original religious impulse, Weber saw only the dissipation and possibly perversion of that impulse.

German academia effectively simulated the Comtean assault on theism by the formal separation of the strictly epistemic from the pastoral functions of theology, the origin of what Max Weber would a century later canonize as "value-free" inquiry. This distinction, associated with Friedrich Schleiermacher's ascendancy to the theology chair at the renovated University of Berlin in 1810, was a largely self-protective move by theologians who wanted to preserve a distinctive "religious" sentiment necessary for the pastoral mission from its possible erosion by both political indoctrination and academic criticism (R. Collins 1998: ch. 12). But this move also freed theology faculties to inculcate "critico-historical" approaches to sacred texts, which served to "naturalize" them. Thus, by the 1830s several theologians claimed that their study of these texts effectively falsified most, if not all, of the sacred mysteries of Christianity that were still a source of political legitimacy. In the fore-front was Ludwig Feuerbach, a former student of Hegel's, whose intel-lectual pilgrimage from theology to the natural sciences resulted in a "humanism" rather close to Comte's religion of humanity that strongly influenced his younger contemporaries, Karl Marx and Friedrich Engels. The final twist in this tale is Ernst Mach's (1960) application of "critico-historical" to his late nineteenth-century account of how a church-like physics establishment managed to suppress two centuries of empirical and conceptual objections to classical mechanics – a thesis that in turn inspired Einstein, Heisenberg and others to revisit those objections and thereby revolutionize the physical sciences in the early twentieth century (Fuller 2000b: ch. 2).

An important question clearly runs through this general account of sociology's vexed relationship to theism: *Does the "secularization" of modern society mark a sharp break with or a sublimated extension of Abrahamic religious ideas and sentiments?* The two implied alternatives were given canonical formulation by, respectively, Hans Blumenberg (1986) and Karl Löwith (1949). Blumenberg imagines secularization in terms of the "religious world-view" on one side of a historic divide and the "scientific world-view" on the other, whereas Löwith envisages secularization as the con-tinuous process of purifying the human spirit from its base, a Gnostic ideal that science has expressed as the elimination of error in pursuit of the one ultimate truth. For Löwith, writing in exile in the wake of the second of two science-based world wars, secularization simply channels Abrahamic absolutist impulses by more technologically enhanced means. He takes this to be a bad thing. Blumenberg, writing somewhat later and in a more conciliatory mode, takes a position akin to Kuhn (1970), which traces science's rapid technical advancement since the late seventeenth century to the exclusion of religious differences from the public grounds of epistemic justification. He takes this to be a good thing.

My own view is that Löwith's perspective is probably closer to the truth though I do not share his pessimism. In contrast, Blumenberg's position is more politically correct but perhaps captive to wishful thinking, given the further secularization that science itself has undergone since the end of the Cold War, whereby both commercial and religious forces – sometimes in tandem – have resisted general explanatory concepts that undermine or preclude the self-understanding of significant segments of the population. Unsurprisingly, given their direct bearing on our mental and physical well-being, the biomedical sciences have been the main sites of contestation. More specifically, devotees of complementary medicine and intelligent design theory (aka scientific creationism) have developed considerable academic skills (though perhaps not in the core disciplines of the orthodoxies they are challenging) as well as political, cultural and economic clout. The situation here bears comparison with the socio-politico-economic base that evolved in Europe from the sixteenth to the eighteenth centuries, in which the Reformation evolved into the Enlightenment: namely, an emergent educated middle class with dissenting religious views but a clear financial stake in the handling of civil affairs that appeared to be unduly influenced by state protected clerical interests (Wuthnow 1989: pts I–II). However, nowadays the "protected clerical interests" are those of the scientific establishment, which has led to the rise of what I have called "Protestant Science", or "Protscience" (Fuller 2010: ch. 4).

The strongest arguments for seeing secularization as constituting a sharp break with theism have always been institutional, not intellectual. Moreover, they have been related to sociology's own defining problematic. All of the works that now constitute the canon of classical sociology (e.g. Marx, Durkheim, Weber) were preoccupied with the demarcation of something called "modern society" from prior "traditional" forms of social life. The omnibus use of the word "religion" to cover what had held together complex forms of social organization prior to the rise of the modern nation-state also dates from this period, the third quarter of the nineteenth century (Masuzawa 2005). At that time the phrase "world religions" is first invoked to include not only the Abrahamic religions – Judaism, Christianity and Islam – but also Hinduism, Buddhism, Confucianism and Taoism, despite their rather disparate views on the nature and even existence of a personal deity. Against this backdrop, what makes us "modern" is the removal of "religion" in this new omnibus sense as publicly acceptable grounds for political and epistemic legitimacy. In this respect, "religion" was invented as a residual category to give a face to the "other" of modernity.

A full appreciation of the precedent for this mentality requires observing two phenomena that occurred in parallel over the previous

58   *Epistemology as divine psychology*

(eighteenth) century but are not normally associated together: on the one hand, the legal constitution of new republics in both the Old and New Worlds, most notably (and durably) that of the United States of America, which functioned *de facto* as sacred texts for a civic religion; on the other hand, the construction of colonial territories, most notably British "India", whose integration of peoples of traditionally conflicting faiths was designed to demonstrate values of fairness and efficiency that transcend entrenched religious differences and serve as a template for eventual collective self-rule. Science grew into a comparable role of secularizer as it enabled people of diverse ideological origins to unify for common purpose without first having to resolve their doctrinal differences. The English Lord Chancellor Francis Bacon had first projected such a role for science in the early seventeenth century, partly in a failed effort to prevent a religiously based civil war. Shortly after the war's end, in 1660, the Charter of the Royal Society of London institutionalized a version of Bacon's vision (Lynch 2001).

Over the next 350 years, science came to be more explicitly identified with secularization as it sided with the state against religious authorities in matters of education and public policy. This stance was rhetorically clearest in countries with strong religious ties to the Roman Catholic Church, perennially a potential source of divided political allegiance, given its attempt to command universal allegiance from a particular location. In this respect, Comtean positivism served as a basis for secular nationalism not only in France but also throughout Latin America, where the Pope was equally seen as a menacing foreign force (Zea 1963). Indeed, the Comtean motto "Order and Progress" remains inscribed in the Brazilian flag. Recalling this history helps one to appreciate the irony of the topsy-turvy politics that beset Latin America in the 1960s, when a left-leaning "liberation theology" originating from within Catholicism joined forces with a global Marxist revolutionary movement in trying to upend locally entrenched elites, typically beholden to the United States. Here the forces of universalism, regardless of church allegiance, were arrayed against particularist forms of secularism that had failed to deliver political autonomy for their people (Gutierrez 1988).

Although the Latin American case is extreme, it nevertheless points to the partly illusory character of "secularization", at least as understood sociologically. As a matter of fact, "secularization" has been strongest in the nations of northern Europe, where the (Protestant) Christian church continues to enjoy state privilege, albeit at the cost of considerable state oversight and clerical self-constraint. Where there is no such clearly institutionalized relationship (some might say "co-optation"), the churches lie in wait for when the secular state fails to command spontaneous moral legitimacy. Thus, evangelism flourishes in times of low voter turnout, when a call to return to "fundamentals" can mobilize the disaffected to support perspectives missing from the political landscape (Micklethwait and Wooldridge 2009). However, it is to the credit of secularization as an "institutional" force that these conflicts are waged for the most part by means established by secular authorities, namely, elections and judicial decisions. Whatever violence has been caused by "religious" elements has usually been focused on the alleged failure of secular authorities to abide by their own rules.

Sociological interest in theism has been focused on the institutionalization of, on the one hand, ideas and theories about God and, on the other, God-oriented practices. Weber (1963) and Durkheim (1961) may be seen as standing for those two positions, respectively. Interestingly, neither position takes "atheism", in the strict sense, as a serious proposition. God never fully disappears from the scene, as secularization appears as an extended exercise of pouring old wines in new bottles. This point is sometimes difficult to see because the disciplines involved in providing a modern translation of theistic concepts – most notably theodicy and natural theology – have fallen into disrepute, accused of ineptly trying to co-opt new ideas for purposes of apologetics. When, say, Karl Marx identified theology with "ideology" and Vilfredo Pareto with "derivatives" of a residual religious instinct, this is what they had in mind. Indeed, even theologians routinely ignore, if not condemn, theodicy and natural theology for their heterodoxy while failing to credit them for fleshing out divine agency in terms of entities and forces that enabled the scientific imagination to transcend the realm of common sense. Nevertheless, if we take the internet in the twenty-first century to be comparable to the printing press in the sixteenth century, science appears to be in the process of repeating the institutional history of Christianity (Fuller 2010: ch. 4). At the end any Catholic-like science establishment will be forced to live in an intellectual ecology populated by "Protscience" denominations that interpret the same scientific research in radically different ways, both in terms of ultimate explanations and practical implications. Kuhn's (1970) long influential idea that a science is defined by the presence of one dominant "paradigm" will thus go the way of "Christendom" as the most natural interpretation of universal Christianity. It is something that today's liberal ecumenists have yet to come to grips with.

Why naturalism is too conservative to explain science

Naturalism is the broad metaphysical position that defines reality in terms of what has been and will be experienced by ordinary empirical means. The position typically presupposes continuity in nature, such that the past is presumed to be a reliable indicator of the future. On this view,

60 *Epistemology as divine psychology*

experiments are cognitively necessary not to challenge this knowledge base but to extend it into new contexts. Here naturalists routinely underestimate the decisive role that experiments have played in the history of science: Experiments are less about enhancing our natural modes of understanding than providing access to new modes of understanding that we might otherwise lack, were it not for the intelligent design of the laboratory. Indeed, I would even argue that experimentation is a general method for transcending ordinary experience to access deeper, counterintuitive aspects of reality that over time come to be "naturalized" – but only after having disciplined the mind and senses of successive generations of scientists. Relativity and quantum theories in physics are the obvious twentieth-century examples. In contrast to this radical even "supernaturalist" view of experimentation (one that was shared by Roger and Francis Bacon), the naturalist is biased towards a kind of methodological conservatism – what Karl Popper disparaged as "inductivism" – in which "what you have seen is what you are likely to get" (e.g. Quine and Ullian 1970).

From that standpoint, I am a "reflexive naturalist" who takes the historical track record of science as offering second-order guidance to how we should extrapolate from past to future experience (Fuller 1992a; 1993: 211–17). It turns out that history teaches that while all knowledge may be ultimately "naturalized" in the sense of rendered reproducible in ordinary thought and experience, no major breakthroughs come about this way. In this respect, the difference between what philosophers of science call the contexts of *discovery* and *justification* is the epistemological equivalent of what metaphysicians mean by the distinction between *supernaturalism* (or "transcendentalism") and *naturalism*. Here it is instructive to consider naturalism alongside Hegelianism. There are two ways of interpreting the Hegelian motto, "What is real, is rational." Whereas the "Right Hegelian" mode holds that what has been already realized defines what is to be rational, the "Left Hegelian" mode holds that the real is whatever is rationalizable (in the future). Naturalism and reflexive naturalism stand in just this relationship.

Naturalism as a first-order philosophy can generate resistance to the very idea that a substantially different vision of reality is to be found by adopting the typically indirect and artificial means offered by the experimental method. (Consider the scientific establishment's ongoing scepticism towards parapsychology experiments and intelligent design theory.) As a point of historical reference, recall that while Aristotle is the paradigm case of a naturalist in the ancient and medieval worlds, the people who overthrew his hegemony in the seventeenth-century Scientific Revolution were more or less Platonists who saw in experimentation's pursuit of unrealized possibilities a privileged portal to the mind of God. Indeed, these people, notably Galileo, may not have even clearly distinguished thought experiments from concrete ones (Koyre 1968). For them a vivid imagination matched by a potent rhetoric simulated the unrealized possibilities that some future round of experimentation would ultimately vindicate. And certainly in the case of Galileo, that bold conjecture proved correct (Feyerabend 1975).

But let us take naturalists at their word that their position is the default metaphysical stance of the natural sciences. Then that fact must be itself explained by the theories and methods of the natural sciences. But how does one do that without begging crucial questions? For example, it is tempting to argue that the natural sciences are simply a somewhat more disciplined version of common sense, which itself is an extension of the problem-solving skills that all animals deploy in adapting to their environments. Such a view was explicitly promoted in the twentieth century by the American pragmatists John Dewey and W. V. O. Quine, both of whom invoked "naturalism" to name their own positions. It had the virtue of bringing science down to earth, by making it seem to be part of our evolutionary heritage, given Darwin's view that the cognitive capacities of organisms are adapted to their normal habitats, including the threat of extinction if the environment changes suddenly. However, the power afforded by scientific knowledge is decidedly non-Darwinian: It takes us out of our natural habitats, leading us to radically transform and even replace them, while we extend our horizons to the heavens. Indeed, from a Darwinian standpoint, it remains a mystery why the most highly valued form of human knowledge – first in the West and then the world – should be a science of mathematical physics that aims to understand all of reality from a cognitive standpoint that does not approximate that of the average human, even today.

Taking mathematical physics as my exemplar, let me highlight three senses in which science aspires to *universal* knowledge, the motivation (*not* the justification) of which defies naturalist scruples (for greater elaboration, see Fuller 2010: ch. 2):

1 Science aspires to knowledge of all things, under conditions potential and actual, regardless of their relevance to our everyday lives, let alone personal or species survival.
2 Science aspires to articulate all things in a common language, no matter how different these things may appear to our senses.
3 Science aspires to be knowledge for everyone, regardless of where and how we live, a universal human legacy.

The Abrahamic religions – Judaism, Christianity and Islam – provide the only clear historic basis for conceptualizing science as "universal" in this

62 *Epistemology as divine psychology*

robust tripartite sense of aspiring to knowledge of all things by and for all people. That basis is the Biblical doctrine that humans are unique as beings created in the image and likeness of God. To be sure, the doctrine has been variously interpreted, but it has been generally read as a call to epistemic empowerment – at the very least, that humans can know (and do) much more than what is necessary to maintain their animal existence. Notwithstanding the various obstacles that organized religion has placed in the way of science over the centuries, the best explanation for the shape and persistence of science's fundamental questions is theological. The point is driven home in the various questions of "origins", "ends" and "design" that have framed scientific inquiry into the nature of life, mind and the universe as a whole. Unsurprisingly, naturalism's most trenchant adherents – from the ancient Epicureans to moderns like Hume and Darwin – studiously avoided reaching any firm conclusions on these matters and denied that science could ever contribute substantially to them. As we shall see below, every argument raised against natural theology could always be turned against "natural science", understood as the name of systematic inquiry into fundamental explanations.

Thomas Nagel (1986) famously identified this universal standpoint in non-theological terms as "the view from nowhere", which certainly captures the spirit of points (1) and (2) above. But it captures point (3) as well, since the range of experience – both real and imagined – of any given individual human is in fact quite limited vis-à-vis that potentially available to all of humanity. To be sure, a naturalistic explanation may be given to the "view from nowhere", especially if it is seen as a rather extreme and disciplined version of an "out of body" experience. Such hypotheses are the purview of the emerging field of *neurotheology* (Newberg 2010). For example, the attentiveness of medi-tating Franciscan nuns involves not only an abstraction from their own sense of locality but also a verbalized stream of consciousness – called "prayer" – that subjunctively mimics divine creation, understood as John the Evangelist did, namely, as *logos* declared (Burns 2012). But here the neurotheologian may wish to explore the hypothesis that the neural circuitry underlying Franciscan meditation is akin to that which attends, say, a physicist constructing an abstract mathematical model in her mind. While the formal objects of thought and the institutional practices that give them meaning may be different, the fundamental thought processes accompanying religious and scientific understanding at the highest level may be one and the same, as, say, Arthur Koestler (1959) notoriously maintained in the case of Johannes Kepler and (by implication) other seventeenth-century Scientific Revolutionaries. This is a naturalistic conclusion that would dumbfound the naturalist – simply because it suggests that phenomena that might otherwise be

Epistemology as divine psychology 63

classed with dreams or hallucinations turn out to provide the bases for exceptionally fruitful empirical research programmes.

To grasp my rather sympathetic portrayal of theology's presence in scientific epistemology, the reader must understand that "secular" does not necessarily imply "naturalistic". "Secular" mainly refers to the devolution of authority, specifically devolution from the idea that all knowledge descends in a path-dependent way from one source and is currently concentrated in a church with absolute power, including the power to absolve one from sin (or, in epistemological terms, confirm that one's errors have been corrected). In terms of a distinction drawn at the start of this chapter, secularism denies the Petrine but not the Pauline tradition in Christianity. In this respect, Kuhnian paradigms and *ex cathedra* invocations of a "scientific consensus" would count as Petrine naturalism, something I have spent my career opposing. However, secularism may still retain the idea that there is an ultimate origin to all things that in some sense determines how things have been and shall be, while allowing for a multiplicity of interpretations that then need to establish legitimacy on their own terms. This Pauline perspective is the normal self-understanding of Protestant churches, which over the years has been adopted by independently minded scientists (of the sort Popper valorized) and democratic nation-states. However, it leaves open – perhaps even radically open – the question of how unity is to be restored, if all these increasingly disparate inquirers are to return to their common source of being. This question is one that very much concerns me, as it did Hegel and Marx. However, it need not trouble the naturalist who travelling under the banner of "Darwinism" effectively picks-and-mixes Peter and Paul, accepting both the path-dependency of Peter and the multiplicity of outcomes of Paul as "natural". The patron saint of this approach is David Hume (1711–76), the dead philosopher who exerted the most influence in the English-speaking world in the twentieth century, though I doubt that will be the case in the current century.

David Hume: naturalist philosopher of diminished expectations

Hume's status as a naturalist philosopher of diminished expectations was sealed by John Maynard Keynes, whose *Treatise on Probability* (1921) canonized "Hume's problem of induction" in the way it is taught in philosophy today; namely, as a question about the grounds for generalizing from past to future experience. Keynes's point was that human life was all about dealing with this uncertainty by developing a theory of rational risk-taking. Indeed, life is the game of beating the odds against death. In that case, Hume's option of scepticism in the face of inconclusive evidence

64 *Epistemology as divine psychology*

is at best a formula for bare survival – not a flourishing existence. That Hume should have thought otherwise reveals his relatively low expectations for the human condition – that is, we should preserve what we know from experience to work rather than try to leverage it into some unknown future state.

David Hume's enduring philosophical popularity is puzzling. A noteworthy figure in his own day, Hume makes several appearances in Boswell's *Life of Johnson* as one of the leading eighteenth-century Edinburgh wits. However, his reputation was mainly as one of the original Scottish Tories, someone who gave historical legitimation to the United Kingdom, which had come into existence only a few years before his birth. His view of history somewhat anticipated today's evolutionary psychologists, who underwrite the force of precedent and tradition with remarks about their adaptive character vis-à-vis the race and environment of the people concerned. Indeed, Hume believed that humanity had multiple origins – indeed, that different races may constitute different species. Thus, his arguments against black enslavement anticipate today's opponents of cruelty to animals who would stop short of granting animals legally binding rights. Blacks are adapted to one sort of environment and whites to another – and each race does best where they belong.

Hume only started to acquire a specifically philosophical reputation with T. H. Huxley's 1879 popular presentation of him as a precursor to Darwin's naturalistic world-view, including its agnosticism with regard to ultimate causes. Nowadays, Hume is regarded still more positively, even to philosophy's own disadvantage. He appears as a great therapeutic thinker in the lineage of Epicurus, Montaigne and Wittgenstein, who aims to deflate metaphysical pretensions by revealing their futility, as evidenced by the mental anguish that their pursuit causes. In effect, we are now asked to respond to Hume in the exact opposite way to how Kant did: Instead of looking to Hume for a challenge to our sense of species privilege (which is worth defending), we should be looking to Hume as a means to escape that privilege altogether – or at least, so would today's received wisdom have us believe.

Prior to Huxley's book, the spectre of Hume was raised in philosophical circles to illustrate the sceptical dead-end to which empiricism led. This view had been popularized in Oxford in the third quarter of the nineteenth century by Thomas Hill Green, the doyen of British idealists who shortly before his death in 1882 also produced a critical edition of Hume's philosophical works, the introductions to which have been gathered under the title of *Hume and Locke* (Green 1968). Green was less interested in Hume *per se* than in the claims of the nascent science of psychology, which he took to be the legitimate heir of Hume's proposal for a "science of human nature" that was in some sense modelled on

Epistemology as divine psychology   65

Newtonian mechanics yet claimed Lockean empiricism as its foundation. (We shall return to consider the exact sense below.) Hill treated Hume as the *reductio* of this line of thought: If you take the sensing individual as the locus for knowledge, then you will be forced to conclude that knowledge is impossible because your mind does not stand apart as a separate entity, empowered to judge the combination of sensations that it receives. At most, there will be shifts between phenomenal states relative to a given body that may or may not overlap with those of other similarly embodied beings. Instead of Locke's free agents, the Humean "individual" (if that is still the right word) is dissolved into a site for shifting passions.

Nowadays we regard Hume's view of the self as a "bundle of sensations" as prescient of a variety of anti-essentialist views on personal identity that became popular in the final quarter of the twentieth century, including Derek Parfit's (1984) time-slice utilitarianism and Daniel Dennett's (2003) self-justifying narrativism. However, to understand Green's original animus to Hume, one might consider the outrage initially expressed when Richard Dawkins claimed that organisms were simply more or less adequate vehicles for the propagation of genes. In Hume's case, the idea is that our "selves" are no more than convenient animal-shaped parcels for registering and expressing sensations for a certain period of time (i.e. the span of our life) and then dispersed (given no underlying soul or afterlife). Whenever he had the opportunity, Hume stymied any pretence that a faculty called "reason" might have in either inferring deep causes or predicting the relatively distant future. In both cases, he claimed, we fall back on that enhanced collection of habits he called "animal instinct".

In Green's day, Hume's position was widely seen as based on a conflation of the "is" of predication and the "is" of identity. In other words, while the self does indeed possess sensations, it is not exhaustively constituted by them. This point had been driven home most forcefully by James Ferrier (1875), the Scottish idealist who introduced "epistemology" into English in the mid-nineteenth century. Ferrier, under the influence of Fichte and Hegel, saw the self as a god-like, second-order entity that captured the blindspots missed by first-order perception. Properly deployed, the self was capable of providing normative focus to experiences that might otherwise be treated with equal significance simply by virtue of appearing before the mind's eye.

It is worth recalling that "consciousness", the term normally used to capture this second-order "standing above" relationship to experience, was only coined in the generation before Hume's birth by Ralph Cudworth, a friend of Locke and one of the Cambridge Christian Platonists (Passmore 1951). The idea of consciousness was designed to provide a sense of ownership to one's mind by obliging it to organize otherwise contradictory

66   *Epistemology as divine psychology*

experience into a coherent whole, the internal logic of which would then mark one's own identity. One implication, which became increasingly important for the history of epistemology, was the purposefulness with which one comes to know "objects" (i.e. the "objective" of thought, aka "intentionality"). In other words, it is not simply a matter of the mind allowing itself to be receptive to the world – either intellectually or experientially – but that a quasi-ethical demand was placed on the thinker to take the initiative to organize his mental life.

Here Green was using philosophy to score political points (Offer 2006). In his day, psychology was being promoted as a scientific metaphysics with quite discernible political consequences, namely, support for a form of laissez-faire individualism that embedded humanity firmly in the animal kingdom – *à la* Herbert Spencer. Green presented Hume as the ironic culmination of this tradition: individualism self-deconstructed. Although Green's influence turned out to be quite limited in philosophy, his viewpoint strongly coloured the constitution of the British civil service ethic and later facilitated the Labour Party's split from the Liberals. Green saw Hume as having reduced the "person" to the individual body, only then in turn to reduce that body to a site for registering clearly body-related experience. While such a view might work in a world in which individuals are understood as members of a population whose identities are determined purely in terms of overlapping properties (e.g. shared genes, shared experience), it does not work in a world where individuals are valued in their own right, in which case the relevant relationships with other individuals are not in terms of occurrent natural properties but formally undertaken arrangements. This then became the principal metaphysical basis on which sociology split from biology across Europe a century ago.

Despite failing to provide an adequate metaphysical basis for the autonomous individual required of social liberalism, Hume has remained the darling of philosophers because of his consistent scepticism in the face of all forms of authority, be it religious or scientific – even if at the end he leaves us with relatively little "common knowledge" on which to found an epistemology. The key to his appeal may rest on his capacity to provide sharp "observational" judgements in the most literal sense. In other words, Hume appears to use his memory to translate what he sees – which would otherwise be a set of fleeting impressions – into a clear and distinct object of thought. (It may also explain Hume's fondness for journalism as a "philosophical" activity.) This is not a trivial point. After all, on the one hand, one's memory might be regarded as generally unreliable, if not simply degenerate over time; on the other, one's vision might be held to be inherently partial, and hence routinely failing to encompass the entire relevant spatio-temporal context for understanding what one sees. Had Hume taken these liabilities seriously, he would have been driven to invoke either authoritative testimony or some higher "rational" faculty – one not driven by sensation – to modify, critique or overrule whatever passes before one's eyes. On the contrary, it turns out that Hume was sufficiently convinced by memory-focused observation that he used it to resolve the profoundest metaphysical disputes.

A good case in point is his dismissal of the argument from design in nature in *Dialogues Concerning Natural Religion* (published in 1779), which combines four observations: (1) in order for the idea of an "intelligent designer" of nature to be intelligible, said "designer" must engage in an indefinitely extended version of what humans do when they intelligently design; (2) in that case, we should recognize the handiwork of such a designer in nature, yet we are presented with imperfection and change over time; (3) moreover, whatever evidence for design we detect in nature appears to have come about in a manner quite different from that of human design, so as to cast doubt on whether what happens in nature is by design at all; (4) in light of the foregoing, we might reasonably conclude that the very idea of an intelligent designer is nothing more than an anthropocentric – if not outright egocentric – delusion (Hume 1935).

Modern atheism – especially the current strain of "New Atheism" of Richard Dawkins (2006) and other Anglo-American public intellectuals – is founded on these "arguments", a term I place in scare quotes because Hume is really expressing a normative attitude about how we should use our brains, or interpret the products of our brains. Thus, when Hume advocates a moral science based on "experimental reasoning", he is not referring to either the spirit or the practice of the "experimental method" as it is understood today (or arguably even by Francis Bacon). Rather, he simply means the process by which we discount the evidentiary weight of authorities and then test against new experience what our "free" (from authority) memory-enhanced observation would have us expect. Hume does not imagine that someone like Newton – let alone a latter-day scientist – might successfully simulate, in either the "controlled" (aka intelligently designed) environment of the laboratory or the code of a computer programme, conditions that would have given rise to nature as we experience it now.

In other words, Hume could not imagine adopting the creator's standpoint in an attempt to reverse-engineer divine creation – perhaps because he felt he would have to believe in God first. But of course, such a task makes eminent sense, if we take literally that we have been created "in the image and likeness of God". Like most latter-day atheists, Hume does not even entertain this possibility, which leads him to fall back on the fact that to our memory-enhanced observation, organisms appear to come about, develop and die quite differently from machines. He never

68 Epistemology as divine psychology

considers that this difference in appearance might be superficial – in particular, that organisms are more machine-like than our "natural" senses would have us believe. To be sure, in the second half of the eighteenth century, this would have been a heroic hypothesis (Fuller 2010: ch. 2). Nevertheless, it was increasingly pursued in the nineteenth and certainly the twentieth centuries, and it bore remarkable fruit – not least the molecular revolution in biology. In retrospect, we might even say that the long-standing metaphysical dispute between "mechanism" and "organism" has been simply one of perspective, in which the mechanists look at nature from the side of the creator and organicists from the side of the created. Here it is worth recalling that while Hume is popularly regarded as a pro-science philosopher, his esteem for Newton is limited to his having identified durable, general empirical regularities in nature – not that Newton had fathomed nature's *modus operandi*, let alone the levers of divine agency.

Here Hume is usefully contrasted with two of the leading dissenting Christian ministers and scientists of his day, David Hartley and Joseph Priestley (Laudan 1981: ch. 7). In particular, Priestley, who (despite theoretical errors) is normally credited with the discovery of oxygen, took the aim of experiment to be to reproduce, not conditions that somehow emerge spontaneously in nature, but the physical parameters within which the divine plan is implemented. Unlike modern accounts of the experimental method, which tend to discount the experimenter's personality (if not treat it as an outright liability), Priestley regarded the experimenter's participation in a laboratory demonstration as crucial to capture not only how nature behaves but also how God meant it to behave. Since Priestley included the creative side of the experimental process as part of its official record of scientific evidence, his method is nowadays often characterized as "sloppy" or (when polite) "phenomenological" (Boantza 2007). But again, this is merely because we do not take experiments to reveal anything about some hypothetical "natural experimenter" (aka God) – only about some hypothetical "nature".

Finally, let me say something a bit more about the rival conceptions of the brain that distinguished Hume from Hartley and Priestley, since all three philosophers are normally lumped together in history of psychology textbooks as members of the "associationist" school of thought (Allen 1999). For Hume, the brain's associative powers are simply an expression of our animal natures. To be sure, our mind is regularly exposed to competing and contradictory experiences but over time these "animal spirits" eventually settle into habits, reflections upon which become the bases for the laws of nature that we discover. In contrast, Hartley and Priestley were both somewhat aligned with the "enthusiast" wing of the Christian Enlightenment (which included Methodism), which even

Hume had realized in his essay "On Superstition and Enthusiasm" managed to marry a fiercely pro-God and pro-science attitude (Hume 1987).

The enthusiasts interpreted our animal spirits as forcing upon us decisions to resolve these conflicting associations with which experience normally presents us. This was the context in which Priestley first introduced the utilitarian principle of weighing costs and benefits to secure maximum benefit with minimum pain, where the emphasis was placed (*contra* Epicurus) on the maximization of benefit and hence an acceptance of a certain level of pain in the process. (In this respect, the enthusiasts attempted to simulate a divine standpoint by achieving a state of "ecstasy", which literally means the experience of standing outside oneself, or self-transcendence, in which one realizes in a single moment how all the disparate pains and pleasures in one's life constitute a meaningful whole.) Such calculation was seen as a physically necessary yet normatively defining process, as it focused the brain in a way that both integrated and displaced the original conflicting experiences in a more edifying direction. Indeed, this process may have provided the psychological prototype for the idea of dialectical synthesis found in the German idealist tradition. Certainly this was the impression left by Friedrich Engels (2005) in his singular praise of Priestley in his late work, *Ludwig Feuerbach and the End of Classical German Philosophy* – and it anticipates Keynes's rationalization of the animal spirits, in respect to which the Humean conception of the human condition appears safe, slow and satisfied.

The need for theism to explain science

Once we recognize the inadequacy of an unreflexive naturalism such as Hume's to explain the aspirations – and success – of science, the meanings of many of the key metaphysical, if not ideological, positions associated with the scientific world-view start to look less secure. In particular, materialism starts to look problematic. Marx's co-conspirator, Friedrich Engels got it exactly right when he characterized the nineteenth-century revolution in thermodynamics as heralding a "dematerialized materialism" in both science and society (Rabinbach 1990). Here Engels was expressing approval that the English word "work" had come to mean human labour (*Arbeit* in German) and mechanical power (*Kraft*), both of which could be understood in the same mathematical terms as the release of energy over a certain distance for a certain duration. For Engels, a true believer in conservation principles, thermodynamics proved that any increase in production would require an increase in productivity – that is, an efficiency saving in energy expenditure. The only way that could happen would be through a more intelligently organized workforce. Though hardly a spiritualist, Engels nevertheless recognized that humanity's species-distinctive

70 *Epistemology as divine psychology*

sense of intellectual progress lay in its increasing ability to do more with less over time. This intuition continues to be respected in the pivotal role played by new technology in models of economic growth.

But exactly how does the requisite intelligence come about – through some sort of self-generated reorganization of the current system or through the introduction of a wholly new factor from outside the system? The economists' way of posing the question has acquired more general currency: Is technological innovation "endogenous" or "exogenous" in origin? Throughout its history as a political practice, Marxism has struggled with a version of this problem, namely, how to manage the transition from capitalism to socialism: Should one wait patiently until the material factors and social relations of production rearrange themselves in some appropriate manner (e.g. during a war or a depression), or should one strike decisively with a top-down strategy that activates elements of a system that might otherwise remain dormant indefinitely? In sum, we have the difference between social democracy and revolutionary communism: Karl Kautsky the politician in office *versus* Lenin the leader in exile as rival heirs to the legacy of Marx and Engels.

For those who like their conceptual distinctions to bear less political freight, analogous cases are readily found. Consider cybernetics, a field that aimed to understand system maintenance in terms of information theory, an application of thermodynamics to communication under suboptimal conditions, as in the noise generated by field telephones ("walkie-talkies") in wartime. Cybernetics captured the imaginations of a broad range of interdisciplinary polymaths in the third quarter of the twentieth century, including the mathematician Norbert Wiener and the anthropologist Gregory Bateson, who debated whether the difference between, say, good and evil, right and wrong, ordered and disordered could be exhaustively explained by the self-regulated rearrangement of the components ("servomechanisms") within a given system (Heims 1991). Wiener was tempted by this position from his reading of *Paradise Lost* and *Faust*, in which evil emerges from a shift in the selection pressure on qualities that in an earlier environment would have resulted in good (Wiener 1950, 1964; cf. Mirowski 2002: 54–68). In contrast, Bateson (1972) leveraged some ideas derived from the paradoxes of set theory to argue that a higher-order system may need to operate in ways that are at odds with the system on which it acts.

In the contemporary intellectual landscape, we might contrast Stuart Kauffman's (1995) "order for free" defence of a self-organizational approach to evolution that downplays the role of natural selection (or, for that matter, any *deus ex machina*, including a deity) with William Dembski's (2002) "no free lunch" argument against the self-sufficiency of evolutionary algorithms, which implicitly allows for a theologically inspired idea of intelligent design as the source of genuinely new information in nature. However one ultimately stands on the various issues at stake, it is clear that we have moved a long way from the idea that nature can be understood as if it were the product of no intelligence at all. The long march from the blind chance and mindless necessity of classical materialism to the intelligently organized work that Engels adumbrated for a dematerialized materialism began with the explicit introduction of the engineering mentality into physics through thermodynamics, which quickly spread to political economy and physiology, the dominant biomedical science well into the twentieth century. Later in the century, this trajectory acquired forward momentum from the mathematical formulation of information theory and the invention of the solid-state transistor, culminating in the discovery of DNA as the biological precedent for this feat of miniaturized storage and transmission of information, a point that has been long stressed by Stephen Meyer (2009).

From the standpoint of intelligent design theory, the true scientific revolution in biology that allowed the discipline finally to break away from natural history (as both physics and economics had already done) so as to catch up with developments in the physical sciences would be recounted as follows. First, respect would be paid to the mid-nineteenth-century Moravian monk Gregor Mendel, who first discerned interesting mathematical patterns in inheritance that, after some neglect, became the basis for population genetics in the early twentieth century. He is reasonably counted as the Copernicus figure in this revolution. However, the story starts to acquire serious momentum with the molecularization of genetics in the 1930s once Warren Weaver, a pioneer in information theory and director of the natural sciences division of the Rockefeller Foundation, funded the re-tooling of Cambridge's Cavendish Laboratories to enable the discovery of the structure of DNA, the downstream effects of which continue to this day in the mechanical sequencing of genomes from various species (Fuller 2011: ch. 3).

In terms of this alternative historiography, the Darwinian "tree of life" image of phylogeny may no longer be treated as a self-sufficient account of the actual descent of the species, say, as suggested by the *au courant* hypothesis of the "molecular clock", whereby differences in the genomes of different species are taken to imply when they divided from a common ancestor in evolutionary history. Rather, phylogeny may come to be understood as a prototype for, so to speak, a periodic table of biological elements, whereby the macromolecules of the genes are correlated with the expression of traits that may recur at several moments and in different creatures in natural history. In retrospect, Darwin's evolutionary approach to taxonomy may come to be seen as a temporary diversion from the original strategy put forward by Carolus Linnaeus in the eighteenth century to classify life forms according to a design-based logic, the legacy of which continues in the Linnaean coinage, *Homo sapiens* ("man the wise"), a shorthand attempt at a functional definition of our species.

While none of these challenges to the conceptual default settings of Darwin's account of natural history undermines evolution *per se*, it does re-open questions about whatever ends might unfold in the evolutionary process as well as its *modus operandi*. Moreover, one may remain a naturalist and harbour such counter-Darwinian thoughts. For example, a quarter-century ago, two systematic taxonomists drew on thermodynamics to equate the trajectory of evolution with an overall increase in biological entropy (Brooks and Wiley 1986). It follows that whatever direction evolution seems to be taking is simply a reflection of the elimination of the "free energy" available for radically different life forms to develop. We might think of this limitation of life-options as nature gradually expending itself. Thus, any semblance of progress is an illusion created by the path-dependency of a process in the wake of which lies a lengthening trail of extinct precursors. This rather gloomy view of things envisages humans as possibly the last surviving species in an always already dying world. Although neither Darwin nor the biologist of recent times whose work was closest in spirit to Darwin's, Stephen Jay Gould, were signed up to the entropy theory, it captures their own rather pessimistic sense of evolution's naturalistic endgame, which Lord Kelvin had popularized in Darwin's day as the inevitable "heat death of the universe".

But what naturalistically looks like a mere contingency may also provide evidence for purpose, understood from a transcendental standpoint. Consider Cambridge's Professor of Palaeobiology, Simon Conway Morris (2003), an Anglican Christian who nevertheless joins the atheist Richard Dawkins in rejecting the exaggerated sense of contingency that Gould (and Darwin) associated with evolutionary history. But where Dawkins seems satisfied that natural selection is sufficient to explain the adaptation of species to their environments, Conway Morris argues that larger forces are also in play that, in effect, *overdetermine* evolutionary outcomes. Contrary to the spirit of Gould's (1989) famous thought experiment, replaying the tape of natural history would very likely produce more-or-less the same run of species. In support of this claim, Conway Morris reads the palaeo-biological record as implying the long-term convergence of life-forms – a hopeful spin on the entropy theory's "elimination of life-options". Although Conway Morris's mobilization of evidence is impressively diverse and up-to-date, the claim that life-forms tend to converge, rather than diverge, over time is the oldest and most persistent scientific objection to Darwin's construal of evolution. Indeed, over the past century, it has been associated with a variety of heretical Catholic biologists from St George Mivart to Pierre Teilhard de Chardin (Fuller 2008a: ch. 3).

Conway Morris (2003) subscribes to the view that over the aeons "life" has "navigated" the space of biological possibilities to reach similar solutions to similar problems of environmental adaptation. The image of navigation is not new to this general discussion. Not only is it embedded in the very word "cybernetics" (from the Greek for "helmsman"), but, more to the point, it recurs in Neo-Lamarckian accounts of evolution that stress both the uniqueness and the ultimacy of humanity. Taken to its extreme, the image suggests that everything worth preserving about evolutionary history eventually finds its way into our own biological makeup – perhaps in the future with the explicit help of biotechnology in the spirit of an exploratory "synthetic biology" that treats the genome as a zone tolerant of trial and error (Church and Regis 2012).

While Conway Morris himself fails to draw such a provocative conclusion, it can be found in the work of Teilhard de Chardin (1955) and that of his most significant mainstream defender in biological science, the geneticist Theodosius Dobzhansky, the person most responsible for converting the Neo-Darwinian synthesis into biology's dominant paradigm (Dobzhansky 1937). In a late work designed to combine his Ukrainian Orthodox Christian faith and his life-long advocacy of eugenics, Dobzhansky (1967) invoked the idea of *theosis*, namely, Jesus's discovery of his own divine nature, which Christians regard as the "Transfiguration" of Jesus into Christ (cf. Garner 2006: ch. 3). For Dobzhansky, the scientific discovery of biological evolution constitutes a secular and universalizable version of this moment, as we come to acquire godlike powers by understanding the principles and conditions under which life may be created and destroyed.

Recalling our earlier brief discussion of neurotheology, *theosis* should be understood as the moment when one comes to see the world from outside one's own body – from a distance that would render all of history equally present, which is how God presumably sees the matter. Understood as a kind of human experience, it has a clear neuroscientific basis (Eagleman 2009). While often expressed in mystical terms, *theosis* is arguably none other than an articulation of what is called, after John McTaggart, the "B-theory of time" – the homogeneous sense of temporality that Newton made integral to mathematical physics (Funkenstein 1986: ch. 2). The two most common representations of the journey to *theosis* are as either a world-historic sequence of stages over several (but finite) generations culminating in the collective realization of *theosis* or a sequenced course of study undergone as a discipline for the individual realization of *theosis*, the former corresponding to Joachim of Fiore and the latter to St Bonaventure (Passmore 1970: ch. 11).

As it happens, what Bonaventure (1993) originally dubbed "the mind's journey to God" follows what the German idealists would recognize as

74　Epistemology as divine psychology

the logic of the dialectical method: prima facie polar opposites are divested of their polarity and incorporated as complementary parts of some greater whole. Thus, Bonaventure's first two stages of this intellectual path are taken up with natural and social science, respectively, which in Hegel's *Lectures on the History of Philosophy* turns into the study of being *an sich* ("in itself") and *für sich* ("for itself"). In both cases, the first moment of the dialectic focuses on potentiality, the second moment on actuality – that is, the range of directions in which something may go (but of which it is not aware) and the specific direction in which it realizes it is going (but without knowing the alternative directions). The third "synthetic" moment is knowledge of where one is going, understood in terms of the alternatives (i.e. "in and for itself").

For Bonaventure, such knowledge was the product of theology, for Hegel philosophy, and for Marx revolutionary praxis (in which political economy functions as the materialist surrogate for theology and philosophy when it comes to elaborating the scope of the possible). In the twenty-first century, for all we know, the same function may be served by synthetic biology. Presented in its best light, the synthetic moment of the dialectic is the realm of informed free choice. But of course, that is not the only light in which it may be presented. A long tradition of conservative – if not reactionary – political theory recoils at what it demonizes as the "Gnostic" tendencies implicit in this entire line of thought. Gnosticism is a Christian heresy that not only regards any condition of humanity short of divine reunion as inherently evil (i.e. including our embodied and embedded natures) but also believes that our divine potential is realized through our own steadfastness, whereby violence to established political and physical orders is considered an acceptable consequence of a genuine "revolution of the saints" keen on creating a "Heaven on Earth" (Voegelin 1952; cf. Fuller 2006a: ch. 5).

The awkwardness of natural theology in the secular world

In an era when "ecumenical" approaches to religion function as proxies for global diplomacy, calls for the revival of *natural theology* would seem to throw caution to the wind. Natural theology purports to provide the scientific basis for theodicy by comprehending nature in functional terms, the product of "intelligent design" (Fuller 2007b: ch. 1). It is a specifically Abrahamic discipline that takes literally the Genesis idea that humans are created "in the image and likeness of God", according to which humanity differs from God by degree not kind – that is, we are not merely a divine output but, in some sense, an outright representation of the Creator, whose creative powers are of the same sort (but to a much

Epistemology as divine psychology   75

greater extent) as our own (Fuller 2008a: ch. 2). This in turn requires a belief in the literal overlap of the human and the divine mind – specifically, that by advancing the frontiers of human knowledge, we might become more like God (Fuller 2010). Malebranche wrote of this as our "vision in God", by which we are able to think God's thoughts (Pyle 2003: ch. 3). Our anticipatory powers exceed those of the animals by going beyond mere generalization from personal experience to forms of understanding that are clearly imagined but have yet to be encountered in experience. It is this trans-, or at least counter-, inductive capacity, however fallible, that marks our divinity.

In the context of today's intelligent design (ID) debates, it is worth remarking that were the original theodicists asked for evidence of an intelligent designer, their first response would *not* have been to look to indirect evidence in nature – though they did that too, and indeed Malebranche's account of the constitution of heart anticipated Behe's irreducible complexity argument (cf. Pyle 2003: ch. 7). Rather, the theodicists thought that we could have *direct* evidence of the designer through an examination of our own constitution, as creatures in *imago dei*, where "*imago*" was interpreted in a sense stronger than "analogy" and closer to "partial identity". This point becomes especially clear when Nadler (2008) details Antoine Arnauld's objections to the very enterprise of theodicy, as practised by his fellow Catholic priest Malebranche, who argued that our "vision in God" implied that human nature and divine nature substantially overlap, perhaps in the same sense as a human and a chimpanzee genome "substantially overlap".

The key to this argument lies in a metaphysics that respects a strict separation of mind and body, where mind is the seat of humanity's divine nature. Our minds overlap with God's but, of course, also contain powers that are proper to our animal nature, just as God's mind also contains powers that are proper to divine nature. In this respect, whatever their other disagreements, theodicists claimed legitimacy from Descartes, whose *cogito ergo sum* proposed an example of human-divine overlap, namely, humanity's repetition of how the deity establishes its own exis-tence. Genesis may be read as suggesting that Creation is necessary only because God originally exists apart from matter, and so needs to make his presence felt in the world through matter. So too with humans. The products of our own re-enactment of divine thought patterns are still discussed in philosophy today as "*a priori* knowledge".

The open question, then, is how much of our knowledge might fall under this category, since whatever knowledge we acquire from the senses is clearly tied to our animal natures, which God does not share. Here a mental faculty was specifically proposed as triggering the spark of the divine in the human, *intellectual intuition* – that is, the capacity to

76 *Epistemology as divine psychology*

anticipate experience in a systematic and rational fashion. We would now say the capacity to generate virtual realities that happen to correspond to physical reality, the sort of thing computer simulations do all the time, courtesy of their programmers. In the seventeenth century, people were especially impressed by the prospect of Descartes's invention of analytic geometry projecting a rational world-order governed by universal laws of mechanical motion that could be plotted for times and places with which we were not – and perhaps could never be – in direct sensory contact. Seen in terms of ID's dialectical challenge to Darwinism, intellectual intuition promised to specify the "I" in "ID" that connected us to God as a form of knowledge that was reliable and comprehensive yet was grounded in a way that was unrelated to our experience as individuals and irrelevant to our survival as an animal species.

But the promise was ultimately not redeemed. Leibniz, the most ambitious of the theodicists, used his own intellectual intuition to propose an understanding of space, time and cause that Newtonian mechanics refuted. While Leibniz and Newton were largely engaged in the same enterprise, Newton, sensitive to the political implications of religious dissent, backpedalled the theology and took greater care with his calculations. A century later, also living in a time fraught with religious tension but now invoking the undisputed authority of Newton, Immanuel Kant famously denounced theodicy in *Critique of Pure Reason* as displaying an arrogant faith in the human intellect that leads to error in both science and theology. This view has continued to prevail – even though Leibniz was at least partly vindicated with Einstein's theory of relativity. But by the time that happened in the early twentieth century, theology had lost any strong claim to providing the basis for the cognitive unification of human knowledge.

However, nowadays natural theology tends to be defended on much weaker grounds. Thus, the UK's most publicly visible natural theologian, Alister McGrath (2011) begins with a quote from a late-nineteenth-century precursor: "It is not too much to say that the Gospel itself can never be fully known till nature as well as man is fully known." This is as clear a statement of natural theology's historic self-understanding as one is ever likely to get. But instead of interpreting the quote as saying that science is poised to provide the details of the outworking of divine agency in nature (a thesis in the spirit of intelligent design theory), McGrath dilates on how science points to a reality beyond the reach of its own methods, for which theology then provides a necessary resource, if not an answer to everyone's satisfaction. In this way, McGrath ensures that theology rationalizes science but not the other way round.

To his credit, McGrath concedes that the divines who aligned themselves with natural theology for two centuries after Newton's grand synthesis of the physical universe were barely distinguishable from Deists and other Christian dissenters who indulged in Biblical criticism and anti-clericalism. All of them gravitated towards a calculating and contriving conception of God, The Ultimate Mechanic. It was just this rationalistic view of the deity that Charles Darwin came to reject as a result of his studies of natural history. McGrath nimbly argues that Darwin was right to do so but wrong to have despaired of theology altogether, raising a telling point against Darwin's source on natural theology, William Paley's *Natural Theology* (1802), which still influences today's arguments for intelligent design in nature via Paley's famous example of the watch found on a heath. A series of UK Parliamentary debates over the use of evidence in criminal law in the 1830s sent a ripple effect throughout the empirical disciplines. Out went the rhetorical demonstrations of self-evidence that were favoured by Paley and, indeed, the early experimentalists of the Royal Society. In its place came a more inferential conception of evidence, one in which facts drawn from disparate and partial sources are collected together and interpreted before drawing an overall conclusion. Championing this new approach was William Whewell, the natural theologian who coined the word "scientist" and was Darwin's main source on scientific method.

Although appeals to *evidence* figure prominently in the rhetorical armament of both supporters and opponents of natural theology, it is philosophically naïve to conclude that such appeals are capable of resolving their differences (*pace* Thomasson 2011). The disputants leave the concept of evidence unanalysed, even though most philosophers agree that it does not make sense to speak of evidence outside specific contexts of theory choice: Who sets that context and how are the relevant theoretical alternatives defined? Indeed, the strong forensic sense of "evidence" that tends to drive the debate finds its natural home in the law courts, not the scientific laboratory. A very clear example of this is the 2005 US Circuit Court case *Tammy Kitzmiller, et al. v. Dover Area School District, et al.* (400 F. Supp. 2d 707, Docket no. 4cv2688), in which intelligent design theory, understood as a sophisticated version of scientific creationism and heir apparent to natural theology, had its scientific credentials challenged.

In a backhanded way, the verdict against ID in *Kitzmiller* reminds us that, under normal circumstances, scientists test hypotheses whose outcomes are compatible with a variety of larger theoretical frameworks, some of which are mutually antagonistic, as in the case of intelligent design and blind natural selection. Under normal circumstances, scientists happily live in a state of suspended disbelief – that is, until a judge decides to intervene. But of course, the judge is not alone. It is no accident that the person who turned this sense of evidence into a proper tool of organized inquiry, the *experimentum crucis*, was Francis Bacon, a trained

78   *Epistemology as divine psychology*

lawyer. A classical aim of the philosophy of science has been to get scientists to take more decisions and pass more judgements than they might otherwise (Fuller 1993). One does not need to pledge allegiance to what philosophers call the "Duhem–Quine thesis" of underdetermined theory choice to recognize scientists' spontaneous theoretical tolerance. The point is routinely made whenever one opens a scientific journal and sees that its content rarely rises above the level of the technical.

Moreover, scientists who wish to embed their findings in more explicitly theoretical agendas are limited by the peer review process. This leads ID/creationists to complain (rightly) of a "naturalistic" philosophical bias that allows scientific authors to use their articles' introductions and conclusions to articulate their findings in terms of broader Neo-Darwinian research themes but not those of ID/creationism, even though the same findings could be understood in those terms too. As a result of this asymmetrical treatment at the reviewer stage, ID/creationism is effectively censored before it can enter the scientific literature – unless ID/creationists manage to come up with testable hypotheses the success of which could *not* be explained equally well in Neo-Darwinian terms. Most impartial philosophers would find this a ridiculously high standard of evidence.

However, the preferred ID/creationism strategy of forcing the scientific literature to stay closer to what has been empirically demonstrated would succeed only in throttling science's dynamic character, which always aims to transcend the currently agreed data base with fallible yet corrigible theoretically informed inferences. An unfortunate confusion in this entire discussion is that the word "evidence" is often broadened from its strict forensic sense, whereby one gathers evidence specifically to discriminate between the probable truth of alternative hypotheses, to the simple idea of a generally agreed data base, which serves the exact opposite epistemological function – namely, to reduce the difference between theoretical alternatives, if not to render such differences undecidable. It amounts to a slide between two key moments in the modern history of science–religion relations: from Francis Bacon to Pierre Duhem – that is, from a practically minded Lord Chancellor who wanted to extract some cognitive illumination from the heat of religious differences in the run-up to the English Civil War to the devout Catholic physicist whose revenge on France's secular Third Republic would be to show that even in science decisions must be taken on the basis of an unprovable faith. Here one might position Karl Popper as trying to strike a balance between Bacon's demystification and Duhem's remystification of the epistemic status of "belief" in science by appealing to the "acceptance" of a corroborated hypothesis that becomes more acceptable as it is subject to more stringent tests, with the emphasis placed on the originality of the hypothesis to the scientist and not the expression of some pre-established understanding of reality.

Sometimes ID/creationists appear to be closet Duhemians who are less interested in an outright victory for their own view of science – which would amount to the resurrection of natural theology – than a stalemate in which the epistemic pretences of science are forced to yield to unshakeable metaphysical commitments in, say, naturalism or supernaturalism. In this context, Darwinists are right to query the ID/creationist appeal to design in nature in terms of a pre-theoretical sense of "evidence" via some sort of "common sense". A properly "scientific" idea of design must grant that the appearance of design in nature could indeed have resulted from a very drawn out chance-based evolutionary process. Nevertheless the onus would still be on Darwinists to demonstrate the likelihood that such a process has actually characterized natural history. To be sure, Darwinists have demonstrated the *plausibility* of such a process through a combination of fossil-based inferences, generalizations from laboratory experiments and computer models that take current mutation rates and other analogous factors as indicative of what has happened across all of natural history. Thus, the great ID champion Michael Behe was mistaken to have challenged Neo-Darwinism at that level (Fuller 2008a: ch. 5).

Yet the scientific orthodoxy itself – not only ID/creationists – continues to act as if a higher standard of evidence is to be had that would put the ID/creationist threat to rest once and for all. I doubt it. Instead the debate will probably continue with duelling computer models, as organized inquiry continues to migrate from the field (aka nature), through the increasingly artificial environments of the laboratory and the computer (Horgan 1996). The interesting questions then centre on the construction of the models – the parameters used and the range of possible scenarios countenanced as compatible with some variously sourced and weighted configuration of evidence (cf. Fuller 2008a: ch. 5). All of this presumes that Neo-Darwinism does not enjoy a proprietary hold over the evidence that is normally mobilized in its support. Other research programmes, like ID/creationism, are free to appropriate the same evidence, weigh its significance differently and do research that moves in a different direction.

Moreover, as Behe (2007) has observed, the difference between ID and Neo-Darwinism may ultimately rest not on the simple acceptance or rejection of chance-based processes in nature but on the constraints that each theoretical framework places on the operation of such processes, with ID imposing more constraints and hence permitting less variability in possible outcomes – certainly nothing close to what below I associate with "Primitive Darwinism". Indeed, we can identify two "edges", along which the division of the labour of cosmic creation occurs between divine (aka intelligent) action and natural (aka spontaneous) behaviour.

The first is associated with what Behe (2007) calls the *edge of evolution*. It refers to the point in geological, and perhaps even cosmological, time when

80 *Epistemology as divine psychology*

intelligent design, in the form of finely tuned physical parameters, yielded to the chance-based processes of natural selection that govern the evolution of life. It harks back to *The Fitness of the Environment*, the 1913 work by Harvard biochemist Lawrence Henderson, who performed a kind of intellectual one-upmanship on Darwin by suggesting that had not the quantity and distribution of carbon in the universe been as it is, natural selection would never have been able to produce life-forms such as ourselves. In that respect, the universe appears "fit for life" (Barrow *et al.* 2008). More recently, this idea has been developed in terms of what physicists call the "anthropic principle", namely, the idea that whatever principles underwrite the physical universe, they must be ones that enable the existence of humanity (Barrow and Tipler 1988). In Chapter 4, we shall discover Henderson to have been the formative influence – even the intelligent designer – of the Harvard environment that bred Thomas Kuhn.

The second edge is the *edge of uncertainty*, the phrase coined by Warren Weaver, pioneer information theorist and the research director of the Rockefeller Foundation in the middle third of the twentieth century. He meant to capture molecular biology's early promise of enabling us to beat the odds of population genetics, but it continues to be used by promoters for the convergence of nano-, bio-, info-, and cogno-sciences in support of technologies that will enable us to re-engineer nature, including ourselves, thereby overcoming – if not reversing – millions of years of evolution. More specifically, Weaver's edge refers to the "nano-level" of reality, i.e. matter at the scale of a billionth of a metre, just above the level of quantum indeterminacy, which is the smallest unit at which matter retains its functional properties for purposes of intelligent design and manipulation (Fuller 2008a: ch. 6; 2011: ch. 3).

The juxtaposition of these two "edgy" projects reopens the question of exactly what are the limits of the idea that humans have been created in *imago dei* – and how much of our "natural" human condition must be retained as we take increasing control of the creative forces of life. Most creationists, including many ID supporters, shy away from posing these questions, even though historically they seemed quite reasonable once people took seriously, as Behe (1996) does, that, say, a cell could be literally designed like a mousetrap. Moreover, if the concept of God as Artificer – a literal intelligent designer – has been so badly off the trail, then modern science, despite its many problems and excesses, should not have become so integral to humanity's self-understanding and well-being. Any version of ID that cannot honestly accept that judgement reveals itself to be a science-stopper, just as its Darwinist critics suspect.

From a social epistemological standpoint, an obvious feature of the contemporary debates surrounding evolution is that the seriousness with which objections to Darwinism are taken depends on the objector's identity. For example, there is widespread agreement among practising biologists that whatever else "natural selection" is, it is a destructive not a creative force. Moreover, there is agreement that the "destruction" concerns the inhibition of traits in a population of organisms that happen to be unsuitable to the organisms' habitat. Indeed, nowadays one speaks of certain genes being "knocked out" as a consequence of natural selection, understood as the reproductive failure of organisms with the unsuitable genes. And as for the mutations spontaneously generated in the normal reproductive cycle of organisms, the vast majority of these fail to leave an evolutionary trace. So, as it turns out, despite the vast timeframe of evolutionary history required by contemporary Neo-Darwinism, the vast majority of genes have stayed in place. This means that the differences separating supporters and opponents of the Neo-Darwinian orthodoxy pertain to the interpretation of the relatively few genes whose changes over possibly billions of years have resulted in the panoply of organisms that have populated the Earth.

It is telling that the vast differences in interpretation triggered by these agreed facts are more explicitly and suggestively played out in the mass media than in academic journals (Segerstrale 2000). However, if you are espousing views that in one way or another are reminiscent of ID/creationism, it is much better that you are a member of the scientific establishment. Consider the quarter-century transatlantic spat between Stephen Jay Gould and Richard Dawkins, which only ended with the former's death in 2002. I have characterized their difference as one of, respectively, "Primitive Darwinism" (with a nod to "Primitive Christianity", the phrase often used by those who believe that the Church distorted the message of Christ) versus "Genetically Modified Darwinism" (Fuller 2008a: intro.). To compress a long and complex story told elsewhere (e.g. Fuller 2008a), ID/creationism supporters have gravitated to the atheistic Gould because of his stress on the insufficiency of Darwin's original vision to justify the faith in science's capacity to give meaning to the human condition. This then opens a logical space for a non-cognitive "religious" framework (Gould 1999). In contrast, Genetically Modified Darwinists take twentieth-century breakthroughs in genetics and molecular biology as heralding an era of anthropocentric "eugenics" and, more recently, biotechnological "enhancement" that in the past would have been the exclusive preserve of the deity (Esposito 2011). Perhaps then Dawkins (2006) is so militantly atheistic because he is contesting ground – the explanation of the appearance of design in nature – the non-existence of which Gould believed Darwin had already demonstrated.

Gould, sticking largely to Darwin's own expertise in natural history and minimizing the subsequent contributions made by laboratory-based biology, especially after the molecular revolution, was so convinced that

82 *Epistemology as divine psychology*

nature lacked teleology that he suggested that if history happened over again, humanity would probably have never come about (Gould 1989). In Gould's favour was his fidelity to Darwin's pessimistic mindset, which enabled him to resist the temptation of letting evidence for "adaptation" in the strict sense (i.e. the differential survival rates of organisms exhibiting a variety of traits) slip into conclusions about *optimization* (which would imply an ideal fit between successive generations of organisms bearing certain traits and their habitat). This pessimism was born of Darwin's Malthusian legacy, which gave him a very vivid sense of the mutual independence of the organism and the environment, which leads to the periodic overrun of population, resulting in mass extinctions as nature restores its equilibrium (Brooks 2011). The profound blindness of natural selection to the wishes of humans or any other species means that our sense of a meaningful direction to evolution – of the sort fostered by design-based thinking – is a local illusion, a historical mirage based on overestimating the fact that we are here as we are. Thus, it is somewhat mysterious that the rump end of Marxism that takes refuge in the American academy should find Gould congenial, given that those ardent teleologists Marx and Engels always swallowed their Darwin with a strong dose of Lamarck (cf. Foster *et al.* 2008).

In contrast, the slippage from adaptation to optimization is endemic in Dawkins, who reads Darwin as a man of exceptional foresight who somehow anticipated that twentieth-century biology would be led from the field back to the laboratory under the command of interloping physicists and chemists to discover the mechanisms that enable organisms to be adaptive to their habitats. Thus, Dawkins differs significantly from Gould in the ultimate lesson he draws from the long view of history. Whereas Gould followed the letter of Darwin in stressing the inevitability of extinction, regardless of how well adapted a species may seem to a given place and time, Dawkins takes what Darwin himself would have regarded as a more wishful stance, namely, that the sheer longevity of evolutionary history enables organisms to acquire stable design-like features that over time constitute a sense of directionality. In this context, Dawkins (1996) is especially fond of the metaphor of the "ratchet", which supposes that a progressive sense of evolution can be simulated by playing on the fact that every so often a chance configuration of genetic changes acquire a stickiness in a particular environment – what Dawkins (1982) calls the "extended phenotype" – that subsequently channels natural selection in a more focused direction. In lay terms, some organisms are born with a knack that they can turn to their collective advantage, which subsequent organisms either need to know or somehow get around.

However, as Brooks (2011) points out, the evidence for this indirectly generated sense of progress boils down to natural selection affecting different aspects of organisms differently, leading to differential rates of biological change. In that respect, "progress" is a historical illusion generated by the emergence of a temporary bottleneck on the paths available for further genetic change. After all, there is massive overlap between the human genome and the genomes of not only all other animals but also all other plants. Moreover, the species that are regarded as both older and simpler also tend to have the largest genomes. So the appearance of progress in evolutionary history is most persuasive if we imagine watching evolutionary history unfold before our unaided eyes, as opposed to the causal level of genomic changes in populations over time. In the latter case one sees a picture of overwhelming biochemical perseverance in the face of a wide range of environmental pressures – excepting of course the marginal genomic changes that do occur, which have resulted in the Earth's biological diversity. From this standpoint, Dawkins's claim about the more "complex" character of human adaptation vis-à-vis other species looks like an anthropic conceit that one might normally associate with an ID/creationist.

In short, debates over the scientific probity of ID/creationism and Neo-Darwinism have little to do with evidence *per se* but a lot to do with who speaks for the evidence, which in turn is a matter of permissible explanatory frameworks in science. In this context, the Popperian phrase, "metaphysical research programme" comes in handy, since the closer one inspects the genuine points of disagreement between ID/creationism and Neo-Darwinism, the more metaphysical they become. Thus, Gould was perfectly happy to postulate several game-changing ecological catastrophes in evolutionary history and Dawkins continues to take seriously the hypothesis that an alien intelligence seeded life on Earth. Each hypothesis in its own way is controversially related to the body of natural historical evidence but gains an intuitive foothold on the scientific imagination as a naturalized version of the creationist principle of divine intervention – minus the reference to a deity, of course! If that turns out to be the sense in which "naturalism" has triumphed in the history of science, then the logical positivists were right after all that there was little of cognitive significance to play for. It is a "naturalism" that in less politically correct circles would be instantly recognized as "natural theology".

Here is a more explicit argument for the project of natural theology, which draws attention to its inevitably controversial character:

1 As creatures *in imago dei*, we are empowered to understand the nature of reality.
2 That God creates through an outworking of *logos* vouchsafes this point. Thus, we should expect that reality's structure is ultimately rational, even language-like.

3 Hence in some sense we learn about the *modus operandi* of the divine plan by monitoring the workings of our own minds in both theoretical and practical settings.
4 In terms of modern secular sciences, psychology and technology provide clues to physics and biology, respectively, understood as products of God's handiwork. (This helps to explain the ease of metaphorical traffic between the natural and human sciences starting in the eighteenth century.)
5 However, since our grasp of *logos* is necessarily finite and fallible (courtesy of Original Sin), we should also expect that our understanding will always need to be improved; hence science is primarily concerned with the proposal and testing of hypotheses, in search of an intelligible response (Harrison 2007).
6 That the experimental method allows us regularly to generate such responses is a secular variant on Divine Grace. After all, in principle God could simply choose not to communicate at all through our experiments (Fuller 2010: ch. 8).
7 But a consequence of our divine gift of free will is that we must decide how to interpret the result. Even if nature corroborates our hypotheses, the question remains of how to go forward: Do we simply persist in our prior beliefs, refine or radically alter them – and if so, how? The problem of theory choice in science is thus ultimately an existential one, a point that the young Karl Popper grasped from his reading of the German translations of Kierkegaard published in the 1920s (Fuller 2003: ch. 10).

In practice, such a cognitively oriented approach to religion did much to promote science and modern rationalism. In its heyday, from the late seventeenth to the late nineteenth century, the nowadays emotively charged binary "supernatural/natural" was seen as a fluid boundary under continual negotiation as scientists succeeded in resolving divine agency into reliable mathematical equations associated with gravitation and electromagnetism (Knight 2004). In this respect, supernaturalism's proof lay in its eventual assimilation to the naturalistic world-view, such that even people without faith come to accept the workings of extraordinary forces that cannot be validated through unassisted sensory experience. In this respect, science functions as an unfolding *Summa contra Gentiles* for the modern world, to recall Thomas Aquinas's great Christian playbook against pagans and doubters. Thus, a newly resurrected James Clerk Maxwell – someone who quite explicitly evangelized his science – would find in today's dogmatic claims for science's "methodological naturalism" a systematic mistaking of the effect for its cause: Even if in principle everyone can now grasp and benefit from electromagnetism, the very countenancing of its existence had required a belief in the supernatural (Fuller 2010: ch. 6).

Nevertheless, no one can deny that the animus behind natural theology has been also responsible for the heresies, schisms and other conflicts that have especially plagued the history of Christianity. The presupposed divisive idea is that we must agree on God's nature before we can agree on how best to conduct our own lives, since our nature is sufficiently close to God's to be capable of reaching such an agreement. Indeed, our capacity in this regard provides a test of our recovery from Adam's fall (Harrison 2007). In practice, this has meant that controversies over the nature of God have stood proxy for arguments about the normative grounds of the human condition. These controversies at once crowd the space left open by modern science's studied refusal to pass value judgements of personal or societal relevance (Proctor 1991). Yet, they also expose a crucial ambiguity: Do the laws of nature allow for choice because they do not bear on the specificity of our lives (i.e. they do not constrain at the level that most matters to us) or simply because it is within our power to negate their hold on us normatively? The former prospect suggests that God has divided the labour of Creation with us, while the latter prospect suggests that God is testing our worthiness as beings capable of transcending nature's default settings. Again we seem to be led back to natural theology.

Indeed, the surveys and in-depth interviews reported by Ecklund (2010) suggest that while scientists tend to oppose, albeit often without properly understanding, conventional religious belief systems for their allegedly latent anti-scientific motives, they themselves, when pressed on the normative implications of their own views, come perilously close to "New Age" religions in envisaging an impending science-induced paradigm shift in our way of being that will sweep away many secular and sacred orthodoxies. In this respect, scientists are remarkably rather unlike the "separate but equal" dualists who would divide the labour between science and religion in terms of answering "how" and "why" questions, respectively, à la Gould (1999). Indeed, professional scientists differ from the "Protscientists" mentioned earlier in this chapter only in their opposition to the de facto libertarianism of Protscientists, who exercise discretion on the bits of science they wish to stake their lives on.

Faced with the inevitable frustrations of justifying religious sentiment in terms of natural theology, a broad inter-faith coalition has called for the renunciation of Abrahamic literalism. Instead it has argued that religion should not be in the business of second-guessing God but provide meaning in a world ultimately governed by forces beyond one's control. Karen Armstrong (2009), perhaps the most publicly visible champion of this approach, associates it with a reversion from *logos* to *mythos* in religious thinking, that is, from what sets apart Judaism, Christianity and Islam from other religions to what they share with them. The strategy aims to strike the

86 *Epistemology as divine psychology*

right existential balance between hubris and despair, where natural theology is taken to have erred towards the former. Historical evidence for the efficacy of this strategy may be seen in that "Christendom" as a unified secular and religious Christian empire has come closer to realization during periods when the *imago dei* doctrine was interpreted – as Thomas Aquinas did – as specifying an *analogy* rather than an *identity*. This move circumvented vexed discussions about, say, whether we should aspire to "superhuman" – what are now called "transhuman" – modes of being that might bring us closer to the divine. Perhaps the most influential secular version of this analogical approach flows through the hermeneutical tradition in the human sciences, which beginning with Giambattista Vico in the eighteenth century has argued that we can "understand" (i.e. in terms of original intention) only that which we could have created. The natural world is excluded from such intimate knowledge because only God could have created it. It follows that nature can only be "explained", in the sense that its law-like regularity can be grasped without comprehending the intentions of the cosmic lawgiver. On this basis, the modern distinction between the "human" and the "natural" sciences was born (Fuller 2011: ch. 2).

Intelligent design: a "Left Creationist" affirmation of science

"Intelligent design" (ID) is more than a long-winded way of saying "design". The phrase implies the presence of mathematically interesting patterns in the constitution of life and the cosmos whose patent functionality provides evidence for a creative intelligence behind the design, whereby "intelligence" already implies a continuum within which both we and the ultimate creator sit. Contrast this epistemological starting point with that of a "design science" that claims an artefact to be designed simply because it functions in certain capacities in certain environments. In that case, "design science" is about identifying such things and making inferences about their functions in various settings, nothing more. If ID were really nothing more than "design science" that happens to keep bad (aka "creationist") company, then the ID debate would have been a waste of time. Card-carrying evolutionists engage in "design science" in that limited sense all the time under various guises, most fashionably these days as "evo-devo", which grants that evolution occurs within significant developmental constraints (Carroll 2005). The controversy starts only once people talk about origins, whether design arose intelligently or unintelligently.

To keep intelligent design intelligent, we must take seriously the idea that theology is, as the word's etymology suggests, the "science of God". And insofar as the *imago dei* definition of humanity is true, then we can

Epistemology as divine psychology   87

improve our understanding of God by better understanding at least some aspects of our own being. In particular, the more our own mental and physical creations turn out to model what actually happens in nature, the closer we get to understanding the "intelligence" behind divine creation. In this respect, the very recognizably mechanical rendering of the bacterial flagellum that graces the masthead of the leading ID website, *Uncommon Descent*, epitomizes the true spirit of ID. Machines, simulations and other artifices of the laboratory are not merely toys, artworks or conveniences. They are instruments that provide access to a larger reality, if not outright representations of that reality. Such deep epistemic trust in human creations, so characteristic of the seventeenth-century Scientific Revolution, amounts to a demonstration of humanity's trust in the reliability of the divine creative process, an incentive to use science as a means to become closer to God. But at a practical level, by refusing to hypothesize about the intelligent designer, ID not only denies itself the cognitive utility that such a concept might offer to a unified explanation of disparate designed phenomena but also perpetuates the suspicion that ID is no more than an "anti-Darwin" movement with no positive contribution to make to fundamental questions about the nature of life. Turning ID into a God-free zone at best reduces the theory to a toolkit of concepts and techniques for reliable design detection of the sort associated with the so-called forensic sciences.

To be sure, ID is in the unenviable position of being damned as both bad science and bad theology (e.g. Alexander 2008; Giberson 2008). However, if those charges are true, then the basis for belief in *both* science and God may be irrational. (Here "irrational" should be understood in its descriptive not evaluative sense: I am not presuming that an exclusively faith-based belief in either science or God would be bad, though it would certainly raise questions.) ID not only suggests that belief in the two may be interdependent but also develops that possibility with a vengeance – specifically, by offering heretical readings of both theology and science, as in the case of Dembski (2009), perhaps in spite of what its author might think. In any case, I shall defend ID in this doubly heretical sense, specifically as reinventing the spirit of the original Scientific Revolution for our own times. I identify this spirit with the *Creationist Left*. The "Creationist Left" should be understood as the historically strongest justification for the aggressive modern use of technology to both understand and reconfigure nature: to wit, human artifice is marked by the intelligence of the divine artificer in whose own image we were created, which in turn gives us the confidence to persevere through many misgivings, setbacks and disasters on the path to overall species progress, and ultimately salvation.

ID's doubly heretical character is traceable to its assuming that science and religion should shape each other, such that science pursued properly enables us to understand what is distinctive about us that renders the world so intelligible. ID's starting point is markedly different from what normally passes as "theistic evolution", the politically correct face of the science–religion relationship, which assigns to science and theology two discrete realms of being that, following Aquinas and Kant, are often epitomized as "how" and "why" questions (e.g. F. S. Collins 2006). I dub this position "politically correct" because its segregationist epistemology protects both atheists and believers from the effects of any radical shifts in scientific understanding to their respective world-views, as science only deals with the means not the ends of the cosmos. ID, by contrast, posits a more reflexive relationship between our understanding of the cosmos and of our own role within it: The greater our scientific understanding, the more we learn about ourselves as the sort of being who has been created "in the image and likeness of God", which in turn carries implications for how we should act. Even if one upholds the normal Christian view of God as inhabiting a field of possibilities transcendent of space and time, our understanding of what that divine condition means may shift quite radically over time with our understanding of science (e.g. if we see that "field of possibilities" as a quantum field), which in turn has consequences for our relationship to the deity so conceived.

The most basic formulation of ID is that biology is divine technology, with God understood as the ultimate engineer. In other words, God is no less – and possibly no more – than an infinitely better version of the ideal *Homo sapiens*, whose distinctive species calling card is art, science and technology (Noble 1997). This opening gambit reflects a more general ID commitment to a "univocal" use of language that in the High Middle Ages was associated with the Franciscan scholastics John Duns Scotus and William of Ockham, whereby differences between God and humans are conceptualized as matters of *degree* not kind. At the time, this view carried mystical overtones because of its strong emphasis on the still esoteric medium of writing as the privileged medium through with the deity communicates with his privileged creatures, the "People of the Book", as the Abrahamic religions are still called. The rise of mass literacy in the modern era has largely removed writing's mystical overtones, while retaining its unique role in the comprehension of all beings, including God, in one universal discourse, which at times has been identified with mathematics, logic or some ideal scientific language – again, in terms of which anything worth saying can be said.

In practice, ID's commitment to a univocal view of language means that when, say, Behe (1996) claims that an organic cell is as "intelligently designed" as a mousetrap, he means it literally – and as a compliment. This point alone goes a long way to explain ID's natural constituency among engineers, chemists and computer programmers (Fuller 2007c: ch. 4).

For them the scientific fruit borne by a literal understanding of phrases like "genetic code" and "genetic information" is epitomized in the discovery of DNA's relevance to the constitution of life in 1953. For ID supporters, this event – not Darwin's publication of *Origin of Species* in 1859 – marked the true turning point in the history of biology when it finally became a science. It confirmed the language-like character of nature, making it no longer necessary to rely on Darwin's purposeless account of life based on pure historical contingency (Meyer 2009). This orientation has been taken still further in recent years by the synthetic biology – or "do-it-yourself biology" – movement, in which a "reverse engineering" mentality is applied to genomes, very much in the spirit of "open source" computer coding. In this context, the phrase "intelligent design" is explicitly used to characterize the genome's construction, deconstruction and reconstruction (Church and Regis 2012).

But I would be remiss not to mention that for some ID is simply the latest attempt by fundamentalist Christians to get the Bible taught as science in US high school classrooms. In this guise, ID looks like a "science-stopper", which is meant to imply that it would arrest if not pervert science teaching and research in the name of "Creationism". This is a popular view of ID for which a diligently researched backstory has been produced, one that portrays the "Creationists" as a misguided rearguard effort to recover a disappearing sense of the sacred in the wake of modern science (Numbers 2006). Notwithstanding the grain of truth to this assessment, it is hardly the whole story. It is probably not even most of the story. Just because some (but by no means all) religious fundamentalists and cultural conservatives have been attracted to ID, it does not follow that the theory necessitates their normative stances. Indeed, if history is our guide, ID is most naturally read as having politically *progressive*, perhaps even radical consequences. Far from stopping science, ID raises the spectre of our species transcendence, what I have called "Humanity 2.0", a being that perhaps abandons much of its carbon-based biological inheritance to be resurrected in a form that permits a less impeded version of our divine qualities (Fuller 2011). At the very least, this prospect suggests that we need to distinguish a *Creationist Right* from the Creationist Left that is the party of Humanity 2.0, which I propose to defend here.

Many ID defenders – myself included – are not "fundamentalist Christians" (as that phrase is normally understood by both its advocates and opponents) but recognize the historically deeper, theologically rooted questions about the ends of science addressed by ID that continue to be avoided by defenders of science, regardless of religiosity (Funkenstein 1986; Harrison 1998). In this respect, the Creationist Right and Left are agreed in wanting a science that does justice to the distinctiveness of our humanity. Creationists seek a science they can live with. That includes, as I shall suggest below, a science that actually encourages its own pursuit. It is simplistic and misleading to see in this requirement a failure of nerve on the part of Creationists to face the unvarnished scientific truth. On the contrary, it is about according science the seriousness it deserves, which involves considering the reflexive implications for what could count as rational behaviour in beings such as ourselves who would be explained by this science. This point must be addressed even by the "realist" who believes that the truth is ultimately independent of our beliefs – whether that truth resides in God's mind or Kant's *Ding an sich*. Realists still need to decide how to access this truth, however fallibly, if they expect to do science of any sort. The historical answer has involved science making epistemic access increasingly mediated by technology: The independent "fact of the matter" of a spontaneous natural occurrence has been effectively replaced by the outcomes of ever more "intelligently designed" situations, starting with the controlled experiment and more recently the computer simulation. The more intelligently designed the site of knowing, the more intelligently designed the objects of knowledge appear. This is the trajectory that resulted in molecular biology becoming the fundamental science of life, a lab-based, physics-minded discipline completely alien to Darwin's own natural-historical way of thinking (Fuller 2008a: ch. 4; Fuller 2010: ch. 2).

Darwinism's own anti-humanist theodicy

Darwinists must be credited with rhetorical savvy for having already spun the point about the reflexive implications of science in the opposite direction from what I have argued so far: Their stress on our exclusively animal natures, as dictated by evolution, is rightly read as calling for a more benevolent attitude towards animals, perhaps even according them rights previously limited to humans (e.g. Singer 1999). Moreover that very same stress on the reflexive implications of Neo-Darwinism might also make us question the wisdom of developing and valorizing the highly abstract and risky modes of cognition and action that have been pursued by physics, the flagship science of the modern world. Physics has taken us increasingly away – in both intent and effect – from those animal roots. Indeed, Darwin's great champion, Thomas Henry Huxley (1893), was right to question whether humanity's diminished ontological status in the grand evolutionary narrative would be sufficient to sustain the ongoing physics-led Scientific and Industrial Revolutions, faith in which had been grounded in humanity's divine entitlement to comprehend and even complete nature (Fuller 2006b: ch. 12). Lest the reader find Huxley's concern exaggerated, it is worth recalling Darwin's personal

Epistemology as divine psychology 91

reluctance to support such Victorian efforts at human self-improvement as eugenics (*pace* Galton), unlimited vivisection (*pace* Huxley) and even contraception campaigns (*pace* Mill). In each case, Darwin held that too much suffering would come from what he regarded as epistemically unfounded human hubris vis-à-vis nature born of an overdeveloped cerebral cortex (Fuller 2008a: ch. 2).

Darwin's misgivings remain quite recognizable. A latter-day Darwin would probably be among the biggest proponents of an ecologically sustainable "little science" – a cross between the animal liberation theorist Peter Singer (1975) and the "small is beautiful" economist Fritz Schumacher (1973). However, had these precautionary attitudes been dominant over the past 350 years, science would not have taken the shape or acquired the significance it has. Indeed, the signature achievements of humanity as a whole have been scientific projects, especially those that presuppose what the philosopher Thomas Nagel (1986) has called "the view from nowhere". I mean to include here not only the achievements of Newton and Einstein, which allow us to comprehend a universe only a tiny fraction of which we will ever experience directly, but also Charles Darwin's conceptualization of natural history for a period long before humans first walked the earth.

Yet, from a strictly evolutionary standpoint, it is by no means clear what adaptive advantage any of this knowledge has provided members of a species (*Homo Sapiens*) whose members still struggle to survive on Earth for 70–80 years without killing each other. On the contrary, the Second World War – if the First had not already – demonstrated the levels of global risk that we have been willing to tolerate in the pursuit of science and technology. And that faith in science remains unabated. Nowadays what passes for "anti-science", be it New Age movements or ID itself, mostly reflects distrust in established scientific authorities. It is no more anti-science than the original Protestant reformers were atheists. If anything, these developments – which I have dubbed "Protscience" in deference to the original Protestants – speak to the increasing desire of people to take science into their own hands in the twentieth and twenty-first centuries, as they did religion in the sixteenth and seventeenth centuries (Fuller 2010: ch. 4). In this context, the internet today functions very much as the printing press did five centuries ago.

Suppose we continue to put aside our misgivings that science might destroy us – and the planet. In other words, we pursue nuclear energy despite the threat of atomic warfare, genetics despite the threat of genocide, and social science despite brainwashing and surveillance. In all these cases, we are trading on a residual sense of our closeness to God. Indeed, the Christian doctrine of Providence, which was designed to instil perseverance in the face of adversity, is the model for this curious, and some

92 Epistemology as divine psychology

would say, blind faith in science (Fuller 2010: ch. 8). Certainly such a view makes *more* sense if God is thought to reveal his handiwork in nature, as ID supporters presume, than if the deity is inscrutable or non-existent, as ID opponents normally do.

Let us delve a bit more into the deep intellectual difficulty in justifying the economic and cultural resources spent on promoting science, given its massive disturbance to the course of humanity, not to mention other forms of life on Earth. It is common to argue against this claim that the tangible benefits of science associated with medicine and technology outweigh the costs. But that is only if we listen to the voices left standing after the costs have been paid. Anyone easily persuaded by these voices should take a course in economics and learn the difference between "historical cost" (i.e. the investments made in research and development) and "opportunity cost" (i.e. the investments forgone because of the investments made). Clearly some other background belief is offsetting the salience of the opportunity costs involved in promoting science. Here humanity's self-confidence in its godlike powers to right past wrongs comes to the fore. Insofar as we continue to see science as the vanguard and ultimate saviour of the human condition, we remain true to the original doctrine of "optimism", as put forward by Newton's great rival Leibniz. The word literally means that things are getting better – to be sure, after the less than auspicious start represented by Original Sin.

In this context, so I shall argue, what had specifically concerned Huxley as a shift from Newton to Darwin as the "patron saint" of the modern scientific world-view might be better seen as a shift from Leibniz to Schopenhauer in terms of a general philosophy of life. The change in question is not, as philosophers often say today, from physics to biology as the paradigmatic science, but rather from an optimism grounded in our capacity to inhabit "The mind of God" to a pessimism based on a realization that, however hard we try, we remain animals unto death. (Here it is worth recalling that Schopenhauer cut his philosophical teeth by doing a brilliant systematic critique of the signature Leibnizian doctrine in *The Fourfold Root of the Principle of Sufficient Reason*.) When the transition is cast this way, Darwin's empirical account of the inexorable trail of extinction in nature supplies decisive evidence for the probity of pessimism, which if taken to heart would serve only to diminish human ambition to recover its divine entitlement as favoured by the Creationist Left, a secular consequence of which would be a loss of faith in scientific progress.

To appreciate the challenge here, let us recall the sorts of life-destroying practices that have been enabled by science. They constitute the flipside of our increasing ability to move more ideas and goods over longer distances in shorter times – to wit, the twentieth century's two world wars. They established new benchmarks of military achievement in terms of the quick and pervasive destruction of life and land, which culminated in the invention of nuclear weapons. Equally, the combined forces of the natural and the social sciences have set new precedents in invasiveness, as we become capable of intervening in life processes at increasingly multiple levels: from on high (through surgical air strikes) to below the skin (through the introduction of nano-bio-agents). Moreover, the onset of industrial capitalism has driven an increase in population as poor families with high mortality rates try to make ends meet. To be sure, this development spurred the growth of modern medicine – a by-product of which has been a tendency to sustain large numbers of economically marginal people, thereby raising the level of the world's ambient misery amidst brilliant (albeit growing) pockets of wealth. Last but not least is an issue that would focus the mind of a latter-day Darwin – the number of animals that have been killed in aid of extending the human condition in the production of food and medicine.

Enter Arthur Schopenhauer, modernity's great defender of suicide, who asked: *Would it not be better never to have been born than to suffer a normal life?* This question truly comes into its own in a lifeworld colonized by science, where control over whether and how life is generated and terminated is subject to rational deliberation. In light of the issues raised in the previous paragraph, I believe that the only rational way to say "no" to Schopenhauer's question is to embrace the Creationist Left version of ID. We must somehow believe that all the human and non-human lives lost through science-induced aggression, negligence and obliviousness have contributed to a world that has maximized the welfare of more humans, understood as the highest form of life – and is likely to do so in the future. In other words, we must take *all of time* as our moral horizon, treating each moment as of equal value, a position that I earlier associated with *theosis*. Taken to its logical conclusion, if eternal life in a perfect state is a serious prospect, then any pain suffered in a finite interim is arguably a fair price to pay. This position captures what *optimism* technically means as a philosophy of life: namely, however bad things may seem now, they can only get better because this is the best of all possible worlds. Such is the position of the Creationist Left.

Schopenhauer posed his question as an ironic response to Leibniz. To be sure, optimists have been acutely aware of the seemingly endless cycles of violence and hardship that mark the human condition, some self-induced but much not. Leibniz and his late seventeenth-century correspondents, most notably Malebranche, asked how all this misery could be, in some sense, the product of a just deity. Schopenhauer's pessimism was founded on a complete rejection of the general sort of answer that Leibniz and his colleagues developed under the rubric of *theodicy*. To the student of

94   *Epistemology as divine psychology*

theodicy, the weight of the world so acutely felt by pessimists such as Schopenhauer and the Epicureans before him is no more than the expression of an ignorance that we can relieve by using our ingenuity to make a virtue out of necessity, revealing our divine origins by acquiring a state of knowledge that transcends immediate animal impressions, if not by giving God a helping hand with our own creative efforts. (For a sociological inquiry into a similar set of sentiments in our own secular times, see Bourdieu 1999.) In short, to the problems for which the Epicureans had promoted therapy and Schopenhauer suicide as solutions, these original ID theorists recommended scientific inquiry and technological innovation, the latter especially coming to the fore in the eighteenth century, as "industriousness" was advanced as a virtue friendly to capitalism before that nascent economic system had proved itself (Hirschman 1976).

Theodicy's original timing was significant. It arose among theologians as Europe's Scientific Revolution was in full bloom. The strategic aim was to reconcile Biblical statements about the unity and order of divine creation with modernizing tendencies in secular metaphysics and science. In particular, Greek-inspired ideas about nature as beset by accidents and violent motions, not to mention "Asiatic" ideas about the existence of Evil in some Manichaean struggle with Good, did not sit well with the idea that Newton eventually brought to fruition, namely, that all of nature – including the wayward bits – is subject to a common set of laws laid down by the one God whose handiwork humans have been entrusted with understanding and possibly completing. In that case, what might initially strike us as a deity who is a sloppy or callous craftsman is no more than a symptom of our own ignorance of the overall plan in terms of which these apparent imperfections make sense, either in their own right (say, as means to higher ends) or as prods to our own divinely privileged wellsprings for action. Thus was born optimism's most intellectually profound legacy – the strategy of *optimization*, the construction of the best solution under specific material constraints, the hallmark of "bounded rationality" in economics and engineering (Simon 1977; cf. Fuller 2008a: ch. 5).

In popular and technical settings, respectively, optimism and optimization each forces the observer to expand his/her epistemic horizons beyond locally defined terms to a more global perspective. In this context, apparent deficiencies in, say, an organism's design (including its mortality) really reflect deficiencies in our own imaginations. After all, if something is good only by virtue of its capacity to contribute to God's overall plan, then there is no divine mandate that it be designed as well as it could be, understood outside of the context of that plan. Of course, for the divine plan to be meaningful to us, we must be cognitively equipped, at least in principle, to make sense of the judgements that God has had to make to allow just as much suffering as he has in the world. In this respect, entry to the mind of God requires that we understand suffering as energy expenditure or even cost in some overall "natural economy", a phrase coined alongside "political economy" in the second half of the eighteenth century (Bowler 2005). The plausibility of theodicy always turned on our presumed capacity to extend our epistemic horizons indefinitely, something that Kant had condemned in the *Critique of Pure Reason* but only to resurrect in the *Critique of Practical Reason* in the form of the self-legislating categorical imperative. In essence, Kant argued that even if we cannot prove the existence of an intelligent designer, we nevertheless need to presuppose such a universal standpoint in order to live meaningfully – that is, in a scientific manner, given what Kant purported to have established in his first *Critique*.

The controversial theological point lurking beneath theodicy's optimism is that God is in some sense – logically or materially – "compelled" to create in a certain way because the very act of creation imposes certain constraints, if only by virtue of the requirement that creation happens in time, which is not God's natural habitat (Fuller 2008a: ch. 3). To be sure, at a verbal if not conceptual level, this point can be finessed by arguing that, even under those circumstances, the deity is unique in its freedom to create the best possible world, whereas lesser creators would be put off by the intermediate costs (suffering). However, from the public relations standpoint of pastoral theology, the result is an unattractive picture of God as indifferent to the suffering of particular individuals, given deity's single-minded focus on an overall creation strategy. Indeed, this may be the main reason for the decline of theodicy among theologians in the eighteenth century, after which the field's concerns quite naturally migrated to the nascent science of political economy, most notably in the person of Thomas Malthus, the cleric who studied under the Unitarian Joseph Priestley and inspired William Paley (Harvey-Phillips 1984). Paley is nowadays portrayed as the godfather of the modern ID movement, since Darwin rejected ID largely after having read Paley at Cambridge. However, in so rehabilitating Paley, today's ID supporters tend to downplay the fact that Darwin could not believe in Paley's cosmic utilitarian deity, whose "intelligent design" of nature justified senseless death and destruction into the indefinite future (Fuller 2010: ch. 7).

It is worth underscoring that Malthus was an ordained minister whose theory of population control was endorsed by Paley because it provided evidence for the multiple levels on which nature is designed – not only at the individual but also the collective level. Paley thus welcomed Malthus's rationalization of persistently high mortality rates among the poor. But neither Kant's critique of Leibniz nor Darwin's rejection of Paley spelled the end of theodicy. A "folk theodicy" remains embedded in science, insofar as, say, malaria is treated specifically as a problem of disease

96 *Epistemology as divine psychology*

control and eradication (i.e. a problem in medicine) rather than itself a solution to a larger ecological problem (i.e. how to cull the surplus population of poorly adapted humans). Malaria is a challenge from which humanity may learn and ultimately overcome – say, through improved living conditions, vaccines, etc. While modern medicine rests on secular scientific foundations, its basic hostility to anything that threatens human life is a residue of an Abrahamic world-view. In contrast, a strict Darwinian rooted in Malthus's views of population control would find this "folk theodicy" a bit sentimental and might even object to the very term "disease" as displaying an anthropocentric prejudice against the effectiveness of malaria-carrying mosquitoes as vehicles of natural selection.

Indeed, the "racial hygiene" movement in German medical faculties in the half-century leading up to Hitler decried the proliferation of vaccines as creating "counter-selective" environments that threatened ecological instability in the long term (Proctor 1988). For them, mosquitoes should be allowed to do the job for which they were designed. The racial hygienists had a unified conception of science, in which the principle of unification came from regarding medicine as an adjunct to a global environmental science. Its theodicy instructed the physician to treat patients in terms of not only relieving their suffering but also assessing the impact of their continued existence on the ecology. After all, one may read the Hippocratic imperative "to do no harm" in the narrow sense of trying to minimize the patient's pain, which may entail allowing patients to die rather than keeping them alive with treatments that may still cause them some pain, while threatening to destabilize the ecosystem, with the potential to harm many others. In this context, euthanasia appears as a merciful medical means to bring about population control. In the coming years, there is likely to be a major secular dispute with clear roots in theodicy over whether the universally anticipated increase in the quantity and quality of human lives on the planet is seen as a positive or negative indicator of the long-term viability of humanity as such. In the twentieth century, this divide was clearly marked in terms of "positive" and "negative" eugenics policies (Bashford and Levine 2010). The difference that the twenty-first century makes is that mainstream politics will no longer be able to avoid taking sides (Fuller and Lipinska 2014: ch. 3).

Recap: the Creationist Left's challenge to the science–religion nexus

The Creationist Left aims to get around Darwin's morally unpalatable deity with an optimistic belief that the future will be better than the past, if only because our value orientation to the world will have changed in ways that in retrospect will be seen as a correction to both who "we" are and where "we" are heading. In short, the march of progress is itself morally cleansing as we learn from our mistakes. The point is most easily seen as being about what Joseph Schumpeter (1942) called the "creative destruction of markets" under capitalism. For example, after some debate at the turn of the last century about the risk to human and natural life posed by the automobile, it managed relatively quickly to supersede the horse-drawn carriage once it became affordable. Over time, consumers have come to value speed and efficiency over direct sensory contact with the natural world when evaluating alternative modes of transport. Social psychologists regard such a shift as an "adaptive preference formation", which carries a strong sense of rationalization, namely, that we routinely train ourselves to desire what is already available or appears inevitable, so that the next generation is always amazed by the existential struggle that the previous generation underwent to accept a lifestyle now considered normal (Fuller 2002: ch. 3).

Perhaps unwittingly, this analysis adds rhetorical force to Schopenhauer's hypothesis that it might be better never to have been born. It reinterprets the optimist's radical value re-orientations as a desperate survival strategy. Seen in the cold light of Schopenhauer's day, future humans will not live substantially better lives than would have been lived by the many other humans and non-humans sacrificed or forgone on their behalf. The value of all life remains constant, given the transient nature of material beings in the world. In that respect, our actions add no value in any absolute sense. The dead would not have laid the groundwork for a better sort of living. It would simply be a case of one form of life having impeded and superseded the existence of another – the "law of the jungle" raised to the level of metaphysics. Thus, the best we can do is to leave a world that is at least in as good a condition as when we arrived. From here, it is easy to see how Schopenhauer might be regarded as a patron saint of a steady-state view of ecological sustainability, intergenerational justice and even animal rights and the precautionary principle.

In the face of this quite pervasive and persuasive pessimism that would render illusory all dreams of epistemic and social progress, it is incumbent on a defender of the Creationist Left to explain how, given his/her broad adherence to Abrahamic theology, humanity is to rise from its fallen state. The explanation begins by arguing that the difference between God and us is simply that God is the one being in whom all of our virtues are concentrated perfectly, whereas for our own part those virtues are distributed imperfectly among many individuals. Such is the legacy of Original Sin (Harrison 2007). The expulsion of Adam and Eve from the Garden of Eden did not constitute a uniform demotion of humanity. Rather, the deity amplified our ill-fated decision to follow the path of least resistance (succumb to temptation) resulting in the disparate

98 *Epistemology as divine psychology*

development of our various godlike virtues without any thought of how they might contribute to some overall human project. The result is a humanity mutually alienated and internally conflicted, as epitomized in Genesis by the story of the Tower of Babel.

This image of humanity's Fall – a dispersion of the self rather than a collective demotion of the species – is due to the fourteenth-century Franciscan philosopher and theologian, John Duns Scotus, who is arguably the first "modern", at least in terms of taking seriously that because the virtues are unequally distributed across society, if humanity is to return to a godly state, then it must do all it can to enable individuals to re-integrate those virtues in themselves (Fuller 2011: ch. 2). It is easy to see the intuition guiding Duns Scotus's argument, since rather different, perhaps even discrete, sets of people would be normally counted as among the most powerful, good, knowledgeable, etc. Thus, as long as it is possible, say, to be very intelligent and yet commit great evil, we remain in a fallen state. Nevertheless, projects for reunifying these virtues to come closer to God have generated many trenchant academic and political disputes: Is the promised reunification to happen within one's own lifetime or only across several generations? Does the success of this project depend on everyone – or only a select few – achieving the desired unity of being? Finally, the question classically posed to heretics: should the project be understood as driven exclusively by human effort or does it depend crucially on God's involvement?

But a basic Scotist point remains radical to this day: in important ways, the divine and the human are comparable. Notwithstanding Adam's Fall, we remain created "in the image and likeness of God". From this Biblical claim it follows that we are capable of deploying the powers that distinguish us from the other animals to come closer to God. Such is the theological template on which the secular idea of progress was forged during the Scientific Revolution, on the basis of which the Creationist Left was launched. Thus, the science–religion relationship is one of neither mutual hostility nor simple complementarity, but outright continuity. Specifically, Abrahamic theology provides the basis for a conception of humanity sufficiently close to the source of all being to make scientific inquiry possible and feasible – and arguably necessary, if we are to fulfil our potential as creatures *in imago dei*. The following five paragraphs distil the Creationist Left into a set of propositions that make explicit the multiple challenges that it poses to more conventional understandings of the science–religion nexus – as it re-positions epistemology as "divine psychology".

(a) Reality is constructed on the model of language, understood either in New Testament terms as an instantiation of the Holy Spirit (the *logos* of

Old Testament terms as a generalization of the privileged written medium through which Moses made God's intentions evident to the people of Israel with whom he entered into Covenant. Taken together, these language-led images of reality justify science's search for both overarching explanatory principles (syntax) and contextually specified understandings (semantics). The seventeenth-century Scientific Revolution was thus about Nature coming to be read literally as a book, indeed, an alternative Bible (Harrison 1998). Updated for the twentieth century, molecular biology should be understood as the science that explores the divinely available possibilities for life (i.e. the syntax of creation) and natural history as simply the possibilities actualized that have made us as we are (i.e. the semantics of evolution). This position is closer to the discourse of "genetic information" proffered in Schrödinger (1955), the inspirational text for the DNA Revolution, than anything Darwin could have imagined, given his radically path-dependent view of life (Gould 1989). That the genetic code might be literally "cracked" confirms science's Biblically inspired epistemic claim to comprehensiveness, suggesting that we may come to be fluent in the language of Creation so as to read the "signature in the cell" (cf. Meyer 2009).

(b) There are two general ways to engage in a "literal" reading of the Bible that correspond to what the late nineteenth-century Neo-Kantian philosophers called an "idiographic" and a "nomothetic" approach to the study of the empirical world. To the "idiographic" approach corresponds the "literal" reading of the Bible as a historical document that details unique events, as in Bishop Ussher's notorious dating of the Creation to 4004 BCE. To the "nomothetic" approach corresponds the "literal" reading of the Bible as an abstract theory of the cosmos presented in narrative form. This latter reading is sometimes called "allegorical" or even "anagogic" (both terms suggesting a second-order level of interpretation); and in terms of modern philosophy of science we might call it "model-theoretic". In this respect, the literal truth of the Bible lies in the depiction of patterns of ideas and relationships that are repeated regularly throughout nature. Although some might balk at calling this way of reading the Bible "literal", it is the sense in which we say of mathematically formulated scientific theories that, when empirically confirmed, they "literally" capture the structure of their target realities (Harrison 1998). Indeed, it was this sense of "literal" that motivated Newton and a host of radical thinkers from the sixteenth to the eighteenth centuries – from Giordano Bruno to Emanuel Swedenborg – to read the Bible and nature as alternative accounts of the same reality. The secular philosophical descendant of this quest for Biblical literalism is "scientific realism" (cf. Fuller 2014).

100 *Epistemology as divine psychology*

(c) However, the privileged nature of the linguistic medium does not mean that it is error-proof, given the imperfect nature of its human recipients. As humanity reduces its spiritual distance from God in a temporal journey over many generations (scientific progress), we may discover that we have overgeneralized, if not outright misunderstood, features of the divine message. Proper correction may require rewriting, or even redrafting, the sacred text. From that standpoint, Christianity's redaction controversies over the Bible's composition are part of a process that includes the Bible's supplementation if not replacement by covenants in the form of declarations of human rights and national constitutions as well as the mathematical laws of nature. However, the regulative ideal of this redactive enterprise is a text that communicates to us ultimate truths in a way that enables us to reclaim fully our divine entitlement. This general turn of mind was epitomized by the US founding fathers, not least Thomas Jefferson, who stripped down the New Testament into an enlightened tax revolt that escalated into a mandate for self-governance (I. B. Cohen 1997).

(d) The reasonableness of this ideal presupposes that some (typically mental) aspects of human and divine being remain identical, even after the Fall – what Malebranche vividly called our "vision in God". Historically these aspects have been associated with so-called *a priori* knowledge, especially mathematics, in which arithmetic and geometry permit us to calculate, measure and predict features of reality to which our normal human bodies are unlikely ever to have direct empirical access. In short, *a priori* knowledge enables us to inhabit what nowadays is called "virtual reality". But between Malebranche's original theological concerns and those of today's computer simulators lies the modern history of "scientific realism", whereby speculative projections of causal mechanisms come to be operationalized as testable models. Herein lies the most interesting secularization of the theological imagination, whereby the search for God goes beyond the mere finding of "gaps" in scientific accounts to outright second-guessing the divine *modus operandi*. Thus, throughout the eighteenth and nineteenth centuries, "natural philosophers" more or less explicitly focused on the means by which God creates, notably Newton, Leibniz, Boscovich, Hartley, Priestley, Faraday, Maxwell, Boltzmann (Laudan 1981: ch. 2). Indeed, it is during this period that probability theory is developed – largely in a theological frame of mind – to chart both the gradual reduction of our uncertainty about the nature of physical reality and the gradual growth in our understanding of the stochastic processes built into the design of such reality: in short, subjective and objective probability (Hacking 1975).

(e) It follows that the conflict between free will and determinism – a metaphysical conundrum traditionally confronting both God and humans – is largely illusory: God can create through us because we already spontaneously think some of the deity's thoughts; hence, the old Stoic maxim, "freedom is the recognition of necessity". In other words, our sphere of rational action increases as we more fully inhabit the divine standpoint. This invariably involves self-transformation, ranging from the "vocational" sense of hearing God's voice (common to monastic and academic callings, as Max Weber stressed; see Weber 1958b) to the outright performing – that is, acting out – of divine intentions in materially novel ways ranging from socially engineered utopias to bio-engineered transhumans (Fuller 2008a: ch. 7). At both ends, we are engaged in re-making ourselves "in the image and likeness of God". The "dark" side of this process is that humanity realizes its role as what the Neo-Platonist philosophers called the "demiurge", the entity that God delegates to do the "dirty work" of creation, which may include sacrificing some current forms of life in the name of some improved future forms. Here "principal-agent theory" in political economy may offer some insight into the moral logic involved. According to the theory, the "principal" (God, in this case) knows the end-state (Creation) but not necessarily the particular means to achieve it (i.e. the strictly temporal knowledge that humans possess but which does not overlap with the *a priori* knowledge they share with God). However, God is capable – perhaps even obliged – to will the most efficient means available, which requires employing the "agent" (humanity, in this case), who *does* have direct acquaintance with the consequences of pursuing particular means. Over time humans grow into the role of the faithful agent – and in the process acquire the ends of the divine principal as their own – by pursuing means that often go against the grain of conventional morality and perhaps even their own self-interest, as in the case of sacrifice and just wars (Fuller 2011: ch. 4).

3 Epistemology as psychology of science

In the beginning the psychologist was the self-conscious scientist

Experimental psychology began as the psychology of the scientist, specifically the pivotal role that intersubjective differences in astronomical observation – the so-called personal equation – played in laying the foundations of psychophysics in the mid-nineteenth century (Boring 1950: 31). It was assumed that science's special epistemic powers resulted from scientists' heightened self-consciousness about human cognition in general. This assumption was taken in two different directions in the early twentieth century. The first, championed by John Dewey (1910), amounted to advising teachers that children should be exposed to the "scientific method" (i.e. hypothesis testing) in order to learn how to think. The second, relevant to the subsequent development of psychology as a discipline, was that scientists may be expected to be more articulate about what non-scientists always already do whenever they think. This view, shared by the physicists Max Planck and Albert Einstein, justified the Würzburg School's controversial application of the introspective method to themselves and each other, very often using complex philosophical problems as stimuli (Kusch 1999). Here it is worth recalling psychology's dual institutional origins as the applied wing of the philosophy faculty and the theoretical wing of the medical faculty, which helps to explain the pivotal role of William James, someone trained in medicine who migrated to philosophy where he established a psychology laboratory (Ben-David and Collins 1966; Bordogna 2008).

These early Würzburger steps in what is now called "cognitive psychology" were followed up in the 1920s and 1930s by the Gestalt psychologists Otto Selz and Karl Duncker, who departed from their Würzburg forebears in clearly separating the experimenter and subject roles. (As we shall see in the next chapter, Karl Popper was a fellow-traveller who was distinctive in returning to philosophy.) They studied scientists' notebooks to construct general testable accounts of problem-solving (Petersen 1984; Wettersten 1985). Moreover, the Gestalt thought leader Max Wertheimer

Epistemology as psychology of science 103

(1945) probed the directive nature of Einstein's own discovery process in a quarter-century correspondence with the revolutionary physicist. This work in turn inspired the field of "protocol analysis" and other techniques to infer thought processes from verbal behaviour that are still used by a wide range of psychologists today (Ericsson and Simon 1985).

In philosophy of science terms, this original version of the psychology of science treated in a "realist" fashion what psychologists themselves might normally treat as "methodology", a general set of principles designed to amplify truth-tending and minimize false-tending inferences in the scientific community (Campbell 1988). The implied difference here is between taking scientists' self-accounts of their reasoning as recapitulating their actual thought processes (psychology) and as rationally reconstructing those thought processes for purposes of peer evaluation (methodology). To be sure, the treatment of methodology as literal "rules for the direction of the mind" recalls the original seventeenth-century sense of "scientific method" promoted by Francis Bacon and René Descartes as extending the Protestant Reformation's call for the faithful to become more personally accountable to the deity (Yates 1966). This psychologically realist sense of the scientific method was formalized (and secularized) in the eighteenth and the nineteenth century as a quest for "the logic of discovery", paradigmatically the train of thought that culminated in Newton's grand synthesis (Laudan 1981: ch. 11).

However, by the start of the twentieth century, the failure of such philosophers as the pragmatist Charles Sanders Peirce to provide a compelling account of a distinct mental process that at once genuinely advances our knowledge and is reliably self-correcting – what Peirce had called "abduction" – resulted in the more psychologically antirealist or constructivist stance towards the scientific method that persists in philosophy to this day (Laudan 1981: ch. 14). Thus, methodological principles such as the logical positivists' verifiability, Popper's falsifiability and probability-based formulae such as Bayes's Theorem have been primarily proposed as *ex post* tools for evaluating hypotheses, not for hypothesis generation. This helps to explain, and perhaps even justify, the radically reconstructed accounts of the history of science in which philosophers have indulged to make their case for one or another such method (e.g. Lakatos 1981).

Something of the original Würzburg and Gestalt sensibility returned to the psychology of science that emerged, now as an independent field, in the wake of the so-called cognitive revolution in psychology that began in the 1950s and peaked in the 1970s (Baars 1986). However, this work, typically indebted to the experimental paradigms developed at University College London by Peter Wason and Philip Johnson-Laird in the 1960s, shifted the focus of inquiry from the introspective reports of scientists to the verbal behaviour of non-scientists confronted with scientifically structured tasks (Wason and Johnson-Laird 1972). The first work to self-consciously identify itself in terms of this lineage was Tweney *et al.* (1981), which showcased research from Bowling Green State University. Its epistemological legacy remains conflicted to this day. On the one hand, the very idea that subjects might be tested for, say, their propensity to look for evidence that disconfirms a hypothesis suggested that they could and should do such a thing in everyday life. Here the new cognitive psychologists of science appeared to be one with the Würzburgers and Gestaltists. Yet, on the other hand, most of the work done under this paradigm ended up showing just how different canonical forms of scientific reasoning are from the ways of ordinary cognition.

While one might have hoped that these results only show that scientific reasoning requires specialized training, in fact scientists themselves turned out to be no better at, say, falsifying their hypotheses than non-scientists. Similar points had been long observed and theorized by Paul Meehl in the context of the unreliability of clinical judgement. At first Meehl (1967) understood this problem as limited to psychologists' tendencies to over-estimate intuition and individual differences, at least vis-à-vis what he had presumed to be the superior – broadly Popperian – practice of physicists. However, Meehl student David Faust (1984) subsequently incorporated the emerging literature in the new cognitive psychology, drawing generally sceptical conclusions about human cognitive capacities, both lay and expert, when compared to, say, actuarial tables and computerized expert systems capable of ranging over large and varied data sets.

Reflecting on this research with hindsight, one might conclude that the new cognitive psychology of science never quite escaped the shadow cast by behaviourism on mid-twentieth-century experimental psychology. In particular, it could never quite decide whether it wanted to treat mental representations of the scientific method (either by the experimenter or the subject) as revisable models (i.e. prototypes for some presumed cognitive process) or testable hypotheses (i.e. accounts for predicting behavioural regularities). In the next section, we explore the source of this ambivalence as alternative responses to Bertrand Russell's critique of the introspective method, but some recent researchers have tried to turn this ambivalence into a virtue (e.g. Gorman 1992). In any case, by holding subjects accountable to one or another version of the scientific method, psychologists appeared to have unwittingly revealed a deep sense of human irrationality intrinsic to the cognitive process, and not simply the product of motivated interference, say, from conscious self-interest or unconscious defence mechanism.

In the past quarter of a century, there have been two general responses to this development, one social constructivist and the other more strictly social psychological. The first aims for no less than a deconstruction of the very idea of the scientific self-consciousness, according to which, absent independent behavioural corroboration, any scientific self-reporting should be presumed to be entirely the product of rationalization, better explained by the norms of self-accounting at the time the scientist is writing than any generally identifiable psychological processes (Brannigan 1981; Fuller 1993). Arguably this sort of critique served to undermine the epistemological basis for the most systematic attempt at founding a "social psychology of science" (Shadish and Fuller 1994). Stephen Turner (1994), a social theorist active in science and technology studies (STS), observed that the repeated finding of discrepancies between psychologists' normative expectations of what scientists should do and what scientists actually do, whether studied in experimental or field settings, placed psychologists of science in the tricky rhetorical position of arguing that scientists do not know how to do science properly, a conclusion that would then rebound on the epistemic authority of the psychologists of science themselves, just as it had on followers of Karl Mannheim in the sociology of knowledge earlier in the twentieth century. An honourable attempt to carry on as a practising psychologist reflexively aware of the various levels at which this problem arises – from personal encounters with subjects to formal peer review processes – may be found in the corpus of Michael Mahoney (2004).

The second response to this apparent irrationality of scientists was already foreshadowed in the first major systematic presentation of the cognitive limits research: It is to argue that all of the formally fallacious forms of inference observed in the laboratory must serve some sort of "adaptive" function for the human organism (Tversky and Kahneman 1974). Here "adaptive" may be understood in a purely social psychological sense, namely, as referring to a body of "lay knowledge", roughly an articulated version of "common sense", that offers a coherent world-view in normal settings. However, such knowledge tends to be culturally sensitive and does not handle extreme cases especially well. Some self-styled "experimental philosophers" have tried to redefine the task of philosophy as the systematic probing of those limits (Knobe and Nichols 2008), while some social psychologists have examined how those limits are negotiated and perhaps even transcended by scientists who, after all, are lay people for all but their specific area of expertise (Kruglanski 1989: ch. 10). Since the advent of evolutionary psychology in the 1980s, it has become customary to contrast the *adaptive* character of our comprehensively flawed normal modes of reasoning – typically dignified under the rubric of "heuristics" – with the *exaptive* character of methodologically sound scientific reasoning, which casts it as the "co-opted by-products of adaptations" (Feist 2006: 217). In short, science is a humanly significant unintended consequence of the overall evolutionary process.

106 *Epistemology as psychology of science*

To be sure, this response has done nothing to eliminate the apparent strangeness of scientific modes of thinking. However, it has inspired research into the difficulties that children face mastering scientific concepts in ways that have served to undermine the plausibility of Jean Piaget's long influential "genetic epistemology", which had portrayed the maturing child as recapitulating in its own cognitive development the increasingly counter-intuitive character of the history of science (Feist 2006: ch. 3). Perhaps a more straightforward normative response to dealing with the alien character of scientific reasoning has been to reassert the need for strong, methodologically driven scientific institutions to counteract our default cognitive liabilities (Fuller 1993). However, scientists who studied the psychological and sociological evidence for the "unnatural nature of science" tended to interpret this charge narrowly to involve requiring scientists to stick to what is "evidence-based" and not consider "value-laden" issues – thereby leaving the weighting of evidence to public debate and policymakers (Wolpert 1992). A relevant precedent for thinking about the matter is the US Constitution, which is subject to various "separations of powers" and "checks and balances" to ensure that people's inevitable conflicts of interest and short-sightedness do not undermine their collective capacity to serve the public good (Fuller 2000a). Popper held a similar view but did not believe that "facts" and "values" could be separated so neatly, as scientists were no different from others in overestimating their own views and underestimating those of their opponents. Indeed, "science" for Popper is the organization of those liabilities in aid of producing epistemic virtue, via "the method of conjectures and refutations", as imperfectly regulated by the peer review process (Jarvie 2001).

The genealogy of validity: from the bank to the lab bench

"Judgement" understood as a distinct mental process allowed scientists to be seen as self-conscious psychologists who made decisions with an aim in sight. This framing implied that science is a goal-directed activity with a clear objective, the ultimately comprehensive account of reality, what physicists continue to dignify after Einstein as the "grand unified theory of everything" but philosophers know more simply as "the truth". Recalling the late nineteenth century, when physicists were routinely claiming to be on the verge of such an account, Max Planck characterized scientific theories as *Weltbilder* ("world constructions" or "world pictures"). Indeed, a secular legacy of Newton's own crypto-millenarian aspirations is that at the end of every century in the modern era, science has been seen as near the realization of a very grand *Weltbild* through its own initiative

Epistemology as psychology of science 107

that would provide the basis for transcending humanity's intellectual if not physical burdens (Passmore 1970: ch. 10; Horgan 1996). In the heyday of this conception – roughly, the quarter-century on either side of 1800 – Condorcet, Comte and Hegel exemplified the guiding intuition here – that the history of science systematically records humanity's collective self-reflection, unreflective versions of which occur in the ordinary thought processes of individual humans.

However, the relativity and quantum revolutions in physics that Planck himself helped to usher in in the early twentieth century caused the *Weltbild* approach to science to retreat from first-order characterizations of scientific practice to second-order metaphysical interpretations that remain relevant even after a scientific revolution. Thus, Gerald Holton (1973), a student of Percy Bridgman, the Harvard professor of thermodynamics who wanted to reduce all scientific concepts to logical and instrumental "operations", relocated *Weltbilder* to the heuristic value provided by perennial philosophical questions – such as whether matter is continuous or discontinuous – to the conduct of scientific inquiry. These *themata* function as auxiliary constraints or desiderata that guide the empirical elaboration of scientific theories but are never conclusively proven by them. Unsurprisingly, the *Weltbild* conception of science was pursued most actively not by professional scientists but by philosophers, especially as a pragmatic interpretation of "convergent scientific realism", ranging from Peirce to Wilfrid Sellars and Nicholas Rescher (Laudan 1981: ch. 14). However, all of these figures stressed not only the increasing distance that the scientific world-view takes one from common sense but also the diminishing epistemic returns of scientific effort as one continues down that path (e.g. Rescher 1998). Moreover, once Kuhn (1970) installed a properly Darwinian model of scientific evolution, whereby inquiry endlessly exfoliates into ever greater specialization, never to converge in some summative epistemic achievement, even the idea of *themata* as regulative ideals of science started to lose its appeal.

A deep intellectual history of human reasoning would focus on the etymologies of *judgement* and *validity*, the one taken from the law courts and the other from the financial sector. (It is also an important project in the social epistemology of philosophy, part of which should be concerned with the re-inscription of historical social relations in universal conceptual space.) I have discussed the etymology of "judgement" elsewhere, focusing on the German *Urteil* (Fuller 2009b), and I shall discuss the etymology of "validity" more fully below. The guiding intuition dividing the two concepts is that, on the one hand, a judge's verdict decides under which legal principle a particular case should fall, and on the other, a bank sustains the value of currency across all the transactions of that currency's users.

108 *Epistemology as psychology of science*

This difference is preserved in the discourse of philosophical logic. Thus, whereas "truth-values" are judgements of "true" or "false" assigned to particular propositions, a "valid" inference preserves the truth-value of the premises in the conclusion. "Validity" in this sense is the hallmark of deduction, the historic gold standard of all reasoning. It captures the fact that content has been neither lost nor gained in the translation from premise to conclusion. In this context, judgement is always "enthymematic", which is to say, a direct inference from the case to the principle without specifying what the scholastic logicians called the "middle term" of the syllogism (e.g. the moment you infer that Socrates is mortal by observing that he falls under a class of mortal beings known as humans). In more contemporary parlance, judgement always has an "unconscious" character that validity then tries to make explicit and, in that sense, "justify".

Historians of logic normally chart a decline in the concept of judgement after Kant, as what we now call "psychology" and "logic" gradually parted ways, the former concerned with empirical reasoning patterns and the latter with ideal normative ones based on mathematics. On this account, judgement increasingly fell between these two stools, except for interest in what Charles Sanders Peirce called "abduction" and, more generally, the "logic of discovery" (Laudan 1981). To be sure, the story is more subtle, complex and worth revisiting, starting with the informed and sympathetic rendering of the transition in Passmore (1966: chs 6–8). Arguably the last original theorist of judgement with lasting effect was Wilhelm Wundt's main rival for establishing psychology as an empirical science in the final quarter of the nineteenth century, the reformed Neo-Scholastic philosopher, Franz Brentano.

Brentano's legacy remains strongest in contemporary analytic epistemology, especially its non-naturalistic side – courtesy of his post-Second World War American translator and explicator, Roderick Chisholm. Suitably "Chisholmed", this legacy amounts to the idea that one is in a state of knowledge when one explicitly affirms that which is true and rejects that which is false, and in both cases for just the right reasons: aka "justified true belief" (Jacquette 2004). In the Lotzean terms to be introduced below, this state of mind must access both what is true and what is valid, which suggests the survival of judgement as an epistemological concept. But notice that while Brentano (and his analytic-philosophical admirers) characterize his particular brand of psychology as "empirical", it is neutral on the nature of "right reasons" (i.e. they may come from natural or supernatural sources, depending which provides the best explanation).

Psychoanalysis and phenomenology, the influential schools founded by two of Brentano's students at the University of Vienna in the 1880s (Sigmund Freud and Edmund Husserl), may be understood as alternative ways of undermining the paradigm status of judgement – and therefore

Epistemology as psychology of science 109

science – as the form of thought. On the one hand, Freud accepted the disruptive character of science to our ordinarily unreflective modes of self-understanding, yet realized that it may only be a Sisyphean imposition of structure on the wilfully unstructured nature of our mental life. On the other hand, Husserl held that the fixation on judgement impeded our ability to let the phenomena of consciousness fully reveal themselves. Science in this respect, travelling under Husserl's pejorative use of "naturalism", limits rather than enhances the horizons of our spontaneous experience of the world. By the time we reach the existential phenomenology of Husserl's radical follower, Martin Heidegger, thinking has lost any sense of its involvement in a self-affirming project of world-making; rather it has become simply an emergent feature of humanity's abject condition, a periodic flickering of discovery in the original Greek sense of *aletheia*, whose authenticity science destroys through its own methodology and its technological extensions. Overall, then, the trajectory from Brentano on the European continent has been to treat science as more rationalization and psychic artifice than authentic self-consciousness.

The distinction between judging truth and valdating arguments, which proved decisive in driving a wedge between psychology and logic in the late nineteenth century, was canonized by Gustav Fechner's most influential and underrated student, the physician-turned-philosopher Hermann Lotze (Schnädelbach 1984: 107). Although Lotze failed to found a school in his name, from his professorial perch in Göttingen he taught both the pioneering mathematical logician Gottlob Frege and the dean of the Heidelberg Neo-Kantian philosophers, Wilhelm Windelband, as well as two of Wundt's proto-Gestaltist rivals in the development of experimental psychology, G. E. Müller and Carl Stumpf.

According to Lotze, psychology deals with *ideas*, the origin of which may come from inside or outside a given human mind, and logic with *concepts* whose meanings are determined by objective relations within a system of thought. (It is worth recalling that even such mid-nineteenth-century mathematical logicians as George Boole, Augustus de Morgan and William Stanley Jevons still defined logic as normative psychology.) In short, psychology deals with matters of *truth* and logic with matters of *validity*. The subject of the former is the scientist, the latter science. Lotze's sharp distinction between psychology and logic provided the basis for what in the 1930s would be canonized by Karl Popper and Hans Reichenbach as, respectively, the context of "discovery" and "justification" (Ash 1988: 30). In particular, one may come to apprehend a genuine truth but by means that do not generally contribute to the validity of a system of thought. Scientific inquiry is about integrating psychologically compelling yet logically accidental discoveries of truth into the maximally comprehensive valid system of thought.

110 *Epistemology as psychology of science*

Interestingly, Lotze himself identified this system with the mind of God, which to his late nineteenth-century liberal Protestant admirers meant that he managed to place science in the centre of the human condition while avoiding the materialist reduction of theology to projective group psychology, advanced by, say, Ludwig Feuerbach. (One such admirer was the theologian Adolf von Harnack, the minister for higher education who oversaw the creation of the Kaiser Wilhelm Gesellschaft, the original academic public–private partnership that is the forerunner of today's Max Planck Institutes.) It also endeared him to the US pragmatists, including the decidedly irreligious Peirce, for whom scientific inquiry strives for an ideal state that would integrate the collective insights of humanity without simply being the theory on which the latest generation of scientists happen to agree (Hookway 2009).

The subtle difference between the two states observed by Peirce, which philosophers re-packaged as "scientific realism" nearly a century later, is indebted to Lotze's careful attempt to update the Biblical idea that we are created "in the image and likeness of God" (the "microcosm", to recall the title of Lotze's *magnum opus*) without thereby claiming that we might become God. In upholding theological probity, Lotze was also denying the possibility of a middle realm between psychology and logic called *epistemology* that deals with all that is knowable. This realm had been canonized in 1854 by Lotze's German-idealist trained Scottish contemporary, James Ferrier, who regarded the very idea that some things are intrinsically unknowable (as in Kant's *noumena*, or "things-in-themselves") as a contradiction in terms (Passmore 1966: 51–54). For Ferrier, "ignorance" simply reflects our failure to know which possible world God has actualized. But, in principle at least, we are divinely endowed to explore all the possibilities. To be sure, Lotze ensured that the human did not so easily blur into the divine, but he still appeared to relegate the specific truth of human experience to mere inputs of a larger world-system. At least that is how it seemed to Heidegger, whose youthful 1919 lectures, *Towards a Definition of Philosophy*, formally launched what became an influential pushback from philosophy's increasing accommodation with science by insisting on the radical ontological status of our sheer being-in-the-world (Schnädelbach 1984: chs 6–7).

However, a more mainstream academic response to Lotze's rather transcendental conception of validity was represented by the Neo-Kantian philosopher Heinrich Rickert, a student of Lotze's student Windelband, as well as friend of Max Weber and teacher of Heidegger. Rickert was perhaps the most influential epistemologist prior to the rise of logical positivism. He argued that the sciences are to be distinguished not by their objects but their validity conditions (Zijderveld 2006). Thus, a study of human beings may be "valid" (or not) in many different senses

Epistemology as psychology of science 111

depending on the intensity of the normative force attached to the study itself and the extent of the study's normative reach. Moreover, these two dimensions may trade off against each other in a way that was canonized by Windelband as the distinction between *idiographic* and *nomothetic* inquiry. Someone immersed in a particular native or historic culture (i.e. idiographic) more reliably knows that culture than someone who regards it as simply one of a kind, yet that superior knowledge is unlikely to be generalizable to other cultures (i.e. nomothetic).

The clearest contemporary legacy of this perspective is Jürgen Habermas's (1981) four "validity claims" (*Geltungsansprüchen*) relevant to human action, which implies that research may be (in)valid in terms of the accuracy, appropriateness, sincerity and/or comprehensiveness vis-à-vis its target reality. According to Habermas, the existence of relatively self-contained yet equally enlightening schools of sociology, each dedicated to establishing one of these validity claims, demonstrates that validity is not a univocal concept and that so-called threats to it may be best understood as an attempt to mix different validity claims in a single study. Research design in psychology recognizes this point, as a study may provide an adequate model of either other studies of exactly the same kind or a range of rather different studies done in conditions more closely resembling the target reality one wishes to capture or affect.

This is the basis of the distinction between *internal* and *external* validity. In the former case, valid research designs are called "reliable", in the latter "representative", without any general expectation that these two qualities will be positively correlated. Indeed, they may be negatively correlated, thus leading to what the twentieth century's greatest social science methodologist, Donald Campbell, called "threats to validity" (Campbell and Stanley 1963). After all, any experiment or ethnography, simply taken alone, is a statistically improbable act in the normal run of human events. How then is it possible for knowledge gained by such means ever to be expected to have sufficient "validity" to be built upon by future researchers, let alone applied in policy contexts? Here we need to delve into the spirit in which "validity" is supposed to convey "normative force".

The German word that Lotze used for "validity", often translated as "justification", was *Geltung*, a generic term for "normative force", an etymological abstraction of the idea behind "valid legal tender", that is, the state's backing of banknotes that enables them to retain their face value as they change hands in transactions over a wide variety of goods and services. But of course, banknotes are used not only to *measure* but also to *accumulate* wealth. It was in this dual spirit that William James famously spoke of the "cash-value" of ideas, indeed, in a context that anticipated W. V. O. Quine's (1953) ontological slogan, popular among recent analytic philosophers keen to prove their minimalist metaphysics: "To be is

112 *Epistemology as psychology of science*

to be the value of a bound variable". Translated back from Quine's algebraic turn of phrase to James's more psychologistic formulation, the cash-value of your sense of self lies in what it enables you to do in some larger scheme of things (James 1977: 85).

The intuition behind this line of thought derives from Kant's concession to Hume that the bare fact that something exists has no normative force *per se*. Normative force depends on whatever else it manages to empower: "Ought implies can", as Kant memorably put it. Nowadays this principle tends to be interpreted in naturalistic terms as limiting the scope of moral obligation to an agent's capacity to act. However, it was originally given a more performative spin – that one's normative legitimacy rests on the capacity to enforce one's will (Fuller 2008a: ch. 7). Again the ultimate source of the idea is theological, specifically the divine voluntarism of John Duns Scotus: *God is entitled to act as he does because only he can do so* (Funkenstein 1986: ch. 3). According to Blumenberg's (1986) influential account of the rise of modernity, God's omnipotence came to be divided – without remainder – between civil law and natural law. Nevertheless, the original problem of how normative force is both sustained and rendered productive in the social and natural worlds has remained throughout the modern era. Much of this concern has simply secularized Biblical worries about the divine *logos* becoming corrupt through repeated transmission and translation in the material world – be it in the form of semantic inde-terminacy or thermodynamic entropy – resulting in ultimate epistemic and ontic meltdown, pure chaos (Stigler 1986).

In this respect, the advantage of experimentally based inquiry lay in the skilled scientist's capacity to conjure up the normative force of nature through a public demonstration that, at least in principle, may be wit-nessed by others – a kind of socially responsible magic (Shapin 1994). By seeing with one's own eyes, one no longer had to rely on authoritative testimony whose validity naturally depreciated over time and space. However, this solution, which served rhetorically to establish experi-mentation as the gold standard of scientific inquiry, continues to have its doubters even today, as seemingly solid findings appear notoriously diffi-cult to replicate only a few years later (Lehrer 2010). Moreover, already in the seventeenth century, the probability calculus threatened to undermine the long-term validity of scientific findings by treating them as indepen-dent events, whose cumulative impact would be eroded by multiplying their fractional truth-values (L. J. Cohen 1977). But throughout an alternative interpretation of probability has argued that the probity of independent strands of inquiry is reinforced if they tend towards the same conclusion. This view, which sits more comfortably with Francis Bacon's own original modelling of scientific method on legal forensics, came to be championed in the nineteenth century by the British natural theologian

Epistemology as psychology of science   113

William Whewell, who portrayed it as the key to the Newtonian synthesis (McGrath 2011: ch. 5).

This divided verdict on the external validity of experiments is also familiar from economics, especially thought experiments about what the ideal rational agent *Homo economicus* would do under various hypothetical conditions. On this basis, Carl Menger, who brought the marginalist revolution in economics to the German-speaking world in the late nineteenth century, sharply distinguished between the rationality of *Homo economicus* and the imperfect rationality of real economic agents. The phrases "normative" and "positive" economics were invoked to stress the gulf between these two states (Machlup 1978). Clearly *Homo economicus* was not an ecologically valid construct. But additionally, and more importantly from a policy standpoint, Menger held that the interconnectedness of markets and the unique array of forces influencing each agent's decision-making meant that even claims to functional validity could never be achieved, certainly not at the macroeconomic level. Such scepticism underwrites the continued aversion of the libertarian Austrian school of economics to the use of statistics as a basis for major policy interventions, as notably expressed by the opposition of Menger's disciple Friedrich Hayek to Keynesianism (Fuller 1993: pt 2).

When compared with the methodological scruples displayed in these social science discussions of external validity, the natural sciences appear downright speculative (Hedges 1987). For example, whereas Darwin himself was interested in reconstructing the Earth's unique natural history, Neo-Darwinists are mainly concerned with demonstrating evolution by natural selection as a universal process. Thus, over the past 150 years, the centre of gravity of biological research has migrated from the field to the lab. In Neo-Kantian terms, this results in a tension between idiographic and nomothetic modes of inquiry. However, Neo-Darwinian biologists rarely register the tension as such. Rather, they routinely treat contemporary laboratory experiments as models of causal processes that repeatedly happened to a variety of species in a variety of settings over millions, if not billions, of years (Sober 2008). But if Milgram's or Zimbardo's experiments fail in their attempt to model causal processes across cultures and history, why should one believe that Neo-Darwinian experiments succeed in an even more heroic generalization across species and aeons (Fuller 2008a: ch. 4)?

While most "threats to validity" pertain to the generalization of a single research event, the phrase can be understood in both more macro- and micro-terms. Macro-threats to validity derive from what logicians call the fallacies of *composition* and *division* (Fuller 1988: Introduction). In other words, properties of the parts may be invalidly projected as properties of the whole and vice versa. Economists following Menger's lead were especially sensitive to the fallacy of composition, since individuals acting on their own sense of self-interest routinely generate both positive and negative unintended consequences that constrain a society's subsequent range of action. Conversely, it is equally fallacious to infer that a society's overall strength or weakness is due to some particular strength or weakness in each or the majority of its members. Thus, those who stress ideological change as a vehicle of social reform, as if it were necessary for everyone to think the same way to move in the same direction, are often guilty of the fallacy of division. But at the ultimate micro-level – namely, inferences that a single individual makes from psychological states to epistemological judgements – a still insufficiently appreciated source of invalidity is the tendency to use the ease and/or vividness of one's personal response to an external event or recall of a past event as a basis for inferring its representativeness of a larger reality that it purports to address (Fuller and Collier 2004: ch. 6).

It would be a mistake to conclude that the loss of unified knowledge and ultimate truth as explicit aims of science in the second half of the twentieth century undermined the idea of validity in scientific inquiry altogether. The key witness here is Donald Campbell, who figured prominently at the three main conferences expressly dedicated to launching a "psychology of science" (Gholson *et al.* 1989; Fuller *et al.* 1989; Shadish and Fuller 1994) prior to the establishment of the International Society for the Psychology of Science and Technology in 2006. Campbell was important in translating the epistemic aspirations of the scientific method into operating procedures for fallible inquirers. Most notably, Campbell and Julian Stanley (1963) introduced the "quasi-experimental" research design in response to demoralized education researchers who despaired of ever identifying a "crucial experiment" that could decide between rival hypotheses, each of which could claim some empirical support in explaining a common phenomenon. Campbell and Stanley concluded that such despair reflected an oversimplified view of the research situation, which demanded a more complex understanding of research design that enabled rivals to demonstrate the different senses and degrees in which all of their claims might be true. But opening up the research situation in this fashion legitimized the loosening of the various controls associated with the experimental method, which in turn re-invited versions of the traditional problems of naturalistic observation. It was these problems that Campbell and Stanley attempted to address as "threats to validity".

Most of the twelve threats to validity enumerated in Campbell and Stanley (1963) involve insensitivity to the complex sociology of the research situation. For example, research may be invalidated because the researcher fails to take into account the interaction effects between researcher and subject, the subject's own response to the research situation over time, the subject's belonging to categories that remain formally unacknowledged in the research situation but may be relevant to the research outcome, salient differences between sets of old and new subjects, as well as old and new research situations, when attempting to reproduce an outcome, etc. The "quasi-experimental" research design that Campbell and Stanley advocated as a strategy to avoid, mitigate and/or compensate for such potential invalidations can be understood as a kind of "forensic sociology of science" that implicitly concedes that social life is not normally organized – either in terms of the constitution of individuals or the structures governing their interaction – to facilitate generalizable research. In effect, methodologically sound social research involves an uphill struggle against the society in which it is located and which its "valid" interventions might improve.

This rather heroic albeit influential premise has come under increasing pressure as insights from the sociology of science have been more explicitly brought to bear on research design. Presented as a reflexive application of the scientific method to itself, the resulting analysis can be quite sceptical (e.g. Brannigan 2004). Underlying this is ambiguity about how the aims of research might be undermined in its conduct. This may happen because a hypothesis fails to be tested in the manner that the researcher intended – a situation not to be confused with the researcher's failure to obtain the result she had expected. Much is presupposed in this distinction. Research is not a linear extension of common sense or everyday observation but rather requires a prior theory or paradigm that yields an appropriate hypothesis, on the basis of which the researcher selects relevant variables that are then operationalized and manipulated in an environment of the researcher's creation and control. Two matters of validity arise: first, the reliability of the outcomes vis-à-vis other experiments of similar design; second, the generalizability of the outcomes to the population that the experiment purports to model. The clarity of this distinction is due to the statistician Ronald Fisher (1925), who recommended the random assignment of subjects to groups of the researcher's choosing, given the variables that need to be operationalized to test her hypothesis.

Two features of Fisher's original context explain the prima facie clarity but long-term difficulties of his approach (Ziliak and McCloskey 2008). First, Fisher developed his paradigm while working in an agricultural research station, which meant that the things subject to "random assignment" were seeds or soils, not human beings. Second, the station was operated by the British government and so not for profit. While the former feature pertains to the concerns originally raised by Campbell and Stanley (1963), to which Fisher was perhaps understandably oblivious, the latter suggests a more general challenge to statistical significance as a

116   Epistemology as psychology of science

meaningful outcome of hypothesis testing. Fisher's experiments on the relative efficacy of genetic and environmental factors on agricultural output were conducted in a setting where matters of utility and cost did not figure prominently. A state interested in acquiring a comprehensive understanding of what is likely to make a difference to food production presumed that every hypothesis was equally worthy of study. Thus, "statistical significance" came to be defined as the likelihood of an experimental outcome, given a particular hypothesis, which is tested by seeing whether the outcome would have been the same even if the hypothesis were false (i.e. the "null hypothesis"). In contrast, had Fisher been more explicitly concerned with utility and cost, he might have treated hypothesis testing as a species of normal rational decision-making. In that case, the validity question would be posed as follows: Given the available evidence, what is the cost of accepting a particular hypothesis vis-à-vis potentially better hypotheses that might require further testing? Indeed, Ziliak and McCloskey (2008) credit this stance to W. S. Gosset, lab director for Guinness breweries in the early twentieth century, who was a student of the founder of modern statistical inference, Karl Pearson.

The opportunity costs of not exploring alternative hypotheses raised in the economic critique of Fisher threaten to blur his distinction between internal and external validity by forcing the researcher always to calibrate the knowledge gained from a particular design in terms of the goals it is meant to serve. For their part, psychologists have tried to address the issue by following Campbell's Berkeley teacher (and Bühler's student) Egon Brunswik (1952) and distinguishing *ecological* and *functional* validity, the latter being "external validity" in the strict sense of extending the laboratory to the larger world rather than trying to capture the pre-laboratory world (Fuller 1993: pt 4). The distinction addresses exactly what should be reproducible in a piece of research: Ecological validity pertains to an interest in reproducing causes and functional validity effects. Very few experiments meet the standard of ecological validity but many may achieve functional validity, if they simulate in the target environment the combination of factors that produced the outcome in the original experiment, even if that means altering the target environment's default settings (cf. Shadish and Fuller 1994: ch. 1).

The key epistemological point made by dividing external validity this way is that experiments may provide valid guides to policy intervention without necessarily capturing anything historically valid about the underlying causal relations. Instead they would test the limits of a hypothetical model of the world that has been already proven within specific lab-based parameters. Indeed, Meehl (1967) appealed to this use of experimentation to explain the scientific superiority of physics to psychology, a field that by his lights too often relied on research designs that aimed simply to mimic rather than genuinely test (and hence potentially extend) what the researcher already thought he knew about the target environment. But as Hedges (1987) subsequently observed, ignoring the ecological dimension of research validity tends to be accompanied by an omission of outlying data that may be crucial to identifying relevant contextual differences that point to other, perhaps even countervailing factors at work to the ones hypothesized. This point bears on the scepticism generated by proposed "evolutionary" explanations of the experiments conducted in the 1960s and 1970s by Stanley Milgram and Philip Zimbardo that demonstrated the relative ease with which subjects submit to authority and torture their fellows (Brannigan 2004). However, one may grant the lack of ecological validity in such experiments, while acknowledging that they suggest how a different combination of factors might reach an equivalent outcome, say, in the context of wartime intelligence gathering. The success of such an extension of the original research paradigm would demonstrate its functional validity.

The need for psychology of science to improve the conduct of science

The crucial step taken in the research design of the new cognitive psychology of science from its Würzburg precursors was to study scientific thought processes in a manner alienated from the scientist as a psychological agent. After Kant, the teleological character of science had been underwritten by a conception of thinking as *judgement* that stressed its self-generated, self-directed, discriminating, and determining character. (As we shall see below, William James understood this very well.) The paradigm case of judgement was the assertion of the truth or falsity of a proposition, what logicians still call, after the psychophysicist Gustav Fechner's student Hermann Lotze, "the assignment of a truth-value" (Fuller 2009b). The Würzburg School had attempted to found experimental psychology on the study of judgement in its most primitive form, namely, between two sensations (of weight), in which subjects detected an "attitude" or "determining tendency" associated with task but no corresponding image (Kusch 1999: ch. 1). For them the fundamental difference between "scientific" and "lay" thought resided in neither the content nor the processes of thought but in the subject's degree of self-consciousness (Gigerenzer and Murray 1987: ch. 5). In this respect, Karl Popper (1959), though rightly seen as more methodologist than psychologist of science, was true to his own Würzburg roots – Karl Bühler was his doctoral supervisor in Vienna – when he proposed that a mark of a truly revolutionary scientist such as Einstein was his capacity to conduct in his own mind stringent tests of a pet theory (i.e. "thought-experiments") for purposes of reaching a critical

118   *Epistemology as psychology of science*

judgement (Wettersten 1985). This is in sharp contrast with the nemesis of Popper's later career, Thomas Kuhn, who held that even great scientists lacked the psychological wherewithal for such potentially paradigm-shifting feats (Fuller 2000b: ch. 6; Fuller 2003).

However, Bertrand Russell's (1927) popular work, *An Outline of Philosophy*, launched a two-pronged attack on the very idea of scientifically studying mental contents, based on the then vanguard fields of symbolic logic and behaviourist psychology, which together effectively eliminated introspection as a method in scientific psychology. The first call for a dedicated field of "psychology of science" emerged as a subtle response to Russell's critique. The key figure was Arne Næss (1965), eventually the *magus* of Norwegian philosophy, who was one of two graduate students (the other being W. V. O. Quine) present at the original meetings of the logical positivists' Vienna Circle. Næss heard E. C. Tolman promote the need for such a field in an address given to the 1936 International Congress for Unified Science in Copenhagen (L. Smith 1986: ch. 5). Næss had been visiting Tolman, founder of Berkeley's psychology department, who had studied with Ralph Barton Perry, the successor to William James at Harvard's philosophy-cum-psychology department. Tolman's self-styled "purposive behaviourism" involved endowing the full range of organisms he studied – from rats and apes to humans – with "cognitive maps" that supposedly inform their responses to experimental tasks. Here Tolman was following up the Jamesian insight that each individual has its own spontaneous way of organizing the data it receives prior to any experimenter-driven protocols or stimuli.

Originally James (1884) was arguing for a more self-critical sense of introspection, which he then developed into a general account of "conceptual schemes", his influential expression for how the mind processes data as objects that then function as means to the individual's ends (James 1983: ch. 12). Features of the environment that fail to be captured in such patently functionalist terms – to mix two Jamesian metaphors – may escape through the mesh of the scheme, eventually only to blindside the individual altogether. However, James was clear that conceptual schemes do not change "naturally" but only as a result of individuals having to accommodate these previously ignored features in order to realize their goals. In this respect, James treated conceptual schemes as rigid but also replaceable, assuming that the organism has a strong sense of purpose. Although James was widely interpreted as retreating from idealism and opening the door to behaviourism, in fact he wanted to do almost the exact opposite – namely, to extend the locus of intentionality from the thinking head to the entire organism operating in the world (Bordogna 2008).

True to the original spirit of James, Tolman (1932) held that the "psychology of science" should help the scientist become psychologically closer to the object of investigation – including not least, as Tolman himself stressed, by coming to understand how a rat thinks of its maze-running task (Maslow 1966: 112). Despite being criticized by fellow behaviourists for conflating hypothetical constructs with real psychological states, Tolman insisted that the capacity to think like the experimental subject (whatever the species) provides a crucial source of clues for operationalizing hidden psychic processes that govern behaviour, what Tolman called "intervening variables". This approach resonated with the Gestalt psychologists, who distinguished themselves from both introspectionists and behaviourists by denying that the subject necessarily frames the experimental task as the experimenter does, such that the only behaviour worth examining would be that which bears directly on the task (Ash 1988: ch. 5). Perhaps because the most systematic Gestaltist, Wolfgang Koehler (1938), shared a medical background with James (and Freud), he recognized the importance of such "unobtrusive measures" as blood pressure, rate of breathing and other incidental behaviours unrelated to the experiment's official task that nevertheless may provide clues to the subject's wider existential horizon (or "baseline"), which in turn may serve to amplify or subvert the experimenter's own assumptions about the subject. These measures provided evidence for the intervening variables that Tolman sought, a point that was not lost on his most distinguished student, Donald Campbell, who worked directly with the Gestalt psychologist who migrated from the Vienna Circle to Berkeley, Egon Brunswik (Campbell 1988: ch. 13; cf. Brunswik 1952).

Russell's critique of introspection was still more strongly felt in the radical behaviourism that would prevail at Harvard itself in the middle third of the twentieth century, courtesy of W. V. O. Quine in philosophy and B. F. Skinner in psychology (Baars 1986: 62). A key mediator in this transition was the psychophysicist E. G. Boring, the founding head of Harvard's free-standing psychology department, who underwent what he described as a "Damascene" conversion from the introspective methods that he had learned at Cornell University from its leading US proponent, E. B. Titchener. Generalizing from the phenomenon of time delay associated with the transmission of both electro-chemical impulses in the nerves (Helmholtz) and light rays in the heavens (Einstein), Boring came to believe by 1930 that any act of outer or inner perception amounted to a bifurcation of the self into two relatively independent parts, one largely a stranger to the other (Boring 1955). He saw the perceiver-part as captive to a *"Zeitgeist"*, the totality of the scientist's cultural heritage that functioned as a cognitive unconscious that inhibited his ability to see the perceived-part in all its significant novelty. (Intuitively the *Zeitgeist* might be seen as the time lag that results from taking one extended moment in

120   Epistemology as psychology of science

history as a stationary frame of reference.) Here Boring specifically referred to Joseph Priestley's failure to abandon phlogiston in favour of the oxygen-based chemistry promoted by Antoine Lavoisier, an example he credited to James Bryant Conant (1950), then Harvard president who had torn asunder William James's original unification of psychology and philosophy, so as to render psychology a purely experimental unit. Conant's teaching assistant, Thomas Kuhn (1970), would later infer from the Priestley-Lavoisier example a more restricted, discipline-based sense of *Zeitgeist*, the "paradigm".

Together the two responses to Russell's *Outline* – purposive and radical behaviourism – generated the two main problematics of the philosophy of science of the final third of the twentieth century: what after Quine (1960) is called the "indeterminacy of translation" and after Kuhn (1970) the "incommensurability of paradigms" (Fuller 1988: ch. 5). While philosophers have tended to define these matters in strictly logical terms (i.e. in terms of whether truth is preserved as the same data are processed by different conceptual schemes or theoretical languages), the psychological implications were more vivid. Both Quine and Kuhn suggested that any piece of evidence might be regarded in any number of logically self-consistent ways, such that its most "natural interpretation" would depend largely on the personal history of the interpreter in question. Arguably philosophy has failed to make progress as a field precisely because its history has been subject to the simultaneous propagation of several qualitatively different "world hypotheses", each with its own way of configuring what might appear, from a "common sense" standpoint, the "same evidence". This point was associated with Tolman's Harvard classmate and chair of Berkeley's philosophy department, Stephen Pepper (1942), who originally used it to counter the logical positivist claim of theory-neutral data. However, one of Pepper's key hires in the late 1950s would go on to show how science has historically solved the problem that Pepper had identified in philosophy – namely, that science is governed by a succession of distinct paradigms, each dominant for a given period (Kuhn 1970). Thus, Kuhn gave an overriding role to disciplinary socialization, which reorients the scientist's world-view to such an extent as to make it difficult, if not impossible, for her to alter her working assumptions later in life, even in the face of cognitively better alternatives. The exceptions to this rule, originally stressed by Max Planck, were those scientists who have made relatively little existential investment – say, by virtue of being young practitioners or cross-disciplinary interlopers (De Mey 1982: ch. 6). It follows that a radically new science may require radically new scientists – though *pace* Planck it would be a mistake to interpret the relevant sense of "newness" primarily in terms of age (Simonton 1988).

Conclusion: how scientific creativity went from being abundant to scarce

If E. C. Tolman's original call for a "psychology of science" in the 1930s was made in a broadly positivistic spirit of ongoing improvements to the conduct of science, the first book actually to bear the title "psychology of science", published thirty years later, was concerned mainly with the very motivation for doing science, which suited a time when a science-based "Cold War" placed humanity at the brink of self-destruction (Maslow 1966). The book's author, Abraham Maslow (1908–70), was a thought-leader in humanistic psychology, a school that aimed to provide an account of mental health that complemented Freud's psychodynamic theory of neurosis. Although Maslow is nowadays remembered for a cluster of concepts – "self-actualization", "hierarchy of needs", "peak experiences", etc. – that continue to inform the positive psychology movement, this legacy was very much informed by Maslow's own training as a scientist (originally as a primate behaviourist and then as a devotee of Alfred Adler's brand of individual psychology) and his encounters with natural and social scientists whom he came to regard as paradigm cases of self-actualized human beings (Albert Einstein, Max Wertheimer, Ruth Benedict). When the core thesis of Maslow (1966) was first delivered as the annual invited lecture to the John Dewey Society for the Study of Education and Culture, Maslow's words were clearly received as a challenge for those who considered themselves "scientists" to determine how much of their personal experience might enhance the epistemic power of their research (Maslow 1966: foreword).

Underlying this challenge was Maslow's broad commitment to science as "hypothesis testing" but understood in a particular way, namely, that hypotheses are artificial constructions that approximate but not substitute for reality. At the start of the book, Maslow cites the influence of a Brandeis University colleague, the psychohistorian Frank Manuel (1963), who wrote of Isaac Newton's secret interest in sacred history as reflecting an awareness of a deity perpetually dissatisfied with his own creation, whose "laws of nature" were an ideal that regularly needed to be enforced against the recalcitrant ways of matter. Far from reading divine order directly from the heavens, Newton had to postulate God's periodic interventions to square his mathematics with the astronomical data. As this sensibility was secularized in the modern era, the Biblically fallen character of nature came to be internalized as humanity's sense of its own subordination to nature, a viewpoint that easily shaded (e.g. in Nietzsche) into nihilism, potentially undermining the motivation to study nature in Newton's systematic fashion. To be sure, Maslow was not the first to discover the problem of motivating a commitment to science. At the end of the nineteenth century, no less than "Darwin's bulldog", Thomas

122   Epistemology as psychology of science

Henry Huxley (1893), turned Herbert Spencer's confidence on its head by arguing that instead of providing a scientific basis for ethics, evolutionary theory – with its radically demystified ("species egalitarian") view of humanity – could subvert any belief in future scientific, let alone ethical, progress. After all, if Darwin is correct, extinction is the only long-term guaranteed outcome to any collective project in which a species might engage (Fuller 2010: ch. 6).

Maslow took this general existential anxiety to have direct consequences for actual scientific practice. In a world where people no longer believe that they have been created "in the image and likeness of God", a Newton-like capacity to abstract heroically from an array of data points – so necessary for success in modern science – may reflect a psychological estrangement from concrete human existence, which in turn may lead to the application of methods that can be justified on theoretical but not phenomenological grounds. Thus, the fact that Neo-Darwinism says that humans, genetically speaking, differ very little from other animals does not mean that studying humans according to methods normally used to study apes or rats will yield equally interesting results. More specifically, Maslow diagnosed radical behaviourists' lack of openness to differences in the individual histories of their human subjects in terms of a "fear of knowing" that failed to alleviate the behaviourists' own anxiety about the ultimate truth of their own hypotheses but simply kept that anxiety in check – so to speak, Cold War-style. Maslow dubbed this defence mechanism *safety science*, in contrast to the psychologically healthier *growth science*. He drew a clear distinction between the safety scientist's need for a method that achieves attestable results and the growth scientist's greater tolerance for uncertainty and error – only the latter of which provides the relevant psychic environment for creative effort.

Interestingly, Maslow explicitly cast the two scientific world-views as glosses on Kuhn's (1970) normal and revolutionary science. However, he went against the grain of Kuhn's own argument by associating the latter, not the former, with the fully self-actualized growth scientist. Indeed, Maslow saw the safety scientist as subject to arrested development and regarded the relative rarity of revolutionaries in science as symptomatic of massive untapped human potential. Focusing on just its cognitive implications, Maslow's safety–growth science distinction would seem to drive a wedge between "expertise" in the strict sense (i.e. knowledge that results from trained experiences of a certain sort) and a more authentic scientific existence whose comprehension of reality extends beyond glorified pattern recognition. Here it is worth recalling that an important sense of "paradigm" in Kuhn (1970) is the kind of pattern recognition associated with the normal scientist's tendency to solve problems by finding textbook exemplars for their solutions. Kuhn had learned of this approach from the self-styled "new look" to the study of thinking then championed at Harvard by Jerome Bruner *et al.* (1956). However, it involved just the sort of self-imposed cognitive boundedness that was anathema to Maslow but which by the 1960s had come to be popularized in advertising as "subliminal perception". Accordingly, one would overcome fear of the new (experimental stimulus, scientific finding, consumer good, etc.) by unconscious assimilation to already familiar things that had satisfied corresponding needs in the past. In this respect, one might see Maslow as providing an implicit methodological critique of the new cognitive psychology of science.

In the nearly half a century since the publication of Maslow (1966), support for the presence of the two scientific world-views has come through the concept of the "self-regulatory focus", which social psychologists claim structures a person's cognitive motivation to enable one to remain in equilibrium with one's environment. In this context, safety science corresponds to a "prevention" focus and growth science to a "promotion" focus (Higgins 1997). The distinction turns on what people take to be the greater evil: a harm that could have been avoided or a good that could have been realized. From the standpoint of statistical inference, the contrast is easily captured in terms of living one's life so as to err on the side of either missed opportunities or false alarms. In terms of the broader cultural context of science, one might distinguish, respectively, *precautionary* and *proactionary* uses of science, the former stressing the damage potentially done from not correctly anticipating the consequences of a science-led intervention, the latter the benefits (including learning from mistakes) potentially reaped from taking a chance on just such an intervention, regardless of its consequences (Fuller and Lipinska 2014). These perspectives are routinely played out in public debates about the impact of new technology on the future of the planet (Fuller 2010: ch. 1).

Although Maslow anchored the safety–growth science distinction in Kuhn (1970), his principal source for the psychology of the growth scientist was, perhaps surprisingly, the philosophical chemist Michael Polanyi, again deployed in ways that stressed the differences from Kuhn. Nowadays Polanyi (1957) is remembered as Kuhn's great precursor on the role of "tacit knowledge" as the aspect of scientists' socialization that enables them to judge intuitively what is normal and deviant practice in their fields. However, Polanyi (1963) had criticized an early version of Kuhn (1970) for suggesting that successful revolutionary science never occurred deliberately but only as an unintended consequence of the self-implosion of normal science. In contrast, Polanyi believed that science differed from "mere" technical expertise in its drive to test the limits of its fundamental assumptions. In this respect, Polanyi sounds very much like Karl Popper – except that Polanyi parted from Popper in stressing the scientific establishment's authority as the final arbiter of any revolutionary proposals a

124 Epistemology as psychology of science

particular scientist might make. Here Polanyi was probably reflecting on his own experience as a chemist whose research failed to make headway with its non-mathematical, visually based approach just when his field was being absorbed into the decidedly non-visual, mathematically driven paradigm of quantum mechanics (Nye 2011). Unlike Popper, who continued to contest the correct interpretation of quantum mechanics and evolutionary theory into his old age, Polanyi conceded that, in some definitive sense, his field's research frontier had moved on, and so he migrated from a chair in chemistry at the University of Manchester to one in "social studies", where he forged an equally creative second career, indeed, the one for which he is now more widely known.

Interestingly, Maslow turned a blind eye to Polanyi's social conformism, which was based on an extended analogy between the scientific community and a monastic order, while agreeing with him that the difference between science and religion was "merely" institutional, a distinction that was drawn to the detriment of both. Indeed, one of the most jarring features of Maslow (1966) for today's secular reader is the ease with which the religious nature of science is maintained. Indeed, his concluding chapter calls for the "re-sacralization of science" (cf. Fuller 2006a: ch. 5). However, Maslow does not identify religion with a church or dedicated clergy but with the basic need to understand the ground of one's being. In tune with his times, he explicates this need in terms of complementary attitudes represented by the Eastern ("Taoistic") and Western ("Judaic") world-religions: on the one hand, a receptivity to the structure of reality; on the other, a refusal to be satisfied with first appearances. What distinguishes religion and science in practice is simply the means by which they pursue these general regulative principles of inquiry, which then has implications for what one means by "success", "validity" and "progress". The chapter of this book on epistemology as sociology of science opens with a now forgotten dispute in the "psychohistorical" vein encouraged by Maslow that illustrates how to argue about the contribution of religion to the motivational structure of modern science.

The Maslovian vision of untapped human potential was not the one to dominate in the psychology of science. To be sure, Maslow was President of the American Psychological Association (1967–68), but tellingly his life ended five years later as a highly sought after management consultant, a specialist in cultivating what he dubbed "gold collar workers", people with intellectually stimulating, well-paid jobs who nevertheless do not regard their work as capturing the fullness of their being. The question then is how to provide outlets for expressing such "existential excess". The ancient Athenians famously proposed politics as the answer, though Aristotle specifically targeted philosophy as something that ought to fill one's leisure time. In the modern period, capitalist society, under the influence of the Protestant Ethic, had come to colonize this space in terms of both profit re-investment and financial speculation, depending on whether one wished to build a heaven on Earth or imagine a radically different Earth. Maslow's contribution was to suggest the development of consumer products that may be marginally different at the material level but which nevertheless point to alternative futures based on lifestyle signification. For example, genetically modified and unmodified foods may look and taste pretty much the same but the difference matters in terms of other associated life-choices that together confer an overall pattern of meaning that could scale up to a major transformation of the human condition. Maslow termed the increasing number of people susceptible to this sort of marketing "transcenders" whose *modus operandi* could be fathomed via "Theory Z" (Maslow 1998).

What I would call a *deep liberalism* can be developed from this perspective, one in which the well-heeled, self-interested agent may be drawn to adopt self-transcending values through a surfeit of choice that then forces the agent to be more discriminating. In this respect, Maslow differed from his Neo-Freudian contemporary Herbert Marcuse (1964) who suspected in the expansion of consumer choice the emergence of "repressive desublimation", as consumers were presented with an array of options that indeed fostered self-expression but in a way that simply reinforced late capitalism's concentration of power in a few producers. In contrast, Maslow saw this development in more optimistic terms, as consumers would now be forced to raise their game in the spirit of resolving diverse desires – and diverse expressions of those desires – in a unique and thereby self-defining way. The model here was the US poet Walt Whitman's "Song of Myself", a popularization of Ralph Waldo Emerson's Transcendentalist philosophy that celebrated the personal resolution of contradictory pulls as a critical moment in the formation of character (Bloom 1992). Unsurprisingly, both Emerson and Whitman figure among Maslow's paradigm cases of "self-actualized" people. They, in turn, hark back to perhaps the original self-actualizer, Johann Wolfgang von Goethe, who attempted to incorporate within himself all of the academic disciplines in search of a uniquely synthetic mode of being, one that dared to call into question the adequacy of the Newtonian worldview to the fullness of humanity (Fuller 2013).

What Maslow envisaged – and what in fact has happened – is that the advertising agencies and public relations firms that have been marketing goods in increasingly sophisticated ways since the 1920s are now in the lifestyling business, which encourages people to think about goods as part of a larger world-view package that then becomes the product on offer. Thus, if one buys, say, "green" or "Fairtrade", not only are a set of potential purchases implicated but also a system of values. One might

126   *Epistemology as psychology of science*

then consider "value-led product development", in which an entire range of goods beyond the stereotypical "green" ones might be countenanced with the collaboration of the potential consumers. While Marcuse would condemn this as the co-optation of people who, given their greater education and income, would otherwise be best placed to critique capitalism, Maslow saw it as a market-driven way to become more self-conscious about one's underlying principles. Interestingly, this perspective appears to have influenced the metaphysical horizon of the deepest libertarian philosopher of recent times, Robert Nozick, who locates the metaphysical basis for the self in the resolution of heteronomous desires in a hierarchy of needs that in turn functions as one's sense of autonomy (Nozick 1981: ch. 5). The implication is that without the challenge to compose competing demands into a unified and purposeful whole, we would never acquire the self-consciousness that distinguishes humans most clearly from animals.

Unfortunately the current wave of work in the psychology of science that originated in the 1980s has not been especially kind to the research agenda originally outlined in Maslow (1966). In the intervening period, psychoanalysis has fallen from grace as a source of authoritative scientific knowledge of psychodynamic processes. Indeed, one touchstone volume in the field opens by observing that "fortunately" psychology of science was no longer dominated by Freudian psychohistories (Gholson *et al.* 1989: 10). However, it should be quickly added that the genre of psychological biographies of significant scientists was largely the innovation of E. G. Boring, who was quite critical of psychoanalysis, especially after having undergone it himself in the 1930s (Runyan 2006). In any case, psychoanalytically inspired accounts of psychology of science suffered from the stigma of seeming to stress idiosyncratic features of a scientist's life in ways that were both ultimately unverifiable and ungeneralizable. While this criticism may have applied to some work done under the rubric of "psychohistory", it is unfairly applied to Maslow (1966), which repeatedly stressed the need for an eclectic mix of methods that allowed for the scaling up of the phenomenological to the objective. Thus, Maslow himself developed tests for creativity and endorsed the controversial electrode-based attempts by psychoanalyst Lawrence Kubie to find neural correlates for creativity-relevant psychodynamic processes such as free association (Winter 2011: ch. 4).

Beyond the issue of psychoanalysis, a more fundamental difference between Maslow (1966) and today's psychology of science may lie in the conceptualization of scientific creativity. Rather unlike Freud, but in line with such Neo-Freudians as Adler and even Herbert Marcuse, Maslow believed that what requires explanation is not what makes particular individuals creative but, on the contrary, what prevents more if not all people from being creative. Thus, neurosis is associated with the

Epistemology as psychology of science 127

inhibition not the promotion of creativity (Kubie 1967). This position was developed quite explicitly against the more popular view – on which Freud appeared to confer his authority – that creative individuals possess a unique genius that reflects their tortured souls. In contrast, Maslow would diagnose what prevents people from realizing their full creative potential and then advise how they might change their relationships to other people and their environment. Philosophically speaking, this "emancipatory" approach to creativity, which continues in the positive psychology movement, was informed by the then recent English translation of the early "humanist" writings of Karl Marx, which argued that all socially relevant forms of inequality are not merely "unjust" in some abstract political sense but reflect the arrested development of the human species. Maslow (1966) held that this point applied no less to the uneven distribution of creativity in the population.

However, more recent psychological research has tended to take the uneven distribution of creativity as given rather than a problem as such. To be sure, some of the elitism inherent in the old "tortured genius" view has been mitigated by a more explicitly social psychological approach to creativity. For example, drawing on some of the earliest cognitive limitations work, Ian Mitroff (1974) identified in the case of the Apollo moon scientists three styles of inquiry that displayed complementary strengths and weaknesses that worked together best in certain proportions, in certain research environments. Mitroff, who went on to found the field of "crisis management", thought about the fostering of creativity from a systems design perspective that was indebted to C. West Churchman, founder of the journal *Philosophy of Science*. Perhaps the heyday for this approach appears in the first handbook in science and technology studies, whose review essay on "psychology of science" (Fisch 1977) focuses on the recruitment and retention of people with the right traits. Indeed, personality inventory tests targeting the nexus between "creativity" and "achievement" of the sort championed in McClelland (1962) formed the basis of the review. This version of the psychology of science continues to flourish in human resource management studies of research and development recruitment that, given our neo-liberal times, are not any longer so clearly focused on retention.

More recent social psychological studies present a mixed verdict on the approach to scientific creativity taken in Maslow (1966). While creativity clearly needs to be self-motivated and may be outright undermined by external incentives, nevertheless "effective creativity" is increasingly defined in terms of the judgement of presumed peer communities rather than (*per* Maslow) a test administered by the psychologist that is designed to control for the inevitable conservative bias of such communities (e.g. Amabile 1996). A more fundamental challenge to the Maslow world-view, especially

128   *Epistemology as psychology of science*

its assumption of a great untapped store of human potential, is the broadly "historiometric" approach that descends from Francis Galton's search for "hereditary genius", which presumes that society contains a scarce amount of human creativity, which needs to be genetically conserved and cultivated, lest it be dissipated through default patterns of mating and breeding. Galton saw his "eugenics" as an updating of Plato's own anticipation of human resource management, but where recruitment and retention of creative individuals occurs at quite an early age. This idea attracted many in the technocratic left in the early twentieth century, including the Fabian founders of the London School of Economics, who envisaged a eugenically inspired "social biology" as the foundational social science (Renwick 2011). Moreover, Galton's programme was well received by both Marxists and positivists in the 1920s (Otto Neurath was Galton's German translator), until falling into disrepute with the rise of Nazism. But in recent decades, armed with a wider and better array of data, improved statistical methods and formal recognition (and systematic measurement) of the increasing dimensions of "big science" (Price 1986), historiometry has been given a new lease on life, one pursued most vigorously for the last four decades by Dean Simonton (1988).

A good sense of the strongly anti-Maslovian cast of this entire line of research may be seen in Cole and Cole (1973), a statistically based study of "social stratification in science". Cole and Cole counterpose two hypotheses concerning the distribution of talent in science: one, the so-called Ortega Hypothesis, which argues that every scientist, however mediocre, contributes to the storehouse of knowledge from which "geniuses" draw together into a synthetic whole; the other, inspired by the authors' mentor Robert Merton, proposes that scientific talent travels in specific lineages (i.e. schools, jobs, achievements, rewards), implying that most actual scientific research is in principle eliminable noise. They clearly plump for the latter hypothesis, though neither hypothesis presumes the existence of a massive untapped scientific potential. Into the breach stepped Simonton (1988) with an equally anti-Maslovian resolution. His "chance-configuration" theory, based on Campbell's (1988) "selective retention" model of evolutionary epistemology, agreed with Cole and Cole on the elite nature of scientific talent but argued that it needs to be more carefully disaggregated from actual track record, which may not do the scientist's talent justice and could inhibit the ability of others in the future from benefiting from it. Thus, scientific talent should be assessed somewhat independently of lineage so as to catch these talented "outliers" (Simonton 1988: 97).

The turn against Maslow may boil down to a shift in attitudes to human biological evolution over the past half-century. Campbell and Simonton, as well as Feist (2006), treat the Neo-Darwinian account of

Epistemology as psychology of science   129

natural selection as a background material constraint on human evolution that in turn shapes their sense of what the psychology of science can be. But given that in strictly Darwinian terms, the species-adaptive character of science is far from secure (i.e. it is not clear that more scientific creativity would increase the chances of human survival), it is perhaps not surprising for them to conclude that science is relatively unrepresentative of human psychology in general. The overall view of *Homo sapiens* implied here is tantamount to an *in vivo* "anti-fragile" investment strategy, whereby all but 10–20 per cent of the population rightly plays it safe, since the species can only afford relatively few of its members to take the sort of large risks in which those who succeed will redeem the effort of the majority who fail (Taleb 2012). In contrast, Maslow's main source for biological inspiration was the founder of general systems theory, Ludwig von Bertalanffy (1950), who started with the assumption that since our native biological equipment deprives us of a natural habitat, our species identity is tied to continuing to beat the odds against our long-term survival by turning a hostile nature into an anthropocentric life-world – or to put it in Dawkins's (1982) more contemporary terms, the species mark of the human is the will and the competence to extend its phenotype indefinitely. Whether von Bertalanffy's proactionary view of the human condition trumps Darwin's more precautionary one in the long term will be of interest of course not only to students of scientific creativity but also to the rest of humanity that is bound to feel the effects of such creativity in the future.

4 Epistemology as philosophy of science

By misunderstanding Kuhn, we misunderstand our own times

The details of the life and career of Thomas Kuhn (1922–96) are now well known. The American historian and philosopher of science was probably the most influential theorist of science in the second half of the twentieth century. Like many of his generation who were trained in physics but experienced first-hand the role that its expertise played in the Second World War, Kuhn left the field shortly after receiving his PhD in 1946. He then joined the new "General Education in Science" programme established by Harvard President James Bryant Conant. There Kuhn developed the general theory of scientific change for which he is best known, according to which a science's theories and methods are dictated by a "paradigm", which is replaced only once it accumulates too many unsolved problems. At that point, it enters a "crisis" phase that eventuates in a "revolution", resulting in a successor paradigm.

At Conant's recommendation, Kuhn published the full version of his theory in 1962 as *The Structure of Scientific Revolutions*, which appeared as the final instalment of the International Encyclopedia of Unified Science, the main postwar project of the logical positivist movement. The book became a mainstay in non-science courses about science upon its second edition in 1970. The second edition reflected both Kuhn's political resonance at the time – an era of widespread student protest – and the appearance of a landmark volume edited by Imre Lakatos that positioned Kuhn as the main challenger to the "critical rationalist" approach to science championed by Karl Popper (Lakatos and Musgrave 1970). The debate turned on whether science should be understood as an "open" (Popper) or a "closed" (Kuhn) society in its own right. Whereas Popper supported a "permanent revolution" in the foundations of science, Kuhn held that revolutions were best seen as unintended consequences of normal scientific problem-solving.

Just over twenty years ago the journal *History and Theory* invited me to publish an assessment of *The Structure of Scientific Revolutions* in its first

Epistemology as philosophy of science 131

thirty years of publication. The result, Fuller (1992b), provided an unflattering picture of Kuhn – and, by implication, his followers – as an unwitting vehicle of the world-historic spirit, which in this case was a Cold War environment that promoted a nominally free science that was nevertheless also placed in the service of a geopolitical strategy that presumed the likelihood of a third world war. Kuhn, in both text and person, exemplified a "heads down" approach that detached the ultimate aims of science (which was left to the powers that be) from the solution of paradigm-specific puzzles (which the scientists decided as a collective). Based on this premise, I interviewed Kuhn at his home, consulted the archives at Harvard and MIT, and subsequently published two widely received works: Fuller (2000b) and Fuller (2003), the critical discussion of which is gathered in Gattei (2003) and addressed in Fuller (2004).

Below I review the reception of these works, which are now benchmarks for more recent discussions of Kuhn's historical significance (e.g. Gordon 2012; Mayoral 2012). In particular, the emphasis I have placed on Kuhn's intellectual and institutional dependency on Conant (discussed briefly below) has been borne out in subsequent historical work, not least by George Reisch (2012), who flatters by repeating my original claims as if they were his own (cf. Fuller 2000b: 179–82). In addition, recognition of Harvard's overall importance in defining the *Zeitgeist* in the middle third of the twentieth century has resulted in a small cottage industry of scholarship that tries to cast the Conant–Kuhn milieu at Harvard in terms, alternatively, more diabolical (Chase 2003) or more benign (Isaac 2012) than I originally argued.

Kuhn's theory of scientific change undoubtedly turned out to be much more influential than its author had anticipated. Kuhn saw it as applying mainly to the physical sciences, especially when Newtonian mechanics served as the paradigmatic theory – which is to say, roughly 1620 to 1920. Indeed, Kuhn's examples from chemistry cease after the mid-nineteenth century, his discussion of physics ends in the 1920s and he does not discuss the biological or social sciences at all. Yet Kuhn was more influential in the fields that he did *not* discuss (Gutting 1980). Much of that is due to the politically evocative language associated with "scientific revolutions", especially in the context of student unrest in the late 1960s, though Kuhn made a point of discouraging all such associations. Indeed, in retrospect Kuhn's refusal to comment on – let alone condemn – the complicity of science in the "military-industry complex" of the period appears striking. His interest in science lay exclusively in its status as a self-organizing, self-contained mode of inquiry.

But despite the many misguided attempts to harness Kuhn's theory of scientific revolutions to revolutionary politics, his theory remains politically interesting for at least four reasons.

132   *Epistemology as philosophy of science*

1   Kuhn's fundamental idea of "paradigm" as a collectively agreed set of theoretical discourses, problem-solving strategies and empirical data. His singular case in point was the two-century hegemony of the Newtonian paradigm in the physical sciences, during which theologically freighted concepts related to divine agency – captured by the omnibus notion of "action at a distance" – issued in scientific accounts of not only gravity, electricity, magnetism but also (after Einstein's relativity revolution) light, space and time. Here Kuhn drew on the legacy of Francis Bacon, but somewhat differently from Bacon's popular image as the promoter of induction as the method of science. As legal advisor to the English king, Bacon's original ambition was to find a means to sublimate, if not resolve, ongoing civil and religious wars in seventeenth-century Europe, during which valid empirical insights would be often presented as the exclusive property of one or another competing world-view. In this context, "science" held the promise of a kind of social contract, or at least high court, in which a "crucial experiment" served as an honest broker of differences, since the experiment's outcome would unequivocally support only one of the competing theories. Thereafter "scientists" would be forced to cast their knowledge claims in terms of such agreed findings, thus rendering testable any remaining differences with their rivals, as well as overall collective intellectual progress (Shapin and Schaffer 1985). To be sure, Bacon envisaged that a state agency would function in this capacity, whereas the Royal Society of London, the body founded in his memory after his death, was independent of both church and state. Kuhn's innovation was to identify the academic discipline as the paradigm's institutional vehicle. In this move, he appears to have been influenced by Wilhelmine German ideas of the project of science as the completion of a "world picture" (*Weltbild*).

2   Kuhn's Baconian fixation on paradigms as vehicles for resolving potentially intractable disputes encouraged a "linear" view of the relationship between science and technology, whereby a paradigm must mature before its theories and findings are harnessed for practical applications. Most major state-based science policy agencies after the Second World War were organized around this idea, most notably the US National Science Foundation, resulting in the rise of "peer review" as the principal means of securing not only publication but also funding. Technology was thus no longer seen as simply the product of eccentric inventors or industrial innovation; rather, it was the direct application of proven scientific principles, or what MIT Vice-President Vannevar Bush famously dubbed "basic research". (Bush and Conant had administered the successful American bid to build the atomic bomb, the exemplar of effective technology built on sound science.) In the late 1970s, this

Epistemology as philosophy of science 133

view, trailing its Kuhnian pedigree, was championed by German followers of Jürgen Habermas as "finalization" – that is, to "finalize" science by giving it an explicitly socially relevant focus once it appeared that the rate of return on the paradigm's efforts at solving its own technical problems had diminished (Schaefer 1984). At the time, this policy was portrayed as a social democratic solution to the prospect of scientific revolutions de-stabilizing society at large, were it allowed to proceed in Kuhn's original undirected manner.

3 Kuhn's theory of scientific revolutions applies ideas from a theory of political revolution that were in vogue during his Harvard undergraduate years in the 1930s (Fuller 2000b: 162–69). The account, associated with the Italian political economist Vilfredo Pareto, was developed in explicit response to Marxist predictions of the fall of capitalism with the Great Depression. Pareto had adapted Machiavelli's circulation of elites, in which revolutions occur only when the establishment self-destructs but soon thereafter a version of the old order is restored. A "Pareto Circle" was organized by his English translator, the biochemist Lawrence Henderson, who taught the first history of science courses at Harvard. Henderson, a pioneer in the study of homeostatic systems, was attracted to Pareto's similarly minded theory. On this basis, the main historian attending the Circle, Crane Brinton (1952), proposed a theory of modern revolutions that presented stages akin to those now associated with Kuhn, including "crisis" to name the period of paradigmatic meltdown that precipitates a revolution. Key to the anti-Marxist slant of this theory is that the paradigm shift is both initiated and concluded in terms internal to the science undergoing the change: hence, the vision of one set of elites superseding another set. A paradigm's long-term viability comes to be questioned as the rate of return from investing in the paradigm diminishes for younger, cutting-edge practitioners. Despite the paradigm's venerable track record, if it provides relatively little insight into current scientific problems, that standing inadequacy – not unexpected findings, external social pressures, let alone disenfranchised masses or their interests – will provide grounds for radical change. While a paradigm in crisis presents a fractious and inconclusive picture of intergenerational conflict, the scientific revolution itself corresponds to the younger generation's ascent into leadership roles in the discipline.

4 Among Kuhn's subtlest yet most influential claims is that a new paradigm secures its scientific hegemony by monopolizing how the history of science is presented to students, the paradigm's latest recruits. Kuhn went so far as to describe such histories as "Orwellian", alluding to the preoccupation in *1984* of continually rewriting

134 *Epistemology as philosophy of science*

history – specifically, by rewriting newspaper articles – to place the current regime's decisions in the best possible light (Kuhn 1970: 167). Thus, the histories of science promoted in not only textbooks but also popular works tend to show that everything worth talking about from the past contributed to the cutting edge of current research. The "real" history of science – warts and all – is something left to professional historians, with whom normal scientists rarely have any contact. An implication of Kuhn's view is that disciplines lacking a paradigm – as in the humanities and social sciences – will not be able to distinguish so neatly histories "for" the science from those, strictly speaking, "of" the science. Thus, historians of the humanities and social sciences are still typically housed in the disciplines they write about, where they function (often unwanted) as their critical conscience, full of stories of suppressed alternatives and missed opportunities that undermine any sense of clear, steady progress. While most historians of science continue to celebrate Kuhn's effective call for their field to become autonomous from the epistemic legitimatory concerns of particular sciences, the cost – felt especially in the natural sciences – has been to inhibit the capacity of historians to reform the fields they write about.

Kuhn's legacy of prescriptive/descriptive confusion

Given its overall influence, it is striking that Kuhn's model of scientific change has been invoked much more in pedagogical, policy, and other normatively inspired contexts (such as legitimating the scientificity of one's discipline) than in the explanation of actual cases of scientific change. In one sense, this is not surprising, since from a strictly *empirical* standpoint, Kuhn (1970) is best seen as an exercise in "syncretism", specifically a combination of aspects from different moments in the history of science into a single narrative cycle. If divine memory were an indefinitely extended version of the dynamic and reconstructive character of human memory (as opposed to an immutable record-keeping with infinite storage, which is nothing like human memory), then his consciousness might well be syncretistic (cf. Eagleman 2009). In any case, syncretism is most familiar from the structure of myths, which aim mainly to reinforce, not challenge, the audience's sense of identity – who they are, where they came from, and where they are going (Fuller 2000b: 195; 2003: ch. 17). Nevertheless, this empirical shortcoming has not prevented Kuhn's model from exerting enormous influence.

In textbook philosophy of science, the Kuhnian mythos is often presented as a blurring of the "prescriptive" and "descriptive" dimensions that follows once scientific inquiry is acknowledged to be theory- or value-laden. Yet, Kuhn's way of acknowledging the theory- or value-ladenness of inquiry

Epistemology as philosophy of science **135**

marked an ironic departure from its most famous precedent – namely, Max Weber's methodological remarks on the status of social science research. For Weber, as well as most of Kuhn's critics in Lakatos and Musgrave (1970), the fact that research always reflects the researcher's theory and value commitments implied the need for a broadly falsificationist ethic that allows for the testing of knowledge claims by those who do not share the researcher's commitments but are part of the same community of inquirers. Yet, after Kuhn, it is no longer clear that such people can exist.

In these Kuhnified times, all admission of theory and value commitments in science are simply excused, effectively narrowing the focus of criticism to contradictions and disagreements that arise only once the commitments are assumed. The commitments define the outer boundary of the paradigm within which "normal science" – the real stuff – is conducted. This Kuhnified image is shared by self-avowed "underlabourers" in contemporary philosophy of science, who take the conceptual foundations of an established discipline like physics or biology as their object of inquiry, and the more explicit relativists in postmodern cultural and social studies of science (what is referred to below as "STS"), who are often (misleadingly) portrayed as "anti-science". The two groups share an epistemology and rhetoric that appeals to "naturalism", which implies what sociologists call a more "grounded" approach to theorizing, namely, that one tries not to introduce any theoretical notions that would be alien to the subjects – in this case, the scientists – under investigation (Fuller 2006a: ch. 3). Naturalism is relevant to Kuhnification by justifying the intuition – familiar to evolutionary epistemologists – that science would not be as it is, for as long as it has, were it not functioning as it should.

Philosophers of science should recognize the turn to grounded theory in the quarter-century decline in projects concerned with providing generalizable accounts of reduction, explanation, rationality, and progress. Indeed, nowadays there is considerable interdisciplinary support for rewriting the history of the philosophy of science as the gradual recognition of the "disunified" nature of science (e.g. Galison and Stump 1996). According to this perspective, unity is something that philosophers have had to impose on science against its "natural" tendency to diverge into multiple forms of inquiry, a process Kuhn himself likened to speciation in biological evolution (Kuhn 1970: 205–6). I have criticized this move, even when done by such philosophically sophisticated revisionists as Michael Friedman (Fuller 2001, a review of Friedman 2000; cf. Fuller 2000b: 264, n. 11). The revisionists fail to observe that philosophers and scientists have long known – often quite intimately – that organized inquiry has moved in many different directions. But usually both philosophers and scientists have deplored this state of affairs and consequently proposed various normative correctives (Fuller 2007b: chs 1–2).

136 *Epistemology as philosophy of science*

Admittedly, most of these "unity of science" projects have failed. But I believe that is only because of shortcomings in the particular projects – and more often due to a lack of adequate resources than a lack of a suitably comprehensive vision. (Revealing here is the correspondence between the lawyer Paul Otlet and Otto Neurath in the Weimar period, when the movement for universal documentation temporarily joined forces with logical positivism: Fuller 2007a: 69–73.) Going against the grain of Kuhnification, the agenda of my own "social epistemology" involves re-incarnating the spirit of these projects in a guise that takes seriously the advances in history and sociology of science (Fuller 1988). However, this task of unity – which is a set of successive projections of the ultimate ends of inquiry – should not be confused with the short-term search for a "scientific consensus", a post-Kuhnian project that I discuss later in this chapter. I may decide that the long-term prospects of a scientific concept or research programme are doomed long before the current consensus has dissipated. In that case, I treat intellectual life as a kind of "futures market", in which it is equally likely that dominant modes of thought will self-expire as continue indefinitely.

To appreciate the legacy of Kuhn's confusion of the prescriptive/ descriptive distinction, consider his own attempt to capture the spirit of his enterprise, when confronted by critics:

> The structure of my argument is simple and, I think, unexceptionable: scientists behave in the following ways; those modes of behavior have the following essential functions; in the absence of an alternate mode *that would serve similar functions*, scientists should behave essentially as they do if their concern is to improve scientific knowledge.
>
> (Lakatos and Musgrave 1970: 237; italics original)

While this confused appeal to science's "functions" has been treated as a virtue of Kuhn's approach by those who favour a broadly sociological or evolutionary approach to the history of science, it was seriously questioned when first presented. Paul Feyerabend went so far as to suggest that Kuhn was writing "ideology covered up as history" (Fuller 2000b: 71, n. 90). While Kuhn is clearly treating science as a historically realized normative category, the means of realization remains mysterious – as in most contemporary naturalized accounts of science – because of a studied refusal to link science's intellectual trajectory to any clear sociological vehicles. It should come as no surprise, then, that when sociologists have taken up the challenge by identifying "science" with specific research teams, professional societies, or university departments, they have often failed to find the relevant philosophical norms in place. For his part, Kuhn's own sense of "paradigm" corresponded to a somewhat abstract version of an academic discipline.

The philosophical burden in the post-Kuhnian world, then, is to define sociological vehicles capable of conveying these norms, a task that would bring philosophy of science closer to political philosophy and eventuate (I believe) in criticism of much of what currently passes for "science" (Fuller 2000a). However, in Kuhn's day, these concerns were never adequately addressed. Rather, they were largely forgotten, as *per* Kuhn's own "Planck effect" account of paradigm shift, once the next generation of historians, philosophers and sociologists of science simply came to presume the appropriateness of Kuhn's blurred perspective, albeit without embracing the details of his project. Consequently, the original criticisms now seem quaint, crude, or beside the point – again, as one would expect the previous paradigm to look to its successor. Thus, the critics, especially Karl Popper and Imre Lakatos, are relegated to historical curiosities, not front-line topics of philosophical research. Thankfully, professional historians have not been so obliging, as evidenced in two expansive accounts of Popper and Lakatos, who are cast as unfulfilled intellectual revolutionaries from whom we have much to learn today (Hacohen 2000; Kadvany 2001). Nevertheless, the damage has been done, at least on a generation of science and technology studies (STS) scholars, to which we shall return in the next chapter.

A good benchmark of how Kuhn (1970) has changed the philosophy of science is the fate of the "demarcationist" project. Though often presumed dead, the task of demarcating science from pseudo-science continues apace, as intelligent design theorists and alternative medicine practitioners know all too well. However, that task has been relegated to Platonic guardianship, a policing of the perimeters of the dominant paradigms. Demarcationism is no longer a cutting-edge philosophical problem, whose solution might embarrass segments of the scientific community who find themselves on the wrong side of the divide (cf. Hempel and Popper on evolutionary theory: Fuller 2000b: 14, n. 30). This is not because, as is often maintained, post-Kuhnian philosophers are more sensitive to historical and contemporary practices of science than their predecessors. Such a view does a disservice not only to the positivists and Popperians, but also William Whewell, Ernst Mach, Wilhelm Ostwald, Pierre Duhem and the other philosopher-scientists of the last 200 years who delved deeply into the history of science to draw normative lessons with contemporary policy relevance (Fuller 2007b: chs 1–2). Nevertheless, the impression remains among post-Kuhnians that anyone with strong normative philosophical concerns must be either an apriorist or, worse, wilfully ignorant of the diversity of scientific practices.

Where the pre-Kuhnians genuinely differed from post-Kuhnians was in their belief that just because the history of science has provided normative exemplars for organized inquiry, it does not follow that the appropriate

138 Epistemology as philosophy of science

lessons have been drawn by those who claim to follow those exemplars: Why should we think that self-proclaimed Newtonians are necessarily Newton's legitimate heirs? Accordingly, the pre-Kuhnians use exemplary episodes from the history of science to criticize past and present scientific practices. This is the tradition that, after Stephen Brush, I call "Tory historiography" (Fuller 2003: ch. 9). It provides the thread that joins in common cause Mach's (1960) "critical-historical" approach to mechanics, Lakatos's "rational reconstructionist" approach to research programmes, and my own "philosophical history" of Kuhn (Fuller 2000b).

Another way to view my appeal to this thread is as an enrichment of Popper's association of his own pre-Kuhnian conception of science with Trotsky's idea of "permanent revolution" (Popper 1981). Whereas Popper meant to exhort philosophers and scientists to *create*, not simply await (*á la* Kuhn), opportunities for scientific revolutions, I would add the pragmatic import of Trotsky's thesis, namely, to reveal publicly the Soviet Union's betrayal of Marxism's world-historic mission, or, in my own case, the deviation of the reality from the ideality of science over the course of its actual history, which has entailed two world wars, a cold war and – now – a war on "terror". All of this is in marked contrast to Kuhn's own vision, which was that the unrealized normative potential of the history of science should be restricted to specialists, out of fear of dispiriting the next generation of scientists who require an "Orwellian" (roughly, Whiggish) history to remain motivated in their less-than-world-historic quotidian pursuits (Kuhn 1970: 167).

Many of Kuhn's admirers stumble at the outset in their understanding of *The Structure of Scientific Revolutions* by failing to appreciate the spirit of its first sentence: "History, if viewed as a repository for more than anecdote or chronology, could produce a decisive transformation in the image of science by which we are now possessed." Readers should attend more closely to the counterfactual cast of the statement. Kuhn, far from endorsing his hypothesis, believed that science's day-to-day operations, and especially the intergenerational reproduction of its practices, would be *undermined* if something closer to a historian's sense of history played a prominent role, as it would end up leaving scientists with a very confused sense of the direction that their current research agenda should take in light of what had come before it.

Take John Gunnell (2009), a distinguished "critical" US political theorist, who errs in supposing that Kuhn wanted the actual history of science to be incorporated into science education, which would (were it to happen) have revolutionary consequences for the social sciences, whose orthodoxies are most closely tied to the image of science that Kuhn's theory overturns. Gunnell's thesis is misdirected at three levels: (1) Kuhn did *not* want the history of science incorporated in natural science education.

Epistemology as philosophy of science   139

(2) He had no particular interest in the social sciences, let alone designs on their transformation. (3) Pro-Kuhnian social scientists did *not* succeed in transforming their fields. At best they found ways to create niche specialities that could justify their existence without conforming to the field's dominant tendency. Gunnell's career – not to mention the journal in which his critique first appeared – unwittingly makes this point, as "political theory" has become autonomous from "political science" yet without returning to philosophy.

One concept that has stood me well in academic life makes sense of Gunnell's Kuhn-induced intellectual blindness: *sweet lemons*, the inverse of sour grapes (Elster 1983). Whereas Aesop's fox concluded that the grapes were probably sour anyway once they turned out to be beyond his reach, the victim of sweet lemons comes to believe that what happens to be within his reach is what he had wanted all along. Seen in this light, Kuhn has had the last laugh – at least for now. Gunnell is certainly correct that Kuhn located the truth and objectivity of science in its actual practices rather than in some transcendental ideal of inquiry. He is even correct that this view is now widely endorsed across academia. However, it is by no means clear how any of this has benefited scholars such as Gunnell, whose stock in trade is radical critique of his discipline's scientific pretensions. What I earlier called the "Kuhnification" of academic life means that criticism is nowadays directed at fellow critics rather than the putative objects of criticism, in effect alienation masquerading as autonomy.

Despite his enthusiasm for Kuhn, Gunnell missed the man's deepest point, which remains a challenge to critics such as myself who are pro-science but nevertheless believe that scientists should operate with a demystified sense of their own history: Indeed, contrary to the logic of demystification, science's progressive self-understanding has rested on the streamlined, "Orwellian" view of its history alluded to above that is not only transmitted in science textbooks but also promulgated and embellished in popular science writing. Hence, I have situated Kuhn's insights within the "double-truth" tradition that reaches back to Plato, passes through all the Abrahamic faiths – Judaism, Christianity and Islam – and in the twentieth century was most overtly championed by Leo Strauss (Fuller 2000b: ch. 1). In Kuhn's case, the two truths refer to the history of science as told by and for historians *versus* by and for scientists. However invidious this framing may appear, it is not a figment of my imagination. Within five years of *The Structure of Scientific Revolutions*'s publication in a popular second edition, a Kuhn-inspired article in no less than *Science* queried whether the history of science should be rated X for scientists (Brush 1975). The proposed answer was *yes*.

Moreover, half a century after Kuhn (1970), his double-truth historicism appears to have triumphed, given that history of science as a discipline is

140   *Epistemology as philosophy of science*

now completely differentiated from the original science disciplines, as evidenced by its dedicated journals, assessment boards, training programmes, student pools and career trajectories. Indeed, one can judge the relative "hardness" of a science by the extent to which it has become institutionally segregated from its history; hence, historians of natural science talk mainly to other historians, while historians of social science can still cause trouble by resurrecting repressed memories of "paradigms lost" (e.g. Mirowski 1989). Thus, today one can become a very respected and successful historian of a science without the corresponding scientists ever learning of – let alone being bothered by – one's existence. Thus, Steven Shapin (2005), grandee of the self-styled radical "sociological" turn in the history of science, recently proposed a "cocktail party" standard of communication in order to redress this sense of lost audience. Shapin and others who followed closely in Kuhn's footsteps may wonder where the promised social revolution in science went. But Kuhn himself was always quite clear that it was not supposed to happen – and did whatever he could to prevent it from happening (Fuller 2003: 141, 193, 202, 212).

However, the most potent ideological function performed by Kuhn (1970) occurred in the philosophy of science, where it has provided protective colouration for the field's de-politicization in the middle third of the twentieth century. What became the analytic philosophy of science establishment in post-Second World War America began life as the "logical positivists" in the "Red Vienna" days of the 1920s and 1930s, when they attempted to revive a metaphysically neutral yet still politically progressive scientific world-view from the ashes of German materialism's defeat in the First World War (Proctor 1991: ch. 9). George Reisch (2005) has chronicled this transition, which predates Senator Joseph McCarthy's early Cold War, anti-Communist hysteria and reaches back to such unlikely suspects as John Dewey and especially his student Sidney Hook, two "social liberals" who were profoundly put off by the positivists' socialist credentials when they first arrived in America. But once ensconced in the US, the head positivist, Rudolf Carnap, in one breath discouraged Popper's emigration to America given the latter's aggressive promotion of science as the paradigmatic "open society", and in the next breath, praised Kuhn's understanding of science as drawing clear boundaries around its own distinctive sphere of freedom prior to any user involvement (Fuller 2000b: 286, fn 51).

Together the two judgements suggest that Kuhn enabled the positivists to support the autonomy and integrity of science, even if it would be at the cost of abandoning the Enlightenment ideal of science as the vanguard of social and political progress. Over time this trade-off justified the increasingly technical turn in the philosophy of science that is associated with the discipline's "analytic" tradition. In this respect, then, Kuhn's impact on the history and the philosophy of science has been complementary, yet each in its own way self-negating: The historians have become more autonomous from the scientists and hence alienated from the scientists' "Whiggish" normative impulses, while the philosophers have morphed from second-order critics and directors of science to the scientists' spiritual alter egos and *amicus curiae* brief writers; hence, the title of chapter 6 of Fuller (2000b): "The World Not Well Lost: Philosophy after Kuhn".

Popper's (pre-)challenge to Kuhn and Kuhn's anti-rationalist response

I have suggested that Karl Popper's marginalization as, so to speak, a "rogue positivist" is part of Kuhn's ascendancy in re-focusing the cognitive orientations of the history and the philosophy of science. To appreciate what was lost in the process, let us start by tracing Popper's longing for "permanent revolution in science" to his principled *anti-inductivist* approach to inquiry, which I believe was basically on the right track. A good way to get into Popper's understanding of induction is through that old warhorse of analytic epistemology, the so-called grue paradox. According to Nelson Goodman (1955), "grue" is the property of being green before a given time and blue thereafter. This property enjoys just as much empirical support as the property of being green when hypothetically applied to all known emeralds.

For Goodman, this was a "new riddle of induction" because unlike Hume's original example of induction – how do we know that the sun will rise tomorrow just given our past experience – his problem suggests that our propensity to inductive inference is shaped not simply by our prior experience but by the language in which that experience has been cast. Popper could not agree more. Unfortunately Goodman proceeds to draw a conservative conclusion from this situation, namely, that we are generally right to endorse the more familiar predicate "green" when making predictions about the colour of future emeralds. Why? Well, because that predicate is more "entrenched", which is a bit of jargon for the rather unphilosophical stance of "if it ain't broke, don't fix it".

Popper's anti-inductivism may be understood as an attempt to render Goodman's riddle philosophically more interesting. The prospect that a predicate like "grue" might contribute to a more adequate account of all emeralds (both known and unknown) than "green" is certainly familiar from the history of science. It trades on the idea that the periodic inability of our best theories to predict the future may rest on our failure to have understood the past all along. In short, we may have thought we lived in one sort of world, when in fact we have been always living in another one. After all, the "grue" and "green" worlds have looked exactly the same until now. In this respect, Goodman showed that induction is about locating the actual world in which a prediction is made within the set of possible worlds by proposing causal narratives that purport to connect past and future events, "green" and "grue" constituting two alternative accounts vis-à-vis the colour of emeralds.

This is a profound point, especially for scientific realists, the full implications of which have yet to be explored – even now, more than half a century after Goodman's original formulation (cf. Stanford 2006 on the problem of "unconceived alternatives" to the best scientific explanation at a given time). In particular, seen through Popperian lenses, Goodman suggests how the "paradigm shifts" that Kuhn identified with "scientific revolutions" should be expected if we take the fallibility of our theories as *temporally symmetrical* – that is, that every substantial new discovery is always an invitation to revise what we had believed about the past. In other words, as science increases its breadth by revealing previously unknown phenomena, it increases its depth by revising our understanding of previously known phenomena so as to incorporate them within the newly forged understanding. Newton did not simply add to Aristotle's project but superseded it altogether by showing that Aristotle had not fully grasped what he thought he had understood. Indeed, if Newton is to be believed, Aristotle literally did not know what he was talking about, since everything that he said that we still deem to be true could be said just as well – and better – by dispensing with his overarching metaphysical framework.

Put in starkest terms, Kuhn's advice to scientists wishing to advance their fields is to bury the past as deeply as possible, so that only historians can recover it, whereas Popper's advice is the exact opposite – namely, to resurrect the past in order to follow through on objections and misgivings that the dominant paradigm has failed to address adequately (Fuller 2003: ch. 9). Regardless of whether you follow Kuhn or Popper, counterfactuals are involved in both cases. Interestingly, the leading philosophical critique of my deconstruction of Kuhn's position (Fuller 2000b) turns precisely on my heavy reliance on counterfactual reasoning about history of science to score normative points (Andersen 2001). Yet, counterfactual reasoning was equally formative in Kuhn's own philosophical project, as he tried to fathom what Aristotle had been up to, once scientists had come to believe that Aristotle was no longer relevant to concerns (Fuller 2000b: 202–3).

To be sure, Kuhn and I appeal to counterfactual reasoning in diametrically opposed ways, which in turn reflects a difference in our sense of the relationship between the history and the philosophy of science. I believe that the two pursuits are artificially separated and mutually alienated, whereas Kuhn saw them as functionally differentiated and best

Epistemology as philosophy of science 143

pursued independently of each other (Fuller 2000b: 15, n. 33). Kuhn's appeal to counterfactuals here has the advantage of tracking the *entente cordiale* that currently exists between history and philosophy. The "smart thinking" today likes history to counterfactualize from present to past, where the historian is an observer or re-enactor of past events who, like a guest in a foreign land, tries to learn the natives' customs. But equally, the "smart thinking" likes philosophy to counterfactualize from past to present, so that were (say) Aristotle reincarnated as the ultimate adult student, he would be sufficiently rational and obliging to see how to get from his physics to ours through a combination of logical inferences and empirical observations that he himself would have made, under the right conditions. However, the implied clarity with which the past can be divided from the present is explicable in terms of the "later Wittgensteinian" legacy to contemporary philosophy, which overemphasizes the need for guests to be polite to their hosts, something that a psychoanalyst might trace to a residual worry born of Jewish assimilation in Christendom, as in the case of the Wittgenstein family in late Habsburg Vienna (cf. Gellner 1998: ch. 21).

But setting aside such apologetics, the *entente cordiale* between history and philosophy stretches credulity as a model for how alien visitors should approach native norms. (I elaborate my own opposition to this *entente cordiale* when discussing "epistemology as counterfactual historiography" in Chapter 6.) Since virtually all societies manifest internal conflicts, any public display of what a society "normally" does is bound to be an official story (perhaps even one "made for export") that represents an expedient resolution of those conflicts (Fuller 1993: 191–207). Kuhn himself seems to have modelled such normative displays on the late Habsburg and Ottoman Empires, whose accumulated political anomalies eventuated in the First World War (Fuller 2000b: 146–49). But from a strictly philosophical standpoint, there is no reason to suppose that the alien visitor could not criticize or even change native norms by appealing to these internal conflicts. In other words, why must counterfactual time-travel be asymmetrical, with historians always transporting themselves to the past and philosophers always importing the ancients into the present? Why not portray the ancients as our historians or us as philosophical missionaries in the ancient worlds? In both cases, we would be forced to persuade the ancients that we could bring (or have brought) out the best of their scientific projects, and defend ourselves against the charge of taking (or having taken) them in wayward directions. Recovering this pre-Kuhnian appeal to counterfactuals, which I associate with Popper, would be a valuable first step in reviving the fortunes of the normatively integrated history and philosophy of science that the success of Kuhn (1970) has made us forget.

144   *Epistemology as philosophy of science*

In sum, from a Popperian standpoint, science may be defined as the form of organized inquiry that is dedicated to reproducing Goodman's new riddle of induction on a regular basis. To be sure, speculatively conjured predicates like "grue" rarely lead to successful predictions, so some skill must be involved to make them work, whereby they acquire the leverage for rethinking inquiry's prior history. Such skill in devising "projectible" predicates, to use Goodman's jargon, is displayed in first-rate scientific theorizing. In this way, scientific revolutions metamorphose from Kuhn's realm of the unwanted and the unintended to Popper's positive vision of deliberately instigated "permanent revolutions".

To be sure, Kuhn's intellectual motivation did not significantly differ from those of Popper and his other interlocutors. Like many of his generation, Kuhn was sufficiently put off by the emergence of "Big Science" that he transferred his original natural-philosophical interest in physics to the humanities. He appealed to episodes in the history of science only insofar as they exemplified a pattern in the conduct of organized inquiry that he found normatively desirable. Kuhn differed only in being less explicit about the normative ideal he was defending and more forthcoming with the historical episodes that exemplified it. However, the number and arrangement of the episodes did not make them any less self-serving than those of his interlocutors. The debate recounted in Lakatos and Musgrave (1970), for all its empirical and historical suggestiveness, was still about the normative ideal of science: In his own terms, Kuhn privileged normal science, his opponents revolutionary science. Nevertheless, Kuhn's strategy of foregrounding the descriptive and backgrounding the prescriptive dimensions of science has been widely imitated, though its origins in the more esoteric reaches of the Platonic tradition – in Kuhn's case, Alexandre Koyré – have generally gone unnoticed (Fuller 2000b: 38–95).

The long-term effect of this aspect of Kuhnification is that the original normative dispute has been displaced by competing philosophical and sociological attempts to explain the actual history and practice of science. The question of how organized inquiry should best proceed has been reduced to a matter of second-guessing the dominant research trends and chronicling their ascendancy. The relevant dialectic no longer turns on "ought" versus "is", but "universal" versus "particular". Consequently, easy points can be scored simply by revealing the lack of empirical generalizability in a proposed normative model of science once it strays beyond the designated exemplar, as in the case of a physics-based account that is extended to biology. Before Kuhn, this objection would have been seen as tantamount to epistemic relativism, given physics's historically vanguard scientific role. Nevertheless, over the past half-century, "naturalized" philosophers have become both more technically adept at the practices of the special sciences and more reluctant to abstract from those practices altogether, implicitly conceding to historians and sociologists that any general normative pronouncements are bound to be arbitrarily selective.

In short, philosophers have become not only *of* but also *for* science. By this I mean that philosophers have increasingly surrendered their historic prerogative to dictate the terms of normative engagement with science. In Weberian terms, they have shifted their orientation of rationality from "substantive" to "instrumental" vis-à-vis science. I first made this point at the American Philosophical Association, in its 1996 Eastern Division symposium dedicated in memory of Popper and Paul Feyerabend. There I contrasted alternative interpretations that pre-Kuhnian philosophers *of* science and post-Kuhnian philosophers *for* science would make of various claims that might just as easily come from the mouth of either one. The argument is summarized in Table 6.

In retrospect, Kuhn may turn out to have been the most influential *anti-rationalist* philosopher of the second half of the twentieth century. The fact that he was a philosopher of *science* is the most striking feature of this claim. What makes Kuhn so "anti-rationalist" is his denial of the dynamic character of reason, what is sometimes called its "reflexive" capacity for self-application (Will 1988). What I mean here is that reason learns from its own activity to discover its optimal expression (aka its "true end", which is usually equated with the ultimate representation of reality). A broad range of thinkers – from the sophists through Comte

Table 6 Philosophy of science or for science?

Common claim	Philosophy "of" science	Philosophy "for" science
"Philosophy derives premises from science"	Only at the Meta-level: Philosophy is no more or less probable than science	At the Object Level: Science provides new foundations for philosophy
"Philosophy is critical like science"	Philosophy applies science's critical scrutiny to itself	Philosophy criticizes within science's framework
"Philosophy solves problems like science"	Philosophy's problems defy specialization and hence may interfere with science	Philosophy's problems are specialized and hence do not interfere with science
"Science's problems originate in philosophy"	These problems are deep and cannot be offset by empirical success	These problems may be ill-formed and may be offset by empirical success
"Philosophy is necessary for science to flourish"	Philosophy always needed to prevent science from ossifying into dogma	Philosophy not needed for science once it has cleared away dogma
"Philosophy articulates the norms of science"	The norms are whatever it takes to realize the goals of science, even if scientists don't like it	The norms are already implicit in what scientists do

and Hegel to Peirce and Popper – have adhered to this general conception of reason. It is fairly called "dialectical" by virtue of accepting reason's self-correcting character – that is, not only its fallibility but also its "corrigibility". Thus, when our most popular theories meet empirical resistance, our rationality is marked by correcting *both* the theories themselves, so as to make them more representative of the phenomena to which they lay epistemic claim, *and* whatever underlying presuppositions of those theories allowed the errors to be committed in the first place. The former, first-order process re-calibrates our sense of reason's end-state; the latter, the second-order process, re-calibrates our sense of how to get to that now re-defined destination.

While both adjustments result from the same encounter, they need to be addressed separately. In particular, the second-order process involves a radical re-thinking of how past precedents should be taken forward in the future in the guise of "methodology". My earlier re-interpretation of Popper's anti-inductivism in light of Goodman's "new riddle of induction" is a clear example of how one philosopher has dealt with this side of the problem. After all, the scientific method, whether officially expressed as a form of deductive or inductive inference, is ultimately about collecting known cases to achieve a common understanding that can be then extended to unknown cases. In this respect, we are still playing the game to which Larry Laudan introduced us a quarter-century ago (Donovan *et al.* 1988).

It is worth stressing that among the "historicist" philosophers of science who flourished in the Anglo-American academy in the second half of the twentieth century – including Popper, Feyerabend, Lakatos, Joseph Agassi, Larry Laudan, Russell Hanson, Stephen Toulmin and Dudley Shapere – Kuhn stands out for his refusal to attribute such reflexivity to science. To be sure, Kuhn's philosophical defenders outside his immediate field have charitably associated Kuhn with a rather different version of reflexivity, what economists call "path dependency", which consists in reinforcing what already works so as to eliminate all competitors and thereby dominate an environment. For example, this is what Alasdair MacIntyre (1981) defined the "traditional" element of disciplinary practices. According to Kuhn, it is what happens when an exemplary scientific achievement, such as Newton's *Principia*, serves as a "paradigm", on which all subsequent research in the physical sciences is modelled. It becomes "entrenched", to recall another term of Nelson Goodman's, one designed to underscore its conservative presumption.

However, the shortcomings of Kuhn's vision had been adumbrated by *cybernetics*, the interdisciplinary field concerned with the intelligence embodied in artefacts, which also came of age in Kuhn's lifetime. Cyberneticians recognized the perils of path dependency, which they dubbed "positive feedback" (Wiener 1950). An entrenched paradigm – be it

Epistemology as philosophy of science 147

understood as a research tradition or in a more extended sense of "life-world" – tends to amplify its own distinctive properties indefinitely, ignoring that long-term survival requires equilibrium with the environment, which in turn entails an understanding of the limits of one's own mode of being. "Negative feedback" was coined to capture this idea, through which systemic resilience may be developed. When modelling the behaviour of organisms, cyberneticians suggested that a body's immune system served as a micro-model (or "simulation") of the selection environment to which the organism as a whole must ultimately prove adaptive. Similarly, at an intellectual level, one recalls Popper's (1972) view of hypothesis testing in science as allowing theories to die in our stead. In contrast, to all this, Kuhn was very clear that a change in paradigm requires a change in population, since relatively few scientists who started working under one paradigm ever make the switch to a successor. This is what gives "scientific revolutions" the appearance of a generational shift.

To be sure, there have been attempts to discredit the close link implied between age and openness to change. Perhaps the correct thing to say here is that what really matters is not chronological age but the number of years invested in a specific tradition, such that a recent cross-disciplinary interloper may be intellectually "younger" than a chronological junior who has spent his whole life in the field (Fuller 2000b: 289, n. 59). Nevertheless, any charitable interpretation of Kuhn requires a strong "naturalization" of science, in the sense that he ontologizes what a predecessor like Popper would have treated as epistemological. Thus, very *contra* Popper, for Kuhn, a strongly held theory in science is likely to constitute the theorist's death sentence. Exactly when that sentence is carried out depends on the stage of the paradigm's development. Here Popper's insistence that science tests hypotheses *as opposed to* beliefs proves salient. Popper clearly saw science as a simulation of life in the full sense of both "simulation" and "life": On the one hand, hypotheses function as simulated beliefs; on the other, an experimental outcome functions as a simulated version of lived experience.

Evolutionary naturalists can interpret the Kuhn-Popper debate in two ways: Either *à la* Kuhn, that people (who essentially live their paradigms) are the units that are ultimately selected by the history of science; or *à la* Popper, that ideas (which are only hypothetically associated with people) are ultimately what are selected. What from Kuhn's standpoint appears principled, to Popper's appears dogmatic. Conversely, what from Popper's standpoint looks like an openness to learn from whatever the world has to offer, to Kuhn's looks like a counsel of unrealistic flexibility, if not (given the evolutionary context) Lamarckism. My own "reflexive naturalism" (Fuller 1993) clearly sides with Popper in the view that the more we

148 *Epistemology as philosophy of science*

learn from nature, especially through scientific experimentation, the less "natural" nature turns out to be. Put less paradoxically, empirical regularities that originally appeared to define the structure of reality – *à la* induction – turn out to be dependent on conditions that, as science progresses, may come to be manipulated at will so as to reveal previously hidden aspects of reality.

A useful way to see the difference between Kuhn and Popper here is in terms of their perspectives on both Gestalt switches and linguistic relativity. In these matters, Kuhn was famously influenced by, respectively, Jerome Bruner and Benjamin Whorf; whereas, less famously perhaps, Popper completed his doctorate (in educational psychology) under the supervision of Karl Bühler, who made significant early contributions to both fields. Whereas Kuhn follows Bruner and Whorf in stressing the sense in which subjects by default inhabit only one perceptually or linguistically defined world-view, Bühler taught Popper to think of alternative world-views as conditional constructions over which subjects ultimately have control. This difference may be understood in terms of the paradigm shift that took place in, so to speak, the "sociology of method" underwriting experimental psychology in the twentieth century (Fuller 1992a). Reflecting the dominant line, Kuhn treats the scientists studied by historians with the same detachment of a psychologist vis-à-vis a subject. This means that Kuhn's notorious concept of "incommensurability" is actively manufactured in the research context via a "double blind" situation in which the experimenter and the subject start by being ignorant of each other's epistemic horizons. In contrast, Popper echoes the earlier practice in psychology whereby the same person functioned as both scientist and subject and was thus capable, at least in principle, of controlling the conditions under which s/he frames a situation one way rather than another (cf. Fuller 2000b: 266–80).

Of course, from a normative standpoint, the two stances may obtain as two parts of a single process, as the Kuhnian double-blind set-up enables the presumptive causal factors in one's world-view to come to the fore, which then allows for a Popper-style reflexive manipulation of those factors. Indeed, underlying Kuhn and Popper's common interest in perceptual and linguistic relativity may be a metaphysical perspective they shared. I originally discussed this as a dualistic account of modality: Both Kuhn and Popper were realists about possible worlds (a paradigm, say, constituting one such world) but antirealists about the actual world (Fuller 1988: 87–89). In other words, based on the evidence at their disposal, agents may inhabit any of a number of worlds but at any given moment they can only inhabit one such world, each of which is determinate and self-contained (cf. the many-worlds interpretation of quantum mechanics). In that case, Kuhn and Popper differ only insofar as the former portrays this state of affairs as something that happens to agents (e.g. a "conversion experience") whereas the latter sees it as something that agents decide for themselves (Fuller 2003: ch. 11).

Kuhn's contemporary legacy: the naturalization of consensus in science

Kuhn is increasingly invoked in the context of claims for a "scientific consensus" vis-à-vis some policy-related issue, in terms of which attempts to stir up controversy are treated pejoratively as "manufactured". This curious deployment of Kuhn has been given its most articulate expression by Leah Ceccarelli (2011), a distinguished rhetorician of science, whose earlier work argued that three key twentieth-century revolutions in the life sciences were "manufactured" by virtue of proposing interdisciplinary syntheses that eluded the sort of peer review processes that are emblematic of the normative structure of a Kuhnian paradigm (Ceccarelli 2001). I shall return to this earlier research at the end of this section, since it tells so much against Ceccarelli's current Kuhnified preoccupations. However, her current volte-face says a lot about how the American left has come to rely on some wishful account of scientific consensus as a *deus ex machina*, a trend started by the *Washington Post* science reporter Chris Mooney (2005). In this respect, as we shall see, Ceccarelli is a sort of "Ultra-Kuhnian" who is not simply content with science governing itself but would also have science settle disputes (*à la* Bacon's juridical ideal) among competing ideological factions in society.

Ceccarelli's phrase, "manufactured scientific controversy", would seem to presume that there is something wrong when scientific controversies have not come about in some "natural" way. The phrase also invites a complementary consideration of "manufactured" and "natural" scientific consensus. The philosophical paper trail on this latter issue starts with Charles Sanders Peirce and runs through Karl Popper and eventually to Jürgen Habermas. Peirce set this inquiry on the right footing when he proposed that scientific validity is governed not by the moment-to-moment epistemic drift in scientific opinion but an envisaged agreement in the ultimate set of inquirers "at the end of time". This normative horizon encourages us to go beyond merely extrapolating from present trends into the future (i.e. a fetishization of the current orthodoxy) to imagining that the shape of long periods of change in the past will be reproduced in the future. Such reasoning is akin to the sort of knowledge that financiers aim to have of the firms in which they might invest, and corresponds to the vision of would-be scientific revolutionaries who happily risk collective past achievements on behalf of a bolder if speculative future (Haskell 1984).

150 *Epistemology as philosophy of science*

Seen from that second-order perspective, those angling for a Peircean consensus should endorse what Hilary Putnam dubbed the "pessimistic meta-induction", according to which, based on science's historical track record, most of what we believe now as fundamental explanatory principles – though not necessarily the evidence invoked in their support – is likely to be superseded in a century's time (Putnam 1978: 24–25). Here we need to take the Gestalt switch model of scientific revolution seriously: What makes a previously duck-looking figure suddenly appear rabbit-like is a change not in the figure's details but in the overarching frame of reference used to interpret it. But if Putnam is right, why even wait a century to witness this radical change in frameworks? Why not manufacture controversies, the outcomes of which will get us nearer that ultimate consensus? This was certainly the spirit in which Popper offered falsifiability as the mark of the scientific: It was meant to expedite progress, perhaps even at a rate faster than the scientific establishment would wish, especially considering how the outcomes might affect investment and employment patterns in science. (That alone may explain why science is not Popperian in practice.) Of course, not every attempt at falsification is destined to succeed – in fact, most fail. But assuming that the results are publicly available (*per* Popper's "open society" vision of science), everyone will have benefited from the lessons drawn from these tests to established thinking.

There is no reason to presume either that consensus is normal in science or that whatever consensus exists in science is anything more than an institutionally sanctioned opinion about theories whose ultimate prospects are still up for grabs (Shapin and Schaffer 1985). If science is ultimately about following the truth wherever it may lead, then one should expect inquirers to diverge in their paths, as they extend the same knowledge base in various directions, only some of which will bear substantial fruit, sway colleagues, etc. Indeed, my own support for intelligent design theory follows very much from my opposition to the Kuhnian presumption of "one science = one paradigm" that has been used to great rhetorical effect by defenders of the Neo-Darwinist orthodoxy (Fuller 2008a: ch. 1; cf. Segerstrale 2000).

However, this inertial tendency to diverse paths of inquiry is periodically interrupted by the perceived need for the scientific community to present a united front. The source of this need may be at least threefold: (a) resource constraint, (b) legitimation crisis, and (c) policy relevance. The first threatens to turn alternative research trajectories into potential competitors, the second corresponds to the self-generated "crisis" of a Kuhnian paradigm, and the third refers to the situations on which Ceccarelli focuses. In this last set of cases, there is a general expectation that "science" must speak in one voice to a pressing matter of public concern.

Epistemology as philosophy of science 151

The difference between the second and third sources of consensus formation in science highlights the rather restricted sense in which Kuhn envisaged the matter. While Kuhn stressed the consensual nature of science, he tended to restrict the object of that consensus to an exemplarily solved problem, the sort of thing that could be routinized as a textbook exercise for students entering the field. This explains the emphasis that he increasingly placed on "symbolic generalizations", especially mathematical formulas that can be applied in a variety of settings to extend a paradigm's reach. However, for Kuhn, the exact epistemic interpretation given to these formulas (e.g. are they representations of reality or instruments of control) is normally a matter for philosophy, not science, unless the exemplars persistently fail to tackle significant problems set by the paradigm. In that case, science – for a relatively brief "crisis" period – becomes open to foundational epistemic discussions (Fuller 1988: 207–32). In the 1980s, partly under the influence of the emerging social studies of science, Ian Hacking (1992) generalized Kuhn's sense of exemplar to cover laboratory practices that reliably produce objects that are then subject to multiple theoretical interpretations.

My point here is that one need not hold my own agonistic view of science to find Ceccarelli's understanding of "consensus" as semantic or ideological closure problematic. Even the more mainstream STS tradition that flows from Kuhn through Hacking limits the relevance of consensus in science to focal objects for the community of inquirers, that is, literally *res publicae*. Interpretation of these objects is expected to vary across research contexts, which in turn explains the prominence of ethnography as an STS methodology. By this logic, the claims to scientific consensus to which Ceccarelli refers are manufactured in specific locations – say, the offices of the National Academy of Sciences – and then placed in circulation to be appropriated for local purposes.

Moreover, the politics of Ceccarelli's three high-profile cases differ substantially, as well as the nature of whatever "scientific consensus" might exist relating to them. To be sure, there is very probably a consensus over (1) the HIV–AIDS causal link, (2) the impact of human-based carbon emissions on Earth's climate and (3) the evolution of species over a very long timeframe. But that still leaves open whether whatever "scientific consensus" exists in these fields is sufficient to dictate policy. The answers vary:

1 The easiest case concerns the administering of antiretroviral drugs to treat AIDS sufferers, even though that depends on a rather unholistic, almost "magic bullet" approach to medicine that is generally eschewed these days. I raise this point because the most influential and scientifically distinguished "AIDS denialist", Peter Duesberg, Professor of

152   *Epistemology as philosophy of science*

Cell Biology at Berkeley, was trained in the holistic approach to cancer research that made Germany the leader in that field until the Second World War (Harrington 1999; Proctor 2000). Accordingly, systemic cellular dysfunctions were understood and treated at the level of the "lifestyle". When applied to AIDS sufferers, this approach put in the spotlight, *inter alia*, the relatively higher levels of recreational drug use by homosexuals. Even if one shares my view that the jury is still out on the intellectual merits of Duesberg's position, few can doubt that the gay community's hard won struggle for civil rights in living memory makes it difficult to consider his hypothesis dispassionately. But this is likely to change with time – and further research.

2 In the case of climate change, let us first put aside the nagging meta-induction that the climate theories that say we have fifty years to save the planet have themselves a life expectancy of half that time. Agreement on the facts of global warming and its likely anthropic source still leaves open whether we should try to stop or adapt to it. The two strategies are very different in spirit. The more internationally visible strategy of substantially cutting carbon emissions presupposes a (morally?) negative judgement on capitalism's default capacity to meet the coming crisis. In contrast, the adaptive strategy places much greater faith in capitalism but blames governments for not providing sufficient incentives to develop alternative energy sources and invest in climate-resistant infrastructures. The adaptive strategy, though less publicized, has been taken seriously by economists and the financial press (Green.view 2010).

3 Finally, when seventy national academies of science banded together to oppose creationism on a global level, the definition of "evolution" to which all parties could agree failed to identify any specific mechanism, not even natural selection (Fuller 2008a: 32–33; cf. InterAcademy Panel 2006). The resulting document, though superficially impressive, succeeded only in blocking Young Earth Creationists. If anything counts as a purpose-built "scientific consensus", this does. Moreover, it should come as no surprise, since even evolutionists admit that many long-standing controversies in their field draw on the same conceptual and empirical aporias that also fuel neo-creationist agendas. Often the only way to prevent such scientific undesirables from gaining any advantage is by pricing them out of the market, especially through lawsuits that threaten any would-be creationist defendant with bankruptcy (Fuller 2008a: 35–36). An adept practitioner of the subtle art of determining who is and is not entitled to gain theoretical advantage from Neo-Darwinian anomalies has been the philosopher John Dupré (2012), who heads the UK's Economic and Social Research Council's Centre for Genomics and Society, whose own work has championed

Epistemology as philosophy of science 153

the inclusion of "developmental factors" – stopping short of a divine hand – to complement Ultra-Darwinism's exclusive reliance on natural selection as the mechanism of evolution.

In any case, current scientific practitioners – either in their elite or their mass – do not own science, not even epistemologically. Science's epistemology is ultimately aspirational, an indefinite pursuit for an understanding of reality that goes beyond whatever might be easily comprehended and implemented by a given generation of inquirers. Here Ceccarelli underestimates the epistemic import of *dissoi logoi* (i.e. the representation of an argument as if it had two equally matched sides) if not the entire Protagorean tradition in rhetoric, which is more fully realized in a dialectician like Hegel than a sceptic like Sextus Empiricus. The very presence of conflict in a matter of public concern indicates that each side has a contribution to make that is in some sense excluded by the other. What that contribution turns out to be does not necessarily correspond to the relative standing of the parties but only emerges over the course of the debate, resulting in some rounded synthetic judgement that is then binding on both parties. In this respect, the desire for a "balanced perspective" that Ceccarelli criticizes in the popular presentation of scientific controversies is epistemologically legitimate, especially if Putnam is correct that the fundamental explanatory principles of the future are unlikely to be our own. In that case, one would be wise to err in the direction of open-mindedness in research and educational policy.

I began this section by expressing bemusement at the pejorative cast of Ceccarelli's conception of "manufactured scientific controversy", given her significant work in the rhetoric of interdisciplinary collaboration (Ceccarelli 2001). The most notable feature of Ceccarelli's original rhetorical analysis was her stress on the productive power of what would normally be considered epistemic liabilities, such as strategic ambiguity in the use of concepts, misleading appeals to authority, not to mention ordinary errors of fact. The three cases that she examined – Theodosius Dobzhansky's *Genetics and the Origin of Species*, Erwin Schrödinger's *What Is Life?* and E. O. Wilson's *Consilience* – arguably captured the most important moments of cross-disciplinary synthesis in the life sciences over the past 100 years. To be sure, when her book appeared, Ceccarelli had cast Wilson as a failure. However, that 2001 judgement of a book published in 1998 may have been premature, especially given the rise of evolutionary psychology and Wilson's own metamorphosis from the overlord of sociobiology to a philosopher of global ecological consciousness (e.g. Wilson 2007).

Nevertheless, the three works under consideration are a textbook (Dobzhansky's), a public lecture (Schrödinger's), and a work of popular

154 *Epistemology as philosophy of science*

science (Wilson's). These are not the usual genres of revolutionary science, if Kuhn is taken to be our guide. They all circumvent the strictures of specialist peer review, which very likely would have caught the relevant rhetorical tricks – and thereby blocked their use. And for all we know, those tricks were caught prior to publication but were tolerated because of the larger epistemic ends they served. However, it is difficult to see the author of Ceccarelli (2011) licensing such a conclusion, as she now interprets the phrase "politics of science" in the narrow sense of "politics as usual but as applied to science".

Ceccarelli's eagerness to provide rhetorical services to current liberal causes, while sticking to a Kuhnian view of consensus-based science, has arguably blinded her to science's own longer-term normative horizons. Moreover, in today's neo-liberal political economy of science, scientists' interests may be more closely aligned with those of their employers – be they public or private – than with each other (i.e. the mutually shared consciousness that characterizes a Kuhnian paradigm). In that case, in order simply to achieve the sort of socio-epistemological coherence that Ceccarelli (2011) takes for granted, scientists and their well-wishers may need in the future to engage increasingly in the types of activities to which Ceccarelli (2001) originally drew expert attention.

The problem of positioning Popper on his own terms

A disturbing feature of twentieth-century philosophy is that the dominant figures of the two main European philosophical traditions – Ludwig Wittgenstein (analytic) and Martin Heidegger (continental) – were decidedly conservative thinkers with strong authoritarian tendencies (Gellner 1998; Safranski 2000). The disturbance is only increased when an avowedly liberal thinker like Richard Rorty (1979) explains the significance of his own hero, John Dewey, in terms of the views that Dewey shared with Wittgenstein and Heidegger, as if Karl Popper had never existed. Had Rorty taken Popper's achievement more seriously, we might have acquired greater immunity to the postmodern predicament, whereby the failure to establish logical foundations for all thought opens the door to an endless proliferation of community-based epistemic standards (Hacohen 2000: 2–3). Indeed, a regrettable sign of our non-Popperian times is that the most natural way to interpret the idea of "social epistemology" is as a consensus-seeking approach to inquiry based on a division of cognitive labour and trust in expertise – not, as Popper himself did, a set of mutually critical agents whose thoroughly conventionalist approach to disciplinary boundaries invites them to question and reform even fundamental knowledge claims on a regular basis (Jarvie 2001). Of course, some social epistemologists take Popper seriously (e.g. Fuller 2000a).

Epistemology as philosophy of science   155

If philosophers are judged by their entire corpus, Karl Popper was arguably the most noteworthy if not the greatest philosopher of the twentieth century. It is difficult to imagine a field of academic or public life that his work did not touch directly or indirectly. (Those in doubt should consult Shearmur and Norris 2008, which includes Popper's media interventions.) Indeed, Popperian buzzwords still populate the trading zone between academic and public discourse – "falsifiability", "demarcation criteria", "the open society", "the poverty of historicism", "methodological individualism", "conjectures and refutations", "evolutionary epistemology", "world 3" (i.e. the realm of objective knowledge). To be sure, in many cases Popper was responsible more for promoting than developing the ideas behind the buzzwords. But most remarkable, especially for a twentieth-century philosopher, Popper's ideas remain memorable in ways that have not proven either embarrassing or shameful.

Popper's relative neglect by professional philosophers is arguably more than compensated by the impact of his work on other disciplines, especially the social sciences. In the second half of the twentieth century, Popper stood within academia for the scientific method, objectivity, rationality, liberalism and individualism, just as his English patron, Bertrand Russell, had in the public at large. But Popper's direct style, which communicated easily across disciplinary boundaries, has not worn well with philosophical colleagues, who tend to interpret it as an expression of dogmatism. Yet most of Popper's "positive" views were really negative ones in disguise. His rationalism was tinged by fallibilism that set its sights primarily on the unreflective character of inductive inference. His liberalism was consistently anti-authoritarian to the point of harbouring strong reservations about the deference that his friend Friedrich Hayek showed to the market's "invisible hand" (Hacohen 2000: ch. 10). And Popper's individualism was driven much more by an opposition to the prospect of humanity's absorption into one or another kind of groupthink than any metaphysical adherence to self-interest as the defining feature of human nature. Popper's de facto "oppositional consciousness" meant that he often presented his views as critical sketches that presumed some acquaintance with the details and history of what was being criticized.

Failure to appreciate the profoundly dialectical character of Popper's thought has led to his portrayal – at the hands of no less than the self-avowed keepers of the dialectical tradition – as a relatively simple-minded thinker, such as the standard-issue "positivist" that came across to the self-styled "critical theorists" of the Frankfurt School, Theodor Adorno and Jürgen Habermas, in the *Methodenstreit* of the 1960s (Adorno 1967; cf. Fuller 2003: chs 13–14). But even among the positivists' Anglo-American descendants in analytic philosophy, in whose ranks he is sometimes misleadingly included, Popper is known for having adopted a

156 *Epistemology as philosophy of science*

distinctive, if not altogether transparent, stance on the role of something called "induction" in scientific epistemology. Such cagey language is warranted because for Popper the exact nature of induction matters less than the significance it has for him. In essence, "induction" stands for everything that Popper is against, not only in science but also in politics: *blind conformity to tradition.*

An unintended consequence of Popper's typecasting as a wayward logical positivist or analytic philosopher is that his historically nuanced interpretation of scientific inquiry has been often overlooked. Consider his distinction in the contexts of scientific discovery and justification (or "validation", to use Popper's preferred term), the latter making no reference to a knowledge claim's original circumstances (Popper 1959: ch. 1; Fuller 2003: ch. 15). Popper fully recognized both how necessary and how difficult it is to draw the distinction in practice, since even canonical formulations of knowledge claims often bear hints of their origins and aspirations, which can then easily bias evaluation. Although Popper regularly protested the fuss that positivist and analytic philosophers made about semantics, he himself was very alive to the implicit dangers of taking knowledge claims on their face. A seemingly innocent expression like "Newtonian mechanics" suggests that the theory in question is the legitimate heir of the work of the great late seventeenth-century physicist, an impression that may serve to inhibit challenges to the theory's foundations.

However, unlike the positivists, Popper did not demand a complete regimentation of the language of science. Rather, he proposed that knowledge claimants specify a "crucial experiment" – namely, a situation in which two empirically comparable theories predict opposing outcomes under agreed test conditions (Popper 1959: chs 3–5). Thus, Popper believed in the methodological but not the theoretical unity of science. Put in more philosophically grandiose terms, Popper was an epistemological but not an ontological unificationist. (This point is most developed in Popper 1972.) Popper appeared to believe that we are entitled to our private realities, except when we expect others to abide by them as well. In that case we are obliged to specify what the anthropologist and cybernetician Gregory Bateson (1972), with a nod to the pragmatists Charles Sanders Peirce and William James, dubbed "the difference that makes a difference". In other words, what would it take for you to come to believe something that up to this point only I believe? For Bateson this phrase defined what it means to be "informative" to a given receiver, which is exactly in the spirit of Popper's proposal.

The tricky question for Popperians has been how to understand and institutionalize the outcome of crucial experiments. Francis Bacon, the early seventeenth-century Lord Chancellor of England who originated the idea, clearly intended it as a peaceful settlement to religious disputes that would otherwise – and eventually did – lead to civil war. This was the spirit in which Kant dedicated the second edition of the *Critique of Pure Reason* to Bacon, a fact that bore heavily on Popper's interpretation of Bacon's achievement. Here one might say that Kant saw epistemology as resolving metaphysical disputes – such as those involving theology, medicine and law that he later denounced in *The Contest of the Faculties* (1798) – in the way that Popper now wished the falsifiability principle to settle disputes between rival scientific hypotheses that, left to their own devices, would spin themselves into self-certifying *Weltanschauungen*.

Bacon seemed to imagine that the experimental outcomes would become the property of the state, contributing to a common body of knowledge available to govern society in a more rational and less violent way. Indeed, Bacon's proposed "House of Solomon" is arguably what the Royal Society would have become were it a branch of the civil service rather than a chartered corporation. But otherwise, the larger theoretical frameworks responsible for the competing predictions would be allowed to flourish among their self-organized adherents in civil society. From today's standpoint, scientific disputes in this Baconian regime would seem to be very similar to political disputes, with theoretical frameworks functioning as political parties in modern democracies that survive regardless of their record of electoral success. However, there would be a decisive difference. Whereas the tendency in modern democracies has been towards fixed-interval elections, regardless of the achievements or failures of the ruling party, the sort of scientific "election" implied by crucial experiments for Bacon and Popper is an epistemic "vote of no confidence" that could be raised by an organized opposition at any time.

Notice what is *not* being affirmed here – namely, the winner-takes-all sense of dominance and overriding sense of intellectual purity that is characteristic of a Kuhnian paradigm. For Bacon and Popper, people may form beliefs however they please but the resulting theoretical vision (or "metaphysics") becomes a matter of public concern – and hence a candidate for knowledge – only once a formal challenge is made to an opposing theoretical vision. However, the outcome of that challenge is understood as a gain for the public storehouse of knowledge that works at once to enable and constrain subsequent claims to knowledge: all theoretical visions may draw on this knowledge to advance their interests. But equally, if they wish to contest other theoretical visions they must take this knowledge into account when formulating their bids.

We see here the source of Popper's instinctive antipathy to induction: It is to the very idea of a "legitimate heir" to a well-corroborated scientific theory. For Popper, the whole point of science is that there is no presumption about what counts as an appropriate extension of a theory. In that sense, a theory is no more than a conventionally organized and

158 Epistemology as philosophy of science

strategically focused body of evidence aimed at extending inquiry. Here Popper's stance is usefully contrasted with that of W. V. O. Quine, who also recognized that the body of evidence in support of one theory could be equally used to support another, even contradictory theory. Quine's considered view of this so-called underdetermination of theory by data was, like Goodman, to plump for a conservative presumption that favours the theory that saves the phenomena with minimal epistemic disruption (Quine and Ullian 1970: ch. 6).

Quine, rather like John Dewey (1910), was inclined to regard science as technically enhanced natural cognition, an activity focused on "problem-solving" understood in the rather limited sense of biological adaptation, in which an organism optimally "solves" a problem given by the environment by doing whatever it takes to enable the organism to continue as it has up to that point. In such cases, the "problem" is whether the current case can be addressed entirely in terms of past experience or requires a different frame of reference. Omitted is the more radical possibility that a different frame of reference is needed for *both* past and present cases. In that case, the problem would be treated less as a localized block than a symptom of some deeper disorder that would precipitate what Kuhn called a "paradigm shift". In that case, the subject actively contributes to the construction of the problem-space for which she then finds a solution. In effect, by arriving at a new understanding of her past, she opens up a new horizon of epistemic possibilities, the next generation of normal science puzzles. But unlike Kuhn, Popper was more impressed by those who discovered than solved problems.

Popper was one with the logical positivists in stressing science's tendency to break with default ways of knowing, even within science itself. In other words, a Kuhnian paradigm shift was precisely when science came into its own as a form of knowledge distinct from the dogma promulgated by propaganda ministries in religious and secular regimes. This attitude reflected the lasting impression that the early twentieth-century revolutions in relativity and quantum theory left on the intellectual youth of the time. Recall that in 1919, when Einstein's general theory of relativity passed its most widely publicized empirical test (i.e. that light would appear to bend around the sun during a solar eclipse), the positivists were beginning their academic careers and Popper was still a teenager. In effect, they saw the epistemic horizons of the physical universe reconfigured by an empirically successful redefinition of the problem-space of physics. Moreover, two of the seminal logical positivists, Rudolf Carnap and Hans Reichenbach, had entered philosophy as refugees from physics just when it presented relatively short-lived but significant resistance to relativity. They went on to promote philosophy as defending a scientific attitude in the face of not only various irrationalist and pseudo-scientific tendencies in Weimar culture but

Epistemology as philosophy of science   159

also the default conservatism of the scientific establishment that had ostracized them.

Popper's steadfast opposition to presumption in science may be understood partly in terms of this common sensibility that he shared with the positivists. However, he went much further, refusing to see science as itself a "foundation" on which truth is constructed that in turn might be used as the basis for the conduct of public life, if not the governance of society more generally. Here it is worth recalling the literalness of the logical positivists' "positivism". The Vienna Circle Manifesto, "The Scientific World-View", not only openly acknowledged inspiration from Auguste Comte – the man who aspired to have science exert an authority comparable to that of the Roman Catholic Church in its heyday – but also urged the insertion of vanguard scientific ideas in an envisaged rational reconstruction of post-First World War Europe. These insertions ranged from living spaces to communication systems: that is, from Bauhaus architecture to "Isotype", a visual Esperanto – or "universal slang", as Otto Neurath put it (Galison 1990).

In contrast, Popper's adherence to science was always less to its particular first-order theories than its second-order *attitude* towards the world – that is, a rather content-neutral sense of the "scientific world-view" in which experiment functions as a technically enhanced version of Socratic inquiry, as opposed to the positivist impulse to clarify and propagate scientific ideas that have been already secured by technically approved means. A long-term consequence of this subtle but important difference is that Popper and his followers – most notably, Paul Feyerabend – often found themselves on the less popular if not losing side of many of the leading scientific controversies of the day, including the mind-body problem, the scientific standing of Darwinian evolution, and especially the consensus – the so-called Copenhagen Interpretation – that quickly formed around quantum mechanics in the 1920s, which finesses the ontological implications of Heisenberg's Uncertainty Principle by reducing the goal of physical inquiry to improvement in the prediction of the outcomes of physics experiments. This concordat effectively sealed off from direct scientific consideration wilder yet empirically supported interpretations of what transpired in the key experiments – including radically constructivist views of reality, parallel universes and action at a distance. To be sure, discussion of these theoretical possibilities continued apace but only semi-connected to developments in the empirical side of the physics.

Unlike other philosophers of science who are normally called "conventionalist", Popper regarded the conventional nature of scientific knowledge claims as a standing challenge rather than a *fait accompli*. In other words, conventionalism was less interesting as an alternative theory of the epistemic foundations of science than as an indication of the ease

160   Epistemology as philosophy of science

with which alternative epistemic foundations could be found for science. Here one might say that Popper and his followers exploited the reflexive implications of conventionalism to turn it into anti-foundationalist theory of epistemic foundations (Sassower 2006). It is from this standpoint that the philosophy of science known as *instrumentalism* appears as anathema. For Popper instrumentalism is when science loses its existential boldness and slips into "mere" technology, rendering it intellectually sterile and a pliant tool for the powers that be (Popper 1963: ch. 3).

The spirit of Popper's critique of instrumentalism is worth noting as the mirror image of what Pierre Duhem found attractive in the position: On the one hand, Duhem the committed Catholic followed Galileo's chief inquisitor, Cardinal Robert Bellarmine, in welcoming instrumentalism's humble realization that scientific inquiry could never resolve fundamental differences in theoretical horizons, thereby keeping the door open to faith – hence, Duhem's brand of theism is called "fideism". (An updated version of this sensibility is van Fraassen 1980, esp. ch. 7.) On the other, Popper denounced instrumentalism for selling short science's potential, effectively shoring up whatever happens to be the current paradigm. To be sure, the Catholic Church might justify instrumentalism as a piece of pure realpolitik: Social order is best maintained by opportunistically co-opting the dominant theory by allowing it a carefully delineated domain within which to pursue its inquiries, as long as it does not stray into matters of ultimate spiritual concern. But is such a mollifying attitude necessary in avowedly open societies? Can we not afford to take greater intellectual risks? Popper clearly thought so, which is why he treated instrumentalism as the counsel of those who lack guts and/or imagination.

Contemporary philosophy of science has not seen the problem of instrumentalism in quite this way, mainly because it has not seen it as a problem for instrumentalism – but for realism. This shift in the burden of proof was made possible once philosophers defined instrumentalism as explicitly neutral with regard to the theories that guide scientific research, resulting in a theory-neutral sense of "empirical success". The realist is then forced to defend the value added by science trying to do more than simply achieve and extend such empirical success. However, prior to Hume, it is difficult to find anyone other than Francis Bacon who thought that instrumentalism might provide an adequate account of science on such grounds alone (Laudan 1981: ch. 6). Even Bacon would have realized that the instrumentalist's notion of empirical success trades on a conflation of the mark of success and the means by which it was achieved – that is, a point about theory testing and a point about theory choice. After all, the record of empirical successes chalked up by a science remains the product of a particular history of inquiry (aka Goodman's entrenchment), even after all traces of that process have been removed from official presentations of the science for purposes of further extending and applying its empirical base.

In this respect, as economists would say, instrumentalism is dedicated to masking science's "path dependency", which in turn makes its accounts of science especially vulnerable to the grue paradox. Put another way, for Popper, instrumentalism encouraged a lack of historical reflexivity, what Hilary Putnam (1978) dubbed the "pessimistic meta-induction" from the history of science: that is, if history is our guide, then the foundational explanatory theories of the sciences are likely to be superseded in a century's time, without necessarily undermining the cumulative character of their findings. On this basis, Popper's marching orders to scientists are clear: Hasten history's course by speeding up the rate of criticism. However, these orders cannot be followed if instrumentalist philosophers discourage scientists from accentuating their theoretical roots, which open them to competing ways of organizing (much) the same data to point in different epistemological and ontological directions. Underlying Popper's sensibility here is an existentially rooted anti-foundationalism – namely, the belief that because we could have reached comparable levels of empirical success by alternative theoretical means, we should not fear losing our genuine epistemic achievements by radically changing our theoretical premises on the back of a falsified prediction or some other major empirical setback. Such an attitude permits an epistemic confidence that welcomes regular shifts in paradigms – in science *and* politics.

The key to Popper: the psychologist who never really left the lab

In formulating his philosophical views, Popper may have been helped by not having been formally trained in physics. His PhD was in educational psychology under the supervision of Karl Bühler, a pioneer in the experimental study of "imageless thought", the subject matter of what we now call "cognitive science", which is concerned with forms of consciousness oriented towards an object that is not present to the mind in the manner of a proxy observation (Berkson and Wettersten 1984: ch. 5). Bühler was a product of the Würzburg school, which histories of experimental psychology nowadays tend to present as a transitional stage between Wilhelm Wundt's original sensation-based version of introspective psychology, from which the Würzburgers revolted, and the more holistic but objectivist vision of psychology pursued by the Gestalt school, which most Würzburgers eventually joined (for a good comprehensive philosophical history of the transition, see Kusch 1999: pt I).

In the wake of Kripke (1977), we may think of the objects of "imageless thought" as making "semantic" but not "pragmatic" (or "speaker's")

162 *Epistemology as philosophy of science*

reference. In other words, one seeks an object that satisfies a certain definite description or a solution that meets a specific set of disciplinary criteria without necessarily possessing a mental image from a previous encounter with the object of inquiry. Note that even if the object in question has not been previously encountered, nevertheless most if not all of its defining properties may have been. However, the properties emergent on their combination that uniquely identify the object remain unknown until the object is correctly encountered, which in turn marks the consummation of the act of thought. Popper's account of science as historically extended organized inquiry may be understood as a theory of imageless thought writ large. It provides a context for understanding his dogged refusal to assimilate "verisimilitude" to subjectivist notions of probability, which are too strongly anchored in prior expectations (e.g. Popper 1963: ch. 10).

For a precedent, when the French *philosophes* Turgot and Condorcet characterized the overall "progressive" movement of history, the term they used was *tâtonnement*, based on how they understood how buyers and sellers agree prices so as to clear the market, a process that they believed was continually re-iterated as the economy expanded (Rothschild 2001: ch. 6). A century later Léon Walras abstracted from their historical considerations to make *tâtonnement* the basis for general equilibrium theory, the cornerstone of neo-classical economics. A century after that, Pierre Teilhard de Chardin (1955) appropriated the same term for his version of creative evolution. *Tâtonnement* literally means groping in the dark. It is easy to think of either a settled price (*à la* Turgot) or some "omega" species (*à la* Teilhard) as the object in question. The idea also helps to explain two of Popper's metaphors for the search for truth, one being mountaineers aiming for the same peak via different upward trajectories and the other being the searchlight that a hypothesis shines on nature during an experiment with the aim of revealing whether the sought object has been found (ter Hark 2009). It captured the "world 3" character of objective knowledge, which Popper explained as a long-term, largely unintended consequence of the exigencies facing our collective existence. We enter this realm of being, which transcends the worlds of both matter and mind, when we turn our attention to problems solutions to which are presupposed by our ability to solve the sort of real-world problems that involve the direct engagement of human designs with material outcomes (Popper 1972). In this way science was born – starting with mathematics as a sphere of inquiry independent of its applications (Fuller 1988: ch. 2).

Karl Bühler held the chair in experimental psychology at the University of Vienna just when Sigmund Freud's psychoanalysis, the discipline's private sector competitor, had itself reached its peak of local

Epistemology as philosophy of science   163

influence (Ash 1987). This bit of history helps to explain Popper's rather schizoid attitude to psychology as a discipline in the development of his anti-inductivist views. Never one to neglect youthful experience as a source of philosophical insight, Popper reported a conversation he had in 1919 (aged 17) with Alfred Adler, then Freud's most publicly recognized disciple, whose ideas about the "inferiority complex" and "lifestyle" would dominate the reception of psychoanalysis in post-Second World War America. At the time, just before going to university, Popper was working as a social worker for a Viennese inner city youth project under Adler's auspices. What turned Popper off psychoanalysis was the ease with which Adler could diagnose a child's problems by the simple matching of hearsay to past clinical experience without having examined the child directly. Given that this conversation took place at a party in Adler's home, the rather earnest Popper may have overreacted to his host's bluff manner (Hacohen 2000: 92). Nevertheless, the episode became one of Popper's set pieces for explaining how he came to demarcate science from pseudo-science (e.g. Popper 1963: ch. 1).

By all accounts, Adler was a purveyor of socially progressive views, including egalitarianism in matters of class and gender that eventuated in his expulsion from Freud's circle. In this respect, his politics were quite close to those of the young Popper. However, Popper detected a clear difference between Adler's egalitarian ends and the inegalitarian means that he used to pursue them. In particular, Adler's exceptionally broad – and seemingly exceptionless – explanatory account of psychodynamic development amounted to a high-minded prejudice that circumscribed his interpretation of the child's response to treatment. Thus, a child who failed to respond well to improvements in his or her social environment would be diagnosed as engaged in resistance. There was no question of the original diagnosis having been at fault. The child previously stereotyped as irredeemable remained stereotyped, but now as redeemable under scripted conditions. Given the trust that both politicians and parents placed in Adler, his word carried enormous weight – all the more reason the young Popper found Adler's casual generalization of his clinical practice irresponsible.

Though little remarked, it is striking that when Popper wanted to stress the critical moment of scientific inquiry, the word that always came up was *risk*. Adler never placed his ideas at risk because he could not cede the epistemic privilege of his track record, which was after all the basis of his livelihood. A proper test of his track record to see whether it was based on science or superstition – that is, a genuine causal understanding of children's problems versus a series of lucky guesses – could result in an embarrassing outcome that would result in his losing reputation and hence clients. How much more convenient, then, it is to generate

164 Epistemology as philosophy of science

a pre-emptive feeling of success for any new case, so that if – or when – difficulties arise, social workers are ready to limit any damage to that expectation by excusing, marginalizing or papering over potentially discrepant outcomes.

Ethnomethodologists call this activity, in which the young Popper was loath to become involved, "repair work" (Garfinkel 1967). Its prevalence in everyday life is often cited as evidence that the normative structure of society needs to be actively constructed on a moment-to-moment basis. On this basis, Wittgensteinians and ethnomethodologists have often made common cause in forging a philosophy–sociology alliance in STS under the rubric of that protean term, "constructivism" (Lynch 1994; Sharrock and Read 2002). But whereas Wittgensteinians focus on the conceptual point that, at any moment, a social practice may be taken in any number of different directions, given that its track record may be justified by any number of theories, ethnomethodologists alight on the empirical observation that prior commitment to one such theory can be maintained in the face of any number of outcomes. In both cases, the "normativity" of logic alone appears to pass for that of society, such that what is not logically prohibited is presumed to be socially permissible, so that one simply needs to see what happens in practice.

Such a position is normally dismissed as oblivious to any standards of conduct that the agents may have learned, let alone long established power relations, that intercede between what is logically possible and socially permissible. When sociologists counterpose a "structuralist" or "macro" perspective to the individualist micro-orientation of ethno-methodology, this is what they mean. To be sure, some of Popper's animus can be explained this way, given his default sympathy for social-ism, which led him to keep a studied distance from the more libertarian tendencies of the political economist Friedrich Hayek, the two of whom, in their common opposition to totalitarianism, joined sides on a "my enemy's enemy is my friend" basis (Hacohen 2000: 481–82). Not sur-prisingly, Popperians have excoriated the sort of sociology that would normalize, if not valorize, a process that systematically turns a blind eye to problems deeper than what social agents are normally willing to sto-mach to get on with each other (Gellner 1979: ch. 2). It is one thing to admit that the truth can never be determined with certainty, but quite another to encourage the studious avoidance of testing what one currently presumes to be true. The latter reduces politics to politeness, as tact passes for "tacit knowledge".

But Popper's objections to the probity of "repair work" run deeper in ways that can be explained in terms of his early study of psychology. Popper believed that we are born holding many false ideas about the world, which only come to light as we conceptualize beyond what is necessary for our biological survival (Petersen 1984). In this respect, the epigraph to Popper (1963) is an instance of philosophical insight generated by ironizing irony – which is to say, taking the original statement straight. Popper starts *Conjectures and Refutations* with Oscar Wilde's "Experience is the name that everyone gives to their mistakes". While Wilde was clearly remarking on people's seemingly endless capacity for self-justifying repair work, Popper took the quip to mean that it is only by making mistakes that we acquire "experience" in any epistemically meaningful sense. Everything else is simply operating by default, whereby responsiveness to the external world is, from an engineering standpoint, a redundancy designed to remind us of the original script that we are supposed to follow.

Put this way, Popper is making an ontological point, trying to draw a clear line in humanity's status as what, in the early twentieth century if not today, would be called *machine* and *organism*. A machine maintains itself by virtue of having been programmed to respond to various anticipated states of adversity, whereas an organism can alter the terms in which it confronts adversity, even if it cannot alter its own programme (cf. Rosen 1999: ch. 17). Thus, Joseph Agassi (1985), perhaps Popper's most faithful follower, has built an entire philosophy around the idea that a science turns into a technology once its horizons are limited to where it is reliably effective. Practitioners of such a risk-averse body of knowledge are acutely aware of their comfort zones (aka conditions of applicability) and are determined to stay within them. The mystique of expertise in the public sphere is arguably constructed in just this way (Fuller 2002: ch. 3), which in turn implies that it can be experimentally deconstructed once experts are encouraged to engage in even slightly counterfactual speculations (Tetlock 2005). The machine-like character of expertise also helps to explain the instinctive Popperian revulsion to epistemic deference that has become so popular in analytic social epistemology (Diller 2008), which we shall discuss in more detail in the context of epistemology as sociology of science. The problem here is less to do with the "experts" trying to maximize the applicability of their expertise than with the "laity" falling for the bait-and-switch of thinking that their distinctive knowledge interests are adequately encompassed by any such expertise (Fuller 1988: ch. 12).

Metaphysically speaking, such mechanization becomes a problem once it starts to replace, rather than enhance, the organic dimension of our being. Before the Scientific Revolution, one might say, the problem was trying to get Christians to think of themselves as more than mere divine machines. The revolutionary breakthrough was to infer from a fairly literal Biblical understanding of humans as creatures "in the image and likeness of God" that we are also mechanics, just like God, capable of reverse engineering reality back to first principles. The secular descendant

166   *Epistemology as philosophy of science*

of this attitude remains in the scientific impulse to reduce empirical complexity to the constrained application of a finite set of laws. In the aftermath of the Scientific Revolution, the main problem has been to ensure that we do not slip back from this state of species confidence, this time to an atheist version of the pre-revolutionary condition, a sort of Epicurean revival. It could still happen, in response to the massive risks we have incurred over the past four centuries in the course of reconfiguring our relationship to the environment. The signs are already there, as discussions of global justice are increasingly influenced by the "precautionary principle", which implies the existence of inherent limits to our capacity for action. To Popperian eyes, this principled attempt to circumscribe our "ecological competence" is itself worthy of severe test, which I have been pursuing as the "proactionary principle" (cf. Fuller and Lipinska 2014).

The problem of assessing Popper's philosophical fortunes

Popper's philosophy of science has survived primarily as a glorified rhetorical device – albeit one deployed to great effect, though not necessarily by Popper himself. Foundational experimental work on the presence of "confirmation bias" in the psychology of both lay people and experts starting in the 1970s presumed falsifiability as the normative scientific attitude – which those experiments then proceeded to falsify (Tweney *et al.* 1981: pt IV). Around the same time, early sociologists of scientific knowledge made great sport of the fact that famous scientists bore witness to Popper's heroic image of them as "permanent revolutionaries", while ethnographic studies of normal scientific practice revealed little evidence of falsification in action (Mulkay and Gilbert 1981). Notwithstanding these empirical embarrassments, some who remained convinced that the Popperian ideal captured the spirit of scientific inquiry started to question whether it could be realized in an individual human being: Perhaps a specifically organized social group or a computer programme might prove a more appropriate vehicle (Fuller 1993: pt III).

But even scientists who claim the efficacy of falsificationism in their own fields tend to infer – in a rather un-Popperian way – that because major past scientific errors and even misconduct could be reasonably traced to a failure to falsify one's pet hypotheses, it follows that falsificationism was behind those who escaped such ignominy and perhaps came to be celebrated. This false dichotomy is especially operative in popular presentations designed to demarcate "science" from "pseudoscience". After all, it is usually not too difficult to show that purveyors of "pseudoscience" have clever ways of shielding their hypotheses from direct

Epistemology as philosophy of science   167

refutation. But left unsaid is that practitioners of "science" are usually no less adept. This pleasant superstition has been carried along by a rather loose sense of "falsification", in which an accidental discovery might count as a "falsification" even without specifying the prior theoretical claims that the discovery has supposedly contradicted. People are surprised all the time, sometimes significantly – but attributions of significance presuppose a context for making sense of the event. A surprising outcome that arises under surprising circumstances does not count. Thus, Popperian falsification requires explicit experimental stage setting, at the end of which one can state which one or more previously plausible hypotheses have now been excluded from further consideration.

In short, for all their pro-science attitudes, Popperians are inclined to bet against the scientific consensus. They are most definitely not Lockean "underlabourers" (cf. Fuller 2000b: ch. 6). Indeed, Popper's former student from the London School of Economics in the 1950s, George Soros, the financier-turned-philanthropist, must count as the person who has most successfully internalized his anti-inductivist world-view. Trained in the arts of arbitrage, Soros has managed to stay in business by assuming that, for any commodity, half the market overvalues it and half undervalues it. This means that a profit can be made simply by falsifying both: that is, buying low and selling high. The question then is when the two opposing errors are sufficiently discrepant that one can make the biggest killing. The trick is to figure out what the philosophical version of Soros's winning strategy might look like for a revival of Popper's fortunes.

Compounding the problem of assessing Popper's philosophy is that his own normative judgements about science, as well as those of his followers (especially Paul Feyerabend), tended to veer substantially from those of the scientific orthodoxy. In particular, they erred on the side of levelling the epistemic playing field. To be sure, a cautious falsificationist like Imre Lakatos (1970) worried that Popper's ethic made it too easy to eliminate new competing theories before they had a chance to develop. Nevertheless, as can be already seen in Popper's early encounter with Adler, in practice Popperians have more often aimed their fire on established theories that tacitly incorporate dogmatic elements that render them unfalsifiable. Indeed, they have pursued pseudo-science in a spirit rather opposed to that of most other philosophers, who appear to start with agreed intuitions about what counts as pseudo-science and then differ over the principles of which they run afoul (Hansson 2008). In contrast, Popperians pursue their principles and let the cases fall where they may. In this way, even Lakatos (1981) himself ran roughshod on the scientific establishment's self-understanding by defining the task of the philosopher of science in terms of the "rational reconstruction" of the history of science – the suggestion being that despite science's historic epistemic

168 *Epistemology as philosophy of science*

successes, it could have proceeded much more efficiently had it followed some sage philosophical advice.

Another point that should not be underestimated is the Orwellian historiography that is practised by analytic philosophers of science in their current "postmodernist" phase (cf. Agassi 2008: 158, n. 55). As in the case of Michael Friedman mentioned above, these philosophers tend to be grounded in physics – just like Kuhn, the positivsts and the Popperians – but now with a twist: They treat physics, if not exactly as a historically closed science, nevertheless as a discipline that is no longer the vanguard for others to follow. In particular, thanks to Nancy Cartwright, a very un-Popperian thinker who nevertheless holds Popper's old chair at the London School of Economics, and Friedrich Stadler of the Vienna Circle Archives, Popper's original sparring partners, the logical positivists, have been given an intellectual facelift. As a result, we learn that, despite their renowned rhetoric of "unity of science" and "verificationism", the positivists are now seen as having recognized the epistemologically problematic nature of these concepts, indeed, appreciating the "disunified", "context-bound" and "socially responsible" character of science in ways that just so happen to anticipate the standpoint of the historical revisionists (e.g. Cat *et al.* 1996). Thus, a previously marginalized positivist, Otto Neurath, now emerges as the central figure who anticipated many of Popper's criticisms of the movement – yet again obviating the need to credit Popper properly.

5 Epistemology as sociology of science

In search of the "will to science": from religious inspiration to remunerated research

Robert Merton (1970) and Lewis Feuer (1963), two philosophically minded sociologists and contemporaries at Harvard in the 1930s, arrived at radically different views about what might be grandly called the *will to science* – more specifically, the affective foundations of the seventeenth-century Scientific Revolution. Their differences were enacted in a fraught encounter at the 1956 meeting of the Eastern Sociological Association in New York (Cushman and Rodden 1997). Following Max Weber, Merton argued that Puritan asceticism fostered the necessary self-discipline, now divested from the overbearing authority of the Church of Rome, to enable a comprehensive investigation of nature through experimentation and close observation. The crucial premise – sometimes hidden in Merton's own argument – was that a literal reading of the Genesis-based belief of humans as created *in imago dei* suggested that "we", understood as a species rather than as particular individuals, are likely to succeed in coming to grasp God's plan. Thus, Calvin's Elect was secularized as – to recall a slogan of Newton's that Merton later refashioned for his own purposes – the lucky giants on whose shoulders others great and small subsequently stand. This premise justified the long, arduous and often seemingly pointless work of day-to-day research, central to what Kuhn (1970) later characterized as "normal science".

Feuer countered this with an updated version of a view popularized by Cornell University founder Andrew Dickson White (1896) in the wake of the controversies surrounding Darwin's theory of evolution – namely, that the Scientific Revolution marked an end to the "Dark Ages", a fundamental break from religious attitudes altogether. In particular, Christian routines of self-denial were replaced by a hedonistic openness to a material world that we fully inhabit, a sensibility that Feuer interpreted as a shift in humanity's existential horizons from pessimism to optimism. To be sure, Merton had not denied science's latent optimism. However, he saw its role as sustaining collective effort towards a goal, the beneficiaries

170   *Epistemology as sociology of science*

of which would most likely be not a given generation of scientists but their glorious successors who finally fathom the divine plan. In contrast, the optimism that Feuer attributed to the Scientific Revolution was ultimately self-consuming; namely, the capacity, unfettered by religious orthodoxy, to ameliorate the human condition in one's own lifetime by inventions and discoveries that minimize ambient pain, while increasing personal convenience. Both Merton and Feuer could easily cite the founder of the scientific method, Francis Bacon, for their own purposes. But where Merton clearly saw the Scientific Revolution as culminating in Newton and fostering an ideology of progress that secularized the Christian salvation narrative, Feuer's scientific exemplar from that period is Spinoza, whose spirit has informed the increasingly prominent participation of Jews in science over the last 350 years (most notably Einstein), where "Judaism" stands for the most earthbound and naturalistic of the Abrahamic faiths.

How to resolve this disagreement? First, there is no denying that the Renaissance revival of Epicurean philosophy – its atomic view of nature, its hedonistic conception of all animal life (including humans), and its scepticism about any transparent sense of cosmic design – helped to launch and propel the Scientific Revolution. Disagreement arises only over the spirit of Epicureanism's adoption: Did it destroy and replace the Christian world-view or was it simply assimilated, leaving most of the Christian assumptions intact? That is Feuer *v.* Merton in a nutshell. Clearly there is a hermeneutic problem here. Natural philosophers of the period rarely stressed points of conflict between Epicureanism and Christianity in their own thinking. That was left for opponents who accused them of "atheism", the sacrilege of which largely rested on its perceived psychological aberration (Febvre 1982). But difficulties in imagining sincere and sane atheists must be offset against a decline in substantive references to divine agency in nature – though that may be explainable as an expedient to avoid intractable doctrinal disputes. Merton takes this general line, namely, that Epicureanism was incorporated into a self-disciplining Christianity that subsequently privatized and then secularized matters of faith. In return, Christianity tamed the overriding role of chance in the Epicurean worldview, which had inclined it towards fatalism (Fuller 2008a: ch. 5). The legacy came in the form of probability theory, a field where theologians played a formative role, as they attempted to resolve the uncertainties involved in deciding to believe in God as well as explain how even stochastic processes in nature appear to operate within discernible limits. It is from these roots that modern subjective and objective conceptions of probability, respectively, derive (Hacking 1975).

For his part, Feuer pointed to a freer, anti-scholastic style of discourse that had taken hold in the sixteenth and seventeenth centuries that he associated with the unfettering of the human imagination from the yoke of dogma. In addition, Feuer attempted to portray Merton as outright denying an emotional basis to the Scientific Revolution. But to be fair, Merton was simply operating with a different account of the cognitive work of emotions, one indebted to the Italian political economist and early sociologist Vilfredo Pareto, for whom all ideologies (including scientific ones) are sublimated versions of fundamental affective ties to the world (Shapin 1988). Feuer presupposed a more phenomenological understanding of emotion that led him to doubt the reliability of official professions of faith made by early Royal Society members as indicators of the lives they actually led, given background information about the times – and sometimes the members themselves. What Feuer quite happily explained as hypocrisy on the part of these so-called Puritans, Merton understood in terms of a subtle, perhaps only semi-conscious, retooling of religious beliefs for scientific purposes that over the next two centuries became an unwitting vehicle of secularization. Of course, it is easy to imagine truth on both sides of the argument, but the main question of interest to the psychology of science is which one better explains the character of science as it has actually come to be practised. Here Merton ultimately has the upper hand but the contest is subtle.

On Feuer's side, the Scientific Revolution was striking in its antipathy to the sort of disciplinary specialization that Kuhn (1970) and others have seen as the hallmark of scientific progress. Indeed, many of the seventeenth-century revolutionaries would regard such specialization as a sterile scholastic holdover. To be sure, the period featured many Biblically inspired "trees of knowledge" – not least from Francis Bacon himself – that rationalized various divisions of cognitive labour. But as if to anticipate the "modular" approach to the mind favoured by today's evolutionary psychologists, Bacon organized the pursuit of knowledge to match the organization of our brains, so that we could learn quickly about the world so as to lead optimally adapted lives together. This meant that disciplines had to correspond to innate mental functions, which the artificially defined disciplines of the scholastic curriculum had distorted. Thus, Epicurean sympathizer Denis Diderot was convinced that the future history of science would consist in incorporating more embodied, praxis-based forms of knowledge (i.e. the chemical, biological and social sciences) to supplement what he believed was Newton's overemphasis on our abstract formal capacities that were exhaustively elaborated in the mechanical world-view. Thus, when designing the Enlightenment's great editorial project, *L'Encyclopédie,* Diderot gave arts and crafts unprecedented visibility as forms of knowledge – but understood *à la* Bacon as extensions of memory, not *à la* Newton as applications of physics (Darnton 1984: ch. 5).

172 *Epistemology as sociology of science*

However, what ultimately gives Mertonian asceticism the upper hand are three distinctive features of the "research" orientation to modern scientific inquiry, namely, its *collective, trans-generational* and *indefinitely extended* character. The sociologist Randall Collins (1998) has drawn attention to the emotional energy that sustains intellectual networks, such self-generated and largely self-maintained enthusiasm, which seems to favour Feuer's hedonic approach. But Collins also recognizes that more must be involved to distinguish science from, say, philosophical schools or, for that matter, religious sects. After all, many of the metaphysical ideas and empirical findings of modern science were also present in various intellectual social formations in ancient Greece, India and China. Yet by our lights there seemed to be relatively little appetite for improving and adding to those insights to produce a cumulative epistemic legacy. If anything, while superficially tolerant of diverse perspectives, those societies inhibited the development of science beyond the level of a concrete project, a hobby or other self-consuming activity – out of fear that might otherwise result in self-perpetuating disciplines that claimed to producing reliable higher-order knowledge of greater social relevance than that provided by established authorities (Fuller 2010: ch. 2). Thus, despite their technical and cultural advancement, Greece, India and China lacked a sense of the scientist as a distinct kind of person whose primary social identity might derive from affiliations with like-minded people living in other times and places – and hence potentially subversive of the local power structure. This distinctive pattern of affiliation marks the unique social role of the scientist, popularized by Max Weber in the twentieth century in terms of "science as a vocation" (Ben-David 1971).

Let us delve more deeply into research as the form of intellectual work that is distinctive to science. Like its cognates in French (*recherche*) and German (*Forschung*), the English word *research* carries connotations that distinguish it from older and more general notions of *discovery* and *scholarship*. In what follows, I elaborate these differences and then identify three crucial transition points from scholarship to research as a mode of inquiry, and offer some observations about research as a collective project of indefinite duration. Captured in etymological perspective, the differences in the psychological constitution of discovery, scholarship and research are as follows:

- *Discovery* suggests the revelation of something previously hidden, possibly forgotten, typically for a long time. This perhaps captures the oldest sense of knowledge in the Western intellectual tradition, traceable to the Greek *aletheia*. A discovery usually carries life-transforming significance because it purports to get at the original nature of things that are intimately connected to the inquirer's identity: We find out who we really are by learning where we belong in the great scheme of things. At the same time, while in the words of Louis Pasteur, "Discovery favours the prepared mind", there is probably no method, let alone logic, of discovery. Indeed, discoveries are often portrayed in quasi-miraculous terms as products of a receptive mind encountering a serendipitous event. The implication is that a discovery – as opposed to an invention – points to a reality that is never fully under the inquirer's control.

- *Scholarship* suggests a familiarity with a wide range of established sources, the particular combination of which confers authority on the "scholar". Scholarship thus tends to focus on the personality of the scholar whose powers of discrimination are akin to those of a connoisseur who collects only the best works to perpetuate the values they represent. This makes scholars natural bedfellows of editors and curators. Although some scholarship makes claims to originality, its value mainly rests on the perceived reliability of the scholar's judgement of sources. On this basis, others – especially students – may then use the scholar's words for their own purposes. In this respect, the idea of scholarship already implies a public function, as if the scholar were conducting an inquiry on behalf of all humanity. This point is reflected in the traditional academic custom of annual public lectures and public defences of doctoral dissertations.
- *Research* suggests a potentially exhaustive process of inquiry whereby a clearly defined field is made one's own. An apt metaphor here is the staking of a property claim bounded by the claims of other property-holders. The researcher undergoes doctoral training to acquire a licence to exploit the field for all the riches it contains. This training equips the researcher with methods designed to economize on effort to allow for the greatest yield in knowledge. Whereas the character of scholarship is *individual* yet *public*, that of research is *collective* yet *private* in that it is tied less to the intrinsic significance of what is investigated than the effort invested in the activity, ideally as judged by fellow researchers. (The application of the labour theory of value to the intellectual world?) The transition between scholarship and research is most clearly marked in its public justification. The researcher typically needs to do something other than a version of her normal activities in order to demonstrate usefulness to others because of the inherently specialized nature of research.

Clearly, discovery, scholarship and research are overlapping concepts. For example, research can enhance the conditions of discovery by producing inquirers whose minds are sufficiently disciplined to recognize the true significance of an unanticipated phenomenon. For Kuhn (1970), such recognition constitutes an "anomaly" for the researcher's "paradigm". Moreover, as the information scientist Don Swanson (1986) has observed, relatively little of published research is read, let alone cited. In effect, researchers unwittingly manufacture a vast textual archive of "undiscovered public knowledge" whose depths may need to be plumbed by scholars who, equipped with smart search engines and other "data mining" tools, could then discover solutions to problems that researchers in the relevant fields themselves believe still require further original work. In addition, if Derek de Solla Price (1986) is correct that research activity has so rapidly intensified since the end of the Second World War that most of the researchers who have ever lived are alive today, then for better or worse it would follow research publications mostly manufacture opportunities for knowledge rather than knowledge as such.

Also implied in the above account is that discovery, scholarship and research may correspond to specific phases in the life cycle of scientific activity. Thus, "discovery" refers to the original prospective phase of epistemic insight, "research" to the ordinary work that Kuhn called "normal science", and "scholarship" to the retrospective significance assigned to scientific work. The phenomenon of "undiscovered public knowledge" (Swanson 1986), which gives rise to the need for "knowledge management" (Fuller 2002), suggests that we may soon return to what had been the norm for doctoral level research, even in the natural sciences, prior to the final third of the nineteenth century – namely, the testing of a theory against *a body of texts* (Clark 2006). This reflects not only the surfeit of unread but potentially valuable written material but also the diminishing marginal rate of return on original research investment. Concerns about the unwittingly wasteful repetition of research effort had been already voiced in the 1950s, sparking the US National Science Foundation to pilot what became the Science Citation Index, which researchers were meant to consult before requesting a grant to ensure that they were indeed heading in a new direction (Fuller 2008b).

Implied here is the historic significance attached to establishment of academic journals, especially ones tied not to particular universities or even national scientific bodies but to internationally recognized scientific disciplines. This has greatly facilitated the conversion of scholarship to research by introducing criteria of assessment that went beyond the local entertainment value of a piece of intellectual work. One way to envisage this transformation is as an early – and, to be sure, slow and imperfect – form of *broadcasting*, whereby a dispersed audience is shaped to receive the same information on a regular basis, to which they are meant to respond in a similarly stylized fashion. This served to generate an autonomous collective consciousness of science and a clear sense of who was ahead and behind the "cutting edge" of research. However, there remained the question of how to maintain the intergenerational pursuit of a research trajectory, such that one can be sure that unsolved problems in what has become a clearly defined field of research are not simply forgotten but carried forward by the next generation. Enter the *textbook*.

National textbooks that aspired to global intellectual reach were a pedagogical innovation adumbrated by Napoleon but fostered by Bismarck. They have served as vehicles for recruiting successive generations of similarly oriented researchers in fields that Kuhn would recognize as possessing a "paradigm" that conducts "normal science" (Kaiser 2005). A relatively unnoticed consequence of the increased reliance on textbooks has been that people with diverse backgrounds and skills are regularly integrated into a common intellectual project, not least through the textbook's integration of textual, visual and other multi-media representations. In this way, the ancient and medieval separation of "head" (i.e. book-learning) from "hand" (i.e. craft-learning) is finally broken down: Text is no longer solely chasing text (as in humanistic scholarship, even today), and the skills needed for research design need not be captive to esoteric rites of apprenticeship. In this respect, the textbook has been most responsible for converting the research mentality into a vehicle for both the democratization and collectivization of knowledge production.

But beyond the internationalization of knowledge production that was enabled by the discipline-based journal and textbook, three moments can be identified as marking the transition from scholarship to research in terms of epistemic practice: (1) the *citation*, (2) the *doctoral dissertation* and (3) the *salary*.

1 *The citation*: Before the printing press enabled mass publishing, the growth of knowledge was slow in large part because authors spent much effort literally reproducing the texts to which they then responded (Eisenstein 1979). As books became more easily available and journals circulated more widely, such literal reproduction was replaced by referencing conventions, starting with the footnote (Grafton 1997). Whereas the medieval scholastics had written their commentaries on the margins of the pages of books they copied, early modern scholars dedicated the main body of their texts to their own interpretations, while citing and contesting source works and those of other scholars in often lengthy footnotes. This practice left the impression that scholarship was always a messy and unresolved business, such that whatever was allowed to pass without criticism was presumed true, at least until further notice. The shift from a separate realm of footnotes to author-date citations internal to the main text corresponds to the emergence of a research mentality. In this context, other researchers and their sources are rarely contested. At most, the validity of their work is restricted in scope. But normally such work is cited in service of a positive case that the researcher wishes to make for a hypothesis or finding.

176 *Epistemology as sociology of science*

2 *The doctoral dissertation.* In the older era of scholarship, a dissertation was seen less as an original contribution to knowledge than a glorified examination that provided the candidate an opportunity to display his own brilliance in the mastery of sources, which included the dismissal of alternative interpretations, themselves treated not as definitive refutations but as instances of wit, typically involving the placement of work by earlier authors in an uncharitably ironic light. And this is how it would be understood by witnesses to the dissertation's public defence. Thus, the elevation of a candidate to doctoral status did not by itself constitute a change in the course of collective inquiry, as a future doctoral candidate may ironically dismiss that doctor's arguments by reasserting the authority of the old texts. In this respect, knowledge in the world of scholarship certainly grew but without demonstrating any overall direction. Much of the humanities, including philosophy, arguably still operate in this mode. The doctoral dissertation shifted from scholarship to research once "originality" started to be stressed, a product of the Humboldtian reform of the German universities in the early nineteenth century (Clark 2006). The modern requirement that dissertations constitute an "original body of research" is meant to capture two somewhat different ideas: First, there is the Romantic view – endemic to the modern German university's ideological baggage – that research should be self-motivated and self-sustaining, something done for its own sake and not to serve some other interest. But second, there is the more classically scholarly view of "originality" that one gets closer to the original sources of knowledge by eliminating various interpretive errors and placing salient truths in the proper light. Newton, who by the mid-eighteenth century was already touted as the greatest human intellect to have ever lived, was seen as "original" in both senses: On the one hand, he laid out a conceptual framework for understanding all matter in motion based on principles that he himself had derived. On the other hand, he presented this framework as the *prisca sapientia* ("pristine wisdom") implied in Biblical theology, once shorn of its accumulated corruptions and misinterpretations.

3 *The salary*: Even today scholarship conjures up images of leisure, specifically of someone with the time to spend on reading and writing what he or she pleases. There is no sense of competition with others to reach some commonly agreed goal, let alone a goal that might provide untold benefits to all of humanity. Rather, scholars set their own pace along their own intellectual trajectories. In contrast, it is rare for a research agenda to be pursued by an individual working alone. But simply because research tends to be focused on problems of common interest, it does not follow that solutions will be quickly forthcoming.

Chance plays a strong role in whether research effort pays off for the people doing it. Indeed, major research breakthroughs typically come after many people have been working in the same field, proposing competing hypotheses, for some period of time. Even Newton famously admitted that he saw as far as he did because he stood "on the shoulders of giants". It was just this long-term perspective on the fruits of research that justified the need for researchers to be given regular salaries regardless of the ultimate significance of what they produced (Fuller 2010: ch. 3).

Several historical developments are indicative of this shift in mentality that makes salaries a reasonable form of remuneration for research. First, the segregation of teachers and researchers in separate institutions starting in Napoleonic France enabled research to be conceptualized as a full-time job in the civil service. In addition, the increasing need for complex specialized equipment in the natural sciences, starting with chemistry, forced a greater dependency of academics on support from the business community, which in turn opened the door to knowledge work being seen as a form of high-skill, high-tech industrial labour. The precedent was set by Justus Liebig's establishment of the first university-based laboratory at the Hessian University of Giessen in 1840, soon followed by William Thomson (later Lord Kelvin) at the University of Glasgow. A downstream effect, evident in the global ascendancy of German academic research in the final quarter of the nineteenth century, was the "Harnack Principle", named after the minister for higher education who argued that research institutes should be organized around individuals with ambitious yet feasible research plans even if others end up being employed to do most of the work (Fuller 2008c). This principle is still very much in force in the funding of research teams through the vehicle of the "principal investigator" who acts as an entrepreneur who attracts capital investment that then opens up employment opportunities for researchers, typically on short-term contracts. However, as we shall now see, the concept of expertise has been invoked to paper over the normative dissipation of science – Zygmunt Bauman (1993) likes the term "adiaphorization" – that has resulted from what is essentially an extension of the industrial division of labour into the cognitive and affective realms.

Science and expertise: natural bedfellows or mortal enemies?

Science and technology studies (STS) and social epistemology are types of social theories of knowledge that claim to be both "naturalistic" in method and "normative" in orientation. What is meant by the two

178 Epistemology as sociology of science

quoted terms can vary significantly and may occasionally overlap. "Naturalistic" may range over historical, social scientific and perhaps natural scientific (e.g. Neo-Darwinian) studies of epistemic activities. "Normative" may cover ultimate and auxiliary values that knowledge producers uphold in their own practice, refer to long-term tendencies of beneficiaries and victims or project ideals that are informed by history but may suggest a future that radically breaks from it. While I shall allude to my own views, starting from Fuller (1988), the rest of this chapter proceeds by critically examining two general trends in STS and the dominant school of analytic social epistemology that have resulted in "normative recession" – that is, a retreat from the classical philosophical aspiration of charting the growth of knowledge understood as "science" in the robust sense of systematically organized knowledge made universally available (Fuller 2007b: ch. 2; Fuller 2009a: chs 1–2). The train of the argument begins by showing that both STS and analytic social epistemology, in their own ways, reduce science to expertise, which they themselves then adopt as their own self-understanding. The chapter ends with a discussion of the ascendancy of Thomas Kuhn and Bruno Latour in this general train of thought.

Although science and expertise appear identical in today's postmodern world, not least in the literatures associated with STS and social epistemology, at least as practised by analytic philosophers (Kusch and Lipton 2002), they have been regarded as antithetical forms of knowledge in both the ancient and the modern world (Sassower 1993). The ancient Athenians associated science (*epistemé*) with the contemplative life afforded to those who lived from inherited wealth. Expertise (*techné*) was for those lacking property, and hence citizenship. Such people were regularly forced to justify their usefulness to Athenian society. Some foreign merchants, collectively demonized in Plato's dialogues as "sophists", appeared so insulting to citizen Socrates because they dared to alienate aspects of this leisured existence (e.g. the capacity for articulate reasoning) and repackage them as techniques that might be purchased on demand from an expert – that is, a sophist. In effect, the sophists cleverly tried to universalize their own alien status, taking full advantage of the strong analogy that Athenians saw between the governance of the self and the polis. Unfortunately, Plato, the original spin doctor, immortalized Socrates' laboured and hyperbolic rearguard response to these sly and partially successful attempts at dislodging hereditary privilege.

In any case, science and expertise led a more harmonious existence in the pre-modern Christian era, as everyone was expected to live by the sweat of their brow, an aspect of the labour theory of value that joined Thomas Aquinas to Karl Marx. Medieval monasteries were the original communes, in which the monks alternated between contemplating God and taking turns at the scriptorium and/or the vineyard. A privatized version of this ethic came to be known as the "Renaissance Man", as exemplified by the careers of Leonardo da Vinci and especially Galileo. In this context, the boundary separating science and expertise became more porous, specifically enabling technical arts of instrumentation and experimentation to become constitutive of scientific inquiry itself. The Royal Society of London famously institutionalized that attitude.

However, the unprecedented achievement of Newtonian mechanics led many Enlightenment thinkers to conclude that science had nearly reached the limits of human comprehension, such that our ingenuity is best spent on making the most of this knowledge through applications that ameliorate the human condition and extend our dominion over Earth. The Greek attitude had been turned on its head: Instead of science being the luxury of those who did not need to live by their expertise, expertise came to be seen as a political imperative to make the most of the virtually completed body of scientific knowledge. This shift in attitude was perhaps clearest in the case of mathematics, as championed by Diderot's co-editor of *L'Encyclopédie*, Jean d'Alembert, who regarded his discipline as an adjunct of engineering and political economy, a statistically driven search for tolerable error in socially relevant contexts – not a Cartesian quest for superhuman certainty (Collins 1998: ch. 13). The uncertainty of statistics was tolerable precisely because science, at least to the *philosophes'* satisfaction, had replaced theology as the foundation of knowledge.

This view of science persists in the legal incentives that modern states provide for inventors to turn the "laws of nature" to their advantage – not least in the Enlightenment's most enduring political legacy, the US Constitution, which names patenting as a civil right. A society that took seriously how wrong we might turn out to be about the laws of nature – that science is, in Karl Popper's phrase, an "unended quest" – would never have created a special category of "patents" that confers a privilege on invention beyond what can be fetched on the open market. Instead an invention would be treated as an ordinary good possessing only exchange value, not some deeper value from one's having worked over a parcel of common reality, aka "intellectual property". It follows that the sales registered for the invention prior to its market replacement would be sufficient reward, with no further need to grant the inventor some additional legal protection simply because he brought the idea to market first (Fuller 2002: chs 1–2).

The nineteenth century witnessed the reinvention of the university as the institutional seat of science and the guarantor of expertise, under the aegis of nation-states with world-historic aspirations. This development followed a "secular" and a "sacred" course, the former traceable through Wilhelm von Humboldt's promotion of philosophy as the synthetic

180 *Epistemology as sociology of science*

discipline of citizen education in Prussia, the latter through William Whewell's promotion of Newtonian mechanics as the Anglican Church's scientific face, which justified all other theoretical and practical pursuits. Where Humboldt wanted a curriculum that would shift student allegiance from the church to the state, Whewell aimed to ensure that the church remained relevant to a rapidly secularizing economy. In both cases, the university would "internalize the externalities" of a society that encouraged innovation without having anticipated its long-term consequences: expertise could not be based simply on the personal testimony of either the producers or the consumers of a purveyed good or technique. Rather, expertise must be underwritten by scientific principles, which the reinvented universities would be in the business of nominating, organizing, testing and promulgating (Fuller 2000a: ch. 6).

In the final quarter of the twentieth century, Jean-François Lyotard (1983) fashioned the phrase "the postmodern condition" to capture the "always already" doomed character of the university's mission. Here Lyotard made an invidious but persuasive comparison with the mythically "progressive" status that socialism had acquired, albeit sometimes by violent means, over roughly the same two centuries. For Lyotard "science" (understood as a unified body of knowledge instantiated in the university) and "society" (understood as a unified body of action instantiated in the state) were fictions that had outlived whatever usefulness they ever had in bounding developments whose very nature exceeded all attempts at bounding. Lyotard argued the point in largely empirical terms, observing just how much intellectual innovation in the recent past (e.g. computer science, molecular biology) occurred off-campus in heterogeneous research teams lacking any obvious disciplinary home. He concluded that what universities continue to mystify as "science" – understood as a version of what states continued to mystify as "society" or better still, "welfare" – is really the product of locally developed expertises, which universities – again as extensions of states – only later exploited to their own advantage.

Lyotard drove a stake into the heart of any project that drew sustenance from the Enlightenment legacy, a main beneficiary of which has been STS, notwithstanding Latour (1993), which "doth protest too much" in trying to distance STS's self-professed "non-modernism" from Lyotard's postmodernism. At a general level, STS adopts the standard postmodernist line of denying the canonical historical narratives of scientific knowledge production, not merely because they do not assign epistemic credit properly (as a Marxist might argue) but on the more principled ground that there is no privileged standpoint from which to tell the history of science, due to a lack of normative closure on the ends of science (Fuller 2000b: 365–78).

More specifically, the anti-university vision shared by Lyotard and STS may be contrasted with my own pro-university vision in terms of an analogy drawn from political economy. On the one hand, Lyotard sees the university as the appropriator of surplus value from the truly creative researchers and inventors who work in places kept apart – both conceptually and physically – from the university's inner sanctum, the classroom and the curriculum committee. On the other hand, I see the university as a vehicle of "epistemic justice", precisely through its educational function, which effectively redistributes knowledge-based advantage from the elite clients who are the primary beneficiaries of innovation to a student audience that has historically encompassed a broader range of backgrounds and interests. Thus, whereas Lyotard saw universities as commissioning expertise by granting it epistemic authority, I see them as decommissioning it by spreading that authority widely (Fuller 2009a: ch. 1).

Expertise as site for normative recession in analytic social epistemology

Over the past quarter of a century, analytic philosophy, perhaps *malgré lui*, has moved in a postmodern direction, though largely without acknowledging the corresponding world-historic trends. Indeed, analytic philosophy's two main conceptions of expertise are rarely distinguished, let alone perceived in mutual tension. One is Hilary Putnam's (1979) "linguistic division of labour", the other Philip Kitcher's (1993) "division of cognitive labour". While trading on the sociological idea of "division of labour", they nevertheless divide the relevant labour rather differently. Putnam's point is that speakers normally know what they mean from the context of usage, except for "hard cases" that require experts who spend their time studying what distinguishes p from $\sim p$. Implied here is a theory of expertise that would tell us to seek a physician only when we cannot manage our bodies by the usual means. In contrast, Kitcher's point is that reality is carved up into discrete expertises, such that our claims to know something are always already accountable to those who spend their time studying it. Implied here is a theory of expertise that would tell us to seek a physician on a regular basis, since prima facie the physician knows our body better than we do. Of course, in most cases, our own and our physician's judgement will converge – but the convergence matters, at least epistemologically.

What distinguishes Putnam's and Kitcher's positions? The difference here clearly matters for those who worry that things are done for the right reasons. However, if all that concerns us is that the right things are done, regardless of reasons, then Putnam and Kitcher merely chart alternative routes to destinations that will coincide in the vast majority of cases. The

182   *Epistemology as sociology of science*

sociology of knowledge gives us some initial insight into this matter, since Putnam (born 1926) and Kitcher (born 1947) belong to different generational cohorts. Putnam writes when Marxism was most respectable in Anglo-American academia (and Putnam himself would drop quotes from Mao and Althusser), while Kitcher writes in a post-Marxist, neo-liberal world (which does not think twice about using neo-classical economics to model the science system). Putnam's view presumes that we are epistemic equals unless shown otherwise, while Kitcher's presumes the exact opposite. Behind these presumptions are opposed social-epistemological worldviews that provide alternative answers to the question: Does our status as competent members of society *ipso facto* underwrite our epistemic authority? Putnam says yes, Kitcher no.

For his part, Putnam takes seriously that everyone enjoys equal access to reality. When people disagree, that is simply because they have different evidence at their disposal or weigh the same evidence differently, all of which is tractable to negotiations with other people who are in the same epistemic state. Call this the "primitive communist" approach to social epistemology. It implies that the need for expertise is limited to "technical matters", where an unusually prolonged focus on a specific topic serves to resolve uncertainty and disagreement. Although the Athenians held a notoriously elite view of citizenship, their attitude towards expertise was very much in this vein: mere *techné*. Thus, Plato and Aristotle praised expert craftsmanship for its capacity to realize in matter an idea that would otherwise remain inchoate in the client's mind. But there is no sense that the craftsman is either the source of the idea or the ultimate arbiter of its realization.

The conversion of *techné* to bureaucracy – from commercial trade to civil service – is a signature theme in modern German philosophy, starting with Humboldt, Fichte and Hegel. It is how the Athenian attitude came to be democratized. The German idea was to incorporate more people as epistemic equals through a proactive state-based educational system, with expertise relegated to increasingly detailed and potentially routinized administrative tasks. When Marx and Engels spoke about the "withering away of the state" under Communism, they were refashioning a phrase Fichte had used to chart this trajectory. Indeed, Marx and Engels saw the party carrying on the work of the university as expedited by the industrial development of labour-saving technology – provided that the social relations of production were wrested from capitalist control. In the resulting communist utopia, expertise would be on tap – in a black box? – to remove the drudgery as we explore the multifarious aspects of our humanity.

Before turning to Kitcher's rather different attitude towards expertise, two remarks are in order about Putnam's social-epistemological vision. First, I believe that, despite its empirical failure and unfashionable status, this vision takes seriously the fullness of our humanity. Its revival will not be easy, however, and the tenor of STS research goes largely against it. But "utopian" here should be interpreted to mean "difficult" or "against the grain" – not "impossible", let alone "wrong". Second, seen as a historically unfolding idea, this vision reveals the underrated appeal of an "instrumentalist" philosophy of science and even the "instrumentalization" of scientific practice. These notions presuppose that humans supply the ends on whose behalf those "instruments" would be deployed. By not building ends into the instruments themselves – that is, by denying that science as such or its constitutive practices have ends of their own – we as humans are given a potentially free hand to fashion the ends for ourselves. I say "potentially", of course, because the question of the "ends of science" gets shifted from something about how science intrinsically works to who has the right and power to deploy the relevant instruments without interruption. To be sure, the question of who "we" are remains subject to contestation – but no less so than the question of what it is about a practice that makes it scientific. However, the same question posed in political terms focuses the mind – and action – in a way that it does not when posed in metaphysical terms: The former is about what it takes to be free, the latter about what it takes to be determined.

For his part, Kitcher's conception of expertise is proprietarian, an extension of John Locke's version of the labour theory of value. No one can lay authoritative claim over a domain of reality, even the reality of one's own body, until they have worked it over with intensive study. For Locke, this position constituted, on the one hand, a criticism of the casual instrumentalization of persons allowed by the law of slavery and, on the other, an endorsement of the Protestant idea that persons are obliged to undergo the self-study associated with the cultivation of conscience and the adoption of discipline. The former removed an arbitrary royal privilege, while the latter constituted modes of enquiry that the Protestants had wrenched back from the pastoral mission of the Catholic clergy and, to a lesser extent, secular medicine. Locke, a physician notoriously intolerant towards Catholics, took the "empiric" (i.e. sceptical) view that allopathic intervention should be permitted under extreme circumstances after several physicians had been consulted. Such was the model for Locke's legislative prerogative over either royal edict or personal judgement in a just society (Romanell 1984).

There was a period from, say, 1700 to 1900 when the religious and scientific senses of "discipline" vis-à-vis the human body were largely the same. This period coincides with the secularization of conscience as consciousness, and the ascendancy of "introspection" as a putatively reliable mode of epistemic access. However, the route from Locke to Kitcher starts to get paved in the second half of the nineteenth century, when a

184 Epistemology as sociology of science

scientifically reinvigorated medical profession, including psychiatry, provided new secular grounds for claims to expertise over personal space previously held by the pastoral clergy. As a result, we now routinely defer to the advice of physicians without doing so out of the fear of God or the demands of slave masters. Officially, this decision to cede authority over one's own property – in this case, one's own body – to experts is supposed to be a free one.

Unfortunately, medicine and psychiatry have effectively hollowed out that decision by introducing new distinctions between, say, one's mind and one's body and even one's conscious mind and one's unconscious mind. The underlying idea is that all bodies and all minds (outside of consciousness) share more in common than their surface appearances would indicate, and what they share is more directly available to scientific inquiry than spontaneous experience. Consequently, we have come to approach our own bodies and minds less as seats of agency, let alone sovereign power, than as sites of investigation that are *terra incognita* until staked out by those who have undergone proper training. This typically involves restricting the significance of, if not undoing, the lessons of personal life experience. Such is the epistemic social contract to which lay people and experts agree in Kitcher's division of cognitive labour. It results in the familiar image of the history of science as the colonization of what the later Husserl (1954) called the "life-world". In our times, the lawyer Peter Drahos (1995) has observed the emergence of a second-order version of the same tendency in cyberspace under the rubric of "information feudalism".

So what gives the philosopher the right to pass normative judgements on science, especially those involving criticisms of science's social entanglements? Analytic social epistemologists such as Kitcher basically resort to saying, "That's just what philosophers do (for a living)". Implied here is a *primus inter pares* approach to the other disciplines, which leads them happily to cede authority to the scientific establishment on strictly scientific matters – indeed, "scientific underlabourer" is a badge of honour worn by analytic philosophers (Fuller 2000b: ch. 6). Thus, they confine their critical comments to areas where they can speak in a uniquely "philosophical" voice. This can leave someone who reads across disciplinary boundaries with a distinct sense of analytic social epistemology's artificiality. This point can be illustrated by considering two exchanges relating to social epistemology that were published in the journal *Philosophy of Science* in recent times.

The first exchange transpired at the 2001 Pacific Division meeting of the American Philosophical Association. On that occasion Janet Kourany (2003) argued that philosophy of science needs to recover its sense of social responsibility, which the logical positivists lost when they emigrated to the United States. Moreover, feminism is well poised to redress this normative deficit, not only due to its free-standing political commitment to social justice but also the sheer empirical fact that women constitute most of the human population and an increasing percentage of the scientific workforce and pool of research subjects. On closer inspection, however, Kourany's understanding of the matter turns out to be quite narrow. For example, the entire Marxist tradition – ranging from rather orthodox Bernalists (about whom more below) to such heterodox followers of the Frankfurt School as the early Habermasians of the "finalizationist" school (Schaefer 1984) – is omitted. Also missing is what might be called the "left" wing of the Popperian (e.g. Agassi 1985; Feyerabend 1979) and Kuhnian (e.g. Ravetz 1971; Rouse 1987) schools. Indeed, even within feminism itself, Kourany omits mention of fellow philosopher Sandra Harding (1986), let alone a philosophical historian of science like Donna Haraway (1991).

Common to these excluded sources – and here I might add my own work – is their relatively liberal appeal to substantive claims about the overall trajectory of the history of science. These in turn provide the pretext for a critique of contemporary science. To be sure, many of the claims, which turn on alleged power relations, are empirically contestable. But that fact simply underscores the extent to which these missing sources routinely blurred the boundary between philosophy and the special sciences. But Kourany is not one to blur boundaries. Instead she follows Helen Longino – more about whom below – in grounding her sense of critique in the bare logical point of the so-called Duhem–Quine thesis of the underdetermination of theory choice by data, namely, that a given body of evidence can be deduced from any number of mutually incompatible theories. Armed only with that philosophical premise, Kourany concludes that we can and should promote forms of scientific inquiry that comport with our own values, especially her primary value, egalitarianism. But the underdetermination thesis at most necessitates a role for values in scientific theory choice but not which values they are. This does not disturb Kourany because she presumes that values by their very nature are subjective, which she glosses as "political". Kourany is not one to make ontological inquiries into whether things are valuable because we desire them or we desire things because they inherently possess value.

Nevertheless, whatever ultimate value science might have aside from its immediate practical value is arguably what the metaphysical dispute between realists and instrumentalists has always been about (Laudan 1984; Proctor 1991). For her part, Kourany simply takes instrumentalism as read, revealing the philosophical weakness of her argument, a point politely but firmly made in response by Ronald Giere (2003), himself one of the earliest and most consistent supporters of STS among analytic

186 *Epistemology as sociology of science*

philosophers of science. Giere insists on holding Kourany accountable to their shared analytic-philosophical scruples, which in this case requires strict agnosticism with regard to what might count as "politically correct" inquiry, absent a philosophically grounded argument about the ends of science. And here Pierre Duhem can be counted to testify for the prosecution. After all, when Duhem first proposed the underdetermination thesis roughly a century ago, he did not use it to try to convert his colleagues to his own Roman Catholicism. Rather, Duhem's polemical intent was to rebuff French Third Republic secularists who claimed that science had discredited the knowledge claims of theology.

The second exchange over social epistemology occurred in mutual reviews of two contemporaneous books by leaders in the field, Helen Longino (2002a) and Philip Kitcher (2001), both analytic philosophers of centre-left persuasion. Longino's strongest words of praise for Kitcher are indicative of the entire exchange: "one of the great merits of this book is that it shows how much scope for social and political considerations can be established on the basis of relatively canonical epistemological stances" (Longino 2002b: 568). Well, yes, and that is the *problem*. It seems that the main difference between Longino's and Kitcher's social epistemology of science turns on how the relevant social interests are identified so as to constitute what Kitcher calls a "well-ordered science". Kitcher (2002) is more concerned that all the relevant interests are adequately represented – by as many or few people as it takes – whereas Longino (2002b) is more concerned that people are capable of representing themselves in research that may impact on their lives. If Kitcher's social epistemology suggests that a benevolent philosopher-bureaucrat might design a well-ordered science all by himself, Longino's raises the spectre of direct democratic approval for each research proposal. These alternatives are reminiscent of the working conditions under which, respectively, the US and the French national constitutions were drafted in the late eighteenth century (Fuller 2000a: ch. 8).

Strikingly common to both accounts is a static conception of politics, as if interests were fixed, either objectively (*á la* Kitcher) or subjectively (*á la* Longino). Yet the stuff of politics is the organization of interests for the specific purpose of facilitating collective decision-making. Greater attention to institutional design – a topic now widely studied by sociologists, political scientists and economists – would have made this point clear. Two examples suffice. First, the identification of units of representation with geographical regions inhabited by roughly the same number of people, rather than fixed interest groups, continually forces both the represented and the representatives to think about their interests in terms of those of others. This staple of modern democracies has tended to encourage greater openness to change. While not an unmitigated good, it serves to minimize what under philosophical analysis might appear as irreconcilable value differences. A second example is the constitution of juries by parties relatively disinterested to the issue under deliberation who nevertheless must reach a binding agreement, as in so-called consensus conferences (Fuller 2006a: ch. 6).

Expertise as site for normative recession in science and technology studies

Generally speaking, Philip Kitcher's social-epistemological vision is one with which STS is largely – and regrettably – comfortable. The origins of this attitude lie in issues associated with the most influential school of sociology in early STS research: *ethnomethodology*. Forty years ago, ethnomethodologists had raised the question of knowledge "ownership", partly in response to a perennial problem in the politics of ethnography that had come to a head in the heightened academic consciousness of the 1960s: To what extent is the analyst accountable to the analysed? This problem arises because an ethnographer's subjects are potentially subject to the designs of her clients in government or business who have a vested interest in understanding the movements of such "natives", "deviants", or other key target groups. Does a good ethnographer in the name of "giving voice" to these groups end up betraying whatever secrets had enabled them to elude more powerful forces in society? The fact that even today cooperative subjects are called "informants" suggests that the problem has not been fully solved. In a heated debate with Howard Becker at the US Society for the Study of Social Problems in the 1960s, Alvin Gouldner accused ethnographers of illicitly appropriating the knowledge of vulnerable groups, effectively placing them at risk, while presenting themselves as champions of dispossessed countercultures (Fuller 2000b: 363). Were Gouldner alive today, he would probably make a similar argument against medical anthropologists who work for pharmaceutical industries on bioprospecting projects.

Against this critical backdrop, ethnomethodologists provided a self-protective scholastic response. Thus, Sharrock (1974) identified the possession of knowledge with the production of accounts of knowledge. Insofar as the accounts of the analyst and the analysed are produced in different contexts, in different words and for different ends (which may or may not be achieved), they are different pieces of knowledge, each owned by their respective producer, as a labour theory of value would have it. Ethnomethodologists were especially well-placed epistemologically to make this argument. They broke with traditional ethnography on two crucial points relating to their radical social constructivism. First, ethnomethodologists upheld a minimalist view of knowledge as whatever

188 *Epistemology as sociology of science*

passes for knowledge in a particular social context, without presuming, say, the prior existence of cognitive traditions, unless they are conjured up (discursively) in that context. Second, ethnomethodologists were notorious for their strategic interventions in ongoing social practices, very much in the spirit of experimentation, which deliberately undermined any notion that their accounts "mirrored" or even "represented" the subjects analysed.

At first STS seemed to adopt the ethnomethodologist's pose towards knowledge production unproblematically. The field made a persuasive case that it had staked out its own distinct domain of knowledge that drew on agents' first-order experiences but presented them in a fashion that was at once alien from yet illuminating to those agents. The exemplar of this moment is Jonas Salk's preface to Latour and Woolgar's *Laboratory Life* (1979), whose laboratory in San Diego provided the site for what remains *the* classic STS ethnography. While the book's language was hardly obscurantist by the standards of the late 1970s – the period when Foucault and Derrida were translated into English – it was nevertheless sufficiently indebted to discourses unfamiliar to either their subjects or those who might be interested in their subjects' activities to carry a strong sense of autonomy and integrity.

At the same time, however, the excitement surrounding early STS fed off the frisson of radical critique associated with the rhetoric of "alienation", which tapped into the rediscovery of the "young" or "humanist" Karl Marx, whose unpublished manuscripts were translated into English in the 1960s. This Marx tended to treat social, including economic, structures as alienated ideological formations – "reifications", to recall Gyorgy Lukacs's term – abstracted from concrete practices, or "praxes". The bellwether text was Peter Berger and Thomas Luckmann's *The Social Construction of Reality* (1966), which continues to be fondly cited by STSers of the 1968 generation regardless of their current politics. For a fleeting moment, the cunning of reason greeted the invisible hand: Cold War polarities appeared to self-deconstruct once Marx was revealed to have been an avid reader of Adam Smith before the latter became a capitalist icon.

However, this early flirtation with Marxism came back to haunt STS after the collapse of Communism and the onset of the Science Wars. These two events are connected by science's loss of default generous national funding, once the Soviet Union was no longer seen as a substantial high-tech security threat to the United States. In this shifted context, talk of "material practices" appeared to turn science into an activity whose own practitioners were its primary and perhaps sole beneficiaries. Here STS suggested that work done outside the laboratories was required for work done inside them to acquire scientific status. If so, should not the scientists themselves – rather than an already overloaded state – bear the burden of recruiting allies to advance any research programmes? Intentionally or not, STS promoted the idea that science had to be justified not in some general, long-term, collective sense but in terms of specific, short-term, constituency-based horizons: a shift from a state to a market vision of science.

For STS to evolve into a kind of "metascientific" expertise, an increasing proportion of those competent in the field should enter "science policy", broadly defined, to orchestrate this transition in the mode of science's societal justification. In fact, this has probably already happened. However, in practice, such people have effectively abandoned STS's research arena to an academically based community that has moved in the exact opposite direction. For those steeped in STS, this schism is exemplified in the contrasting trajectories of Bruno Latour (who articulates the ideology of policy-making STS) and Harry Collins (who articulates the ideology of academic STS), neither of which from my own standpoint is satisfactory.

Suppose we ask the pointed question: Who won the "Science Wars", the phrase that *Social Text* editor Andrew Ross (1996) coined for the increasingly visible clashes between scientists and STS practitioners and fellow-travellers in cultural studies that took place in the 1990s over the character and disposition of science in a post-Cold War multicultural world: "them" (the scientists) or "us" (the STSers)? From the standpoint of the normative criteria used in contemporary science policymaking, "we" seem to have emerged victorious. Whenever a funding agency evaluates a grant proposal in terms of the "users and beneficiaries" from outside the peer scientific reference group, STS expertise is vindicated.

Yet at the same time academic STS has increasingly cast its own expertise as simulating, if not approximating, the expertise of first-order science. Thus, Collins and Evans (2002) plot the history of STS as progressing through three stages: no expertise, interactional expertise and contributory expertise. Accordingly, STS charts its success by how much its researchers can contribute substantively to the projects of the scientists they study. Such a narrative would seem to imply that the task for STS researchers is to reinvent by exclusively sociological means the sorts of skills that science pedagogy normally – and more efficiently – provides. But why should sociologists interested in acquiring "contributory expertise" in a science not instead simply acquire a degree in the science? It would certainly be quicker than picking up the relevant knowledge by osmosis over many years by "interacting with" the relevant scientists. For a field like the study of gravitational waves, it would probably result in a more streamlined presentation than the 864-paged Collins (2004). Under the circumstances, the take-home lesson of "contributory expertise" for STS as an autonomous body of knowledge remains obscure if it is not denied altogether. "Contributory expertise" is an unequivocally *progressive*

190   *Epistemology as sociology of science*

moment in the history of STS only if the final court of appeal for the value of STS research are the scientists whom STS studies. In that respect, "they" won the Science Wars. (I shall return to the epistemological significance of the Science Wars in the Conclusion.)

And while Collins may have the most developed record of research in the STS study of expertise, his general orientation to expertise is implicit in how STS judges its own work. I belong to the first generation of people trained in the STS fields who were told that our intellectual credibility would be enhanced by mastering the science of which one would do the history, philosophy or sociology. Whatever one now makes of this advice (which I didn't take), it strongly suggested that STS research could only be as good as the mastery of the studied science that it displayed. Whatever distinctive slant or perspective STS provided was in addition to, and presumably detachable from, the show of scientific competence. Consequently, the least controversially excellent work in STS is by people – say, Donald MacKenzie and Peter Galison – whose intellectual calling card is technical virtuosity presented with a light theoretical touch. As it turns out, MacKenzie, Professor of Sociology at Edinburgh, is the heir of the Strong Programme in the Sociology of Knowledge that began the philosophical career of STS, while Galison, Professor of History of Science at Harvard, is the heir of the department that through its house journal *Isis* established the field as the humanist face of science in American academia through figures like Gerald Holton and I. B. Cohen.

Given MacKenzie's succession of research topics – statistical controversies in genetics, accuracy in military weapons, the computerization of mathematical proofs and the modelling of financial markets – it probably comes as no surprise that he began his academic career with a first class honours degree in applied mathematics from the University of Edinburgh. Indeed, if an overall pedagogical lesson is to be gleaned from MacKenzie's career, it is that very little sociology goes a very long way, if the STS researcher already possesses a first-hand understanding of the science she studies. For his part, Galison bypassed the circumambulations of Collins's "interactive expertise" by going native and acquiring a physics PhD alongside his doctorate in the history of science. He sees "theory" as providing shade and nuance to locally constrained practices, much in the manner of an artist whose technique compensates for potential deficiencies in the observer's perspective on an object (Galison 2004). What theory does *not* do is to place the object in a radically different light, potentially subjecting it to criticism.

Here it is worth recalling that the prehistory of STS consisted of people who approached matters from quite the other way around: They were already expert in the natural sciences and mathematics but they wanted to distance the nobler concerns of their disciplines from their secular

Epistemology as sociology of science   191

entanglements in the First World War, Second World War and Cold War. (I mean here to cover everyone from Rudolf Carnap to Barry Barnes.) That aim forced them to move into history, philosophy and sociology, disciplines that still allowed the expression of rapidly disappearing, if not entirely lost, normative ideals. To be sure the ideals promoted by, say, Carnap and Popper, Kuhn and Lakatos, Barnes and Bloor varied in detail. Nevertheless, they had a shared sense of the task – namely, to justify science by "natural philosophical" standards that Newton would have recognized as his own. However, these were not necessarily the standards to which most scientists in the twentieth century have aspired, let alone realized. Indeed, the prehistory of STS can be read as an invocation of the past to criticize contemporary science for being too fragmented, instrumentalized and otherwise fallen.

All of this stands in striking contrast to the decidedly "anti-critical" stance of STS vis-à-vis science in the wake of *both* Latour and Collins. For example, when MacKenzie (2006) writes of the "performative" character of economic models of financial markets, he is more concerned with how models succeed in shaping markets than with whatever power the models exert as critical forces, especially when they *fail* to shape markets. Yet the epistemic authority of economics, like that of medicine, is evidenced more in the guilt that society feels for failing to live up to its normative ideals than in the ease with which it can make society conform to its explanatory ideals. (Consider attitudes towards inflation and obesity: rarely managed but always regretted.) To be sure, in both cases the same models are at play but they are seen in rather different lights – specifically, in terms of what might be called the "vector of accountability": Are economists ultimately accountable to the markets they help bring into being, or are markets accountable to economists, whose criticism renders markets problematic in ways that demand a concerted social response? Economists in both cases may get their way, but it is only in the latter case that their expertise counts as an independent force countermanding other, locally based and typically elite, expertises.

Let us take stock by drawing together the various strands of the argument. Science and expertise are historically opposed ideas: The former evokes a universalistic ideal meant to be pursued in leisure, while the latter consists of particular practices pursued to earn a living. However, expertise can serve the universalistic ideal of science by undermining the authority of other expertises that would cast doubt on the viability of this ideal. Put bluntly, expertise is "progressive" only when it serves as the second moment of a Hegelian dialectic. *Contra* Lyotard and most STS treatments of science, I see the modern university – specifically through its teaching function – as the place where this moment most often happens. STS has failed to recognize that the project of "democratizing

192   *Epistemology as sociology of science*

knowledge" ultimately means that expertise is not to be conserved but actively decommissioned. It follows that what is still often valorized in STS circles as the "tacit" or "craft" character of expertise should be critiqued as a mystified version of what economists call "path dependency" – that is, in philosophical terms, an attempt by those who originated a robust body of knowledge to conflate the contexts of discovery and justification to maintain their initial advantage.

The challenge here to STS can be posed as an explicit research imperative: If we remain committed to the democratization of knowledge, we should always try to find some less costly alternative path to the modes of thought and action currently licensed by a given expertise – and then ask why that cheaper route is not already dominant. This drive towards intellectual efficiency includes rendering esoteric research pedagogically tractable, transferring skills from humans to machines, converting virtuosity into routine and reassigning the significance of the division of labour from its role in Kitcher to that in Putnam. It also means restoring *breadth* to its rightful place ahead of *depth* as a value in knowledge. We shall see in the next section that philosophers of science have been all too willing to abide by their own expert-centred epistemology, which in turn renders them uncertain allies in the research challenge I have posed to STS.

Learning from the past to redeem a normatively "fuller" social epistemology

In Fuller (2000b), I observed the paradox of Kuhn's achievement: On the one hand, he clearly recognized that the promotion of scientific progress depends on scientists recognizing the peculiar relationship in which they stand to their history; yet on the other hand, it never occurred to Kuhn to apply this insight to his own case, namely, someone who was trained in the dominant paradigm of his day but left it in order to pursue a career in the history and philosophy of science. What Kuhn failed to appreciate, or at least not properly acknowledge, is that scientists in his position might not so much be discarded by the dominant paradigm – as if they were the detritus of Hegel's world-historic spirit – as voluntarily abandon it because of what they perceive as an illegitimate turn in the paradigm's development. Kuhn clearly saw his departure from physics shortly after being awarded a doctorate from Harvard as an active rejection of the field's "Big Science" metamorphosis that he had experienced first-hand in the Second World War (Fuller 2000b: 395–96). Nevertheless, he treated the decision as being no more than of biographical interest – not an opportunity to theorize the distinction between corporate rejection and individual dissent in science.

Kuhn's use of history and philosophy of science as an "exit strategy" contrasts interestingly with that of another scientist-turned-metascientist of his generation, Freeman Dyson (2007), whose involvement in the Second World War did not result in his feeling the same sense of betrayal of physics's world-historic mission. Dyson began life as the most promising protégé of J. Robert Oppenheimer and Richard Feynman on the Manhattan Project, sharing their faith in the efficiency-based arguments for nuclear arms as a deterrent to conventional warfare. Without ever quite renouncing that faith, Dyson has spent the bulk of his career on just the right side of respectability while challenging orthodoxies in physics and biology about life's origins and prospects, typically by fuelling various contra-Darwinian currents, most notably the idea that human life could thrive indefinitely in completely artificial environments in outer space. It would be easy to read such a career ironically as apt atonement for having worked on the project that did the most to underscore the transience of the human condition on Earth. (For Dyson's evil twin, imagine a parallel universe in which the Nazis triumphed, or at least survived, and Albert Speer then out of a vague sense of guilt decided to devote his life to the support of indigenous peoples in "separate but equal" environments.)

The distinction between corporate rejection and individual dissent in science is subtle, entailing different styles of historiographic rationalization. The same situation may be equally characterized as science as a system casting off a dysfunctional part or science as a project losing sense of its mission and hence some of its original followers. The subtlety of this distinction needs to be kept in mind when trying to understand the relationship between the first-order sciences and the second-order "metascientific" disciplines like the history, philosophy and sociology of science. In effect, for all the lip service that continues to be paid to Kuhn, we have merely picked up his bad habits and none of his good ones.

By way of example, consider the following, which appears as the opening paragraph of a recent article that calls for the philosophy of science to become a genuinely "social epistemology" that might usefully inform public debate about science. I single it out because it captures very well a certain "post-Kuhnian" consensus in the philosophy of science that fancies itself to be alive to the social and historical contexts of science:

> There is no more interesting nor sobering chapter in the history of 20th-century philosophy of science than that which tells the story of the discipline's disengagement at mid-century from the social and political concerns that shaped its earlier years. In Europe, near the century's start, conservative Catholics like Pierre Duhem, social democrats like Ernst Mach, and revisionist Marxists like Otto Neurath all understood that science was

194 *Epistemology as sociology of science*

> central to the modernist outlook then asserting its cultural authority and
> that a philosophy of science must, therefore, among other tasks, theorize the
> manner in which science is embedded in a social, cultural, and political
> context and the manner in which it contributes to the transformation of
> the world.
>
> (Howard 2009: 199)

What's wrong with this picture? Briefly put, Don Howard damns with faint praise. It is only in hindsight that Duhem, Mach and Neurath can be so easily lumped together as "philosophers of science" who were engaged with the sciences of their day in order to make them more socially relevant. This characterization presupposes a sharp distinction between what is "internal" and "external" to science that they themselves were loath to admit. All three were trained as – and saw themselves as – practitioners of first-order natural and (in Neurath's case) social sciences, who were "philosophical" mainly in the sense of asking fundamental questions about the *modus operandi* of their disciplines, which in practice meant challenging institutionalized dogmas. As it turns out, each lost his battle and, in this respect, the identity of "philosopher" amounts to a consolation prize bestowed by later generations who implicitly concede that Duhem, Mach and Neurath were indeed wrong about strictly scientific matters but said some interesting things of a general nature nonetheless.

My historiographic squabble with Howard bears on the grounds on which philosophy of science can launch (or re-launch?) itself as a normatively "fuller" (excuse the pun) social epistemology. Drawing on Reisch (2005), Howard bemoans how the logical positivists were driven to increasingly formal and technical pursuits in the foundations of the sciences once they moved to the United States, through a combination of Communist paranoia and collegial spinelessness. (Interestingly, Howard underplays the rather more proactive suspicions of some pragmatist philosophers like John Dewey and especially his student Sidney Hook, who found the positivists' "unified science" agenda potentially subversive of liberal democracy.) He believes that this traumatic transatlantic adjustment set the tone for philosophy of science's politically quiescent attitude towards science in the second half of the twentieth century, out of which the field is now only emerging, thanks in part to the post-Kuhnian influence of history and sociology of science. Again, what is wrong with this picture?

As my comparison of Kuhn and Dyson suggests, the historiographically soundest answer to philosophy's normative legitimacy over science is not one that the analytic philosophy community normally countenances – namely, that philosophers of science adopt the normative standpoint of dissenting scientists. I mean specifically that they purport to uphold the same norms as those of the scientific community, but they accuse the community of having taken one or more wrong turns in the application of those norms over the course of history. The orthodoxy that defines who is in and out of the community merely masks the original error, which if anything has only intensified over time. On this view, philosophers of science, far from being supercilious outsiders, see themselves as directly implicated and affected by whatever mistakes they feel that the majority of their colleagues have made. Were Pierre Duhem, Ernst Mach or Otto Neurath resurrected now, this is the standpoint from which they would make their case.

Needless to say, mine is a controversial position because it dispenses with the usual relativistic pretence that philosophers and scientists are bound to understand science differently because of their different disciplinary perspectives. Instead philosophers and scientists are placed in explicit opposition as rival heirs to the same intellectual lineage. Philosophers are simply dispossessed scientists, and scientists no more than philosophers suffering from tunnel vision. In that case, one would expect philosophers and scientists to avail themselves of the same mix of conceptual, empirical and methodological arguments. Philosophers would not be limited – as they are today – to providing rival justifications for the same canonical historiography of science. (Here I allude to the various schools of "realists" and "instrumentalists" who disagree over everything except the exemplary episodes in the history of science that they need to justify.) Rather philosophers would continue to contest the research choices originally taken by scientists, since the presumptive correctness of those decisions underwrites the legitimacy of the dominant paradigm (Fuller 2003: chs 8–10).

To be sure, there are many styles in which this contestation might occur, most of which are in evidence in Popper and his followers. For example, at various points in his career, Popper was notorious in scientific circles for contesting the Copenhagen interpretation of quantum mechanics and Darwin's theory of evolution by natural selection. Here was a clear case of a philosopher issuing a first-order challenge to scientific authority by contesting whether scientists had applied their own norms correctly as they rallied around particular theories. Although the hardening of disciplinary boundaries in the twentieth century cast Popper from the outset as a "philosopher", he was operating in the spirit of Duhem and Mach, and a generation or two earlier would have been treated as they were, a dissenter from within the scientific ranks. Perhaps unsurprisingly, then, while Popper was admirably forthright in his criticism, he did not succeed in changing many scientific minds.

His students approached the matter more indirectly. In particular, Imre Lakatos's (1970) self-styled "rational reconstructions" of the history of

196   *Epistemology as sociology of science*

science aimed to show that, even if we grant that science is now where it ought to be, it could have arrived much sooner had it made more epistemologically perspicuous decisions along the way. Lakatos aimed to divest the history of science not of its content but of its necessity. In other words, scientists have managed to advance knowledge almost in spite of themselves, given their hit-and-miss ways. Ever the Hegelian, Lakatos believed that philosophy added modal ballast ("necessity") to a pursuit that might otherwise appear desultory. However, he shied away from claiming anything more than wisdom in hindsight – the Owl of Minerva taking flight at dusk – for his rational reconstructions. Paul Feyerabend (1975) pressed home this point by specifically tracing the haphazard character of the history of science not to scientists violating methodological rules but to their taking the rules too seriously, thereby overlooking that the balance of evidence vis-à-vis competing theories is bound to change over time with the introduction of new methods and instruments of inquiry.

However, more ambitious Hegelians like the left-wing British science activist John Desmond Bernal (1901–71) wanted to do more than simply use a philosophically informed understanding of history to highlight the limitations of scientists' current paradigmatic assumptions. Bernal explicitly followed Marx in believing that something like a Lakatosian rational reconstruction of the history of science could provide guidance on science's future trajectory, what nowadays is called "foresight" in science policy circles to suggest an epistemic symmetry with "hindsight". Bernal's *Social Function of Science* (1939), written at the peak of Western enthusiasm for the scientific promise of the Soviet Union, followed by the most comprehensive Marxist history of science ever written, the four-volume *Science in History* (1971), are worthy precursors of social epistemology and are among the earliest works in the sociology and social history of science. Yet Bernalism is nowadays presented as a colossal folly.

Before considering the nature of Bernalism's failure, the exact nature of the argument for what Bernal was happy to call the "science of science" is worth recalling:

1 The history of science displays an overall trajectory of progress, in that, on the whole, we deem it better than not that science has become increasingly prominent in world culture.
2 However, it is equally clear that the history of science could have proceeded more efficiently, which would have resulted in more benefits and less harms for more people.
3 By understanding the various retardant forces that have operated in science's past, we can plan so that neither they nor anything like them are operative in science's future.

This argument contains a hidden premise:

4 The difference between "necessary" and "contingent" features in the historical development of science corresponds to the distinction between its normatively "progressive" and "regressive" features.

The premise is recognizably Hegelian – but not exclusively that. It also reflects the confidence of a whole host of professedly non-ideological historians, philosophers and (Mertonian) sociologists of science who distinguished "internalist" and "externalist" approaches to science prior to the rise of STS (Kuhn 1977, Shapin 1992). For them an idealized account of science is *ipso facto* one that identifies what "really" makes science work. For most other human endeavours, this assumption would appear empirically ill-founded if not naïve. When does steadfastness of purpose guarantee desired outcomes? The answer of course is when there is an unlimited power behind the purpose, such that the end always justifies the means. Only spiritually driven projects in the Abrahamic tradition, and mainly in Christianity and Islam, have consistently had this "progress as purification" character, which in the twentieth century was secularized and technologically enhanced in the totalitarian projects of Communism and Nazism (Löwith 1949). Such projects do not countenance the prospect that, so to speak, any attempt to remove the dirt from one's dirty hands always acquires new dirt in the process.

Thus, Bernal held that scientists could free themselves from the corruption of priests and capitalists without falling into the arms of some other "external" force, as long as they constituted themselves as a high-skilled version of the universal proletariat who collectively set the terms by which science might be steered for the betterment if not perfection of humanity: in short, an updated version of the power for good that naturally flows from a community of true believers. This sentiment is already on clear display in Bernal's youthful science fiction work, *The World, The Flesh and the Devil* (1929), which anticipated the recent science policy turn towards "transhumanism", with its promised convergence of nano-, bio-, info- and cogno-technosciences as a strategy for "enhancing" human evolution in ways that will address long-term problems of economic productivity and national security (Freeman 1999: 126–31; Roco and Bainbridge 2002; Fuller 2011: ch. 3). The properly scientific society will not only cast aside atavistic institutions like the church and the market but will also increasingly turn away from the human body itself, at least in its natural state.

Of course, to Darwinian ears, "enhancing evolution" sounds less like utopian futurism than a Lamarckian throwback, as it privileges humans with the capacity to provide direction to a process that – at least

198   Epistemology as sociology of science

according to Darwin – is fundamentally purposeless, given the high element of chance that has been always at play in species survival. While such Darwinian scepticism is likely to become less compelling in the twenty-first century as we become more expert in reversing millions of years of evolution through biotech interventions (no doubt with unintended consequences), Bernal himself was accused of high-tech wishful thinking with his staunch support of the Soviet agricultural minister Trofim Lysenko, whose Lamarckian approach to agronomy was given free rein on ideological grounds, resulting in many decades of failed farm policies.

Without wishing to excuse Bernal's behaviour, I would draw attention to two aspects of the logic of his situation that show his clear grasp of the meta-level issues involved in social epistemology, despite his faulty first-order judgements:

1 Bernal in his scientific capacity ran one of the laboratories devoted to X-ray crystallography that contributed technical expertise to the quest to crack the genetic code. Like many involved in the early history of molecular biology, he was a physical scientist by training who moved into biology to tackle the ultimate questions surrounding the nature of life that Darwinists, due to their background in more ecological approaches to biology and geology, were inclined to leave shrouded in rather mysterious chance-based historical processes, which in turn gave the impression that artificial selection could never trump natural selection, and hence life could never be, strictly speaking, "manufactured". From this standpoint, Bernal may have prematurely seen in Lysenko's Neo-Lamarckianism a prototype for what is nowadays increasingly claimed – on empirically sounder grounds – for biotechnology.

2 Bernal in his philosophical capacity believed that science was a vehicle for the self-realization of humanity, in which Abrahamic talk of "spirit" was to be understood as a metaphorical rough draft for a project that would be brought to completion by dialectical materialism. In his own day, especially in the aftermath of the First World War, Bernal detected a fragmentation of scientific effort from this universalist aspiration that was largely driven by nationalist and capitalist concerns, the results of which increasingly destabilized the world order, measured in both military or financial terms. In this respect, Bernal regarded science as being in a "fallen" state pitted against society, and both suffering as a result. This perspective led Bernal back to visions of unified science put forward by the likes of Friedrich Engels and ultimately Lamarck (whose views Engels did not distinguish clearly from Darwin's) that were designed to redress various wrong turns taken in science's recent history.

The attractive feature of Bernal's perspective is that his construal of the problem of theory choice in science was not dictated primarily by either orthodox scientific opinion or, for that matter, a strong sense of evidential warrant. At first glance, this seems strange, since most versions of social epistemology practised by analytic philosophers fall back on some combination of authoritative expertise and evidential warrant to support normative conclusions about the direction that scientific inquiry should take. Bernal's rejection of these two epistemic staples reflects his realization that the value of evidence is relative to which authorities one takes seriously, which in turn rests on the reasons one has for pursuing science in the first place. After all, evidence that directly addresses a long-standing problem within a particular scientific field is clearly of high value only if that field is worth pursuing. Otherwise, one might be prepared to downplay or ignore such evidence in pursuit of other ends. In short, both expertise and evidence can be reasonably weighted on many different scales, but in any case the judgements involved are simultaneously scientific and philosophical.

Bernal often looks bad nowadays because he is inserted into a historiography of science that presupposes an axiological horizon quite opposed to his own. That horizon, influenced by Kuhn, takes the purposeless diversification of the sciences as an irreversible long-term tendency. Thus, Bernal's endorsement of Lysenko is typically faulted as an instance of ideological commitment clouding one's vision to unfavourable evidence, as if Bernal's project of unifying science to emancipate humanity were itself to blame. In contrast, I believe that merely Bernal's dogmatic attitude towards the pursuit of his project proved to be his Achilles' heel. After all, Bernal could have declared Lysenko a false prophet of human emancipation after enough crop failures and then moved on to seek new exemplars, instead of tying his project so closely to Lysenko's fate, or perhaps more generally the fate of the Soviet Union as the vanguard world-historic state. In any case, as the "cunning of reason" would have it, Bernal's legacy lived longest where it was most actively opposed, namely, in the scientific establishment norm of "communitarianism", Robert Merton's sublimated version of Bernal's original call for the formation of class consciousness among scientists of all nations (Mendelsohn 1989).

For a larger perspective on the implications of Bernal's normative failure for the history of STS, Gary Werskey (2007) offers a canny diagnosis that respects the intellectual brilliance and political efforts by Bernal and his colleagues on the scientific left. The Cold War division of the Allies into "Liberals" and "Communists" produced two competing scientific "Lefts" with universalist aspirations that spent the second half of the twentieth century squandering enormous financial and intellectual capital on campaigns of mutual suspicion that verged on "mutually assured

200   *Epistemology as sociology of science*

destruction", when they should have been focusing on their points of agreement in order to relieve global misery. The result, to which we bear witness today, is an overall shift to the right in the centre of political gravity that casts aspersions on much of what both sides of the Cold War stood for, not least the idea of science as an emancipatory force. Werskey astutely observes that much of our "postmodern condition", including the ideological cast of STS, can be understood in these terms. I also agree that the "subaltern" forms of knowledge championed by postmodernists may complement, but not replace, historically "Western" science in addressing global problems.

Nevertheless, Werskey skirts a very important blindspot of the Bernalists: They were not "democrats", in the civic republican sense of trusting ordinary people to decide matters of public import through the ballot box. This point is crucial to grasp today because characteristic of our postmodern condition, especially the actor-network theory that dominates contemporary STS, is the tendency to conflate democratic decision-making and consumer choice. To put the matter in terms of the "state/market" binary popularized by welfare economics in the Cold War (i.e. the failure of one elicits the need for the other), democracy is now normally found on the "market" side of the binary (Fuller 2006a: 63–67). The Bernalists unwittingly helped the postmodernists make this point by exemplifying the stereotype to which the equation "democracy = market" seems like a reasonable response. In particular, the Bernalists operationalized the scientific planning of society in terms of the co-optation of right-minded elite scientists to state ministries and select committees. They gave little thought to chains of accountability that reached back to the people themselves.

In terms of "democracy", my concern here is less that scientists constituting the planning board would not be statistically representative of all qualified scientists, let alone the society targeted by their policies, than that the Bernalists failed to see the need for the planning board to subject its judgement to regular public checks, as per elections. This does not deny the Bernalists' democratic credentials by more meritocratic criteria. They clearly believed that talent was equally distributed across social classes, which led them to campaign for "equality of opportunity" to enable the talented to rise up the ranks quickly (Werskey 1988: 243). However, such a policy amounted to a technocratically updated version of Plato's cultivation of philosopher-kings in *The Republic*. Plato also realized that those fit to rule might be of inferior birth and therefore must be given the opportunity to prove themselves (e.g. through examinations). But none of this – in either its Platonic or Bernalist form – challenged the overall vision that the best should be given absolute political authority over the rest.

Here it is worth recalling that the use of "proletarian" to modify "standpoint" or "science" by Marxist theorists after the First World War reflected a general distancing from – and disappointment with – the activities of the actual working classes who were supposed to have led the communist revolution. Consequently, "proletarian" came to refer to the relationship that the working class stands "objectively" (i.e. according to Marxist theory) to the means of production *regardless* of whatever beliefs or desires the workers themselves expressed. This soon generated a "vanguardist" mentality, now associated with high modernism, whereby a more enlightened non-working-class group might be better placed to provide subjective expression of the proletarian standpoint. The history of so-called Western or "critical" Marxism, which increasingly became the preserve of academic intellectuals, captures this transition, of which Bernalism was an important part. Thus, the Bernalists with their Oxbridge pedigrees believed that they might articulate a "proletarian science" better than a working class that had been seduced by capitalist aspirationalism.

In fairness to the Bernalists, however, it must be said that the adoption of the proletarian standpoint suits the scientific class in one sense, given the increasing relevance of scientific training to managing the means of production. Nevertheless, very often the science behind this training is of little more than symbolic value (i.e. a screening mechanism for employers in an overpopulated labour market), since the actual skills employed (e.g. in computer-based work) are just as mindless as anything previously required under industrial capitalism. Thus, the identification of science-based workers with the proletariat turns out to be literally correct – but with an ironic twist unforeseen by the Bernalists, namely, that they are the functional equivalent of the old industrial workers, their superior training notwithstanding. In that respect, the task of raising class consciousness has returned to where Marx and Engels started over 150 years ago.

An interesting symptom of Bernal's obliviousness to the fallibility of scientifically based political judgement appeared in his review of the second edition of Karl Popper's (1945) *The Open Society and Its Enemies* for the *British Journal for the Philosophy of Science* (Bernal 1955). He characterized Popper as a *philagnoist*, a neologism literally meaning "lover of ignorance". It is telling that Bernal took Popper's doubts about the certitude of scientific knowledge to be an embrace of ignorance rather than a recognition of fallibility. It is as if Bernal could imagine only two positions: acceptance of the (Bernalist) truth and its denial – but not its outright falsification. At the very least, this reveals Bernal's instinctive commitment to a positivistic, rather than a dialectical, conception of science, a point that even his admirers have been forced to concede (Rose and Rose 1999: 143–44).

More seriously, in terms of the various ways knowledge and power might be interrelated, Bernal seemed to conflate the *magnitude* and the *irreversibility* of science-based change in order to infer the inevitability of

202 *Epistemology as sociology of science*

social progress. Thus, Bernal accused Popper's piecemeal social engineering approach of "obscurantism" for ignoring the palpably revolutionary difference that modern science has made to our technical mastery of nature. Yet, for Popper, no public policy, however strongly backed by scientific developments, should ever propose social changes that cannot be reversed later, in light of the consequences. What a consensus of right-minded scientific elites gains in power, it does not necessarily also gain in knowledge. My point here is that Bernal's attempt to cast Popper as an anti-scientific thinker reveals Bernal's own limited conception of science's democratic accountability.

Bernal's fate is interestingly contrasted with that of the ecologist Barry Commoner, who figures as an icon of "critical science" in Ravetz (1971). Commoner was inspired by Bernal's *The Social Function of Science* to join the Bernalist American Association of Scientific Workers as a student at Harvard (Egan 2007: 19–20), an organization that Harvard president and soon-to-be Kuhn mentor, James Bryant Conant, saw as a Communist threat (Fuller 2000b: 162–64). However, Commoner's subsequent career can be read – from anti-nuclear to pro-environmental activism – as a call for scientists to shift their political base from the state to the populace. Armed with information supplied by activist scientists, the people could then become more directly involved in science-based decision-making. The result would be a scientific version of what the Protestant reformers urged vis-à-vis the Roman Catholic Church, in light of the Church's own internal problems, the general spread of literacy and the printing of personal bibles. Mindful of this precedent, I have used the phrase *secularization of science* to characterize an approach like Commoner's (Fuller 1997: ch. 4; cf. Fuller 2006b: ch. 13).

Commoner realized that the logical conclusion of his position was to allow the people a free vote on the role that science plays in their life. While this attitude displayed a patience and trust in the wisdom of the crowds, something that Bernal's vanguard elitism – more than any taste for totalitarianism – rendered him incapable of appreciating, it was not without its own faults. Commoner's fifth-place finish as the Citizens Party's candidate for US president in 1980 arguably played a spoiler role vis-à-vis Jimmy Carter comparable to Ralph Nader's role vis-à-vis Al Gore twenty years later. The former resulted in eight years of Ronald Reagan, the latter in eight years of George W. Bush.

The challenge ahead: the legacies of Kuhn and Latour as obstacles

The year 2012 marked the fiftieth anniversary of the first edition of Kuhn's *The Structure of Scientific Revolutions* and the twenty-fifth

Epistemology as sociology of science 203

anniversary of Latour's *Science in Action*, the two most influential works in STS. My attitude towards Kuhn and Latour and their role in the development of this field has changed in subtle ways over the past quarter-century, corresponding to the shape that "the new production of knowledge" (Gibbons *et al*. 1994) has taken in the aftermath of the Cold War. Overall I have been surprised – and disappointed – at the role that their two books have played in short-circuiting STS's normative impulse, including even the philosophy of science.

Asked back in 1987, just when "social epistemology" was being launched as an unapologetically normative project, I would have expected that by 2012 both books would be regarded as having provided useful historically and sociologically inspired correctives to the dogmatic simplicities of what was then called the "received view" of the philosophy of science (Suppe 1977) – but that in the end STS would consolidate as the successor discipline to the philosophy of science, a normative inter-disciplinary metascience of the sort articulated in Fuller (1988). Of course, nearly the exact opposite happened, something that I had seen by the time of Fuller (2000b), which, while officially about Kuhn's impact, also includes a substantial discussion of Latour's ascendancy in its chapter 7. The continuing influence of Kuhn (1970) and Latour (1987) illustrates beautifully the need for a reflexively applied social epistemology as a propaedeutic for any intellectual progress. To be sure, Kuhn lacked it, which may explain why he was unable to deal creatively with his success. In contrast, Latour (I believe) has understood the context of his reception quite well, though of course his response goes counter to what I would have wished! Nevertheless, the basic social epistemological point remains: you need to understand why such books by such persons at such times had so much influence in order to escape their spell.

Given the entrenchment of neo-liberal sensibilities since the publication of Fuller (2000b), I would now stress that Kuhn (1970) had been already warping normative sensibilities for more than a decade before the end of the Cold War. I allude to the "finalization" movement of German social theorists under Jürgen Habermas when he directed the Max Planck Institute for the Study of Living Conditions in the Technoscientific (*wissenschaftlich-technischen*) World (Schaefer 1984). They glossed Max Weber's autonomy of academic inquiry (as protected by tenured university employment) as Kuhn's self-organization of disciplines (as defined by the dominant paradigm). Whereas the former was meant to be comprehensively self-critical, the latter reduced criticism to troubleshooting. It left the impression that any substantial reorientation of scientific effort would have to come from outside science itself, because, following Kuhn, the finalizationists believed that science left to its own devices would continue to pursue technical puzzles increasingly removed from the outstanding problems of the human condition. As followers of Karl Popper quickly recognized, in the hands of the finalizationists, the role of "criticism" had morphed from being a defining feature of science's self-improvement to an external force to serve specific interests – first of the social democratic state and then (after 1989) of the more diffuse neo-liberal social order. The latter came to be championed as "the new production of knowledge" (Gibbons *et al*. 1994), in terms of which market-sensitive "mode 2" knowledge was now presented as an antidote to the paradigmatic rigidities of "mode 1" knowledge (Weingart 1997). Kuhn (1970) facilitated the smooth transition by casting scientists as natural born dogmatists whose single-mindedness inclines them to run their paradigms into the ground, absent the intervention of some relatively disinterested parties – be it the state or a client pool – capable of checking for diminishing returns on scientific investment.

The logical next step was to undermine altogether the ontology underwriting the internal/external distinction vis-à-vis science. That strategy, championed by Latour, turns science (or, more precisely, "technoscience") into multiple, partly overlapping, heterogeneous networks consisting of agents (including the state) that, depending on context, can be either producers or consumers of scientific knowledge – in a word: a market, if not *the* market. In such an environment, "science" is simply the name given to the most extended network. To be sure, this captures the general intuition that for many years we have lived in a world that has become "scientized" to its core (Fuller 2006a: ch. 5). Yet Latour's version of this insight loses – and encourages his readers to forget – the normative sensibility that lay behind the desire to keep science, in some sense, "autonomous" from the rest of society, even if its own practice has failed to live up to that ideal. (My own social epistemology takes off from this point.) As a result, STS has tended to discount the idea of science as a profession or an institution, the two main categories in terms of which the classical sociologists Emile Durkheim and Max Weber – and their main followers, Robert Merton and Joseph Ben-David – were inclined to see it. Indeed, a recent STS book on "the scientific life" goes so far as to argue that the ideal of autonomous science is a figment of the social scientific imagination that reflects social scientists' own historic anxieties about epistemic legitimacy that were never shared by more confident and free-wheeling natural scientists (Shapin 2008).

So how did Kuhn and Latour manage to get us to this state of normative meltdown, whereby science appears to be everywhere and nowhere at once? The basic move was to deny that "science" refers to a way of seeing the world, or even a univocal idea. In a manner not unlike what happened to the concept of species after Darwin, "science" no longer refers to a type of knowledge distinct from other types but to a population of knowers who know other things too. To be sure, this was most definitely not Kuhn's own view but it turned out to be a long-term unintended consequence of perhaps the most admirable feature of the story of the ascendancy of Kuhn (1970), namely, the intellectual matrix in which the book was conceived. Kuhn was the teaching assistant of Harvard President James Bryant Conant, who designed a "general education in science" curriculum in the wake of the Second World War, during which science scaled up in unprecedented ways that at once raised, if not exaggerated, people's hopes and fears (Fuller 2000b: chs 3–4). Drawing on teachers from across the university, Conant's strategy was to train introductory level non-science students to discern invariant features of the scientific mindset in practices as diverse as rolling balls down an incline plane and smashing atoms together in a cyclotron. He dubbed such discernment "science connoisseurship". The point would be to normalize science within the legacy of Western civilization – as opposed to allowing science to loom as a threat to civilization, as many humanists, clerics and ordinary members of the public were prone to see the matter after Hiroshima. Indeed, Conant wanted humanists, who were the bulk of these students, to become actively engaged in the future of science, just as they might any other aspect of public life.

It might be said that, after Kuhn and Latour, three assumptions underlying Conant's pedagogical project have been systematically, if not perversely, deconstructed: (1) Harvard trains tomorrow's elites, so they (not necessarily others) should learn the scientific backdrop of our civilization, because they will be the ones in control of our future; (2) only professional scientists know how to do science, but that is radically different from understanding what science should be for, a topic fit for elite humanists; (3) despite the institutional changes to science over the centuries, a core scientific mentality remains intact and needs to be preserved. In each case, a key binary has gone by the wayside, as STS's deconstructive mode takes the necessary interaction between two terms as revealing their essential indistinctness: respectively, elite versus mass, scientist versus non-scientist, science versus non-science. It is the dissolution of the third binary that concerns me most here.

It is common to locate Kuhn in the intellectual lineage that derives from William James's talk of "conceptual schemes" in guiding scientific inquiry, which was subsequently developed in more analytic terms by his student C. I. Lewis, who chaired Harvard's Philosophy Department in Kuhn's undergraduate days. Lewis may have even been the source of Kuhn's famous example of the Copernican Revolution (Kuhn 1957) as involving incommensurable world-views (Fuller 2000b: ch. 6). Conant, though more experimentally minded than these philosophers, continued to treat scientists' conceptual schemes as basically their cognitive

206 *Epistemology as sociology of science*

horizons. Thus, experiments were important primarily as a means of testing hypotheses generated from an overarching theoretical perspective. Kuhn's decisive break with Conant was less to do with "collectivizing" conceptual schemes as "paradigms" (as in the ritualistic invocations of Ludwik Fleck's "thought-collectives") than with downplaying their cognitive character in favour of a form of knowledge even more practical and embodied than that proposed by Harvard's own pragmatists. Whenever Michael Polanyi (1957) is alleged to be an influence on Kuhn's thinking, this is what is meant.

The primacy of "tacit" over "explicit" knowledge nowadays marks this transition, which the Edinburgh School amplified with readings of Polanyi and the emerging literature in cultural anthropology (e.g. Douglas 1970) that stressed meaning-making as the patterned movement of bodies in space and time. In that case, science is not an idea shared by, say, everyone working in a laboratory. On the contrary, scientists may hold quite different ideas about what they are doing. However, science is whatever turns out to be the emergent product of their harmonized interactions. It is then just a short step to reach the trademark Latourian conclusion that the very idea of science is the effect – not the cause – of scientific activity. Harry Collins has tried to arrest this intellectual slide by reinventing a relatively autonomous normative sphere of science within post-Kuhnian practices, called "expertise" (e.g. Collins and Evans 2007). But it captures only part of the classical concept of autonomy, which in the case of science pertained not only to its technical distinctness from other forms of knowledge but also its supervenience over them and, most importantly for my purposes, the self-directed character of its pursuit – the original legal aspect of academic life that was shared with the trade guilds as medieval "corporations" (*universitates*). This particular omission reflects a telling concession to Latour.

Indeed, in light of STS developments since the publication of Latour (1987), I would put the point more strongly: Latour has effected a transfiguration of values whereby the very idea of wanting to keep science somewhat autonomous from society is nowadays demonized as a refusal to recognize science's dependency on the rest of society – and nature. In a bit of Latourian Anti-Enlightenment Newspeak, "independence of mind" has come to mean "negligence of matters of concern" (Latour 2004). Instead of aiming for an ideal (e.g. "Truth" or some other endpoint of progressive movement) that regards the stuff before our senses as more-or-less means to this greater intellectual end, we should focus directly on our need for things as part of the never-ending quest to strengthen our networks. Latour (1988) has called this position "irreductionist", but that too is Newspeak: the entities proliferated in the name of populating an "ecology of concern" are of equal relevance to the maintenance and extension of the ecology's constitutive networks. Here Latour suggestively extends the ecologist's habit of treating all life-forms as "living" in exactly the same sense – but now to cover all *created* beings, not least human artefacts. As a result, the human organism loses any superior vantage point but is itself always in danger of dissociation from the environment in its quest for some spurious sense of self-purification or "transcendence". I would have thought that such a dogged attempt to tether everything to the same ontological plane, flattening any prospect of a meta-level perspective, is rightly called "reductionist". But I seem to be in a minority (Fuller 2007b: ch. 3). Overall Latour appears to have alighted upon a secular formulation of MacIntyre (1999).

A vulgarized version of the Latourian sensibility has planted the seeds of a counter-narrative of the history of Western culture – Luddism's anti-intellectualist evil twin, as it were – that blames our failure to exploit science and technology's full potential on a disdain for palpable things in the name of abstract ideas. The journalist Timothy Ferris (2011) has recently given it the Silicon Valley spin. On this reading, ideas do not steer but block our access to things. Rather than enabling us to be receptive to what the world has to teach us, ideas censor how and what we communicate. Ferris manifests little of the original constructivist animus, namely, that we might create the world in the image of our ideas by the application of will. But this is not to deny that he has academic fellow-travellers – such are the ways of "object-oriented-ontology", a popular Latour-inspired philosophical project spearheaded by an American in captivity in Cairo (Harman 2009). Political captivity has always been the breeding ground for fabulous, self-incapacitating metaphysics, in this case called "speculative realism", that seduces one into remaining a passive spectator – or "follower" – rather than an autonomous agent in the historical unfolding of reality. A spectator can simply luxuriate in the ontological excess, whereas an agent would need to make a cut in the flow to "participate" in the proper sense of that word.

A darling of the *Wired* magazine set, Ferris plays off "intellectuals" against "engineers", a distinction that eerily recalls the early public valorization of fascism. What intellectuals – not least Karl Marx – extolled as the capacity of ideas to provide unity amidst diversity, engineers (the preferred position) disregard as simply an excuse not to study how things work in practice. The most striking feature of putting things this way is Marxism's shift to the "intellectual" side of the intellectual/engineer binary. After all, half a century ago, as the writings of Bernal, Popper, Polanyi and Hayek could testify, the big hope/threat of Marxism was its "engineering" potential with regard to social and even scientific affairs. What has changed in the interval is a downsizing of the engineer's teleological ambitions to "tinkering", which in turn reflects a shift in overall metaphysical sensibility

208 *Epistemology as sociology of science*

from "determinism" to "indeterminism" – that is, from global to local teleology, from the reason of state to the wisdom of crowds.

To be sure, Latour was hardly alone in promoting this shift in worldview. In France itself, which since the days of Napoleon and Saint-Simon had treated the top-down civil engineer as a national hero, the change had been already signalled within the scientific elite. While Latour was conducting his original ethnography of Jonas Salk's biomedical laboratory in San Diego, which became the basis for *Laboratory Life*, a striking piece appeared in *Science* by the Nobel Prize-winning molecular biologist, François Jacob (1977). Jacob made a point of openly endorsing natural selection as an account of evolution (heretofore not a popular move in France) and then explicitly comparing its *modus operandi* to that of a tinkerer – as opposed to an engineer – a distinction he drew from Claude Lévi-Strauss's (1966) influential characterization of "the savage mind". Wittingly or not, Jacob anticipated Latour's later work by treating the modern top-down "engineering" mentality as an aberration that perhaps marks our humanity but is nevertheless ultimately subject to the rule of nature. I say "wittingly or not" because the spirit of Jacob's piece appears to be that our modernist engineering capacities might improve upon nature's endless tinkering (e.g. *à la* Church and Regis 2012), whereas Latourian narratives seem never to present that prospect. Instead, they suggest simply redistributing agency across ever-extending networks to accommodate new entities. Admittedly, for recent recruits to the neo-liberal academic labour market, such narratives are bound to prove attractive. But to me, this suggests that to promote a metaphysical horizon more conducive to a progressive scientific ideology, we must start by securing an institutional basis for autonomous inquiry that might encourage young academics to think of themselves as inhabiting a "progressive" world.

The trajectory from Kuhn through Latour to today's STS has made social epistemology's task increasingly difficult. It tracks the dissolution of the idea of knowledge as a public good. First, Kuhn reinforced – if not outright legitimized – the "path dependency" of scientific progress: a science's origins circumscribe where it can go; hence the inevitability of anomalies, crises and revolutions in science, which requires a new start – typically by new people. Latour then denied that science displays any clear sense of progress, other than simply enabling the indefinite extension of networks. Thus, science has descended from being a *public good* (the Enlightenment ideal) to a *club good* (Kuhn) to a *positional good* (Latour). STS typically places a positive spin on this trajectory: namely, that science is losing the hegemonic character it had acquired over the past two centuries by hybridizing with non-scientific agendas and forms of life. No doubt, STS has recorded and celebrated many interesting innovations. However, the price of this open-ended pluralism is that the normative regulation of both science and society has been effectively turned over to unconstrained markets, rendering STS the happy face of runaway neo-liberalism. The challenge ahead will come from more extreme explorations of alternative ways of knowing and being that are currently mobilizing personal and material resources – ranging from deep ecologists, on the one hand, to radical transhumanists, on the other (Fuller 2011, 2012; Fuller and Lipinska 2014). Social epistemology's task here will be to provide an academic discourse and policy orientation that allows these vast divergent world-views and lifestyles – many of them "open source" and "open access" – to flourish together within the normative bounds of what Karl Popper (1945) might recognize as an "open society", namely, one that allows criticism to flourish in the name of ideals that all parties putatively share above and beyond their current differences (Sassower 1995).

6 Epistemology as counterfactual historiography

The complementarity of freedom and determinism in the modern world-view

There is a strong but misleading tendency to suppose that determinism is opposed to freedom. On the contrary, some kind of determinism is presupposed by most accounts of freedom. Indeed, the sphere of rational action is composed by placing freedom and determinism in some normatively appropriate, empirically informed, complementary relationship. In what follows, I address the topic from many different angles without pretending to have resolved them all into a single coherent perspective. My guiding intuition is that it does not make much sense to say that people are free to do what they want, unless the options at their disposal are likely to result in meaningfully different outcomes that can be more or less anticipated. The only kind of determinism that is clearly opposed to freedom is the one that William James targeted in his famous 1896 lecture, "The Will to Believe" (James 1960). What James attacks as "determinism" is the belief that unactualized possibilities are illusions, which in Kantian fashion he held would undermine at once our ability to make causal inferences and assign moral responsibility.

I stress the species of "determinism" that James opposed because it is enjoying a revival among those who are partial to Epicurean "minimal suffering" approaches to ethics in an era of rapidly expanding knowledge of our biological nature, including our genetic constitution. An insufficiently examined feature of our times is the schizoid normative response to the probabilistic character of genetic causation. On the one hand, the "proactionary" risk-seekers support the use of biotechnology for not only therapeutic but also prosthetic purposes (Fuller 2011, 2012; Fuller and Lipinska 2014). On the other, the "precautionary" risk-averse treat such technology more diagnostically to minimize the potential for suffering at both the beginning and the end of the life process. Related to this perspective, I have referred to "Karmic Darwinists" and they provide a scientific version of the "determinist" mindset that James thought was resolutely *pre-scientific* (Fuller 2006b: ch. 11). I stand with James in opposing this form of determinism. However, and perhaps more relevant to our own times, I am also launching a second-order attack on those who would deconstruct by strictly mathematical or purely literary means the freedom/determinism binary as a relic of a woebegone scientific modernism. But this does not deny that the fates of freedom and determinism as intelligible concepts hang together, not separately.

Because "determinism" is often associated with some aspect of the modern scientific world-view, I should stress that what James originally attacked was a pervasive *pre-scientific* sensibility that the spread of the modern scientific world-view was supposed to correct. This sensibility held that whatever happens had to happen. Such a sensibility implies nothing about the presence of overarching laws of nature. But neither does the presence of overarching laws of nature imply the fatalistic attitude to the world that passes in the pre-scientific mind for "determinism". In contrast, two versions of the problem of "freedom and determinism" are posed by modern science. The first is associated with the *mechanical* world-view and the second with the *evolutionary* world-view. The former's intellectual centre of gravity lies in the seventeenth and eighteenth centuries, the latter's in the nineteenth and twentieth centuries. It would be a mistake to see the distinction between the two world-views as based on a disciplinary boundary between physics and biology. On the contrary, one should say that the disciplinary boundary emerged over the course of the nineteenth century as those who saw the universe as a machine professionally consolidated around the identity of "physicists" and those who saw it as a developmental process consolidated around the identity of "biologists".

A good way to epitomize the difference between the two world-views is that the mechanical world-view attempts to derive freedom from determinism, whereas the evolutionary world-view attempts the reverse. Table 7 projects the hopes and fears of these two world-views. I shall make more of this distinction in the next section but let me start by focusing on the mechanical version of the problem, with which contemporary philosophers are more familiar. It turns on a distinction drawn by Newton's self-described "underlabourer", John Locke, between *freedom of will* and *freedom to will* (Berofsky 1973).

Table 7 The two modern world-views.

	Mechanical world-view	Evolutionary world-view
Hope	Derive freedom from determinism (overdeterminism)	Derive determinism from freedom (underdeterminism)
Fear	Determinism divorced from freedom (fatalism)	Freedom divorced from determinism (chaos)

Locke adopted a position that has become standard among "naturalistic" philosophers (e.g. Dennett 1984, 2003) – that freedom *to* will is the only freedom worth having. It implies possession of the means by which an effect can be reliably produced, even if the means is not a creation of its possessor. This was the hopeful message for humanity inscribed in Newton's subsumption of all movement in the universe under three laws and one overarching gravitational principle. Finally one might know what God has permitted and prohibited. On the one hand, we would not try to do things that can never be done; but on the other, we might rise to the challenge of exploiting the full range of things that can be done. This captures the sense of "rational freedom" in which the Enlightenment philosophers took comfort, as epitomized in the slogan, "Freedom is the recognition of necessity".

However, Kant insisted on the stronger freedom *of* will, whereby we assume the position of God, authors of our own fate – "autonomous" in the strict sense of "self-legislative". His insistence on this stronger conception had two roots. One was ordinary juridical practice, whereby one's responsibility is determined by both whether an outcome would have happened even had the agent not acted and whether the agent could have acted other than s/he did. The agent's responsibility is established if the answer to the former is "no" and the latter is "yes". Freedom to will demands only the former condition, whereas freedom of will adds the latter. The second root is Kant's unified view of the human mind and resolutely anthropocentric view of reality, whereby the difference between, say, Newton's laws and the Ten Commandments is that the same modes of thought are directed in the former case "externally" and in the latter "internally". In other words, the principles of physics and ethics are *equally* abstract constructions from the indeterminate welter of experience. Thus, in asserting freedom of will, Kant was rendering freedom to will less naturalistic and more conventional than most of his Enlightenment brethren were inclined to do: In his hands, physics became more like ethics rather than the other way round.

Here it is worth remarking on the names given to the philosophical doctrines discussed here. Lockean freedom to will is associated with *libertarianism*, Kantian freedom of will with *voluntarism*. Both doctrines have high medieval roots but are rarely invoked together – and not merely because the one has migrated to Anglophone and the other to Germanophone philosophical discourse. The background metaphysics to freedom is strikingly different. Libertarianism conjures up what Jean Buridan in the fourteenth century originally called the "liberty of indifference"; that is, the indeterminacy that comes from being equally drawn to alternatives because nature does not favour one over the other: you may choose to do either or neither – and may live or die, as a result. The Enlightenment dramatized the idea that this logically open space could be exploited as an opportunity, but equally one could follow the example of the classical sceptic by withdrawing from the situation altogether. In contrast, "voluntarism" – a doctrine earlier developed by John Duns Scotus – conjures up the image of opposing pulls that create conflict in the soul, compelling a decision, which then becomes life-defining. A philosophical genealogy of existentialism would go through Augustine, Duns Scotus, Pascal, Kant, Kierkegaard up to Sartre. Interestingly, "the will" suffered a terminal decline in scientific psychology after the First World War, as it came to be seen as a pseudo-faculty that provided an excuse for the inevitability of war, understood as a "clash of wills" (Ainslie 2001: 202).

To summarize the discussion up to this point, and to anticipate what follows, we have seen that free will presupposes two senses of determinism, the second adding weight to the first. They may be characterized as follows:

1 *Lockean determinism* = "freedom *to* will" = the focus is on a determined effect that requires the agent because it could not have happened otherwise.
2 *Kantian determinism* = "freedom *of* will" = the focus is on an autonomous determiner who could have acted other than s/he did.

The two positions may be usefully seen as complements: The Lockean observes from inside a system what the Kantian observes from outside it. In terms that will become salient in the next section, the Lockean is an *overdeterminist*, the Kantian an *underdeterminist*. We might say that the project of "Enlightenment" consists of moving people from a pre-Lockean state (i.e. the fatalism that James called "determinism") to the Lockean and ultimately the Kantian states. In other words, progress is made once an apparent necessity is revealed to have been the product of contingent choice, which could have been made otherwise to significantly different effect. At this point, humans have retrieved the sense of freedom characteristic of God's point of view. It also captures the demystification of previously esoteric knowledge that characterized critical-historical theology and its secular descendant, Marxist ideology critique. One recent philosopher who has taken seriously this sense of progress as increasing self-determination is Karl Popper. Indeed, in response to critics who suspected Hegelian tendencies in spite of himself, Popper concedes the point made here: "that the world, in becoming conscious of itself, necessarily becomes open and incompletable" (Schilpp 1974: 1057). But before considering Popper further, we must first briefly consider Kant's unique contribution to this trajectory.

In the history of modern philosophy, Kant's status is both pivotal and peculiar. On the one hand, he was clearly a hard-headed supporter of the natural sciences on a Newtonian basis, the metaphysical presuppositions of which provided the basis for his own transcendental philosophy. Yet, on the other hand, Kant's followers spawned various schools of idealism, positivism and pragmatism, movements that had chequered relations with the naturalism (or "materialism") of Kant's Enlightenment forebears, who by the end of the nineteenth century found a descendant in Charles Darwin. In this context, words like "conventionalism", "constructivism" and even "relativism" were used to capture the sense in which Kant's freedom of will seemed to level the difference in the kind of constraint exerted between what the Greeks originally called *physis* and *nomos* – that is, the law of nature and the law of humans. This peculiar aspect of Kant's legacy became German academic dogma in the late nineteenth century, courtesy of the self-styled Neo-Kantians, in whose footsteps Jürgen Habermas was probably the last to walk. Like the Trinitarian God, the complete Habermasian human was equally present in three distinct guises – the technical, the practical, and the emancipatory – each of which constitutes a "cognitive interest" (Habermas 1973).

It is worth noting that over the course of his career, Habermas's relationship to Kant changed subtly, perhaps most noticeably in Habermas (2003), where he comes to terms with the implications of the new biotechnology for human dignity. Here he argues against the idea of "designer babies" as a violation of Kantian autonomy, as such offspring could not imagine themselves as authors of their own fate. They would always be saddled with the knowledge that they were created as a means to their parents' ends. This argument presupposes a much stronger form of naturalism than in Habermas (1973). The younger Habermas was clear that regardless of our knowledge of how we came to be as we are, the only operative question in circumscribing our freedom in particular action contexts is whether we could have done otherwise, and whether it would have made a difference. In contrast, the elder Habermas writes as if our very status as autonomous beings requires certain material preconditions, not least a kind of opacity between our parents' intentions and the traits we possess by virtue of their procreative activities. One wonders what he would think, were he reminded of the crude but no less real genetic sensibility that informed "arranged marriages" long before recent advances in biotechnology.

At the same time, philosophers explored what might be called a "naturalized Kantianism", whereby the self-legislative moral agent is operationalized in its empirical multiplicity, each functioning as a "law unto herself". In a series of works culminating in *The Poverty of Historicism* (1957), Karl Popper published a famous "proof" of the fundamentally unlawlike – in the sense of unpredictable – nature of humans. The proof turned on the "self-fulfilling" and "self-defeating" tendencies in human behaviour. Consider stage theories of progress that predict, say, a world-wide proletarian revolution. On the one hand, those who learn of the prediction may try, out of enthusiasm or coercion or both, to increase the likelihood of its realization and indeed succeed in bringing it about. Indeed, they may do so more quickly and harshly than predicted. On the other, they may try to contravene the prediction with an equal degree of single-mindedness (and perhaps perversity). And they too may succeed. This point is especially problematic for so-called realist theories of knowledge, according to which knowledge claims are not causally rele-vant – either positively or negatively – to the realization of the states of the world they represent.

This so-called proof has been taken as luminous for at least a couple of reasons. At the political level, it was read as a veiled warning to would-be central planners in an "open society" where information is transacted freely. One can never beat the collective intelligence of a distributed knowledge base without resorting to stealth and deception, which is to say, morally objectionable means. At a more metaphysical level, the proof seemed to mark the difference between the limits of natural and social scientific knowledge, since planets, rocks, plants and, for the most part, animals are incapable of intentionally subverting the principles we hypothesize as governing their behaviour. Whatever subversions appear to occur in the natural realm are properly seen as "falsifications" that result from these entities behaving as they would normally, even had we not hypothesized about them. In this respect, Popper appeared to provide a rigorous basis for the long-standing intuitions of "interpretivist" social scientists. It is worth observing, that unlike many who have used his proof for their own pur-poses, Popper was himself a metaphysical indeterminist about *all* of reality, and so his point was limited to the causal efficacy of communicating knowledge claims in the human realm. He regarded the formulation of laws as universal generalizations mainly as a diagnostic tool for calibrating the difference between what we know and what there is (i.e. the method of conjectures and refutations). Popper did not see laws as potential repre-sentations of the structure of even physical reality. This is where he most sharply disagreed with the logical positivists.

But are these conclusions so clear? According to classical definitions of knowledge that clearly distinguish knowledge from less esteemed forms of belief, the sheer publicity of a knowledge claim has no bearing on its truth-value. Philosophers have traditionally given a "realist" spin to this point by speaking of the "fact of the matter" or "state of the world" that obtains regardless of what is believed. The point is most persuasively made when the target of the knowledge claim is not in a position to alter the fact or state that makes the claim true. But doesn't that simply reduce "reality" to the target's sphere of incapacity – specifically, an incapacity to

216　*Epistemology as counterfactual historiography*

generate an alternate state to the one represented in the knowledge claim? That the political and metaphysical issues can combine in curious ways is epitomized by alternative interpretations of the Baconian slogan "Knowledge is power" (or *savoir est pouvoir*, in Auguste Comte). As we learn more about the social world, what is the relationship between such knowledge and the world? If as Bacon literally said, *scientia est potentia*, what sort of potential for action does organized knowledge provide? In today's terms, is it more like a *capital* or a *consumer* technology? Let's consider these options in turn.

On the one hand, we might envisage knowledge as revealing, and hence reinforcing, a sense of order, very much along the lines of the mechanical world-view. In that respect, knowledge – and Bacon referred to *scientia*, formally organized knowledge – would consist of laws that provide the infrastructure of a rational society (i.e. the ultimate capital technology). However, an important reason these laws could function in such a capacity is that they would be *esoteric*. They would be the result of considerable and specialized research, conducted largely in seclusion, the fruits of which would be then turned over to the state for general application. A law so produced would not be subject to public scrutiny in the manner of a proposed piece of legislation, nor would there be the expectation that the knowledge informing the law would be communicated in the normal course of education.

This version of scientific politics aimed to virtualize – or, in today's usage, "model" – the sphere of governance as a closed system, the boundary conditions of which required innovations in the built environment that would allow the populace to be cultivated as an organic unity, aka the "nation-state". Such mid-twentieth-century novels as Aldous Huxley's *Brave New World* (1932) and B. F. Skinner's *Walden Two* (1948) continued to promote this project in its purest form. But even before the second half of the nineteenth century, when the relevant public works projects began to realize the project in the impure forms with which we are familiar, political economists from François Quesnay to Friedrich List and statisticians like Adolphe Quetelet had already defined the conceptual contours of what sociobiologists and evolutionary psychologists nowadays like to call, after Conrad Waddington, "epigenetic landscapes", namely, the sum of naturally and artificially imposed environmental constraints that foster forms of cooperative behaviour, including interbreeding, that tend to render a collection of individuals more species-like, and hence with a common stake in the maintenance of all of its members, no matter how they differ in terms of properties like class, race and creed (Dickens 2000: 111–12).

That Bacon – and Comte – wrote before most people (even males) received the right to vote and mass education became a standard state provision is crucial to appreciating how *scientia* was supposed to confer *potentia*. It amounted to arriving at principles that enabled legislators to deal with people precisely in the way that Newton was able to deal with natural phenomena. We might say that the research question was "How to render people governable like matter in motion?" Among the relevant conditions one would have to include the erection of substantial intellectual barriers between the governors and the governed. Thus, the absence of the kind of work that is routinely performed by a stratified educational system and an increasingly specialized research culture was the main obstacle to successful statecraft in early modern Europe. Indeed, it was the very problem Plato had first identified in the *Republic* – the inability of the rulers to create sufficient distance between the knowledge possessed by themselves and the ruled. This lack of distance made figures like Machiavelli and Hobbes appear so subversive in their day: Their books purported to reveal the secrets of effective governance, not to pre-selected elites *but to anyone willing to listen.* (The informed reader will notice that I'm turning the grandmaster of esoteric philosophical writing, Leo Strauss, on his head: Machiavelli and Hobbes were Strauss's devils for the very reason I valorize them.) To be sure, Hobbes was more inclined than Machiavelli to invoke the specifically lawlike character of the knowledge he claimed to have possessed, but the overall effect of this publicity was to encourage more people to try their hand at becoming rulers, which contributed significantly – perhaps decisively – to the institutionalization of democratic regimes across the world.

This brings us to "the other hand", that knowledge confers power on its possessors by destabilizing the existing social order – an interpretation much closer to Popper's (1945) "open society" mentality. In that respect, it is a consumer technology. The idea that knowledge can be communicated widely, and hence used by people from very different backgrounds and interests, undermines the esotericism that underwrites the first alternative, either because the same message may be conveyed in multiple media or a medium may be designed to enable everyone to receive the same message. Popper would have encountered both ideas in the organizer of the Vienna Circle, the Marxist sociologist, Otto Neurath. The former was captured by the universal picture language, "Isotype", and the latter by the more famous protocol statements and neutral observation language with which logical positivism has come to be identified. However, in either form, this alternative continues to be dogged by whether *any* sense of order is likely to "self-organize" once knowledge is allowed to flow so freely. Of course, this has been the hope of anarchists and libertarians but the Enlightenment's patron saints had their doubts. Here it is worth recalling how the histories of politics and science were seen as interrelated in the Enlightenment to produce the doctrines of progress that were among its signature contributions to the cultural heritage of the West.

Once Islam popularized the idea that God governs the universe by laws that bind even the sphere of divine action, some enterprising individuals grouped together as scientific magicians (or "alchemists") claimed, on the basis of esoteric knowledge, to be able to turn these laws to their advantage. Several Arab scholars and, later, the Christian scholastics condemned alchemy on grounds of empirical unreliability, as the alchemists (some of whom, like Roger Bacon, were themselves renegade scholastics) invariably overstated the field's claims to knowledge. However, the quasi-official status of the scholastic condemnations had the effect of discouraging any further testing of the alchemists' claims – or at least forced such testing underground. Just this sort of dynamic led the Enlightenment philosophers to stigmatize the medieval period as the "Dark Ages" from which Europe was only now (i.e. the eighteenth century) emerging, especially by challenging the Church's epistemic authority and creating alternative knowledge-based institutions, such as learned academies, that competed with theocratic university systems. However, the Enlightenment's relationship to the Middle Ages was complex. It did not challenge the scholastic critique of alchemy *per se*, only the course of action that the critique licensed. That was because the Enlightenment basically shared the alchemists' "freedom to will" mentality and opposed the scholastic tendency to believe that God's hands are never tied. In effect, the Enlightenment stood for a limited sense of freedom that was widely distributed, rather than an unlimited sense of freedom possessed only by one person (i.e. God).

This trade-off was at once secularized and immortalized as the narrative structure of Hegel's philosophy of history, whereby the "Oriental Despot" provides a concrete expression of the abstract possibility of divine omnipotence kept open by the scholastics. Though ultimately the most influential Enlightenment scheme for the evolution of humanity, Hegel's was, of course, one of the last. What is striking about all the schemes proposed from, say, 1750 to 1850 is the way they stagger the introduction of actual people as historical subjects. In other words, they presumed a positive correspondence between epistemic advance and political inclusion. To be sure, in no country have all adults – let alone all humans – been granted, say, the right to vote at the same time. However, that brute fact is not normally given the Enlightenment's epistemic spin. Here, I suspect, we find the dead hand of Plato at work: The Enlightenment's stage theory of human development is simply a dynamic version of the static knowledge-based social structure that Plato presented in the *Republic*. In other words, the Enlightenment appreciated the order that came from an epistemic asymmetry among social classes but at the same time realized that new knowledge tended to redistribute power – in their own day, to manufacturers and merchants, who were better positioned to benefit from technological applications of Newtonian mechanics than aristocrats trained exclusively in theology and the pagan classics.

The open political question in all this is whether one could always count on the ascendant class to push forward the frontiers of knowledge so as to enfranchise a still wider sector of society by effectively redistributing its own power. Those who have said yes tend to be capitalists (sometimes derided as "trickle-down" theorists), whereas those who have said no tend to be socialists who believe that this trajectory becomes increasingly difficult to maintain over time without an explicit countervailing collective effort (perhaps institutionalized in the state). But whether one took a capitalist or a socialist view on the matter, the general Enlightenment perspective came to be updated during the Cold War as the "linear model" of science policy, whereby "basic research" generates the principles on the basis of which reliable applications can be made to improve the human condition. The model was given the name "linear" to stress the discrete sequence of basic research *then* reliable applications – as opposed to research done for the sake of application. The linear model was developed in the US to legitimatize the National Science Foundation as an agency that allocated resources to scientists on a peer review basis (i.e. distributed by and to the basic researchers). The implicit contrast was with the mission-oriented research that was said to have characterized Nazi Germany and the Soviet Union, which supposedly tried to arrive at scientific principles that conformed to ideological imperatives.

The idea that monstrous applications result from the failure to master fundamental principles clearly served as a warning to those who would let their desire for "freedom of will" overtake "freedom to will". But is the problem here really anything other than an updated version of the decline in social order that Plato predicted would happen, once the Guardians and the Philosopher-Kings contaminated each other's activities? However, the positive historical basis for the valorization of the linear model as a science policy strategy is highly selective and, unsurprisingly, self-serving. The most notable example is Kuhn (1970), based on a selective reading of the history of physical sciences from the early seventeenth to the early twentieth centuries, which argued for strong paradigm boundaries as insulators of normal science from extra-mural concerns. In the 1970s, an ambitious group of philosophers and sociologists under Habermas's directorship of the Max Planck Institute in Starnberg built on Kuhn's observation that paradigms eventually accumulate anomalies as they reap diminishing returns on their cognitive and material investments. At that point, these self-styled "finalizationists" argued, it was rational to shift from basic to applied research (Fuller 2000a: ch. 8; Fuller 2000b: ch. 5).

Freedom and determinism as a problem of historical perspective

The question of determinism is intimately connected with historical perspective, a concept best treated by taking the implied visual metaphor with deadly seriousness. I shall introduce two such perspectives, *overdeterminism* and *underdeterminism*, which are projected from the standpoint of an "ideal observer" who is located *inside* history (Fuller and Collier 2004: ch. 6). In contrast, *determinism simpliciter* is represented by God, who observes from a standpoint equidistant from every moment in time, which is to say, *outside* history – as it were, *sub specie aeternitatis*. This is the so-called absolute time of Newtonian mechanics, which along with absolute space formed the "divine sensorium" or, as we would now say, "interface" between Creator and Creation. Here it is worth recalling and amplifying points raised in Chapter 2, on epistemology as divine psychology.

First, the exact location of God in such a framework was subject to heated discussion throughout the seventeenth and eighteenth centuries, as the universe came to be increasingly seen as a self-contained machine whose *modus operandi* was internally maintained and publicly accessible. Second, the idea of God standing equidistant from all of history remains rhetorically compelling. It helps to explain how it is possible that our best guesses about what happened in the 2 or 3 million years of hominid prehistory – or the 4 or 5 billion years of cosmological time – are taken more seriously by the *bien pensant* public and policymakers than, say, what we know much better about the very much smaller period of recorded history. When every moment in time is accorded equal weight, the sheer quantity of temporal moments, or longevity, is easily read as causal significance, such that, for example, our genetic constitution, which has only marginally changed for many thousands of generations, is seen as exerting a "deeper" control over our behaviour than social institutions that have existed for a much shorter period. While such a view may be rational for God *sub specie aeternitatis*, it is not clear that it is rational for the humans whose lives occupy a well-bounded chunk of space–time. Indeed, as we become better equipped to undo several millions of years of evolution (on ourselves, the planet, etc.), the accordance of equal weight to every temporal moment may come to be seen as the last vestige of the theistic mind in the secular world.

In terms of the two world-views introduced in the previous section, the mechanical world-view represents overdeterminism and the evolutionary world-view underdeterminism. Originally, I said that the mechanical world-view attempts to derive freedom from determinism and the evolutionary world-view derives in reverse. Now, recalling Table 7, let us put the same points in negative terms: The mechanical world-view aims to prevent overdeterminism from descending into *fatalism*, while the

Epistemology as counterfactual historiography   221

evolutionary world-view aims to prevent underdeterminism from descending into *chaos*. An example of considerable historiographical interest makes the contrast vivid (Fuller 1997: ch. 5): *Why did the Scientific Revolution happen in seventeenth-century Europe?*

The question may be interpreted in two ways that might be seen as corresponding to a "sacred" and "secular" historiography of science. On the sacred side, overdeterminism may be understood in terms of human rationality being "released" from its material constraints, as opposed to its being "imposed" on an otherwise indeterminate material world, in the case of underdeterminism (Fuller 1993: ch. 2). This sense of the distinction is best understood in terms of the difference between Christianity and its closest "oriental" competitor, Zoroastrianism, in which the former has been inclined to see evil as simply a privation of good that will be overcome in the long run, given the overriding power of God, whereas the latter sees the triumph of good over evil as more evenly matched and hence contingently determined. Nietzsche quite self-consciously pitched his anti-Hegelian philosophy as a secular Zoroastrianism to couner Hegel's own secular Christianity, in which the world-historic spirit played the role of God. On the secular side, there is an overdeterminist historiography of science that reinforces – and, in that sense, legitimatizes – current scientific practice and an underdeterminist historiography that breaks with – and perhaps even de-legitimatizes – those practices. This difference in perspective can be traced to Max Planck (as overdeterminist) and Ernst Mach (as underdeterminist) in their multiply layered debate about the future of German science in the years leading up to the First World War (Fuller 2000b: ch. 2). Basically, Planck used overdeterminist arguments to justify the inherent value of completing the physics world-picture, whereas Mach used underdeterminist arguments to justify shifting out of physics in the manner of the "finalizationists" mentioned at the end of the previous section.

The overdeterminist reads the question as implying "Why did it happen *in seventeenth-century Europe?*" This interpretation presupposes that the Scientific Revolution would have happened eventually – if not in Europe, then somewhere else. Thus, the interesting research questions pertain to why seventeenth-century Europe was first: What *prevented* the Scientific Revolution from happening earlier in Europe or from happening at all elsewhere, especially in places like China that had so many of the relevant preconditions already in place? Moreover, this interpretation has knock-on effects for how the subsequent history is told. For if the seventeenth-century European origin of the Scientific Revolution is a mere accident of history, then the spread of the scientific world-view from that point of origin is expected, not problematic. Again, the interesting research questions pertain to what *prevented* the scientific world-view from

222 Epistemology as counterfactual historiography

spreading to more areas more quickly. Given this orientation, the over-determinist may be quick to turn to the "cognitive unity of humanity" and the various material and ideological barriers that have stood in the way of its full realization.

In contrast, the underdeterminist reads the question to mean "Why did it happen *at all?*" This interpretation presupposes that the Scientific Revolution is a unique event to be explained primarily in terms of particular features of seventeenth-century Europe that have lasted as long as they have only through great effort, typically involving the translation of the original ideas into new social forms that in turn perhaps subtly (or not so subtly) have transformed the ideas themselves. This interpretation presumes that the prior probability of a Scientific Revolution is so low – perhaps even a miracle – that part of what needs to be explained is the persistence of its legacy and the extent of its exportability: Why don't the ideas and practices of the Scientific Revolution survive merely as part of the idiosyncratic baggage of seventeenth-century European culture? The unexpected character of the world-historic significance of these ideas and practices suggests that there were serious odds against their success. Thus, the interesting research questions concern how ideas and practices were introduced to people who, left to their own devices, would have probably otherwise never adopted them.

I focus on the example of the Scientific Revolution because both the under- and over-determinist versions of the question loomed large in the mind of Joseph Needham, who struggled to reconcile his normative commitment to science as "the salutary enlightenment of all men [*sic*] without distinction of race, colour, faith or homeland, wherein all can qualify and participate" with the fact that a "scientific revolution" never occurred in China, the economically and technologically most impressive civilization that the world had known prior to the early nineteenth century (Needham 1963: 149). Moreover, Needham concluded from a lifetime of scholarship that it is unlikely that China would have forged a scientific revolution by purely indigenous means. This is not to deny that China possessed some of the metaphysical preconditions and most of the requisite technical achievements. Nevertheless, it lacked the institutional and ideological incentives to synthesize them into a project plausibly associated in the Western tradition with Hobbes, Descartes, and Leibniz, but unequivocally realized in Newton's *Principia Mathematica*.

Needham clearly wanted to avoid the most obvious consequence of admitting the world-historic underdetermination of the Scientific Revolution, namely, that the subsequent spread of science amounts to the artificial imposition of a culturally specific accident on China, which had survived perfectly well without modern science's distinctive world-view. Needham's concern here is plausibly informed by an overdeterminist impulse. One way to address it is to imagine a world, contrary to historical fact but within the realm of historical possibility, in which the Chinese could have been shown that *their own* interests would be served by adopting the ideas and findings associated with the West's Scientific Revolution. In other words, the actual accident of the Scientific Revolution's occurrence in seventeenth-century Europe would be matched by the imagined accident of some external agent who could have persuaded the Chinese to develop their traditions towards a similar revolution. Whatever success such a strategy might enjoy would embolden philosophers to appeal to an innate rationality common to all humans that can be manifested under the right circumstances. In any case, as our transhistorical dealings with the medieval luminary Nicole Oresme will show below, the normal narrative presuppositions of science historiography already provide grounds for such a melding of under- and overdeterminist concerns. But before turning to Oresme, let us tease out some more of the implications of the two counterfactually driven approaches to history.

The overdeterminist adopts the standpoint of someone in the future looking backward as a descendant, whereas the underdeterminist takes the position of someone in the past looking forward as progenitor. (For some suggestive opening moves towards integrating these two temporal perspectives in what may be called a "reflective equilibrium" approach to historiography, see Dupuy 2000.) In terms of what may be called "the geometry of historical vision", the overdeterminist has a *hyperbolic* perspective of the past and a *linear* perspective of the future, while the underdeterminist sees the past linearly and the future hyperbolically (for this distinction seen in both its original art-historical context and its metaphorical function in modern physics, see Heelan 1983; Feyerabend 1999). This difference provides two radically opposed conceptions of the overall shape of history. Where the overdeterminist envisages history ultimately converging from divergent origins, the underdeterminist sees a common origin increasingly diverging over time into multiple futures. (Think Lamarck *versus* Darwin.) The former is due to different historical trajectories being drawn to a common endpoint, whereas the latter is due to the differentiation of trajectories from decisions taken over the course of history.

In the sacred historiography of Christianity, underdeterminism captures the Old Testament (OT) account of the Fall from Grace and descent into Babel, while overdeterminism captures the New Testament (NT) story of people of diverse backgrounds being drawn to Jesus as pointing the way to Salvation. One might say that the secularization of Christian soteriology has undergone two stages: (1) the secularization of the NT story by simply altering the vehicles of salvation from, say, the Elect to Humanity to the Proletariat; (2) the secularization of the OT story, which has kept

224 *Epistemology as counterfactual historiography*

the vehicles but reversed the value orientation. Thus, in the postmodern condition, Babel is valorized as cultural pluralism.

The metaphysical uses of the opposing conceptual locations of "unity" and "diversity" are also worth noting. Determinism typically presupposes overdeterminism's appeal to a unified end, while free will defences often turn on underdeterminism's appeal to a unified origin. The former stresses how, no matter where you start, you end up in the same place (because of a preconceived plan), while the latter stresses that even with the same starting point, you can end up in different places (depending on the specific decision taken). This difference provides the basis for contrasting views of the value of political freedom (or "liberty", the Roman term preferred by the US founding fathers) in the modern period. The overdeterminist contributes to a "perfectionist" sensibility whereby freedom enables people to become *all they can be*, whereas the underdeterminist contributes to a more "relativist" sensibility whereby freedom enables people to be *exactly what they want to be*. When philosophers from Plato onward have tried to unify The True and The Good, they have invariably aspired to find a way to enable people *to want to be all they can be*. (When politicians attempt a similar feat, they aim to enable people *to be all they want to be*.)

If the overdeterminist conceives of the historical agent as a more or less efficient vehicle for realizing history's ultimate ends, the underdeterminist positions the agent as a judge responsible for her own fate and the fate of those under her jurisdiction. In caricature, the overdeterminist treats people as replaceable because their decisions are bound to be the same and irreversible, whereas the underdeterminist treats people as irreplaceable because their decisions are bound to be different and reversible. The emotional spectrum covered by the two types of agents is correspondingly different. The overdetermined historical agent perseveres in the face of lagging fortunes yet expresses vindication once success sets in – such is the inscrutability of *necessity*. In contrast, the underdetermined agent suffers regret when she appears to have taken the wrong decision, but equally experiences relief when the right decision appears to have been taken – such is the inscrutability of *contingency*. Finally, to put matters in ontological terms, the overdeterminist sees history itself as a fixed set of potentialities, the actualization of which may be expedited and retarded over time, while the underdeterminist takes history to be a series of accidents that lay down paths on which successors then are forced to depend.

The above contrasts are elaborated in Table 8. They suggest that overdeterminism and underdeterminism subscribe to *modal logics of history* that mix freedom and determinism in opposing ways that are epitomized in the following propositions:

Table 8 The two modal logics of history.

Metahistory	Overdetermined	Underdetermined
Disciplinary division of labour	Philosopher's counterfactual: the past should understand us	Historian's counterfactual: we should understand the past
Ideal observer	Future agent looking backward (as descendant)	Past agent looking forward (as progenitor)
Temporal horizon, as seen from the present	Hyperbolic perspective of the past, linear perspective of the future	Linear perspective of the past, hyperbolic perspective of the future
History's natural tendency	Convergence upon one end ("equifinality")	Divergence to multiple ends ("plurifinality")
Constitution of history	Overarching teleology	Series of turning points
Biological equivalent	Lamarckism	Darwinism
Where is "Reason in History"?	Above the consciousness of the agents (i.e. rationality can travel through multiple agents)	Below the consciousness of agents (i.e. each agent is the source of multiple rationalities)
Status of historical figures	Replaceable vehicles	Deciding agents
Extreme version	Vehicles too easily replaced: Fatalism ("All cultures eventually become scientific")	Decisions too easily reversed: Chaos ("It's a miracle that any culture became scientific")
Emotional spectrum	From perseverance when progress lagging to vindication when progress realized	From regret when decision wrong to relief when decision right
The mix of freedom and necessity in history	Y had to happen, but it need not have happened via X	X need not have happened, but once it did, Y had to happen
Prior probability that a Scientific Revolution ("Y") would occur	High	Low
What needs to be explained about the Scientific Revolution	Why it did not happen everywhere (e.g. in China)	Why it happened anywhere (i.e. in Europe)

- *Overdeterminism*: Y had to happen, but it need not have happened via X.
- *Underdeterminism*: X need not have happened, but once it did, Y had to happen.

Thus, the overdeterminist stresses the significance of the overall design of history, whereas the underdeterminist focuses on the pivotal role played by the decision-maker "X" in determining the outcome (at least until the next major decision is taken). The philosophy and the history of science have conventionally divided their labours by splitting the difference between the two modal logics, with the philosophers as overdeterminists and the historians as underdeterminists. This point can be made vivid by appealing to hypothetical time travel. But whom should we visit?

Consider Nicole Oresme (1320–82), Roman Catholic bishop of Lisieux and perhaps the most progressive mind of his century – at least as seen from an overdeterminist perspective that projects history as leading to our current

226 *Epistemology as counterfactual historiography*

scientific attitudes and beliefs. (This judgement was first advanced by Pierre Duhem in many of his writings, most popularly in the entry on "history of physics" in the 1911 edition of *The Catholic Encyclopaedia*.) At least two centuries before Copernicus, Galileo and Newton, he provided the major conceptual arguments against the geocentric view of the universe, for space and time having properties independent of the bodies they contain, and for the modern principle of inertial motion. Moreover, he often formulated his arguments in sophisticated mathematical terms that anticipated Descartes's development of analytic geometry. Indeed, he even deployed these arguments to debunk the authoritative field of astrology, later the bane of the modern scientific world-view. By all accounts, Oresme was taken very seriously in his day, but no scientific revolution occurred on his watch or even in the decades immediately following his death. The reason normally given for this puzzling state of affairs is that Oresme did not regard his own arguments as sufficiently conclusive to overturn centuries of established dogma. In fact, he regarded their inconclusiveness as an indirect sign of the unbridgeable gap between the divine and the human intellect.

Historians and philosophers see radically different things in this episode and make their plans for time travel accordingly. The historian plans to go back to the fourteenth century to learn more about Oresme's context, with an eye to rationalizing the decisions he actually took about how – and how far – to press his arguments. This strategy is familiar as "sympathetic understanding" or, in Popper's terms, discerning the "logic of the situation". A possible consequence – perhaps unintended – of this strategy is that, upon her return, the historian concludes that Oresme was not really trying to be like us and so we should not place unfair burdens on him.

One question the historian would probably *not* have put to Oresme is why he did not try to shift the burden of proof to the Aristotelians more aggressively, say, in the manner of Galileo. However, this question looms large for the philosopher, who would have Oresme himself embark on a temporal voyage, with the philosopher's seminar as his destination. Upon arrival, Oresme would be administered a crash course in the history of physical theory of the intervening years, in which the philosopher would show how each successive stage has improved on its predecessor. Oresme would duly assimilate this information as any clever pupil would, granting the logic of the philosopher's exposition. The success of such a course would demonstrate – at least to the philosopher's satisfaction – that Oresme's mind is sufficiently like ours to permit her to ask Oresme why he had not himself pushed this logic more forcefully. Short of outright confessing the error of his ways, Oresme's response is bound to appear wrong-footed, compelling the philosopher to conclude that Oresme suffered from some unfortunate barriers or blinkers that provide lingering support for the Enlightenment view that he lived in a "Dark Age".

Epistemology as counterfactual historiography 227

Thus, the historian and the philosopher would clearly deploy time travel to opposite effect, subjecting Oresme to quite different types of inquiry. Nevertheless, significantly, they jointly presuppose that the past is a foreign country, separated in time as if by space. The only difference is that whereas the historian treats the boundary separating the past and the present as an object of respect, the philosopher treats it as an obstacle to be overcome. *But what if the past and the present are not seen as mutually exclusive?* In other words, suppose we imagine that the past and the present are overlapping, with the amount of overlap subject to continual, empirically informed negotiation. This is the view I wish to defend here. It entails removing the *cordon sanitaire* that currently exists between the history and the philosophy of science and, more profoundly, overcoming a reluctance to integrate over- and underdeterminism in a common methodological strategy. To explain why we should go down this route, consider the excesses to which both overdeterminism and underdeterminism are prone when left to their own devices.

On the one hand, the Popperian philosopher of science Imre Lakatos took overdeterminism to its logical extreme, arguing that the task of the philosophy of science is to construct an ideal history of science that consigns most of the actual history to footnotes remarking on errors, delays and diversions. Taken on its own terms, the main problem with this policy is the frequency with which the history of science would need to be, in Lakatosian terms, "rationally reconstructed" as particular disciplines shift their goals and hence what previously appeared to be demonstrable errors now look like inchoate truths. This is the big grain of truth contained in Kuhn's view that after a "scientific revolution", the new paradigm engages in an "Orwellian" rewriting of the history of its field in order to motivate novices to the paradigm.

On the other hand, extreme versions of underdeterminism may be found among historical relativists who believe that everything that could have been done is contained in what was actually done. A currently fashionable version of this position, courtesy of Michel Foucault (1970), is that people cannot be presumed to have entertained (and hence be held accountable for) concepts for which they lack an explicit expression. Of course, this then makes epistemic ruptures very easy to see, which in turn proves to be a never-ending source of frustration for scientists who dip into professional history of science only to learn that even relatively recent figures like Einstein and Heisenberg appear as if they were pursuing problems as removed from the interests of current physicists as Oresme. This reflects the larger phenomenon that I dubbed the "inscrutability of silence", which arises because of the apparent delay between the emergence of a concept and a name being assigned to it (Fuller 1988: ch. 6).

228   *Epistemology as counterfactual historiography*

Now suppose that historians mean to convey just this impression. How then would the past have managed to turn into the present? Is it simply a matter of "one damn thing after another" (perhaps highlighting the violence this truism conceals) or does the past contain the seeds of the future as a potential that might have been actualized earlier? I believe that the latter is the way to go, though it entails recognizing that currently the history and the philosophy of science are mutually alienated activities, which should be practised in combination, regardless of whether our official interest is the past or the present. So what does my alternative look like?

At a normative level, of course, it means that disappointment with one's performance implies that one could have done better. In terms of the time traveller's itinerary, it would require, on the one hand, that Oresme be permitted to visit us with the intent of showing how we have forgotten or distorted ideas of his that should be revived today and, on the other hand, that we return to the fourteenth century to persuade Oresme that he should take decisions favourable to our current epistemic situation. Both activities mix history and philosophy in roughly equal measures but heighten the specifically *critical* nature of the exchange, since the burden of proof in both cases is on the persuader rather than the persuaded. After all, the expectation is that Oresme would find it hard to persuade us to change our ways and we to persuade him to change his. Nevertheless, whatever headway he and we would make in the two contexts would increase the degree of overlap between the past and the present. This is in contrast to the original scenario, in which time travel is designed to enable us to *accept* him (the historian's version) and him to accept us (the philosopher's version) for both who he and we actually are. Under this regime of "separate but equal" accorded to the history and the philosophy of science, it is hard to see how further research in both fields would help to make the past and the present mutually informative so as to serve as a guide to the future. This general field of play is depicted in Table 9.

Table 9 The epistemic rudiments of time travel.

Semantic distance between past and present	Increased (minimize temporal overlap)	Decreased (maximize temporal overlap)
Implications for the history and the philosophy of science	They are normatively distinct disciplines	They are normatively fused disciplines
Cognitive means and ends	Learning with an eye to acceptance	Persuasion with an eye to change
Oresme's identity as he travels from past to present	Wayward student	Nagging parent
Oresme's identity as we travel from present to past	Generous host	Tough customer

Epistemology as counterfactual historiography   229

That the past and the present overlap more than both historians and philosophers normally presume may be defended on two interrelated grounds, the first pertaining to the nature of what is possible and the second to the grammar of temporal reference.

First, there is a difference between the strictly *temporal* and the more generally *semantic* sense of "possibility", the former closer in definition to "probable", the latter to "conceivable". To be sure, before John Duns Scotus drew the distinction in the fourteenth century as part of a defence of free will, the semantic had been normally assimilated to the temporal sense. In other words, something is not possible unless it has already happened once, which in practice amounts to holding the future hostage to the past. So expressed, the pre-Scotist understanding of possibility appears very conservative: It is induction on overdrive, whereby the normative is reduced to the normal – the cardinal Popperian sin – which can end up essentializing the nature of a "people" (aka race) with their common history (Fuller 2011: ch. 1; Fuller and Lipinska 2014: ch. 1). Nevertheless, it continues to inform the relativistic refusal to judge people by standards other than those they themselves explicitly upheld, as we shall see below. However, Scotus's innovation was to convert "possibility" from an empirical to a logical category. Instead of "the possible" referring to something that has already happened, it now referred to something, which even if it has not happened is not prevented by logic (i.e. no self-contradiction) from happening in the future. This innovation marks a rare yet unequivocal moment of philosophical progress: It opened the conceptual space for defining a law of nature in counterfactual, rather than strictly inductive, terms. Thus, rather than simply inferring natural laws from spontaneously observable regularities, as Aristotle did, one could imagine how nature would behave under an array of hypothetical conditions that experiments would later simulate, thereby revealing aspects of nature that would otherwise not spontaneously appear.

To see the Scotist legacy at work, consider two different senses of the slogan associated with Plato's *Meno* that "we know more than we can tell". On the one hand, Michael Polanyi (1957) interpreted it to mean that our knowledge may be expressed by other than strictly linguistic means, but it remains largely limited to our "experience", albeit understood in a fully embodied "practical" sense. On the other hand, Noam Chomsky (1966) has taken it to mean that, under the right conditions, we might say more – and indeed other – than we normally do. It is the latter interpretation, reflecting the Scotist expansion of the concept of possibility, which licenses people from different periods and cultures to criticize each other. This is because everyone cognitively inhabits a common conceptual space – a "universal grammar", if you will – only certain parts of which are normally explored in the course of people's lives

230 Epistemology as counterfactual historiography

but is always available to be explored and shared across time and space. Much more could be said about the truly revolutionary character in this shift in the concept of possibility. For example, the plausibility of empiricism and rationalism as all-purpose epistemologies rest, respectively, on interpreting possibility in the temporal and the semantic sense.

A good benchmark here is the experiments that have been conducted to test the validity of the Sapir–Whorf hypothesis on natives lacking the Western range of colour vocabulary (Fuller 1988: 159–61). The hypothesis states that natural languages correspond to distinct conceptual schemes, yet the natives had no trouble matching tokens for our named colours to the colours they perceived. At the same time, however, it was equally clear that they found the experimental task artificial, since our colour discriminations serve no function in their culture. Presumably, left to their own devices, the natives quickly reverted to their usual colour naming practices, recalling their success at the experimental task as akin to winning at a newly learned game. Nevertheless, these experiments could have encouraged more interventionist anthropologists interested in having the natives integrate the new names into their everyday lives.

Human capabilities should not be reduced to the capacities that happen to be favoured by the environments normally inhabited by a group, even if it serves to turn the tables on psychologists who would reduce social knowledge to a single cognitive capacity diffracted through a variety of more or less intellectually hospitable environments, which can then be arranged in a developmental sequence. The two sides of this zero-sum game between psychology and sociology are not the only ones available. A strategy much more in the spirit of a dialectical synthesis would treat psychology as the science of the socially possible, and hence draw attention to how under the right conditions people can think, act or be other than is normally prescribed. In short, people have changed and therefore can change and therefore could have changed.

A vivid case in point may be raised in response to the ethnomethodologists Sharrock and Leudar (2002), who argue that "sexual harassment" was not a concept available to Westerners living in 1950 because no one at that time put matters in those terms. Nevertheless, that culture was similar to ours in so many other respects that it may have had everything necessary, both materially and conceptually, for recognizing the phenomenon. Thus, a time-travelling experimenter would have no trouble getting 1950s denizens to identify instances of sexual harassment correctly, once they were made acquainted with the concept and required to apply it to specific situations. In this context, the explanatory burden is on why they did *not* have the concept rather than how they could have possibly had it. The only remaining question is whether people in 1950 *should* have recognized sexual harassment: does this epistemic omission constitute moral blindness?

Epistemology as counterfactual historiography 231

Given the degree of overlap between 1950 and now, I would say that, until argued otherwise, if sexual harassment should be recognized by us, then it should have been recognized by them. The burden is thus on those who would *withhold* moral censure from the denizens of 1950.

This brings us to the second basis for supposing considerable overlap between the past and the present. Time is grammatically represented not only by *tense* but also by *aspect*. The former orders action discretely in time as being past, present or future, while the latter captures temporal extension, such that, say, an action begun in the past may be either completed or ongoing from the standpoint of the present. Indeed, the significance of aspect comes into view once we realize that "past", "present" and "future" are token-reflexive, which means that they refer equally to the user and the target of usage. When we compare our own condition with that of another time and place, not everything about that time and place is presumed to be different from our own. Presupposed is, so to speak, a "common space in time" that enables us to distinguish ourselves from others whom we include as actors in our own defining narratives, usually as "precursors" but sometimes "exemplars" whose standards we struggle to uphold (e.g. "What would Einstein say here?"). Moreover, the token-reflexive nature of our key temporal terms makes the exact boundary between, say, the "past" and the "present" difficult to draw, as it may vary significantly across speakers and may also change in light of new historical scholarship and empirical research. Intuitively it captures the idea that when we refer to historical agents with concepts we use to refer to ourselves, we are treating them as virtual contemporaries, at least with respect to those matters, which may include licensing both us and them (via hypothetical time travel) to make moral judgements of each other.

At this point, it is worth observing the different ways in which the boundary between the past and the present may change over time. There are simple and complex cases. The simple cases involve the movement of phenomena from one to the other side of the boundary. On the one hand, what had been attributed to the past may come to be seen as properly belonging to the present. This is *anachronism*. On the other hand, what had been seen as part of the present comes to be seen as part of the past. This is *obsolescence*. Thus, Sharrock and Leudar (2002) would have us regard "sexual harassment" as anachronistic for Westerners living in 1950. The concept's obsolescence would entail either the elimination of the phenomena that currently trigger claims of sexual harassment or a reclassification of those phenomena under different categories, which would reflect a revised understanding of the causal structure of the world.

The complex cases involve an actual shift in the boundary between the past and the present, in other words, a temporal extension of phenomena that had belonged exclusively to either the past or the present. On the

232 Epistemology as counterfactual historiography

one hand, something previously restricted to the past may be seen as also continuing into the present. This is *atavism*. On the other hand, something previously regarded as a recent innovation may be seen as having roots in the past. This is *tradition*. Since most people believe that sexual harassment has never formally disappeared, claims of its atavistic recurrence are rarely, if ever, made. (However, sometimes claims of atavism are attributed to present-day racial and religious discrimination.) In contrast, I regard sexual harassment as having existed long before it was formally recognized, albeit in a collectively repressed form, as evidenced by the past's failure to name the phenomenon, even when the semantic resources were available. A complementary contrast to the one portrayed here – namely, between a claim of obsolescence matched by an argument for atavism – was played out by Max Planck and Ernst Mach over the relevance of persistent philosophical problems with Newtonian mechanics to present-day physics research. Whereas Planck argued that the empirical successes of physics rendered the problems obsolete, Mach claimed that they continued to haunt the discipline (and indeed would help seed the Einsteinian revolution). See Fuller (2000b: 124–28).

An interesting consequence of upholding a strict distinction between the modal and the temporal senses of possibility applies to the scope for moral agency. To enforce the distinction is to presume that people inhabiting a given place and time have much more discretion at their disposal than Sharrock and Leudar – and other relativists – would seem to allow. People are not simply prisoners of their pasts. Scotus himself exploited this point in providing one of the strongest defences of free will in the Christian philosophical tradition. But this expanded voluntarism has a downside. People also bear much more "negative responsibility" for their actions. "Negative responsibility", an expression associated with utilitarian moral theory, is the responsibility one bears for what one does not do but could have done (Smart and Williams, 1973: 93–100). Thus, from a normative standpoint, the fact that sexual harassment could have been recognized by Westerners in 1950 overrides the fact that there would have been no precedent for doing so then. The autonomy of the modal from the temporal senses of possibility thus expands the sphere of the moral accountability of the agents under consideration. But then, who ever said that doing the right thing would always correspond to the path of least conceptual resistance? Certainly not "intellectuals" (Fuller 2009a: ch. 3).

Possible worlds as the micro-structure of freedom and determinism

At first glance, most historians do not take counterfactual reasoning more seriously for the simple reason that it is a "fictional" enterprise, in the

Epistemology as counterfactual historiography 233

strict sense of not being sufficiently constrained by the relevant facts. However, if we stop there, it becomes mysterious why counterfactuals should feature so prominently in computer simulations in both the natural and social sciences, ascriptions of motive and responsibility in law, as well as the more quantitative reaches of history ("cliometrics"), not least economic history. Indeed, the 1993 Nobel Prize in Economics was awarded to Robert Fogel for his counterfactual-driven studies of the difference that railroads and slavery made to US economic history (Fogel 1964; Fogel and Engerman 1974). We shall be returning to Fogel's innovative work below.

One way to demystify historians' resistance to counterfactual reasoning is to suppose that they are not hard-headed about facts but soft-headed about causation. The cognitive value of counterfactuals in history comes from the exercise of suspending one assumption about the past and holding as many of the rest intact so that whatever happens in the alternate history is attributable to that hypothesized difference in initial conditions. It is not sufficient to ask, "What if ... " without a procedure for generating a determinate path or outcome. In this respect, counterfactual reasoning is simply experimental reasoning in the abstract, an idea that is preserved in so-called "thought experiments". For philosophers of the inductive method from Francis Bacon to John Stuart Mill and Ernst Mach, "experimental reasoning" was more a general turn of mind than the specific logic of the laboratory. In this original broad sense, experimental reasoning included what historians would easily recognize as the "comparative method", whereby differences in, say, national destinies are related to distinctive features of peoples who otherwise share many properties and propensities. (An important innovation associated with this sensibility was the introduction of parallel time-lines by Adam Ferguson to accompany his entry on "History" in the second edition of the *Encyclopaedia Britannica* in 1780, which permitted comparative judgements about civilizations at a glance. This enabled informed speculations about what would happen, if a given people were to undergo a specific condition – say, slavery – which animated many eighteenth- and nineteenth-century political discussions.)

Despite these historiographical precedents, historians instinctively resist the strong sense of causal attribution implied by counterfactuals. One source of resistance that should not be underestimated is the peculiar combination of expansiveness and narrowness that counterfactual reasoning requires of the imagination. For example, the standard procedure in economic history for establishing the difference a change in the past would have made at some later date is to determine the latest possible moment when the change could have occurred, thereby disturbing as little of the subsequent history as possible. In the case of imagining the fate of the US economy without railroads, the rationale would be to maximize the likelihood that other modes of transport would have been available to address an already emergent need that railroads historically filled. Thus, the historian is asking a rather finely tuned question: What is the marginal difference that railroads made vis-à-vis its potential substitutes (e.g. horse-drawn coaches, shipping, etc.) in contributing to US economic growth? Nevertheless, the question may be very hard to answer because so much of our understanding of US economic history presupposes the causal significance of railroads that to imagine otherwise makes it difficult to imagine US economic history at all. Not surprisingly, Fogel was awarded the Nobel Prize, as he managed to overcome this failure of the imagination by disaggregating the question into many local problems of how various goods and people would be moved from place to place, and the implications that would have for the redistribution of capital across the nation's regions.

But perhaps more fundamentally, an excessive reliance on counterfactual reasoning challenges a norm of the historian's craft. Much of the hard graft of historical practice is conducted in archives, the results of which occupy the lion's share of space in most historical articles and monographs, which are often presented as an extended commentary on these findings. Under the circumstances, it is easy to believe that significance is proportional to evidence: The more documentation for a given idea, event or judgement, the greater its historical importance. Put this crudely, the thesis appears implausible. However, a subtler version of it would seem to inform the suspicion with which historians tend to treat so-called esoteric interpretations of the past, such as those associated with Leo Strauss, that are based at least as much on what is absent as present in the historical record. Implied by such suspicion is that any phenomenon of import would have left a trace, and the historian's job is not completed until that trace is either found or from its absence the phenomenon's non-existence is inferred. A still subtler version of the thesis would treat each evidentiary trace as itself an event, whose absence might have resulted in a rather different phenomenon being evidenced. But to tie one's sense of historicity so intimately to the historical record is to subvert the powers of abstraction presupposed by counterfactual reasoning (Fuller and Collier 2004: 180–87).

However, the efficacy of counterfactual reasoning suggests two alternative ways of thinking about the historical record: On the one hand, a historian's inference would have been valid even if the paper trail were substantially different or reduced from the one she found. On the other hand, events might have easily gone in a slightly different direction, resulting in a radically different set of documents requiring the historian's attention. In what follows, I characterize these two states as implying,

Epistemology as counterfactual historiography   235

respectively, an *overdetermined* and an *underdetermined* sense of history. Both possibilities suggest that there is a deep structure to history, access to which lies somewhere *outside* the actual archives. In that case, the status of the historian's careful recovery and analysis of documentary evidence may shift from craft virtue to tribal idol.

So let us start by stepping back to the meta-level and ask how one needs to think about the relationship between actual and possible events in history in order to acquire the sense of perspective represented by under- and over-determinism. Consider, once again, the case of the Scientific Revolution happening in seventeenth-century Europe. In judging the historical significance of this episode, not even the most idiographic historian means to suggest that *everything* that historically transpired in the episode was necessary for its having the significance it has had. I choose my words carefully here because I do not especially mean to deny the doctrine of "internal relations" associated with idealist metaphysics, according to which everything is so interdefined that to change one thing, however slightly, is to change everything else. This point can be happily conceded because it still leaves open the question *by how much* everything is changed – especially whether the amount of change substantially alters the significance of the episode. For example, a world where Isaac Newton had never existed would have certainly given us a different Scientific Revolution, but exactly how different? It might be that someone else would have come up with roughly the same synthesis around the same time as Newton, had that person lacked Newton's exotic intellectual interests or personal temperament. (The actual Newton obsessed about his originality, deeply resented slights at his genius, was swayed by flattery, and appeared to have spent most of his time trying to fathom the secrets of alchemy and the Book of Revelations.) In that case, the change would not have mattered very much to our understanding of the historical significance of the Scientific Revolution.

Historians and philosophers of science differ among themselves – and also with practising scientists – about how necessary the actual person of Isaac Newton was to the Scientific Revolution. That such disagreement exists already suggests that the very idea of the Scientific Revolution as "historically significant" implies that we are conceptualizing it as a set of properties (e.g. mental dispositions, scientific doctrines, research techniques, etc.) that are likely to co-exist under some circumstances but not others. Someone with rather literal views about Newton's "genius" would say that the relevant properties could only co-exist in the very person Newton. But that would seem to render the generalizability of Newtonian mechanics and the spread of the Scientific Revolution a complete mystery. After all, the vast majority of those who have mastered and used Newton's equations have lacked Newton's idiosyncrasies. So, it would

236   *Epistemology as counterfactual historiography*

seem that part of what makes an episode "historically significant" is that it could have occurred under somewhat different circumstances – which is to say, in some other possible world or as part of some alternate history of our world. Indeed, that Newtonian mechanics did manage to take root in many cultures and contexts rather different from seventeenth-century Europe may be taken as indirect evidence for this claim.

This suggests two general ways of thinking about the Scientific Revolution's historical significance. These two ways are based on alternative conceptions of counterfactual conditionals, or "possible worlds" as they are more popularly known. The 1970s witnessed a renaissance of interest in this topic, marking a general turn in analytic philosophy away from epistemology and back to metaphysics, itself a reflection of the loosening grip of logical positivism on the entire discipline. The two positions to be discussed are roughly based on the views of the two Princeton philosophers of the period, David Lewis and Saul Kripke. (The best introduction for social scientists remains Elster 1979: ch. 6.) Whereas Lewis envisions possible worlds as multiple parallel universes, Kripke sees them as alternate branchings of the one actual universe. This difference in overall conception implies radically different methods for constructing possible worlds, which in turn may influence our judgements about the extent of determinism in a given situation. Let us consider what is at stake in terms of the example of the Scientific Revolution.

To put you in the Lewisian frame of mind, think about the Scientific Revolution that occurred in seventeenth-century Europe as a botanist who comes across a plant, analyses its physical composition and discovers that it includes a stable compound with some interesting nutritional or therapeutic properties that might be worth synthesizing in a different and more widely available form. Those properties are like the ones that cause us to regard what took place in seventeenth-century Europe as "historically significant". So the question then becomes, beyond the specific ecology that bred the particular plant, how many other ecologies and perhaps even material containers (after all, the relevant properties need not be cultivated in plants, they could be simply manufactured as drugs) could sustain the relevant set of properties as a stable compound? The scientific utopias envisaged by Bacon and his successors are best seen as having been conceived in this spirit, where the "stable compound" they claim to have come across is the scientific method itself, which can then serve as the infrastructure for new and improved societies throughout the world.

In contrast, the Kripkean possible world theorist sees herself as intervening in a developmental process that has been already unfolding. Her claim to 20/20 hindsight appears to be the classic "Monday morning quarterback", the American way of conveying Hegel's idea that the Owl of Minerva takes flight at dusk. The basic strategy is to identify a point in the past when, had the relevant agents decided otherwise (and there is reason to think they might have), another more desirable outcome would have resulted. At first glance, this strategy might seem to favour the overdeterminist interpretation of history, except that identification of the relevant decision-point may turn out to be quite difficult, since that moment will always depend on what we know of the actual history. So, if we want to say that China could have launched the Scientific Revolution before Europe did, what feature of its culture would have had to change and at what point in its history would that change have been feasible – such that it would not have undermined the other features of Chinese culture needed to maintain the Scientific Revolution? The nuances packed in this question are not meant to cast doubt on the existence of such decision-points. However, the answer is not straightforward and is likely to shift significantly as we learn more about both the actual character of Chinese culture and what we take to have been so significant about the actual Scientific Revolution. Indeed, whatever resistance China subsequently posed to the introduction of European scientific ideas and practices could be used as evidence that China first had to be Westernized before it could be a scientific culture. However, this conclusion cuts both ways: By denying China's capacity to sponsor a Scientific Revolution, we would have at the same time revealed the limited reach of Western ideas without the Western vehicles to convey them.

To those who believe that history should be understood exactly as it happened – no more and no less – both the Lewisian and Kripkean approaches conjure up strong normative responses, often disguised as charges that the very idea of "possible worlds" is empirically ungrounded. I say "disguised" because Lewis and Kripke are, in the end, simply suggesting imaginative extensions of empirical practices that are integral to, respectively, the trials of the laboratory and the trials of the courtroom. However, the normative concerns remain, indeed, in a form that can be easily cast in ethical terms. On the one hand, the method of analysis and synthesis that is integral to Lewisian possible worlds is normally applied to non-humans, or perhaps parts of humans, but not entire humans and whole human societies. Hence, the Lewisian is open to charges of exploitation and manipulation. On the other hand, the more forensic approach taken by the Kripkean possible worlds theorist is normally restricted to duly authorized judicial bodies. Here one might ask indignantly: Who gives the Kripkean the right to try people from other times and places for things they unsurprisingly failed to do because they had not attempted to do them? Having dealt earlier with the problems surrounding the Lewisian position, let me now dwell on this objection to the Kripkean position.

One research context where the Kripkean approach has been used to great effect is in the so-called New Economic History spearheaded by

238 Epistemology as counterfactual historiography

Robert Fogel. Fogel pioneered an exact use of counterfactual analysis to test the widespread belief that the introduction of rail transport was responsible for the massive economic growth experienced by the United States in the nineteenth century (Fogel 1964). Is it really true that had the railroads not been introduced, the US would not have experienced such growth? Fogel addressed the question by, so to speak, rewinding the history back to 1830, when the railroads were introduced and then playing the history forward without the railroads and evaluating the economic condition of the US in the alternate 1890. Fogel conducted his analysis under severe historiographic constraints. He removed *only* the railroads from his analysis. In other words, everything else about the state of the world in 1830 remained the same – especially the other forms of transport and the capital available to invest in their development. Fogel chose 1830 as the date to begin the branching into the alternate history because that was the latest date the railroads could have been reasonably ignored as a potential spur to economic growth. Counterfactual methodologists call this the "minimal-rewrite rule" (Tetlock and Belkin 1996: 23–25).

In Fogel's analysis, the railroads are not the unique embodiment of some set of properties or ideas; rather, they are merely one of several possible such embodiments that might have been realized in the timeframe under consideration. Indeed, Fogel found that other forms of transport would have taken up the slack, leading to a more intensively articulated network of river and canal transport, which by 1890 would have resulted in a different distribution of population and wealth across the country but the country as a whole would have enjoyed roughly the same level of aggregate wealth and rates of productivity. So, while railroads were probably necessary for the growth of, say, Chicago, they were not necessary for the overall growth of the US. In that sense, the economic expansion of the United States in the nineteenth century was overdetermined, in that it could have occurred under several different economic regimes, including ones without rail transport.

Given Fogel's operationalization of his research question, it is not surprising that the capital tied up in railroads in the actual 1830 flowed to the development of water-based transport in the alternate 1830. What *is* surprising is the projected state of the US economy in the alternate 1890. Of course, the question that begs to be asked is the exact source of the overdetermination that Fogel claimed to have demonstrated. That would require identifying a point in history before 1830 when an alternate decision could have been reasonably taken, which by 1890 would have resulted in an economically diminished US, relative to the actual 1890. That prior decision-point, though it may turn out to be several decades earlier, should be as close to 1830 as possible, on methodological grounds, so as to minimize the number of other aspects of the actual history that would also need to change. However, it is not clear whether the alternate decision would have been taken by "someone" in the US itself or, say, Britain, France, or Spain, as the decision would have major consequences for bounding the United States as an economic system. (My use of "someone" is meant to be neutral on the nature of the agent: It is unlikely to be a solitary individual but rather a "collective decision" taken by individuals distributed in a mutually recognized sphere of influence, as in the case of capital investors in transport, each of whom would recognize the others as engaged in similar deliberations; or a chain of command emanating from the legislature to the administrative apparatus.) Nevertheless, by identifying the latest moment in history when the economic expansion of the US was underdetermined, one would be finally in a position to address what had to be necessary for that expansion to occur.

Despite its methodological scruples, Fogel's work has been subject to severe criticism, not least on normative grounds. The reception of his follow-up work, *Time on the Cross* (Fogel and Engerman 1974), is instructive as an object lesson in the interdependency of causal and value judgements in the constitution of historical significance. I have envisaged an experimental study of such value-cause dependency, called *axioaetiotics*, conceived in the spirit of psychophysics, in which physical stimuli are varied to manipulate sensory response (Fuller 1993: ch. 4, sec. 7). Accordingly, one would construct scenarios that vary the causal modality of a known event (i.e. the degree to which it was under- or over-determined) to manipulate the value placed on it by a subject. Fogel had argued, using a version of this counterfactual method, that slavery could have been easily sustained on strictly economic terms in the United States, had there been no overriding political will to abolish it. Surprisingly (at least to Fogel), his thesis was widely read as racist, when he very clearly had intended the exact opposite.

To be sure, Fogel's argument was partly meant as a polemic against Marxists who held, very much in the spirit of classical political economy, that the agricultural basis of slavery would soon self-destruct because of its reliance on non-renewable resources. On the contrary, Fogel claimed, the political economy of the slave-holding US South adopted new agricultural technologies, engaged in land conservation, as well as treated slaves tolerably well, at least when compared to the living conditions of blacks in the industrial North. Moreover, the South had a powerful overseas ally in Liberal Britain, which regarded a consolidated US economy as a serious economic rival. Given all these factors, plus the traditional American hostility to "big government" imposing on all states a unitary policy relating to the private sphere (what was at the time positively depicted as "popular sovereignty" and "states' rights"), Fogel concluded that it spoke well to Abraham Lincoln's political judgement

240   *Epistemology as counterfactual historiography*

(admittedly made out of mixed motives and backed by military might) that an outcome whose occurrence had a low prior probability – the abolition of slavery – was actually brought about with long-term positive consequences. More reason, then, to rate Lincoln the greatest US president, or so Fogel thought.

But Fogel's readers thought otherwise. They tarred him with the racist brush for suggesting the long-term sustainability of slavery in the United States. He seemed to imply that the default course of history – at least American history – was not necessarily on the side of the angels. He rendered underdetermined an outcome that had been previously regarded as overdetermined. That this feat should have unleashed such a moral panic reveals the extent to which we expect our causal and value judgements to move in the same direction: however long it may take, the good guys should always win in the end. The depth of our value commitments is evidenced by – or perhaps reified as – the inevitability with which we think they will be fully realized. Thus, those who have seen slavery as a moral abomination have also believed that the practice would be eventually terminated, regardless of, say, the Civil War's outcome. Conversely, those political economists who, in the footsteps of Malthus and Spencer, assimilate the persistence of poverty to the workings of natural selection have also regarded welfare programmes as transient exercises in futility, regardless of the number of state-based initiatives. Very often this linking of causal and value judgements has the effect of a self-fulfilling prophecy, say, inspiring action in those who wish to see slavery end sooner rather than later or inhibiting action in those who out of pity might otherwise delay the extinction of the impoverished.

But Fogel was valorizing an entirely different kind of agent, someone who takes action against the odds yet manages to succeed. Had St Augustine been armed with probability theory, he would have interpreted Fogel's perspective as demonstrating how free will can overcome the genetic liability known as "Original Sin". Perhaps God deliberately created the world in an unfinished state to provide humans the opportunity to redeem themselves or, more heretically (but more simply), as an admission of the deity's need for humans to fill in the details of a plan that S/He can only sketch. This general line of thought (with which I have considerable sympathy) is associated with St Irenaeus, the second-century bishop of Lyon, France. It enjoyed a renaissance in Victorian Britain, especially in the later writings of John Stuart Mill, under the rubric of "constructive unhappiness". But of more direct relevance here is the meta-level point that historical revisionism of the sort practised by Fogel, which ultimately amounts to no more than a shift in the probabilities connecting some events with some other events, can have normative consequences that outweigh, say, anything that might be accomplished by the proverbial time traveller to the past. I stress this point because the fascination with time travel associated with the popularization of Einstein's relativity theory often gives the misleading impression that the alleged "changes" the time traveller can make to the course of history are somehow more profound than what has regularly happened when a historian discovers new evidence and/or systematically reinterprets old evidence (Fuller 1998).

In the case of both the exotic traveller in time and the historical revisionist who never leaves her study, what is loosely called "changing the past" involves, strictly speaking, a change in modality: A world other than our own is promoted to actuality, while ours is demoted to an alternate possibility. One's intervention in the past causes an exchange between the world that actually followed from the moment of intervention and an alternate future from that point in time. In the case of both the time traveller and the historical revisionist, the possibility so actualized need not be radically different from the world it demotes. For example, whether one imagines Fogel to be a time traveller who returns to 1830 to stop the introduction of railroads or simply an economic historian juggling counterfactuals, the alternate future turns out not to be very different on the whole – though, to be sure, different in the parts – from the one with which Americans are familiar. Nevertheless, two reasons may be offered for why time travel is typically regarded as more potent than historical revisionism. One is that people today regard the prospects of turning history in an unexpected direction so remote that the very idea comes to be associated with testing the limits of our understanding of physical reality. Another, perhaps more general, reason is that we tend to believe that the past can exert much more control over the future than the future over the past.

Even if the first reason is dismissed (though it should not be) as merely a speculative piece of sociology of knowledge, the second reason is normally seen as compelling. But is it really? It is striking that the favourite destinations of time travellers are "turning points", moments in the past that we regard as significantly underdetermined with respect to the possible futures into which they open up. Had another, reasonably probable, decision been taken at the time, the outcomes of interest would have been significantly different. A good example is the moment John Wilkes Booth shot Lincoln dead at Ford's Theatre in Washington on 14 April 1865. Had Booth's aim been deflected and Lincoln not mortally wounded, the post-war reconstruction of the South might have occurred with greater perspicuity than it did under his hapless successor, Andrew Johnson, which in turn would have significantly ameliorated American race relations. However, were historians of the future to agree that prolonging Lincoln's life would have made little difference, then so too would the point of travelling back to the past to interfere with Booth's aim. Indeed, we might wish to say that, in light of subsequent historical – including counterfactual – investigation, the people at the time of Lincoln's death and for many years afterward were simply wrong to believe that Lincoln's survival would have made a difference. Similarly, we might even someday conclude, as Fogel did about the railroads, that Lincoln's leadership of the Union during the Civil War was not as decisive to the subsequent history of US as Lincoln's contemporaries and we have taken it to be.

In these instances of historical revisionism, the basic facts of the case need not be other than they are (e.g. Lincoln's date of birth and death, his term of office, the duration of the Civil War, the battles of which it consisted, etc.). Rather, the modal character of the key events has been altered – or more precisely, the probability distribution across the relevant set of possible worlds has changed – such that what had previously appeared necessary no longer seems so, and vice versa. In this respect, the only advantage the time traveller has over the historical revisionist is a capacity to observe the original events in more detail, which might lead to a correction in our understanding of what *actually* happened. However, the fundamental power to "rewire" history – the source of time travel's romance – is exactly the same as that exerted by the historical revisionist, since the time traveller's intervention is no more than a realization of a counterfactual. David Lewis elegantly captures this sentiment in the following comment (as quoted in Dupuy 2000: 329):

> What we *can* do by way of "changing the future" (so to speak) is to bring it about that the future is the way it actually will be, rather than any of the other ways it would have been if we acted differently in the present. That is something like change. We make a difference. But it is not literally change, since the difference we make is between actuality and other possibilities, not between successive actualities. The literal truth is just that the future depends counterfactually on the present. It depends, partly, on what we do now.

The normative stakes of a flexibly revisable history

While this chapter has so far highlighted the interpenetrative character of history and philosophy in the construction and evaluation of counterfactuals, the continuing chequered reputations of Hegel and Comte exemplify the risks in trying to blur the boundary between the two fields. These risks have been taken to a new level by science and technology studies (STS), a field that we have seen is normally associated with "social constructivism", which when applied to history of science highlights the malleability of the modal structure of reality. Specifically, changes to what is (e.g. by the addition or removal of ideas or things) implies

Epistemology as counterfactual historiography   243

changes to what has been, can be and might be. After exploring this point, most notably with regard to Latour's account of Pasteur's scientific achievement, I return to the two polar attitudes towards the world's modal malleability: *over-* and *under-*determination, which correspond, respectively, to a belief in the inevitability and the precariousness of science as a form of knowledge, which I illustrate in terms of Karl Popper's and Alasdair MacIntyre's contrasting visions of a post-human world.

It has become customary to characterize the relationship among the three main disciplines that constitute science and technology studies (STS) – history, philosophy, and sociology of science – as follows: History supplies the raw material that is initially understood in terms of sociological categories, which philosophers then "justify" in the relatively limited sense of offering a recurrent rationale that the historical agents could accept as their own (Fuller 2006a: ch. 3). Daston and Galison (2007) epitomizes the sort of work that results from this process. The book collects a variety of scientific practices over the past three centuries, and organizes them according to disciplines and traditions, from which specific conceptions of "objectivity" (e.g. correspondence, independence, etc.) are then teased out. There is no attempt to provide a grand philosophical – or, for that matter, sociological – narrative that supervenes on the history. Rather, philosophy and sociology are deployed simply to find interesting patterns in the historical detail. Sometimes this approach is presented as a revival of Neo-Kantianism because it appears to presume a correspondence between the organization of academic disciplines and the structure of domains of reality (cf. Fuller 2007b: ch. 2).

My own version of social epistemology construes the tri-disciplinary relationship rather differently, but in a way that can also be explicated in Kantian terms. Consider the organization of Kant's *Critique of Pure Reason*. Here the human subject is cast as an epistemic speculator who is less concerned with insuring what she already thinks she knows than leveraging it into higher-order modes of cognition, ideally to achieve universal knowledge. This was certainly how Kant's immediate idealist successors (Fichte, Schelling, Hegel) read him, which in turn inspired them to develop philosophies that systematized all knowledge into curricula designed to empower free persons. One might then think of history, sociology and philosophy as corresponding, respectively, to the three levels of Kant's architectonic of mind: the manifold of experience, the categories of understanding, and the regulative ideas of reason. In contrast to Daston and Galison (2007), for whom the objects of history are "determined" by being captured in discrete kinds that are both sociologically salient and philosophically meaningful for the contexts in which they normally appear, the idealists saw history itself as increasingly "determined" in the sense that objects with distinct historical origins are

244　Epistemology as counterfactual historiography

consolidated into principles of increased scope that then enable access to new domains of objects. "Science" is thus not a property of particular disciplines but rather a form of knowledge that emerges through what Kant's first major English follower, William Whewell, called the "consilience" of different knowledge bases, with the ultimate aim of knowledge of all things for all people.

A feature of this idealist reading of Kant, which I also endorse, is its "dialectical" character, such that as science opens up new cognitive horizons, it also reconstitutes its understanding of how it got to be where it is. Science is not simply about the growth of knowledge and/or power but equally about the periodic recalibration of the standards by which that growth is measured. This thesis is naturally read as a radical form of social constructivism, and it corresponds to the "Orwellian" function of Whig history in Kuhn's understanding of scientific pedagogy (Fuller 2000b: intro.). The difference between Kuhn's and my own take on Whig history is that I see it less as a "noble lie" that scientists need to motivate themselves and a potentially sceptical public than as a publicly owned narrative whose collective contested performance defines the sense in which both scientists and lay people live in a common world. (Kuhn, for his part, is happy to have scientists and historians of science live in separate worlds, each left to their own historiography.)

To be sure, the very idea that social construction might extend backward as well as forward – that we might "change the past" – easily offends epistemological sensibilities, as Bruno Latour learned when he took symmetrical changes in time to be a consequence of the claim that microbes did not exist before Pasteur. In effect, Latour wanted to argue that over time Pasteur not only cleared the way for today's understanding of the nature of disease, but also successfully backdated the historical record, as Winston Smith was employed to do in *1984*'s Ministry of Truth, to make it so that microbes have always existed (Latour 1999: ch. 5). At first glance, to call this "changing the past" may seem to be an imprecise way to talk about the striking but not so unusual fact that we could come to know that people in the past radically misunderstood important features of their own world (Hacking 1995: ch. 17). Without denying the truth in this observation, nevertheless the emphasis that Latour places on the ongoing nature of the backdating task is striking. When he refers to Pasteur's success in terms just as triumphalist as those of any Whig historian, he is not talking about the enduring truths that were revealed by Pasteur's discoveries but the tremendous amount of work across societies around the world that has been unleashed as a result of those discoveries. On this basis, Latour has provocatively argued that science is the most effective form of politics, if only because scientific discoveries serve as market signals or strong attractors in terms of which

Epistemology as counterfactual historiography 245

many others reorient their activities with the minimal application of external force (cf. Fuller 2007b: ch. 3).

When students of post-Einstein physics want to do a reality check on ordinary usage, they observe that one can only change the present, not the past *or* the future. The statement shocks only because by "the present" the post-Einsteinian incorporates much of what is ordinarily counted as the past and the future. Specifically, "the present" is not simply the "point in time" that the speaker happens to inhabit but a possibility space that extends both backward and forward in time and serves to stabilize the identity of the present as "contemporaneous". To register a change in how things are "now" is *ipso facto* to alter how things could be, where "could" is a measure of "feasibility" in the broad sense, that is, how things might have got to be where they are now and, in light of that, how they might go in the future.

For example, our sense of the present involves the recognition both that Kant died more than 200 years ago and that his ideas remain – and are likely to remain – an important voice in philosophical discourse. Were we to deny Kant's status as a virtual contemporary in this way, we would be effectively living in a different world, one whose past, present and future is bounded differently. In other words, our sense of Kant's continuing contemporaneity presupposes that the dates of his life (1724–1804) are an irrelevance: Kant might as well be living now, as far as our treatment of him is concerned. This is striking, since we routinely discount people by declaring them to be mere "products of their time", by which we mean that their ideas lived and died with their bodies. In contrast, we treat Kant as (if he were) capable of resurrection because his ideas live on in us. Of course, at some point Kant may come to be seen exclusively as a product of his time, in which case our sense of the present will have changed substantially.

However, Latour's Pasteur example reminds us that a change of this sort would be no mere exercise in word magic. Given Latour's own self-understanding as an empirical investigator with no normative agenda, it is left to me to recast the Pasteur case as embodying a two-pronged strategy for world-changing:

1 That any claim to have changed the present – as in the case of Pasteur – should be understood more as a promissory note that is being paid off at a variable rate than a *fait accompli*. In that case, the usual way of telling the history of science misleads by giving too much credit to the work of the originator and not enough to those who pave the ways leading both to and from the work.

2 That changing the present is tantamount to changing the modal structure of history. I have likened this task to history's "time-travelling"

246 *Epistemology as counterfactual historiography*

function, in which world-historic discoveries such as Pasteur's systematically *rewire* the inferences drawn from evidence, so as to alter our sense of what is plausible and hence "realistic". The extent to which we live in the same world is a function of the overlap in our modal judgements. Thus, insofar as people continue to differ about the role of microbes in the cause and spread of disease, the Pasteurian revolution remains unfinished, or more precisely, subject to "uneven development".

I differ from Latour in stressing the normative character of such re-wirings of history. Latour often writes as if history properly told would simply enumerate the entities added to the world, a position he once dubbed "irreductionism" (Latour 1988). Thus, Pasteur first introduces microbes in late nineteenth-century France, and then his followers need to insert them backwards and forwards in history. In contrast, I take more of a balance sheet approach, whereby each entity added incurs costs, as the properties of already acknowledged entities need to be redistributed, resulting in some ontological restriction, if not outright elimination (Fuller 2007b: ch. 3). This is in line with what Imre Lakatos (1981) called "Kuhn Loss", namely, that the introduction of new entities in the wake of a scientific revolution invariably undermines the plausibility of some of the most distinctive entities posited by the previous paradigm by depriving them of a semantic role in the dominant causal narrative – case in point: aether, in the wake of Einstein's revolution in physics. At best, they become fictions, derivatives of the real. Thus, angels have not been erased from historical memory entirely but shunted into a theological ghetto that requires some other entity (e.g. a textual or a neural trace) for their realization, since they now lack a freestanding existence. In effect, I treat ontology as a species of political economy, whereby "reality" consists in living on a budget that requires trade-offs between various possible entities (and their associated expertises), none of which can be fully realized if, as Latour wishes, they would all be realized to some extent (Fuller and Collier 2004: postscript).

A host of metaphysical queries may be raised about the nature of this "ontological budget" that cannot be dealt with here. But suffice it to say, the modal character of reality presupposes that we are normally oriented to such a budget, which is captured by the idea that not everything is possible at a given time and place. What is possible, under which conditions (which is to say, at what cost to whom and to what benefits and harms), constitutes the modal structure of the causal order. This issue is of special relevance to the history of science due to philosophical claims concerning science as a universal form of knowledge. Is science a robust form of inquiry that could be independently invented under various conditions, or a relatively unique approach to the world that leads a rather precarious existence? Here our counterfactual intuitions pull in opposing directions: on the one hand, science could emerge even were the world radically different; on the other, even a relatively slight change to the world would eliminate science altogether.

I have cast this distinction in terms of *overdetermination* and *underdetermination* in history. As we have already seen in this chapter, the former captures a sense of historical necessity that overcomes events and the latter a radical contingency that succumbs to events. Moreover, the same historical evidence can be used to support both alternatives. The two positions part company over how this common evidence base – for our purposes, the actual history of science – is integrated with other evidence that is used to establish what has been and will be possible. This integration task, in turn, has a strong normative dimension that is bound to be controversial because of its potential policy implications. For example, by the logic of underdetermination, insofar as we continue to value science as it is done, and we trace it to events that are considered "accidents of" or "unique to" European history, we are providing prima facie grounds for a certain kind of cultural imperialism. In effect, we are claiming that science requires a rather specific cultural support system that needs to be artificially maintained in order to realize its universal aspirations. These claims would be more openly discussed – and contested – if what in the next section I call a *cordon sanitaire* did not exist between the history and philosophy of science, which involves not only turning the two counterfactual intuitions into default disciplinary postures (i.e. historians as underdeterminists and philosophers as overdeterminists) but also dividing the labour between the two disciplines in terms of temporal horizons (i.e. historians as facing backward and philosophers as facing forward from the present).

In my philosophical youth, at the height of the Cold War, I was very much taken by two contrasting images of the post-apocalyptic epistemic world: an optimistic and a pessimistic one. The former, courtesy of Karl Popper (1972), imagined that a new intelligent species could re-create our civilization by accessing the "objective knowledge" contained in our libraries and databases after what presumably would have been neutron bomb-based holocaust. The latter, due to Alasdair MacIntyre (1981), envisaged that such efforts would be more like those of today's archaeologists, who, even were they blessed with a complete set of our texts and artefacts, would still struggle to understand the sorts of lives we led in virtue of possessing these things. I originally cast the distinction as being about the metaphysical make-up of a world in which knowledge is possible (Fuller 1988: 51–52), but the following will re-cast it as a difference in historiographical sensibility.

Despite the futuristic if not science-fictional character of their thought experiments, Popper and MacIntyre were clearly trying to make philosophical points about our own world. On the one hand, Popper wanted to show that knowledge has much less to do with our personal make-up – either mental or physical – than epistemologists have normally supposed; hence, the autonomy of objective knowledge as "world 3", as opposed to the "world 1" of matter and the "world 2" of belief. On the other hand, MacIntyre wanted to show that knowledge is so closely tied to particular practices that, in the absence of the skills, dispositions, sites and occasions for enacting those practices, texts and artefacts are no more than prosthetic corpses. While Popper's thought-experiment was meant to justify the existence of "science" as a distinct form of knowledge (albeit as a spin-off of all manner of interested, biased and error-prone modes of inquiry), MacIntyre's was meant to undermine the existence of analytic moral philosophy (aka metaethics) for having lost touch with the ways of life that gave meaning to the words that now glibly tumble from philosophically trained mouths.

In terms of the alternative philosophies of history counterposed in Karl Mannheim's (1936) classic *Ideology and Utopia*, Popper (perhaps cast against type) appears to be a radical utopian, who sees a tomorrow that manages to retain everything good from today (i.e. the libraries and databases), whatever else it may contain (e.g. a different species of knowers), while MacIntyre is the reactionary ideologue who downgrades the present for its failure to reproduce essential features of past modes of existence in its own practices. Although Mannheim was concerned mainly to provide a genealogy of the bipolar political world-views of "left" and "right" that emerged in the nineteenth century and continued to structure twentieth-century debate, he acknowledged its roots in the ongoing tensions between what Max Weber (1963) called, respectively, the "prophetic" and "priestly" modes of life in the Abrahamic religions. I am inclined to accept Mannheim's general orientation here. However, I would explain it in terms of a distinction between an *over-* and *under*determinist view of history (Fuller and Collier 2004: ch. 6). Thus, Popper (and the utopian/prophetic mode) represents an *overdeterminist* and MacIntyre (and the ideological/priestly mode) an *underdeterminist* approach to history.

Overdeterminism captures a fundamental optimism in the robustness of history's trajectory, such that the actual details of the past could be radically altered and most of what we already value would remain, or at least be available on tap. This is certainly the spirit in which to understand the "rational reconstruction" approach to the history of science recommended by Popper's follower, Lakatos (1981), who was comfortable both affirming a belief in scientific progress and denouncing most of the actual history of science. After all, to say that something could have been done more efficiently is not to deny that it has been done. In contrast, *underdeterminism* reflects, if not outright pessimism, at least concern for the precariousness

Epistemology as counterfactual historiography   249

of all that we have accomplished, which requires sensitivity to and respect for our mutual dependence as the key to the continued survival of what humanity values. MacIntyre's subsequent career certainly embodies this sensibility (e.g. MacIntyre 1999), where he has been joined by more postmodern theorists who stress the "immanent" over the "transcendent" character of the human condition (e.g. Butler 2004).

My own considered view is that *underdeterminism* – especially of the MacIntyre variety – dwells on the most self-debasing features of humanity's divine heritage, namely, our proneness to a state of "nonage", to recall Kant's disparaging characterization of those whose understanding of humanity was based on a pre-critical reading of the Bible, one that left the impression that we are the children of God who never manage to grow up. Here I prefer Kant's rather literal and uplifting understanding of our divine heritage that was indicative of Enlightenment anti-clericalism – that is, as beings created in the image and likeness of the deity, once we become adults, we take full responsibility for our actions without necessarily disowning our parentage (Fuller 2008a: ch. 7). Indeed, we act godlike in our own way, which for Kant amounted to inscribing a "view from nowhere" in his approach to both theoretical and practical reason. However, it is clear that Kant retains one very central feature of underdeterminism: the precarity of decision-making. In other words, we may aspire to a divine standpoint but in the end we remain fallible creatures whose self-regard may prove delusional, just as the Existentialists feared. In contrast, Hegel believed that even if we personally fail, our successors would be able to learn from our mistakes.

As we have seen throughout this book, of special relevance here is the human significance that Kant assigned to a discipline that he believed had failed on its own terms to render God intelligible: *theodicy*, the justification of the world's many specific imperfections as design features of its being the overall best possible world. Kant (along with many of the devout, I should add) found it blasphemous that theologians would try to minimize human suffering by claiming to speak on God's behalf in this way. Nevertheless, theodicy provides the clearest precedent for our valuing all errors – even evils – as learning experiences en route to a just world order, a thesis that Kant developed in his 1784 essay, "Idea for a Universal History with a Cosmopolitan Purpose" (Neiman 2002: ch. 1). Historical moments of suffering correspond to aspects of nature that, albeit suboptimal in their own right, somehow serve God's global optimization strategy. Epistemic progress may be thought about in a similar fashion – namely, as humanity's temporal experience of God's timeless creation, a modern update of the medieval distinction of *ordo cognoscendi* ("order of knowing") and *ordo essendi* ("order of being"): What we know historically, God wills timelessly. The human quest for knowledge is therefore cast as a journey to an always already settled place, the "Mind of God". This phrase was first popularized by Aquinas's main contemporary rival, Bonaventure, who penned *The Mind's Journey to God*, a proposed curriculum for the University of Paris that anticipates late Enlightenment conceptions of history as humanity's collective self-education (Fuller 2010: ch. 8).

Popper's overdeterminism clearly partook of Kant's peculiar strand of optimism, whereby from the ashes of theodicy emerged the modern faith in progress. It testifies to science's ultimate other-worldliness, its providential perseverance in the face of seemingly interminable resistance – not only from error and evil but also from such mundane ways of knowing as prejudice and common sense (Passmore 1970: ch. 11). However, its full realization requires the removal of the *cordon sanitaire* that normally exists between historians and philosophers of science, whereby both disciplines agree to the principle that "the past is a foreign country" (Hartley 1953), separated in time as if by space – a poetic definition of Kuhnian "incommensurability", if there ever was one. The *cordon sanitaire* allows both for historians to argue that past figures held beliefs suited to their times and for philosophers to argue that those same figures would adopt our beliefs, were they transported to our times. In that case, there is no reason for the present to learn from the past or the past to be humbled by the present.

Moreover, historians and philosophers can interpret this state of mutual non-interference (aka tolerance) to their own respective epistemic advantage. What the historian raises to the level of incommensurable worldviews, the philosopher treats as remediable error. If the philosopher demotes the historian's knowledge claim to a quaint piece of trivia, the historian can repay the compliment by accepting the philosopher's claim as an innocuous fancy. This temporal asymmetry in the historian's and philosopher's appeal to counterfactuals perhaps explains how Rorty (1979) could endorse both Donald Davidson's denial of the existence of conceptual schemes and Kuhn's reduction of the history of science to a sequence of just such things. (In this respect, the hostility that Rorty attracted in the latter part of his career may reflect his scapegoat status for having revealed this unresolved tension.)

Giving the past back its future: the ultimate test of "giving voice"

Historians and philosophers enforce their *cordon sanitaire* by denying figures from the past a full voice in their own inquiries as reality constructors. What I mean by a "full voice" will become clear when considering the case of the thirteenth-century Franciscan friar, Roger

Bacon, who has been alternatively seen as a mad medieval or a proto-modernist. To give Bacon full voice would involve setting aside these two stereotypes in favour of taking the future that he envisaged as a normative benchmark for judging our own world. In this way, Bacon the historical agent would be neither quarantined to a foreign realm called "the past" by the historian nor selectively assimilated to an imperial present by the philosopher. Indeed, a fully "re-enacted" Bacon would challenge the normative assumptions of both possibilities with regard to the modal structure of history: His future would prove to be neither so captive to his past nor destined for our present.

As a first approximation, giving "full voice" to a figure such as Bacon involves taking seriously that figures from the past intended their thoughts and actions to have purchase not only in their own lives and those of their contemporaries *but ours as well*. As it stands, both historians and philosophers treat past figures as polite witnesses, resulting in what I originally called, with regard to Kuhn's (1970) historiography of science, a "double truth" doctrine – one for historians and one for scientists (Fuller 2000b: ch. 1). Put provocatively, historians and philosophers can treat themselves as ultimate truth-tellers and each other as purveyors of fiction or incidentals, just as long as the figures from the past common to their narratives are themselves only semi-realized. But once we insist on a more fully developed sense of the past figures that interest us, then the *cordon sanitaire* proves difficult to maintain – indeed, perhaps to such an extent that, depending on where our normative allegiances ultimately lie, we may need to radically revise either our disciplinary boundaries or our attitude to the past figures in question. In any case, the distinction between "the past" and "the present" becomes problematic.

Behind this point is the claim that the past is not simply something to be handled in some normatively pre-approved fashion – say, through the application of the relevant historical or philosophical methods – but is itself constitutive of that normative sensibility. We may be used to saying that the cut between what counts as "the past" and "the present" is relative to the inquirer's interests, but we rarely acknowledge that those past denizens under study might balk at any such cuts, preferring instead to be treated as our contemporaries, even if they prove to be hostile witnesses in our inquiries. Thus, in the case of the historian, it is not enough for us to understand past figures: However well we might do that, it would seem pointless if these figures did not also understand us as meaningfully related to them, such that (at least) they see why we might find them interesting, even if they would not fully accept our interpretation of their ways. Similarly, for the philosopher, it is not enough for past figures to see the errors of their ways: They should also appreciate that we have been trying to make good on what they were trying to do. Only then would the corrections strike our visitors as more than glorified copy-editing of their original texts but an outright epistemic improvement on their original projects.

Bluntly put, my proposal is that, as either historians or philosophers, we need to learn to treat denizens of the past as our contemporaries. This involves adopting a state of mind that in principle enables the past to change our present-day minds in ways sufficiently fundamental to renegotiate our relationship to the past, perhaps extending to the reconceptualization of our own projects. This amounts to pushing the idea of "re-enacting the past" as far as it can go. Here it is worth recalling that, when first advanced by Wilhelm Dilthey as part of a "critique of historical reason" at the end of the nineteenth century, "re-enactment" foundered because the simple assertion of humanity's species unity was insufficient to underwrite a reliable method (Harrington 2001). However, Dilthey's proposal is set to travel much further in the future, by virtue of two developments:

1 Increasing advances in neuroscience and their integration with historiography will provide a more finely grained sense of how exposure to particular foods and drugs, as well as people, places and artefacts, shaped the past's "psychotropic" environment. Even if neuroscience is never capable of identifying the occurrence of particular thoughts in the past, it may still give us access to the cognitive mood of the past, that is, the "spirit" or "mindscape" within which our forebears thought (Smail 2007; Fuller 2014).

2 Advances in virtual reality technologies will enable the psychotropically enhanced humanist to conduct the re-enactment in the presence of simulated versions of the relevant past figures and conditions ("Second Life" style) alongside the surviving cultural artefacts that provide the usual touchstones for humanistic inquiry. The verisimilitude of this endeavour may be enhanced by the hypothesized capacity of the brain to "mirror" the experience of an action simply by observing it (Turner 2007).

Taken together, (1) and (2) are likely to elevate the pursuit of "historical re-enactment" above armchair speculation, amateur recreation (e.g. staging past battles), or at best the sort of archaeological reconstruction on which the main Anglophone defence of re-enactment – Robin Collingwood's – was grounded. Instead it would become a generalized method of inquiry, for which humanist scholars might routinely seek grants to take the time to live lives like those they wish to understand, during which they would undergo strictures not unlike those of method acting (McCalman and Pickering 2010).

Setting to one side whether the historiographical imagination is likely to be prosthetically enhanced in the near future, conceptual objections remain to the proposal that we engage in a mutual recognition exercise with denizens of the past. At the very least, the historian or philosopher who allows figures from the past to talk back is setting herself up for a fight – not least over whether her own latter-day inquiries are properly conceived. But if historians already imagine themselves visiting past figures and philosophers transporting past figures to their seminars, then what principle stops us from fleshing out those counterfactual interactions into give-and-take social interactions based on jointly negotiated epistemic standards, which in turn might range over both the ends and the means of what we jointly agree to be "knowledge"? After all, when we call ourselves "Darwinian" or, for that matter, "Christian", we are presumably not merely taking advantage of the fact that Darwin or Jesus is dead and hence cannot stop us from appropriating his name for our purposes. Rather, we imagine that he would endorse our activities done under his name by virtue of recognizing us as among his legitimate heirs. In that respect, we implicitly invite time-travelling normative judgement, which once subject to a comprehensive historical re-enactment may of course result in disappointment.

In particular, we tend to assume that those in the past who defended theories and practices that we now regard as precursors to our own forms of knowledge would have also defended most, if not all, of the subsequent developments that increased the likelihood that things would turn out as they have. Yet, this assumption is far from obvious and likely to be false in many cases that are important for historically legitimizing contemporary science. For example, we continue to support Newtonian science *in spite* – not *because* – of its theological foundations, yet Newton would regard our efforts at interpretive charity (i.e. not holding his theology against his science) as condescension, if not an outright emasculation of his position (Fuller 2010: ch. 2). Of course, the last 300 years of the history of science has not been entirely a story of increasing deviation from the Newtonian norm. Physics, though now diminished in socio-epistemic status from its nineteenth- and twentieth-century heyday, still largely aims for the sort of empirically comprehensive and mathematically unified conception of nature that drove Newton's own inquiries. Indeed, even avowed atheists like Stephen Hawking cannot avoid Newton-inspired talk of "entering the mind of God" to justify the increasingly esoteric speculations of cosmologists about the origins of the universe.

To be sure, Newton might have greater difficulty reconciling himself to the history of biology. He would be disappointed by the eventual acceptance of Darwin's theory of evolution by natural selection – even in the face of objections by Whewell, Herschel and Mill that Darwin had failed to render the unity of nature fully intelligible. Newton would see this as indicative of the deviant path that history has taken from the methodological example he laid down in *Principia Mathematica* (cf. Manuel 1963). After all, the closer that human cognitive powers are seen to be to those of animals, as Darwin effectively urged, the more mysterious Newton's own "view from nowhere" achievement becomes and the incentive to pursue it in the future diminishes. However, Newton would take heart at the influx of physics-minded scientists who, largely thanks to the Rockefeller Foundation, filled the ranks of twentieth-century genetics and later molecular biology – along with the nearly science of "biophysics" (Rasmussen 1997). Together these Darwin-neutral disciplines managed to reassert the mechanical world-view, most recently evidenced in the rise of "biotechnology". To be sure, all along their practitioners have had to contend with Kant's rhetorical interference, which for the past two centuries has driven a wedge between mechanism and teleology, to reassure first priests but more recently atheists that scientists are not literally in the business of second-guessing God's motives.

However, a time-travelling Darwin would have his own problems with the present. He would wonder why his name should continue to be attached to developments that so resolutely defy his own de-deified view of humanity, which he expressed in his lifetime as a general pessimism about our ability to take control of the deepest forces in nature, not least (as his cousin Francis Galton had proposed) through eugenics, the politically incorrect precursor of biotechnology. In this respect, Darwin might wish to dissociate himself from any of today's "Neo-Darwinian" projects that suggest that we can alter substantially the course of evolution. But of course, on the other hand, he might come to be sufficiently impressed by the biomedical advances made over the past century to conclude that he had radically overstated the "blindness" of natural selection and the "mereness" of its metaphorical basis in artificial selection (Fuller 2008a: ch. 2). Indeed, Darwin may come to believe that his nineteenth-century critics were right, after all: A stronger case for the intelligibility of nature could be made than he originally thought. But such a concession to today's science would provide only superficial comfort to our own contemporaries, since it leaves Darwin closer in spirit to intelligent design theorists, the scientific creationists who make much of the information-like character of the genome, something that was inconceivable to Darwin in his own day and was only fully fathomed in 1953 with the discovery of DNA's double helix structure (Meyer 2009).

The rhetorical quandaries in which a time-travelling Newton or Darwin would land his present-day hosts speak to the extent to which these great scientists must be understood as having held just the right combination of beliefs in order to provide legitimacy for the science we currently practice. At the same time, we have also seen that both Newton and Darwin could be persuaded to change their beliefs, perhaps quite fundamentally, in light of learning what has happened since they lived. That prospect is of potentially considerable normative interest, as it serves to re-negotiate the social contract with aspects of the past that we want to treat as our own. In that respect, it matters less what Newton or Darwin actually believed than what it would take for them to believe something else, especially something that brings them closer to our own beliefs. (Of course, in the spirit of dissolving the *cordon sanitaire* between history and philosophy, our time-travelling scientists may wish to persuade us that our supposed advances are wrong turns in disguise.) Here we might distinguish two general strategies:

1 *Nudging*: We can get them to our position as a natural extension of their own position, say, by showing them advances in research to which they themselves contributed directly. Philosophers tend to overestimate the utility of this strategy by assuming that because we recognize a scientist as our precursor, she would recognize us as her follower.
2 *Incentivizing*: In cases where some of our own position is radically at odds with some of the past scientist's beliefs, we can try to persuade the scientist that our shared common ground is actually more important to maintain, which then provides a basis for having an interest in changing her mind.

A good way to understand my perspective on the philosophy of history is to see why I object so strongly to the following statement, which clearly expresses the post-Kuhnian, anti-Whig sentiment – what Fuller (2000b) decried as a "Priggish" attitude – towards the history of science that was prevalent in my graduate school days:

> Roger Bacon has often been victimized by his friends, who have exaggerated and distorted his place in the history of mathematics. He has too often been viewed as the first, or one of the first, to grasp the possibilities and promote the cause of modern mathematical physics. Even those who have noticed that Bacon was more given to the praise than to the practice of mathematics have seen in his programmatic statements an anticipation of seventeenth-century achievements. But if we judge Bacon by twentieth-century criteria and pronounce him an anticipator of modern science, we will fail totally to understand his true contributions; for Bacon was not looking to the future, but responding to the past; he was grappling with ancient traditions and attempting to apply the truth thus gained to the needs of thirteenth-century Christendom. If we wish to understand Bacon, therefore, we must take a backward, rather than a forward, look; we must view him in relation to his

> predecessors and contemporaries rather than his successors; we must consider not his influence, but his sources and the use to which he put them.
>
> (Lindberg 1982: 3)

Here the medieval historian David Lindberg is expressing what Harry Collins (1981) was then calling "methodological relativism", which was being promoted as a renewed commitment to *objectivity*. In effect, it proposed to shift the epistemic focus of the historian's role from that of constituting the object of historical inquiry (as had been advanced by various Neo-Hegelian and hermeneutical approaches, as well as Whig histories) to that of providing a context for a sympathetic hearing of the original historical agents (on the model of social and cultural anthropologists). Whereas the former presented the historian as a fellow agent – if not the dominant one – in an ongoing dialogue with the past, the latter presented her as an eavesdropper or silent witness to conversations to which she was not meant to be party (cf. Fuller 1988: ch. 6).

At this point, I must observe that, whatever their merits, Lindberg's claims about how to study Bacon formed part of a historiographical dispute that has come to lose its salience in the intervening three decades. A good way to see this is that two theorists of history who we now often see as standing together, Hayden White (1972) and Thomas Kuhn (1970), would have taken opposing sides on the matter that exercised Lindberg. White's stress on the narrative constitution of history – to such an extent that the historian is not unreasonably seen as making history her own – radicalizes the subjective approach to the past that Lindberg opposed, whereas his own position corresponds to Kuhn's stress on the historian's ability to detach herself from present-day scientific concerns as propaedeutic to making sense of past scientists.

However, this debate over whether historical knowledge is, so to speak, *subject*-led (e.g. White) or *object*-led (e.g. Kuhn) was displaced and the corresponding distinction blurred with the onset of postmodernism in the 1980s. These two now "postmodern" positions were seen as united against a common – albeit probably mythical – "modernist" historiographical foe, namely, one based on a strong metaphysical realism modelled on classical physics consisting in "facts of the matter" about the past regardless of what anyone in the past, present or future might think. Nobody interested in the practice of history enthusiastically embraced this position, since it appeared to imply a theory of causation that committed the historian to some odious form of determinism. But it did provide a new basis for re-drawing the lines between the "human" and the "natural" sciences – not to mention a renewed fashion for talking about "ontology" more generally (e.g. Hacking 2002).

Epistemology as counterfactual historiography   257

I wish to revisit the pre-postmodern disposition concerning the epistemology of history, taking the side of the subject-led approach. Consider the dreaded "Whig history". From the standpoint of the object-led history approach championed by Lindberg (and Kuhn), it constitutes the object of history incorrectly because it fails to respect the past in its "pastness". For these objectivists, "the past is a foreign country" operates as a *de facto* demarcation criterion for what is eligible for historical investigation. Thus, despite holding a doctorate in contemporary physics, Kuhn made no historical inquiries into quantum mechanics or relativity theory after the 1920s because most of the paradigm-bounding issues that were open then remained open when he wrote. Implied here is that a proper object of historical inquiry requires a sense of conceptual and empirical closure that is recognized by the relevant community of inquirers. In sociological jargon, the distinction between past and present is a piece of "disciplinary boundary maintenance" performed by historians that advocates of Whig history violate by treating the past as if it were the opening act for the present. Unsurprisingly, the ranks of Whig history are filled with professional scientists who are prone to interpret professional historians of science as somehow trying to render the past irrelevant to current practitioners, when in fact the past is a ready source of examples, albeit ones often teaching negative lessons.

Subject-led philosophers of history such as myself sympathize somewhat with the Whig historian's bewilderment. We too see continuity between the past and the present, and hence reject the very idea that "the past is a foreign country". However, the Whig sees the continuity going only one way: She projects a line back from the present to – recalling Lindberg's example – Roger Bacon. But of course, the line projected may go the other way, namely, from Roger Bacon to the future *he* would have liked to see realized. Indeed, we may decide that some version of Bacon's unrealized past future would have been preferable to the actual future for which the Whig wishes to provide historical legitimation. In any case, the subject-led philosopher of history does not presume the natural legitimacy of the present in dictating the terms for evaluating the past. Even Hegel, who is so often read as justifying the Prussian status quo, never proclaimed "the end of history" – though Nietzsche believed that a Hegelian would need to say that at some point in time. Rather, Hegel held that any successful practices in one's own day are ultimately means to still greater ends that in retrospect may provide a basis for ironic commentary on what had been truly achieved back then. In this respect, the Whig jumps the Hegelian gun, presuming that we are closer to the end of history than we probably are (Francis Fukuyama, call home!)

Given this background, let us now return to the offending passage by Lindberg. The nature of the offence is captured in the question: *If I were*

258   *Epistemology as counterfactual historiography*

Roger Bacon, would I appreciate being given the Lindberg treatment? It is instructive that the figure in question is the mid-thirteenth-century Franciscan friar Roger Bacon – someone who very clearly believed that his theological, philosophical and scientific views would be vindicated in the fullness of time, a point that Lindberg, to his credit, does not hide. Nevertheless, Bacon would find Lindberg's overall portrayal of him invidious, since it reinforces what appears to have been a mid-thirteenth-century consensus that regarded Bacon's Platonically tinged declarations as relics of an approach to natural philosophy whose preoccupations with mathematics and astrology were rapidly being superseded by a generation influenced by the more earthbound concerns of the then-newly translated Aristotle. In other words, Bacon would regard Lindberg as reducing his thoughts and actions to the interpretive treatment they received at the hands of his contemporaries.

Lindberg could try to justify this treatment, as Quentin Skinner (1969) might, arguing *à la* Wittgenstein or Austin that simply by virtue of engaging in the language game of mid-thirteenth-century natural philosophy, Bacon implicitly agreed to have his speech and actions judged by the rules of that game as defined by recognizably competent players. Lindberg might regard this as a historiographical version of "natural justice", as Bacon is judged by his peers (however harshly) rather than those in the future with whom he never had contact (however generously). But in Bacon's defence, it could be argued that Lindberg's specification of the historical context amounts to "micro-Whiggery". After all, Lindberg's evaluative standards, while no more, are also no less than those upheld by a consensus of Bacon's contemporaries. In effect, their utterances are presumed to be normal expressions of a shared cognitive competence, in terms of which Bacon's own utterances are then treated as deviations. However, this presumption relies on a retrospective sense of closure about the nature of Bacon's times as well as his own fate. Such closure is familiar from mid-twentieth-century social anthropology, which justified the ethnographer's extended snapshot view of the tribe by claiming that, unlike "modern" societies, the tribe's normative horizons are historically "frozen" (cf. Lévi-Strauss 1966). This in turn conveniently circumscribed the object of inquiry so that the inquirer might reasonably master it without having to take any responsibility for it. When translated into historical practice, *à la* Skinner, a kind of collective intellectual obituary needs to be written to turn the past into a foreign country. But exactly how long after the original events should this mass death be declared and the coroner's report issued by the attending historian?

Lindberg's methodologically convenient answer is to judge Bacon by what those of his own and the next generation thought of what he said and did. In that case, to include others whose lives did not overlap with

Epistemology as counterfactual historiography 259

Bacon's would be to shift the context of judgement beyond what Bacon could have reasonably imagined. But is that really the case? I do not believe so. On the contrary, Lindberg radically foreshortens the temporal horizon of intentionality: In at least the Abrahamic world, beliefs and desires are not normally limited to what can be realized in one's lifetime but extend into the indefinite past and future. Thus, when Roger Bacon expressed the belief that the cosmos is constituted as a mathematical system unified under the metaphysics of light, he did not also believe that the truth or falsity of this belief applied only to his lifetime – let alone corresponded to the judgement of the leading thinkers of his day. (The same, of course, could be said of his contemporaries – with interesting consequences.)

In this respect, Lindberg's single-minded quest to capture the first-order intentional states of mid-thirteenth-century Christian intellectuals serves to obscure their second-order attitudes towards those states. In effect, he renders them (with a nod to the ethnomethodologist Harold Garfinkel) *transcendental dopes* – that is, capable of generating thoughts designed for their immediate audience but not some larger yet to be determined audience who might be more receptive. *Pace* Lindberg, Bacon and his interlocutors did not think of themselves as inhabiting a spatio-temporal island of intellectual communication that is available for study as a historian's set piece. Such is a guild conceit of the object-led historian, borrowed partly from anthropology but also, and importantly, from behaviourist psychology, which black-boxed if not outright denied the mind's time-spanning capacities (Fuller 1988: ch. 5).

Unsurprisingly, Lindberg interprets Bacon's preoccupation with the impending apocalypse – a commonplace among Franciscans who followed Joachim of Fiore in reading the Bible as providing a model for understanding secular time – as sufficiently pathological to excuse Bacon's house arrest later in his life. However, this is to ignore that both Bacon and his antagonists were generally contesting the identity of the timeless truth. It was something that would only be revealed in the fullness of time, whether or not it conformed to Joachimite strictures – which, for the record, was not some passing monastic fancy but a red thread that runs through modern notions of progress, not least Hegel and Marx's dialectical conceptions of history (Löwith 1949: ch. 8; Passmore 1970: ch. 11).

Here one needs to ask why someone like Bacon would leave such a voluminous written legacy, if he thought he was merely fighting battles with his contemporaries. Surely, his time would have been better spent doing things that would have made a more direct impression on them, whether it involved face-to-face persuasion or public demonstrations of empirical discoveries. To be sure, from today's standpoint, it is difficult to establish that someone is a philosopher or scientist without access to a textual trace simply because writing is presumed to be the most reliable means of pinning down specific beliefs and their justification. But this guild convention of the historian can too easily obscure the author's opportunity costs in having apportioned his life to the historian's convenience, especially given the improbability that Bacon would have anticipated the existence of someone like Lindberg, who is clearly immersed in our document-saturated culture.

Of course, a time-travelling Bacon could make sense of Lindberg's historiography, but he would marvel at the prosaic status accorded to an epistemic standpoint that in his own day would have been explicitly associated with God's, as channelled through his angelic amanuenses. Yet, in the next breath, Bacon would remind Lindberg that beyond the convenience that they afford academic historians, his corpus signifies his own desire for the intellectual contests of his lifetime to be carried forward, in which case the writings serve as potential scripts for extended improvised performances by future combatants. In this respect, Bacon's textual trace constitutes an act of self-positioning, such so that were he to reappear in our midst, he would be able to identify his descendants – and not simply rely on others to claim him as an ancestor. Moreover, Bacon would be hardly idiosyncratic in trying to game the transcendent character of writing: Jean-Baptiste Lamarck was another figure whose rhetorical strategy appeared to write off his contemporaries in favour of a more sympathetic future audience (Burkhardt 1970).

What makes my own anti-Lindberg position non-Whiggish is that I do not presume for a moment that Bacon would choose as his descendants those who claim him as a noble ancestor. Moreover, by reconstructing Bacon's position as a normative standard against which to judge the subsequent history of science – a feat tantamount to method-acting the role of Bacon for the contemporary stage – we have an opportunity to explore how, say, his commitment to the metaphysics of light might have got us quicker, say, to today's quantum information theory, not to mention other yet-to-be-discovered phenomena. Here Bacon would enjoy the advantage of being someone who held optics to be the foundational physical science, but without having been encumbered by the actual institutional history of science, not least one Isaac Newton, whose paradigm-defining work failed to account for nature of light to anyone's long-term satisfaction.

My historiographical proposal entails that we engage in "rational reconstruction" of the past – but in exactly the way that Imre Lakatos (1981) thought was *not* possible, namely, to project an alternative future from a discarded past. (Lakatos, in contrast, retrojected an alternative, cognitively streamlined past from the present as given.) I have called this approach *retro-futurism* (Fuller 2010: ch. 9). It is clearly related to the "alternate history" scenarios that populate the plots of science fiction. Therefore it should come as no surprise that the approach was originally championed by H. G. Wells in his failed bid to be appointed to the first chair in sociology at the London School of Economics (in the UK) in 1907 (Fuller 2011: ch. 1; cf. Lepenies 1988: ch. 5). Wells's definition of sociology as the "science of utopias" does not seem so odd if we imagine, as Wells did, that the great nineteenth-century prototypes for sociology put forward by Comte, Marx and Spencer proposed various social innovations in order to draw alternative futures from inchoate tendencies in human history. While academic sociology ended up not rising to Wells's challenge, it remains a worthy one to which STS's radical constructivist take on the modal structure of historical reality naturally lends itself.

Conclusion
Redeeming epistemology from the postmodern condition

It is still common to regard the ancient Greeks, especially Plato and Aristotle, as having set the fundamental problems of philosophy and science with which we continue to struggle today. While this may be true at the level of discourse, it is certainly not the case at the level of attitude – that is, what is meant by what is said. Plato and Aristotle did not take these "problems" as seriously as we do. What was for them high-minded leisure for wealthy males – a pursuit of mental acuity comparable to physical fitness – has been for us "high moderns" an intergenerational, species-defining project pursued "for its own sake", which the philosophy, psychology and sociology of science have tried to explicate in their own ways. To be sure, my judgement of Plato here may seem unfair, given his belief that a long-lived individual – the philosopher-king who started ruling at age fifty – is capable of harmonizing knowledge and power in ways comparable to our high modern aspirations, except that we tend to expect our descendants rather than ourselves to achieve Plato's goal.

In any case, were we to teleport Plato and Aristotle to the present, they would probably set aside their deep intellectual differences and join in castigating (if not also pitying) our attempts to remake the world in the image of the laboratory, perhaps in the same spirit that many of the older generation today tend to regard those who wish to "gameify" the world and treat virtual reality as the ultimate reality. In this respect, Plato and Aristotle's judgement would match Freud's in *Civilization and Its Discontents*, where he diagnosed socialism as an "infantile neurosis" that confuses a vivid sense of the desired future with the credibility of its realization (Freud 2002: ch. 5). In short, the Greeks would tell us, "Grow up!" Make no mistake: My own view is that these ancients (along with Freud) would be simply showing their age. But I would expect Aristotle to be the much harsher taskmaster of the two Greeks. Our attempts to incubate a "higher" consciousness through forms of cloistered experience – be it via the laboratory or the computer – comport with Plato's own sense that a radical separateness from everyday life is needed for a deeper understanding of its underlying reality. However, Plato would be frustrated by our assumption that philosophers will spend their entire lives as political larvae, that is, without ever maturing into kings.

In contrast, when it comes to regarding our most mind-expanding conceptions as models for concrete reality, the Bible offers a surer guide, especially if one takes seriously the human-yet-divine nature of Jesus, someone who gradually came to act like the deity that he was discovering himself to be, even if by the end of his mortal existence he had failed. Unlike Plato's Socrates, who is normally presented as an exemplar for accepting the limitations of the human condition with dignity, Jesus has represented humanity's aspiration for self-transcendence from its fallen animal state back to its divine birthright. To be sure, no particular form of worship or "religiosity" follows from this abstract rendering of Jesus's significance. But that does not prevent the "Jesus Stance" from functioning as a default attitude in our thinking of knowledge as, in some sense, a "quest" that is unlikely to be completed in one's own lifetime but from which all of humanity might ultimately benefit, as total knowledge will justify all the sacrifices that have preceded it. Even in the twentieth century, this was precisely Max Weber's (1958b) argument for "science as a vocation". Were we exclusively Darwinian creatures, the pursuit of knowledge would not be such a big deal. "Knowledge" would simply refer to the cluster of capacities that enable us to reproduce successfully as a species – for as long as we do: a synonym for "adaptiveness", if you will.

But clearly the philosophical field of epistemology, which is typically seen as providing the foundation for scientific inquiry, has not historically seen its remit in such banal Darwinian terms – at least not until its recent "naturalistic" turn. To be sure, Darwin would find a comrade in Aristotle in opposing the crypto-theological pretensions of epistemology. What makes epistemology "crypto-theological" is that philosophers argue about "knowledge" and "knowing" in terms that are relatively indifferent to the material embodiment of the knowers: Knowers are treated as vehicles of inquiry and repositories for claims. Even in the case of self-avowed "feminist" and "multicultural" epistemologies, their normative force comes mainly from reminding us of forms of knowledge whose inclusion would benefit – even if only to critically check – the more universal sense of "truth" to which everyone is presumed to subscribe (Fuller 2007a: 49–52, 99–105). Thus, the epistemic shortfall between what we know and should know does not constitute a death sentence for ignorant organisms but an opportunity for autonomous agents to transform themselves and quite possibly the world. This is also the position of "transhumanism", which I have been exploring in my most recent work, especially by developing the "proactionary principle", which was briefly discussed at the end of Chapter 1 of this book (see also Fuller 2011, 2012; Fuller and Lipinska 2014).

264 Conclusion

Against all this, for the past four decades postmodernism has left a distinctive anti-epistemological legacy that is present today in both the postmodernists themselves and their opponents. It is best described as an "ironic displacement" of the "high modernist" quest for knowledge that has been defended in these pages. To reassert epistemology in the form that I have been promoting here – which takes seriously why such a branch of philosophy arose in the first place in the nineteenth century – we must begin by being clear about the "high modernism" that the postmodernist "ironizes". It can be distilled into four propositions:

1 *Knowledge is subject to progress, both at the collective and the individual level.* Humanity comes to know more over time, and each person comes to know more over the course of his or her life. There may be diversions along the way but there is overall forward momentum, such that for most points in time, one knows more than at an earlier time.
2 *Any theory, fact or, for that matter, artefact established is understood to be a temporary moment in the progress of knowledge.* In the fullness of time, it is bound to be substantially revised if not outright replaced. While this does not prevent theories, facts, and artefacts from serving our current needs, they must not be turned into dogmas or fetishes. Knowledge is about objectives, not objects.
3 *Epistemic standards are themselves a kind of theory, fact or artefact, which is to say, equally subject to change over time.* Nevertheless, at any given moment, they function as a fixed point in terms of which theories, facts and artefacts may be judged. However, standards are continually shaped by improvements in the instruments used to implement them as well as the weight of precedent, some combination of which might unwittingly trigger a radical shift in perspective.
4 *Errors are unavoidable in the quest to extend human knowledge.* Their existence is not to be denied but welcomed as reality checks that in the fullness of time, as the relevant corrections are made, should not recur in their original form.

In what follows, I shall consider the "postmodernization" of these propositions in roughly reverse order. My aim throughout is not to reject postmodernism out of hand but to engage in a wheat and chaff exercise from the standpoint of ensuring a future purposefulness for epistemology. While the ultimately sceptical cast of the postmodern mind is to be rejected, it nevertheless points to ways in which epistemologists need to become clearer about what matters in understanding and extending knowledge as the dominant feature of the human being.

A mark of the postmodern condition is that *both* the commission and the detection of errors are seen less as necessary evils than as bases for positive identity formation. In effect, "error" loses its etymological sense of straying from some presumptively virtuous path in two distinct ways. On the one hand, the error committed becomes itself a commitment – that is, reconceptualized as a norm in its own right. On the other hand, error detection becomes an end in itself, which is to say, without reference to any larger end that it might serve. These two sides in the post-modernization of "error" correspond to the two sides of the culture wars that first surfaced in US humanities departments in the wake of decon-struction in the 1980s, reached a fevered pitch as the "Science Wars" of the 1990s, and which in recent years may have entered a new phase with the emergence of scientifically credentialled creationism (aka intelligent design theory) and global warming scepticism. Just as emphasis is placed on the ongoing attempts to suppress an alternative point of view whose very existence challenges the "universalism" (aka hegemony) of the dominant point of view, emphasis is equally placed on the sheer existence of a widely reinforced standard (aka scientific consensus) that reliably catches errors, the commission of which is traceable to ignorance and/or deception of the standard.

What makes both sides of this dispute "postmodern" is that they do not conform to the famous theodicy-informed distinction drawn by the great nineteenth-century German historian Leopold von Ranke, who contrasted his own interest in understanding things as they actually happened (*wie es wegesen*) with a divine standpoint (*sub specie aeternitatis*) in terms of which an overall plan determines the significance of particular events: that is, meaning as it appears to the agent and to the analyst of history, respectively. In obviating Ranke's alternatives, postmodernists do not hide their own selective attitude towards the entire historical record. Indeed, in the brief examination of each side of the postmodern divide below, we find evidence for what Jean Baudrillard (1981) called "hyper-reality" effects, as heroic abstractions made from history are set up as stand alone normative structures, a process enhanced in an age when information and communication technologies have enabled the multiple appropriation and mass circulation of signs without requiring their users to possess a historic trace back to an authentic source. In this respect, the broken hyperlink is simply the latest installment in the perennial failure to find a "genesis" moment that might provide an overarching purpose to one's search for meaning (cf. Derrida 1978: ch. 5).

Following the precedent set by Hayden White (1972), those whose identity is wrapped up with so-called error openly support the idea that history is a form of myth – namely, one which tells the story of how a beleaguered people managed to overcome the odds. To have been declared in error in the first place mainly reflects the prejudice and historical myopia of those who made the judgement. Over time what had been previously seen as liabilities come to be celebrated as virtues. The narrative underwriting this myth is borrowed from the original seventeenth-century Whig account of English political history as "The Story of Liberty", referring to the gradual and often painful transition from royal to parliamentary government, over the course of which democratic rule comes to acquire positive connotations that it had previously lacked (Butterfield 1931). The postmodern twist, already present in White, is to remove the original narrative's unique truth claim by turning it into a ready-made template for any oppressed group seeking vindication. A signature technique here involves converting a reversal of fortunes that originally took decades to achieve into a rhetorical device whereby the stigmata of deviance are re-appropriated by the deviant groups as marks of positive identity, perhaps most notably in the case of "queer" (Butler 1990).

In contrast, groups fixated on enforcing epistemic standards *an sich* range well beyond the official organs of the scientific establishment to include such vigilante organizations as the US National Center for Science Education (NCSE), which specifically monitors the teaching of high school science to ensure that creationism does not appear in the curriculum. They effectively adopt a Darwinian attitude towards Darwinism itself. The sheer fact that evolution by natural selection has become the dominant biological paradigm is for them sufficient reason to accept its epistemic legitimacy. It is worth putting the point so bluntly because groups like the NCSE are usually engaged in no more than fitness checks of the alleged offenders. They are rarely front-line contributors to the sciences whose honour they would uphold and sometimes not even trained in those sciences yet nevertheless quite respectful of their authorization (aka peer review) processes. It also goes without saying that they are not trained to interpret the alleged offenders in context. The calling card of this approach is to "cut-and-paste" offending quotes and show their lack of correspondence to an authorized knowledge claim. The reader is offered neither an interpretation of why the offender might have been moved to utter the offensive lines nor any indication that the experts might be inclined to allow the utterance, despite its lack of correspondence to the official epistemic line.

The Science Wars of the 1990s, discussed in Chapter 5, produced a text that might count as a classic of this practice. Sokal and Bricmont (1998) was written as the definitive follow-up to the great "Sokal hoax", in which Alan Sokal, an obscure physicist at New York University, published an article in *Social Text*, then the leading cultural studies journal in the United States, entitled "Transgressing the Boundaries: Towards a Transformative Hermeneutics of Quantum Gravity" (Sokal 1996). Sokal had mastered the jargon and genuflected to all the right French philosophical authorities, and even declared (genuine) leftist credentials as a former mathematics instructor to the Sandinista rebels in Nicaragua. But he also planted errors that only specialists in the relevant branches of physics and mathematics would easily spot. His intent, as revealed on the front page of *The New York Times* shortly after the article's publication in May 1996, was to reveal the "impostures" of French intellectuals and their American admirers in cultural and social studies of science who claimed to see a vindication of postmodernism in post-classical physics and mathematics.

What followed was a predictable level of denial, backpedalling and rebuttal, typically turning on Sokal's deceptiveness. Surprisingly perhaps, *hardly any defence was made by appealing to postmodernism's own avowed epistemic principles*. In particular, few defended *Social Text*'s editorial decision on the straightforward constructivist ground that the meaning of Sokal's text is defined not by his intentions but the text's reception. (An exception is Fuller 2006a: ch. 4.) It may well be that the tacit acceptance of Sokal's authorial privilege in defining his text as a "hoax" will have turned out to be the biggest strategic error made by his postmodern opponents. In effect, they behaved just as Sokal had imagined them – namely, as constructivists merely in theory but not in practice. Now, nearly two decades later, the overall effect of the Sokal hoax has been to chasten humanists, including STS scholars, insofar as the very idea that these fields might provide a "critique" of science without themselves being specialists in the relevant fields has been placed on the back foot (Latour 2004; Fuller and Collier 2004: intro.; Sokal 2008). To be sure, Sokal's ethics continue to be challenged, so much so that a small cottage industry in social epistemology has now emerged on "trust" as an epistemic virtue (Kusch and Lipton 2002). Yet, Sokal's fundamentally authoritarian approach to knowledge remains untouched.

Nevertheless, there remains a case for Sokal and his admirers to answer: *What is the exact benefit of possessing an "expert-approved" standard of knowledge of scientific facts and concepts?* I have chosen this form of words to highlight the significance that dedicated anti-postmodernists attach to sheer conformity to a presumptive standard as a prerequisite for public discussion of science. But what is the evidence that such conformity actually promotes the growth of science, understood either in strict disciplinary or wider cultural terms? In responding to this challenge, the following four points should be kept in mind:

1 Often the technical errors that Sokal and his admirers catch in others may be corrected without substantially affecting the main points that the offending parties are trying to make; hence, the offenders need to be understood in context. Of course, as the linguistic philosopher Jacques Bouveresse (1999) pointed out against Régis Debray in France's

own domestic version of the Science Wars, the very appeal to specialist scientific knowledge in a non-specialist context may be understood as an unnecessarily mystifying appeal to authority. Nevertheless, a proportionate response is needed that distinguishes between saying that it is illegitimate for Debray to raise abstruse twentieth-century developments in mathematics such as Gödel's Incompleteness Theorem to advance certain political and cultural agendas and saying that it is illegitimate for him to advance those agendas at all. The latter claim of illegitimacy does not follow from the former. After all, even stripped of the bogus abstractions and equations, Debray may still make good sense. In his own defence, Debray would probably go further and defend his practice as enabling scientific knowledge to spread while diffusing the power it exerts simply by virtue of its artificially restricted usage – and he may have a point.

2 Science is not so tightly integrated, logically speaking, that the demonstration of error in one field necessarily affects the credibility that the same claim might have in other fields. Defenders of contemporary hot-button stances like creationism and global warming scepticism typically object to the scientific establishment only at either the very highest level of theorizing or the most practical level of policy. They rarely dispute the facts, concepts and practices that guide normal science in the relevant fields on a regular basis. The debate occurs over how they are synthesized into a larger world-view that purports to provide the best explanation for all fields of knowledge drawn together. Thus, with the exception of so-called Young Earth Creationists, creationists do not generally dispute the findings of genetics, molecular biology, paleontology, etc. *per se* but rather that together they uniquely point to the truth of Darwin's theory of evolution by natural selection (Fuller 2007c, 2008a). This point applies equally, if not more strongly, in advanced Muslim countries like Turkey and Iran, which are home to both very strong religious sentiment and high levels of scientific literacy. In all these cases, to know and to resist the scientific orthodoxy go hand-in-hand.

3 Usually the sorts of "errors" that Sokal and his admirers catch involve the transfer of a concept or a finding from one field to another, where it is clear that the target field does not require all of the transferred item's original features. To take a simple example, reference to politics as "chaotic" or "complex" may have force even though it borrows only a qualitative sense of these concepts without any immediate prospect of a clear mathematical formulation. Normally one speaks of such transfers as "metaphorical". Moreover, the history of science is full of metaphors developing over time into analogies and finally models for uncovering deep structural features in the target field (Hesse 1963). Ironically, the

direction of influence has tended to flow from social practice to natural science, not *vice versa*. So, when Sokal *et al.* are tempted to complain about humanistic and social scientific "misappropriation" of ideas from mathematics and physics, they might think of it instead as payment on loans that mathematicians and physicists of earlier generations had secured when they imagined that aspects of reality to which they had no direct access might resemble social practices that they encountered on a daily basis. For a Marxist and a liberal gloss on this phenomenon, respectively, one should examine the processes that result in what Alfred Sohn-Rethel (1977) called "real abstraction" and Karl Popper (1972) "objective knowledge".

4 One should never underestimate the pragmatic or performative animus behind what Sokal and his admirers are inclined to dismiss as "errors". It is quite rational for one to admit that most people believe certain things and act in certain ways – or at least are aware that such is how they should behave – and then decide to try something different because of the perceived distinctiveness of one's own situation. Of course, this distinction may turn out to be illusory, not really making a difference, in which case the individual will suffer the consequences. There is no doubt that the experimental approach to living evinced by such an attitude is risky, and perhaps even risk-seeking. To be sure, I have endorsed it as "proactionary" (Fuller and Lipinska 2014: ch. 1). But such a perspective need not be based on ignorance, deception or, for that matter, self-deception. It may be simply grounded in a sense of self-possession that resists the mediation of experts in decisions concerning the disposition of one's own life. Virtually all of the movements that currently challenge the scientific orthodoxy – from alternative medicine to scientific creationism – have this character, which I take to be the mark of *Protscience*, a contraction of "Protestant Science", a diffuse but growing campaign not to oppose science but to integrate it more personally into one's life (Fuller 2010: ch. 4).

For the past quarter of a century, professional historians of science have found a diplomatic solution to the problems associated with the Sokal hoax and other manifestations of the Science Wars. They have simply focused on the objects of science rather than any objectives science might have. In the process, the historians have evacuated the concept of *science* of any univocal meaning, which is my negative re-casting of what they themselves see as an openness to the multiple representations and concretizations of scientific practice, whereby historiography becomes an elaborate exercise in labelling and arrangement without need for overarching explanations (Daston and Galison 2007). Their *modus operandi* is traceable to Foucault's (1970) archaeology of knowledge. In Foucault's wake,

270 *Conclusion*

historians have acquired a sense of "objectivity" that involves treating everything as remnants of societies long past to which they themselves do not belong. The historiographical significance of the *object* in this context is that, above all, an object is something that has clear boundaries – both spatial and temporal. It is an artefact rather than an art. Foucault himself turned this subtlety to great effect in writing about man [*sic*] as an "object" on the intellectual horizon that was formally launched at the end of the eighteenth century but was gradually disappearing at the end of the twentieth century.

An artefact is something designed for a purpose, which over its life may suffer several fates: Through ordinary wear and tear it may become unfit for purpose; its purpose may change; or it may be redesigned to achieve the original purpose more efficiently. However, once the artefact enters a museum, it loses those fates because it is no longer regarded as living. The artefact's work is treated as completed. This was certainly the original spirit in which books were collected in the famed library that was attached to the museum in Alexandria, Egypt, starting in the third century BCE. Books from all over the Mediterranean were collected so as to draw attention to Egypt as the final resting place of anything worth knowing. While the library certainly hired scholars, and some like the geometer Euclid proved to be original thinkers, most of the "scholarship" consisted in collating and preserving texts that, given their disparate sources, were always on the verge of corruption and misidentification (McNeely and Wolverton 2008: ch. 1).

Epistemologically speaking, the books housed in Alexandria were in suspended animation: they were wrenched from the cultural context that provided their meaning, only to be made available to those with licensed access to the museum. While this situation was responsible for the rise of many of the basic principles of editing and textual criticism, the resulting scholarship was conducted largely in the spirit of mortuary science or taxidermy. Little surprise, then, that Hegel regarded Egyptian art as "monumentalist" in the sense of containing a spirit that is hidden forever beneath its material expression. Lest one accuse Hegel of simply repeating the widespread stereotype of ancient Egypt as promoting a "cult of dead", it is worth recalling its continuing legacy. Even in the modern period, it has been a struggle to make both libraries and museums appear inviting to the public because of these institutions' overriding preservationist impulse – even before considering what it might take to make their contents useful to those who would have contact with them.

I have dwelled on the spirit of the Alexandrian enterprise not only because much of it lives on in postmodernism but also to explain the considerable hostility that it has attracted over the centuries, especially in Islam, which treats knowledge as a living human activity to which all may contribute and from which all may benefit – and, most importantly, receive forward momentum from the Qur'an. Thus, rather than be stored in one central imperial location that would try the resources of a would-be inquirer seeking access, knowledge should be spread everywhere as part of Islam's proselytizing mission. Unfortunately Islam tends to be remembered for only the negative side of this strategy, which culminated in the final burning of the library of Alexandria in the seventh century CE as a sacrilege surplus to purpose (Fuller and Gorman 1987). The positive side of the Muslim strategy was epitomized in the *madrasa*, the prototype of the campus-based college, which introduced books to students early in their lives as an integral part of their maturation into adulthood. Its spirit lives on in the university, a Christian innovation whose legal protections have enabled it over the centuries to weather ideological storms that easily subverted or compromised the *madrasas*.

Now, given the Alexandrian precedent, consider what is arguably the *magnum opus* of the "new objectivist" historiography: Peter Galison's (1997) *Image and Logic*. Without gainsaying Galison's remarkable ability to write about the theory-experiment relationship with an attention to technical detail that merits praise from professional physicists, in the end he is discussing these matters as the outcomes of practices surrounding particular artefacts through which "trading zones" have been managed for the transaction of information. It is as if Galison first dug up the original Monte Carlo simulators from the ground and then endeavoured hard to find a sympathetic interpretation of their purpose. Such a *modus operandi* is very much in the spirit of someone detached from any larger vision that might have been shared by the scientists directly involved in the enterprise. Reflecting the Alexandrian precedent, it might be seen as an exercise in giving those scientists a decent burial – that is, demonstrating respect for their project in terms they might have appreciated, while at the same admitting that the limit of their activities has been reached. While I am sure that Galison has converted many physicists to history, I doubt that he has facilitated the reverse traffic (though that was his own intellectual trajectory).

The "new objectivism" that characterizes so much professional history of science today – most self-consciously, Daston and Galison (2007) – is arguably a half-hearted response to the breakdown of the high modernist metanarrative. Because they largely accept the postmodernist premise that scientific progress is a failed myth, historians nowadays feel no obligation to participate in its perpetuation, and hence are no longer compelled to issue clear judgements about what does and does not matter to the advancement of science. This removes any need for the historian to have a recognizable personality that is ideologically invested in the metanarrative's outcome. Such a "de-subjectivization" of history is a potential impediment to directly addressing a broad audience. Here it is worth recalling that despite the difficulty, if not outright unreadability, of his works, Stephen Hawking's unique selling point as a popular science writer has been his ability to recount the history of physics as culminating in his own ongoing research. The persuasiveness of this subjective appeal, present to varying degrees in positivist popular histories, should never be underestimated. In its absence, history can easily dissolve into a mass of details, each of equal significance, but lacking any overall direction.

The solution to this problem sought by today's new objectivists is reminiscent of those Romantics and Victorians who turned to aestheticism ("art for art's sake") in the nineteenth century to channel their residual religious sentiment in an increasingly secular world. The difference, of course, is that the sentiment now derives from a scientific source, typically physics. But in both cases, one focuses on particular objects as if they were ends in themselves – that is, not serving any larger purpose. The objects are presented as the culmination of various converging processes rather than as transitional stages through which these processes are working in order to achieve something greater in the future. Thus, Leonardo's *The Last Supper* or the Monte Carlo simulator might be presented as a site of multiple influences that are delicately negotiated in terms of the object's construction. This captures the iconographic standpoint favoured by the aesthete who has no instrumental interest in the object, which by definition has already done all that it could do. However, those who see the object as a moment in a living enterprise would want to make judgements about what is worth preserving, removing, and enhancing in future versions. Such is the standpoint of people actively engaged in the project that produced the object. It is how both artists and scientists tend to treat their own past. They personalize their interactions with the object, so that its value is carried over in their own activity and its products.

For what it is worth, aestheticism can be credited with demonstrating that subjective involvement is not the only way to make an extraordinary human activity appear valuable. Just as one can appreciate art without being an artist, one can appreciate science without being a scientist. The latter is certainly implicit in the new objectivism and comes out clearly in the tips on popular science writing offered by Steven Shapin (2005), a distinguished historian of science who also regularly contributes to the *London Review of Books*. Whether one comments on art or science, the process is cast as highbrow entertainment: a self-consuming activity aimed at a self-contained object. In this respect, Shapin's "cocktail party" standard of historiographical relevance might be seen as a latter-day version of Aristotle's principles of good theatre. However, a cynic might observe that such a vision of entertainment functions as a disincentive to follow in the footsteps of the original artists and scientists whose work is depicted, except in the manner of a wake. No cause is given for the audience to "break frame" to play out the logic of the drama in that double of the theatre, sometimes called "real life" (cf. Artaud 1958; Fuller 2013b).

In any case, it would be a mistake to conclude that aestheticism is the only, let alone the best, route for popular science written by those not active in science's own front lines. In fact, the dominant mode of popular science writing in the first half of the twentieth century was a kind of advocacy journalism that leveraged contemporary developments into visions of future utopias. Exemplary works in this vein were penned by H. G. Wells and J. G. Crowther in Britain, as well as by the first dedicated science columnist in a US newspaper, Waldemar Kaempffert of *The New York Times*. Spiritual descendants of these figures are conspicuous by their absence today, their numbers already beginning to decline once we entered the "Atomic Age". However, the reason for this decline is hardly mysterious. Between them, the three figures mentioned above gave ideological forward momentum to much of what turned out to be the most destructive and authoritarian tendencies in the century's history, including Fascism and Communism. Here we should not underestimate the extent to which the avoidance of twentieth-century-style mass harm operates as precautionary principle, if not a regulative ideal, in much postmodern inquiry, not least the aesthetic turn of the new objectivist historiography of science.

However, postmodernism's most profound – and potentially positive – contribution to the high modernist task of epistemology is its elevation of counterfactual reasoning. It comes as a by-product of denying that knowledge makes progress in a specific direction. From it follows that knowledge may move in many different directions, indeed, at any point in time. A corollary is that whatever trajectory knowledge has taken, it could have taken a different one under the right circumstances, some version of which may still be recoverable. This last point may be the most radical and controversial consequence of the postmodern condition: *that the identities of the past and the future are equally open*. Historical narratives are necessarily selective, insofar as everything is subordinated to a main plot line whose starting point is endemic to its overall direction. For the postmodernist, this is an observation about the nature of narrative rather than the nature of history "as such" (whatever that might mean). In that case, if one selects a different starting point in the past, then what appears as normal and deviant in the subsequent history will be different, resulting in a different future – at least in terms of what is taken to be of value in it. While this mode of reworking history is familiar from the law, as judges select different case precedents to overturn a previous ruling, the postmodernist would apply this practice to all intellectual disciplines, not least the natural sciences. Thomas Kuhn (1970) had anticipated such a move

274 *Conclusion*

when he observed how the history of a given science tends to be rewritten after each paradigm shift, so that the current research frontier appears to be where the science has always been heading. He described this narrative re-focusing as "Orwellian" (Fuller 2000b: intro.).

Counterfactual reasoning came to be unwittingly devalued in the high modernist model of knowledge once it was supposed that any discrepancies about how the past might have proceeded would not decisively affect how we think about the present with an eye to the future. For example, we might learn that Darwin stole his theory of evolution by natural selection from Alfred Russel Wallace, or that much of the fossil record has been falsified or misinterpreted or even that anti-Darwinian researchers, such as intelligent design theorists, have been actively suppressed in contemporary biology. Even if any – or maybe all – of these claims were eventually shown to be true, the high modernist still believes that these revelations would minimally alter our attitude to the overall trajectory of scientific progress. To be sure, it may mean that, strictly speaking, any endorsement of "Darwinism" under that name was premature or that the version of evolution that dominates contemporary biology would be somewhat different or, for that matter, it might have taken a bit longer to arrive at our current state of knowledge. However, what the high modernist does *not* countenance is that the realization of these counterfactual situations would result in a radically different horizon for the pursuit of knowledge. Rather, it is supposed that some other countervailing or compensating factors would have brought biology's trajectory back to a course that is recognizably ours.

Whether one calls it "positivist" or "internalist", high modernism envisaged that a very clear sense of the line of causation runs through the history of science that unfolds a logic of epistemic progress. This logic accounts for which details are included and excluded from the narrative that is presented as one insight building upon previous ones, all illuminating some domain of reality that is always coming clearer into view. Thus, one talks about only that which is essential to realizing the overall *telos*. Sometimes such a view of history is called "inductivist" (Agassi 1963), but that can be deceptive unless the term is understood as a synonym for "incremental" (as opposed to "revolutionary") change, but not in its strict logical sense as the opposite of "deductivist". In other words, "inductive" is being used to show that science is not simply another version of religion or politics, which often confers prima facie positive value on radical breaks. Thus, so-called inductivist historians of science are in fact *very* deductivist insofar as they believe that there are foundational universal premises of theory and method that underwrite the entire scientific enterprise, and which history comes gradually to discover. The history of science is a collective learning exercise by which humanity understands the nature of reality.

Conclusion   275

This whole way of thinking about the history of science, which owes more than a small debt to German idealism, was raised to a notoriously ironic level of self-consciousness in Imre Lakatos's historiography of science as "rational reconstruction", according to which the actual historical details that deviate from the logical step-wise narrative are consigned to the footnotes (Lakatos 1978: ch. 2). This meant that often the footnotes were very lengthy and argumentative, as scientists whose word was gospel for many decades in their fields got portrayed as ignoramuses in the making. Much of the moral fervour that informed the empiricist backlash of both naturalistic philosophers (e.g. Larry Laudan) and constructivist sociologists (e.g. David Bloor) of science starting in the late 1970s was fuelled by the perception that the Lakatosian vision was fuelled by a science-worshipping philosophical arrogance that betrayed a casual disregard for the facts. This backlash provided unwittingly fertile ground for the reception of postmodernist themes in the Anglophone world in the 1980s (Fuller 2006a: ch. 3).

Whatever his other faults, Lakatos could not be accused of lacking a clear sense of the object of scientific inquiry. If nothing else, "progress" presupposes a determinate origin and aim. To be sure, the identities of both ends of the process may be contested but that there are the two ends is not contested. If one takes such a view of the history of science seriously, then its facts come to be weighed in a particular way. What to the jobbing historian or sociologist might appear to be a casual disregard for the facts is to someone like Lakatos a willingness to judge certain events as inconsequential, if not retrograde, to the progress of science. In effect, errors of fact acquire an epistemic significance slightly above that of typographical errors: They pertain merely to contingent features of the historical narrative that could have gone one way or another at a particular moment without affecting the truth of the overall trajectory. To be sure, Lakatos-style confidence must be based on a reasonably clear, albeit contestable, sense of where the trajectory of science is heading – at least clear enough to distinguish what has been contingent and necessary to its development. While today's readers may regard this as an impossibly high epistemic standard, if it is not met, does the "history of *science*" retain any proper meaning at all?

To be sure, it is possible to do a history of the word "science" and its various cognates. But given the word's clear normative import, that project would amount to tracking the descendants of Plato's interest in knowledge for statecraft (Fuller 1988: ch. 7). It would thus follow the history of politics a bit more closely than most professional scientists *and* historians of science would find comfortable, since much of what both groups want to talk about as "science" originated in the margins of power and only fitfully made its way to the centres of epistemic authority.

276 Conclusion

Of course, much of this discussion is obviated because at least professional historians have come to accept that social context is integral to understanding the history of science. But that now widely agreed practice threatens to turn the "history of science" into a history of everything as seen through science, the comic potential of which Bill Bryson's (2004) best-selling book has already realized.

In the Einstein-inflected terms favoured by science fiction writers, high modernist historians of science believe that space–time is subject to "positive curvature", whereas postmodernist ones believe that it is subject to "negative curvature" (Fuller 2010: chs 2, 9). The difference turns on whether a modification to the past – be it by a hypothetical time traveller or a flesh-and-blood hermeneutical revisionist – would result in a future that is convergent with or divergent from our current trajectory. Chapter 6 focused on elaborating the *over-* versus *under*determinist logics of historical consciousness that correspond to this distinction. (The issues at play are encapsulated in Table 8.) The postmodernist faith in divergence is interestingly aligned with the context in which counterfactual reasoning received its original endorsement as a distinct source of epistemic authority, namely, the *media scientia* – that is, "middle knowledge" – advanced by the late sixteenth-century Jesuit theologian Luis de Molina.

Such knowledge is, strictly speaking, fictional, yet at the same time it is epistemologically located as a middle modality between conceptual necessities and empirical contingencies. Middle knowledge is needed to keep both God and humans free yet prescient agents – of course, with God infinitely exceeding humans in his capacity for both freedom and prescience (Beilby and Eddy 2001: ch. 3). For example, God's perfect middle knowledge enables him to decide that, warts and all, this would be the best of all possible worlds to have created as a result of having calculated the costs and benefits of creating any other possible world. Human freedom is predicated on a diminished version of the same capacity: we can consider a more restricted range of actions and anticipate their consequences only with varying degrees of probability (Franklin 2001).

The strictly fictional status of middle knowledge has weighed heavily on the modern mind. As we saw in Chapter 2 of this book, the early modern rationalist philosophers Descartes, Malebranche, and Leibniz, not to mention Newton and his followers, made ample if somewhat veiled appeals to this so-called "middle knowledge". They used it to establish the existence of causal relations between regularly occurring temporal events (e.g. were A not present, B would not have happened), a move that continues to be made by realist philosophers of science to justify the idea that mathematically expressed natural laws are true of infinitely many events that no scientist would ever be in a position to observe for herself. However, Kant began to cast serious doubt on the strong legitimatory role that fiction appeared to play in science when he introduced the ironized form of middle knowledge that is nowadays called the "transcendental argument". Instead of arguing that any other world created by God would have been worse, Kant effectively argued that any other world would not have been a product of God's creation. (This is the negative version of saying that science in the style of Newton would not have been possible without presupposing the existence of the Abrahamic God.) In other words, Kant opened the door to denials of this being the best of all possible worlds, in which case bereft of optimal design, our world ceases to be in need of any divine explanation. This inspired a rich vein of antitheological discourse in the nineteenth century that gained an enormous and lasting boost from Darwin's *Origin of Species*, which in turn helped to secure retrospectively Hume's place in the philosophical pantheon.

In undercutting the epistemic authority of middle knowledge, Kant established (perhaps unwittingly) a strong philosophical precedent for treating fiction as non-knowledge or even anti-knowledge, with "knowledge" now defined in terms of the mutually exclusive alternatives of conceptual necessities and empirical contingencies (aka "analytic versus synthetic" or "*a priori* versus *a posteriori*" knowledge). This move had many serious knock-on effects throughout the nineteenth century, which together served to distance art from the realm of knowledge altogether. In particular, imagination was separated from both reason and memory as a mental function, and philosophers became increasingly sceptical of the prospect of finding a "logic of scientific discovery", such that at the dawn of the twentieth century, scientific creativity itself came to be seen as a psychological activity closer to dreaming than to conscious thought (Hadamard 1945). Together these moves provided the framework for defining the "human" in purely naturalistic and ultimately non-theological terms – a true "anthropology", to recall the Kantian coinage that Foucault used to great effect in making a similar point. Instead of our being raised above the animals in virtue of our partly divine constitution, which had provided the ontological precondition for middle knowledge, humanity was now defined in opposition to all "supernatural" forces, be they deities or demons. Such was the high modernist position on humanity against which postmodernism revolted.

In high modernity, middle knowledge came to be sublimated as "historical necessity", a doctrine that is first clearly stated in Hegel's *Philosophy of History* as a secular successor to theodicy, middle knowledge's natural theological home. Thus, in a world without God, we are no longer permitted the privilege of adopting a standpoint detached from our natural existence. This means that whatever truth there might be to the cornerstone theodicist idea of ours being "the best of all possible worlds" would now have to be redeemed in terms of a sequence of stages

278   *Conclusion*

that evinced a logic to human history (Löwith 1949). In effect, what to God would have appeared to be an intellectual judgement about the best of infinitely many worlds appears to humans as a moral compulsion to do the right thing under specific historical circumstances, on the basis of which progress might be made. Marxists have endlessly exploited this translation strategy. Depending on which side of the barricades one stood during the various revolutions that punctuated the nineteenth and twentieth centuries, the attempt to reinvent middle knowledge through some "dialectical" yoking of conceptual necessity and empirical contingency was seen as either a great success or a great folly. In this context, *Trotsky* stands for a belief in (soon to be realized) success, *Popper* for a belief in (already demonstrated) folly and *Sartre* for a belief in an (indefinitely) open verdict. I believe that the continued relevance of epistmemology rests on the field's ability to triangulate around the horizons associated with these figures.

Postmodernism re-opened the question of middle knowledge by taking seriously our capacity for transcendental projection, but now understood as a by-product of our inherently self-constructed natures. Thus, in an era that gave us "identity politics" as a vehicle for reconnecting with traits marked by class, gender, and race that had been submerged in an ideology of universal humanism, we may well identify with a point-of-view that lies outside much of our current material being in order to reconnect with our more divine features. To be sure, postmodernism does not pretend to peer with certainty into "the mind of God". Nevertheless it might simulate the divine standpoint by envisaging that our knowledge of both the past and the future is subject to roughly the same degree of *un*certainty. This has the ironic upshot of engendering a sense of freedom previously lacking in high modernist conceptions of the human, where each moment appeared to be heavy with decision, on the basis of which future generations would judge us. Much if not all of this modernist momentousness would be eliminated if the past could be changed so as to result in a different future.

Leading the postmodern revival of counterfactual reasoning has been the proliferation of computer models in scientific research. Interestingly, journalists were among the first to herald the increasing use of such models as marking the end of the strict modernist divide between the scientific and artistic mindsets, as actual reality comes to be reabsorbed as just one of the many versions of virtual reality contained within a computer model, the programming of which requires considerable creative design (Horgan 1996). In terms of the theology of middle knowledge, such models might be construed as flawed factories for manufacturing the divine mind, as they enable the user to manipulate the initial parameters by introducing new evidence, resulting in different anticipated outcomes that constitute a new actual world. The simulation of global climate change over the centuries is the most notorious contemporary icon of this sensibility, as the degree of urgency with which we must act now to avert future catastrophe is dependent on a seemingly volatile database of past weather conditions.

Much of the sceptical backlash to global warming can be explained as intuitive resistance to the idea that a slight shift in data points entered into a model could justify unprecedented resource reallocations, especially given the frequency with which such data points have shifted in response to new evidence in the past. To be sure, this complaint reveals a modernist sensibility that demands that tough decisions be made on hard facts because of the potentially irreversible outcomes. In contrast, post-modernism represents a shift in what Baudrillard (1981) called the "political economy of signs", whereby a new sort of progress may be measured by a new standard of efficiency, as represented by the "simulacrum" generated by a laboratory- or computer- or media-based simulation (Baudrillard 1994). After all, the shift from the laboratory to the computer as the site of scientific experimentation has been motivated at least as much by mundane considerations about the skyrocketing cost of scientific equipment as any methodologically driven arguments about improved powers of prediction and control (Horgan 1996).

Future intellectual historians may come to see postmodernism's signal epistemic style very much in the image of successful venture capitalists in our times – that is to say, characterized by a willingness by so many who know so little to commit so much, that is, until further notice. Recalling Chapter 1's discussion of Taleb (2012), we refashion ourselves as "anti-fragile" beings facing a reality that continually throws up new challenges, but ones which we are increasingly designed to meet, even if they require that we abandon much of the "stuff" that had been previously constitutive of our identity. Indeed, we may be heading into a world where the ideal rational agent looks like a miser to the late twentieth-century consumer capitalist – that is, someone who continually strives to do more with less, while continuing to accumulate as much capital as possible as insurance against the risky world to which one always wishes to remain open.

Bibliography

Adorno, T. (ed.) 1967. *The Positivist Dispute*. London: Heinemann.

Agassi, J. 1963. *Towards an Historiography of Science*. The Hague: Mouton.

——1985. *Technology: Philosophical and Social Aspects*. Dordrecht: Kluwer.

——2008. *A Philosopher's Apprentice: In Karl Popper's Workshop*, 2nd edn. First published 1993. Amsterdam: Rodopi.

Ainslie, G. 2001. *Breakdown of Will*. Cambridge: Cambridge University Press.

Alexander, D. 2008. *Creation and Evolution: Do We Have to Choose?* Oxford: Monarch.

Allen, R. C. 1999. *David Hartley on Human Nature*. Albany, NY: SUNY Press.

Alston, W. 2005. *Beyond Justification: Epistemic Dimensions of Evaluation*. Ithaca, NY: Cornell University Press.

Amabile, T. 1996. *Creativity in Context*. Boulder, CO: Westview.

Amarasingam, A. 2008. "Transcending Technology: Looking at Futurology as a New Religious Movement". *Journal of Contemporary Religion* 23(1): 1–16.

Andersen, H. 2001. "Critical Notice: Kuhn, Conant and Everything – A Full or Fuller Account". *Philosophy of Science* 68: 258–62.

Armstrong, K. 2009. *The Case for God: What Religion Really Means*. London: The Bodley Head.

Artaud, A. 1958. *The Theatre and Its Double*. New York: Grove Weidenfeld.

Arthur, W. B. 1994. *Increasing Returns and Path Dependence in the Economy*. Ann Arbor, MI: University of Michigan Press.

Ash, M. 1987. "Psychology and Politics in Interwar Vienna". In *Psychology in Twentieth Century Thought and Society*, M. Ash and W. Woodward (eds), 143–64. Cambridge: Cambridge University Press.

——1988. *Gestalt Psychology in German Culture, 1890–1967*. Cambridge: Cambridge University Press.

Baars, B. 1986. *The Cognitive Revolution in Psychology*. New York: Guilford Press.

Barrow, J. and F. Tipler 1988. *The Anthropic Cosmological Principle*. Oxford: Oxford University Press.

Barrow, J., S. Conway Morris, S. Freeland and C. Harper (eds) 2008. *Fitness of the Cosmos for Life: Biochemistry and Fine-Tuning*. Cambridge: Cambridge University Press.

Bashford, A. and P. Levine (eds) 2010. *Oxford Handbook of the History of Eugenics*. Oxford: Oxford University Press.

Bibliography 281

Bateson, G. 1972. *Steps to an Ecology of Mind*. Chicago, IL: University of Chicago Press.

Baudrillard, J. 1981. *For a Political Economy of Signs*. St Louis, MO: Telos Press.

——1994. *Simulacra and Simulation*. Ann Arbor, MI: University of Michigan Press.

Bauman, Z. 1993. *Postmodern Ethics*. Oxford: Blackwell.

Behe, M. 1996. *Darwin's Black Box*. New York: Simon & Schuster.

——2007. *The Edge of Evolution*. New York: Simon & Schuster.

Beilby, J. K. and P. R. Eddy (eds) 2001. *Divine Foreknowledge: Four Views*. Downers Grove, IL: InterVarsity Press.

Beiser, F. 2000. "The Enlightenment and Idealism". In *The Cambridge Companion to German Idealism*, K. Ameriks (eds), 18–36. Cambridge: Cambridge University Press.

Ben-David, J. 1971. *The Scientist's Role in Society*. Englewood Cliffs, NJ: Prentice Hall.

Ben-David, J. and R. Collins 1966. "Social Factors in the Origins of a New Science: The Case of Psychology". *American Sociological Review* 31: 451–65.

Berger, P. 1967. *The Sacred Canopy*. Garden City, NY: Doubleday.

Berger, P. and T. Luckmann 1966. *The Social Construction of Reality*. Garden City, NY: Doubleday.

Berkson, W. and J. Wettersten 1984. *Learning from Error*. LaSalle, IL: Open Court Press.

Bernal, J. D. 1929. *The World, The Flesh and the Devil*. London: Kegan Paul, Trench & Trubner.

——1939. *The Social Function of Science*. London: Macmillan.

——1955. "Has History a Meaning?". *British Journal for the Philosophy of Science* 6: 164–69.

——1971. *Science in History*. 4 vols. Cambridge, MA: MIT Press.

Berofsky, B. 1973. "Free Will and Determinism". In *Dictionary of the History of Ideas*, vol. 2, P. Wiener (ed.), 236–42. New York: Charles Scribner's Sons.

Bloom, H. 1992. *The American Religion: The Emergence of the Post-Christian Nation*. New York: Simon & Schuster.

Bloor, D. 1976. *Knowledge and Social Imagery*. London: Routledge.

Blumenberg, H. 1986. *The Legitimacy of the Modern Age*. First published 1968. Cambridge, MA: MIT Press.

Boantza, V. 2007. "Collating Airs and Ideas: Priestley's Style of Experimental Reasoning". *Studies in History and Philosophy of Science* 38: 506–22.

Bonaventure 1993. *The Journey of the Mind to God*. First published mid-thirteenth century. Indianapolis, IN: Hackett.

Bordogna, F. 2008. *William James at the Boundaries: Philosophy, Science, and the Geography of Knowledge*. Chicago, IL: University of Chicago Press.

Boring, E. G. 1950. *A History of Experimental Psychology*, 2nd edn. First published 1929. New York: Appleton-Century-Crofts.

282 Bibliography

——1955. "Dual Role of the *Zeitgeist* in Scientific Creativity". *Scientific Monthly* 80: 101–6.

Borkenau, F. 1981. *End and Beginning: On the Generations of Culture and the Origins of the West*. New York: Columbia University Press.

Bourdieu, P. 1999. *The Weight of the World*. First published 1993. Cambridge: Polity Press.

Bouveresse, J. 1999. *Prodiges et vertiges de l'analogie: De l'abus des belles-lettres dans la pensée*. Paris. Editions Liber-Raisons d'agir.

Bowler, R. 2005. "Sentient Nature and Human Economy". *History of the Human Sciences* 19(1): 23–54.

Brague, R. 2007. *The Law of God: The Philosophical History of an Idea*. Chicago, IL: University of Chicago Press.

Brannigan, A. 1981. *The Social Basis of Scientific Discoveries*. Cambridge: Cambridge University Press.

——2004. *The Rise and Fall of Social Psychology: The Use and Misuse of the Experimental Method*. New York: Aldine de Gruyter.

Brey, P. 2000. "Theories of Technology as Extension of Human Faculties". In *Metaphysics, Epistemology and Technology*, Research in Philosophy and Technology, vol. 19, C. Mitcham (ed.), 59–78. Bingley: Emerald.

Brinton, C. 1952. *The Anatomy of Revolution*. New York: Random House.

Broadie, A. 2010. *A History of Scottish Philosophy*. Edinburgh: Edinburgh University Press.

Brooks, D. R. 2011. "The Mastodon in the Room: How Darwinian is Neo-Darwinism?". *Studies in History and Philosophy of Biological and Biomedical Sciences* 42(1): 82–88.

Brooks, D. R. and E. O. Wiley 1986. *Evolution as Entropy: Toward a Unified Theory of Biology*. Chicago, IL: University of Chicago Press.

Bruner, J., J. Goodnow and G. Austin 1956. *A Study of Thinking*. New York: John Wiley & Sons.

Brunswik, E. 1952. "The Conceptual Framework of Psychology". *International Encyclopedia of Unified Science* 1: art. 10.

Brush, S. 1975. "Should History of Science Be Rated X?". *Science* 183: 1164–83.

Bryson, B. 2004. *A Short History of Nearly Everything*. London: Black Swan.

Burge, T. 1993. "Content Preservation". *Philosophical Review* 102: 457–88.

Burkhardt, R. 1970. "Lamarck, Evolution, and the Politics of Science". *Journal of the History of Biology* 3: 275–98.

Burns, C. 2012. "Christianity and the Cognitive Sciences". In *The Routledge Companion to Religion and Science*, J. Haag, G. Peterson and M. Spezio (eds), 308–19. London: Routledge.

Bury, J. B. 1920. *The Idea of Progress*. London: Macmillan & Co.

Butler, J. 1990. *Gender Trouble*. London: Routledge.

——2004. *Precarious Life*. London: Verso.

Butterfield, H. 1931. *On the Whig Interpretation of History*. Cambridge: Cambridge University Press.

Campbell, D. T. 1988. *Methodology and Epistemology for Social Science*. Chicago, IL: University of Chicago Press.

Campbell, D. T. and J. C. Stanley 1963. *Experimental and Quasi-Experimental Designs for Research*. Chicago, IL: Rand McNally.

Carroll, S. B. 2005. *Endless Forms Most Beautiful: The New Science of Evo-Devo*. New York: W. W. Norton.

Cassirer, E. 1923. *Substance and Function*. First published 1910. LaSalle, IL: Open Court Press.

Cat, J., N. Cartwright and H. Chang 1996. "Otto Neurath: Politics and the Unity of Science". In *The Disunity of Science: Boundaries, Contexts, and Power*, P. Galison and D. Stump (eds), 347–69. Palo Alto, CA: Stanford University Press.

Ceccarelli, L. 2001. *Shaping Science with Rhetoric*. Chicago, IL: University of Chicago Press.

——2011. "Manufactured Scientific Controversy: Science, Rhetoric, and Public Debate". *Rhetoric and Public Affairs* 14: 195–228.

Chase, A. 2003. *Harvard and the Unabomber: The Education of an American Terrorist*. New York: W. W. Norton.

Chisholm, R. 1977. *Theory of Knowledge*, 2nd edn. First published 1966. Englewood Cliffs, NJ: Prentice Hall.

Chomsky, N. 1966. *Cartesian Linguistics: A Chapter in the History of Rationalist Thought*. New York: Harper & Row.

Church, G. and E. Regis 2012. *Regenesis: How Synthetic Biology Will Reinvent Nature and Ourselves*. New York: Basic Books.

Clark, W. 2006. *Academic Charisma and the Origins of the Research University*. Chicago, IL: University of Chicago Press.

Clifford, W. K. 1999. *The Ethics of Belief*. First published 1877. Buffalo, NY: Prometheus Books.

Cohen, I. B. 1997. *Science and the Founding Fathers*. New York: W. W. Norton.

Cohen, L. J. 1977. *The Probable and the Provable*. Oxford: Clarendon Press.

Cole, J. and S. Cole 1973. *The Social Stratification of Science*. Chicago, IL: University of Chicago Press.

Collins, F. S. 2006. *The Language of God*. New York: Free Press.

Collins, H. 1981. "Stages in the Empirical Programme of Relativism". *Social Studies of Science* 11: 3–10.

——2004. *Gravity's Shadow*. Chicago, IL: University of Chicago Press.

Collins, H. and R. Evans 2002. "The Third Wave of Science Studies: Studies of Expertise and Experience". *Social Studies of Science* 32(2): 235–96.

——2007. *Rethinking Expertise*. Chicago, IL: University of Chicago Press.

Collins, R. 1998. *The Sociology of Philosophies: A Global Theory of Intellectual Change*. Cambridge, MA: Harvard University Press.

284 *Bibliography*

Conant, J. B. 1950. *The Overthrow of the Phlogiston Theory: The Chemical Revolution of 1775–1789*. Harvard Case Studies in Experimental Science, case 2. Cambridge, MA: Harvard University Press.

Conway Morris, S. 2003. *Life's Solution: Inevitable Humans in a Lonely Universe*. Cambridge: Cambridge University Press.

Corbey, R. 2005. *The Metaphysics of Apes: Re-negotiating the Animal–Human Boundary*. Cambridge: Cambridge University Press.

Cushman, T. and J. Rodden 1997. "Sociology and the Intellectual Life: An Interview with Lewis S. Feuer". *The American Sociologist* (Winter): 56–89.

Daly, L. 2006. *God and the Welfare State*. Cambridge, MA: MIT Press.

Darnton, R. 1984. *The Great Cat Massacre and Other Episodes in French Cultural History*. New York: Vintage.

Daston, L. and P. Galison 2007. *Objectivity*. Cambridge, MA: MIT Press.

Davis, E. 1998. *TechGnosis: Myth, Magic and Mysticism in the Age of Information*. San Francisco, CA: Harmony Books.

Dawkins, R. 1982. *The Extended Phenotype*. Oxford: Oxford University Press.

——1996. *Climbing Mount Improbable*. New York: W. W. Norton.

——2006. *The God Delusion*. New York: Bantam.

Deleuze, G. and F. Guattari 1977. *Anti-Oedipus: Capitalism and Schizophrenia*. First published 1972. Minneapolis, MN: University of Minnesota Press.

Dembski, W. 2002. *No Free Lunch: Why Specified Complexity Cannot Be Specified without Intelligence*. Lanham, MD: Rowman & Littlefield.

——2009. *The End of Christianity*. Nashville, TN: Broadman & Holman.

De Mey, M. 1982. *The Cognitive Paradigm*. Dordrecht: Kluwer.

Dennett, D. 1984. *Elbow Room*. Cambridge, MA: MIT Press.

——1995. *Darwin's Dangerous Idea*. London: Allen Lane.

——2003. *Freedom Evolves*. London: Penguin.

Derrida, J. 1978. *Writing and Difference*. Chicago, IL: University of Chicago Press.

Dewey, J. 1910. *How We Think*. Lexington, MA: DC Heath.

Dickens, P. 2000. *Social Darwinism*. Milton Keynes: Open University Press.

Dietz, J. and J. Rogers 2012. "Meanings and Policy Implications of 'Transformative Research'". *Minerva* 50: 21–44.

Diller, A. 2008. "A Popperian Theory of Testimony". *Philosophy of the Social Sciences* 38: 419–56.

Dobzhansky, T. 1937. *Genetics and the Origin of Species*. New York: Columbia University Press.

——1967. *The Biology of Ultimate Concern*. New York: New American Library.

Donovan, A., L. Laudan and R. Laudan (eds) 1988. *Scrutinizing Science*. Dordrecht: Kluwer.

Douglas, M. 1970. *Natural Symbols: Explorations in Cosmology*. London: Routledge & Kegan Paul.

Drahos, P. 1995. "Information Feudalism in the Information Society". *The Information Society* 11: 209–22.

Dupré, J. 2012. "Evolutionary Theory's Welcome Crisis". *Project Syndicate* (4 September), www.project-syndicate.org/commentary/evolutionary-theory-s-welcome-crisis-by-john-dupre (accessed 24 May 2014).

Dupuy, J.-P. 2000. "Philosophical Foundations of a New Concept of Equilibrium in the Social Sciences: Projected Equilibrium". *Philosophical Studies* 100: 323–45.

Durkheim, E. 1961. *The Elementary Forms of the Religious Life*. First published 1912. New York: Collier.

Dyson, F. 2007. *The Scientist as Rebel*. New York: New York Review of Books.

Eagleman, D. 2009. *Sum: Forty Tales from the Afterlives*. New York: Pantheon.

Ecklund, E. H. 2010. *Science versus Religion: What Scientists Really Think?* Oxford: Oxford University Press.

Egan, M. 2007. *Barry Commoner and the Science of Survival*. Cambridge, MA: MIT Press.

Eisenstein, E. 1979. *The Printing Press as an Agent of Change*. Cambridge: Cambridge University Press.

Elster, J. 1979. *Logic and Society: Contradictions and Possible Worlds*. Chichester: John Wiley & Sons.

——1983. *Sour Grapes: Studies in the Subversion of Rationality*. Cambridge: Cambridge University Press.

Engels, F. 2005. *Ludwig Feuerbach and the End of Classical German Philosophy*. First published 1888. Honolulu, HI: University Press of the Pacific.

Ericsson, K. A. and H. Simon 1985. *Protocol Analysis: Verbal Reports as Data*. Hillsdale, NJ: Lawrence Erlbaum Associates.

Esposito, M. 2011. "Utopianism in the British Evolutionary Synthesis". *Studies in the History and Philosophy of Biology and the Biomedical Sciences* 42(1): 40–49.

Evans, D. 2012. *Risk Intelligence: How to Live with Uncertainty*. London: Atlantic Books.

Faust, D. 1984. *The Limits of Scientific Reasoning*. Minneapolis, MN: University of Minnesota Press.

Febvre, L. 1982. *The Problem of Unbelief in the Sixteenth Century*. First published 1947. Cambridge, MA: Harvard University Press.

Feist, G. 2006. *The Psychology of Science and the Origins of the Scientific Mind*. New Haven, CT: Yale University Press.

Ferrier, J. 1875. *The Institutes of Metaphysic: The Theory of Knowing and Being*, 3rd edn. First published 1854. Edinburgh: William Blackwood.

Ferris, T. 2011. "The World of the Intellectual versus the World of the Engineer". *Wired* (13 October), www.wired.com/2011/10/intellectual-vs-engineer (accessed 24 May 2014).

Festinger, L. 1957. *A Theory of Cognitive Dissonance*. Palo Alto, CA: Stanford University Press.

Feuer, L. 1963. *The Scientific Intellectual: The Psychological and Sociological Origins of Modern Science*. New York: Basic Books.

286 *Bibliography*

Feyerabend, P. 1975. *Against Method*. London: Verso.

——1979. *Science in a Free Society*. London: Verso.

——1999. *The Conquest of Abundance*. Chicago, IL: University of Chicago Press.

Fisch, R. 1977. "Psychology of Science". In *Science, Technology and Society: A Cross-Disciplinary Perspective*, I. Spiegel-Rösing and D. de S. Price (eds), 277–318. London: Sage.

Fisher, R. 1925. *Statistical Methods for Research Workers*. Edinburgh: Oliver & Boyd.

Fodor, J. 1981. *Representations*. Cambridge, MA: MIT Press.

Fogel, R. W. 1964. *Railroads and American Economic Growth*. Baltimore, MD: Johns Hopkins University Press.

Fogel, R. W. and S. Engerman 1974. *Time on the Cross*. Boston, MA: Little Brown.

Foster, J. B., B. Clark and R. York 2008. *Critique of Intelligent Design: Materialism versus Creationism from Antiquity to the Present*. New York: Monthly Review Press.

Foucault, M. 1970. *The Order of Things*. First published 1966. New York: Random House.

Franklin, J. 2001. *The Science of Conjecture*. Baltimore, MD: Johns Hopkins University Press.

Freeman, C. 1999. "The Social Function of Science". See Swann and Aprahamian (1999), 101–31.

Freud, S. 2002. *Civilization and Its Discontents*. First published 1930. London: Penguin.

Friedman, M. 2000. *A Parting of the Ways: Carnap, Cassirer, and Heidegger*. Chicago, IL: Open Court Press.

Frodeman, R. 2013. *Sustainable Knowledge: A Theory of Interdisciplinarity*. London: Palgrave Macmillan.

Fuller, S. 1985. "Bounded Rationality in Law and Science". PhD dissertation, University of Pittsburgh, PA.

——1988. *Social Epistemology*. Bloomington, IN: Indiana University Press.

——1992a. "Epistemology Radically Naturalized: Recovering the Normative, the Experimental, and the Social". In *Cognitive Models of Science*, R. Giere (ed.), 427–59. Minneapolis, MN: University of Minnesota Press.

——1992b. "Being There with Thomas Kuhn: A Parable for Postmodern Times". *History and Theory* 31(3): 241–75.

——1993. *Philosophy of Science and Its Discontents*, 2nd edn. First published 1989. New York: Guilford Press.

——1996. "Recent Work in Social Epistemology". *American Philosophical Quarterly* 33: 149–66.

——1997. *Science*. Milton Keynes: Open University Press.

——1998. "Boundaries Not Established". Review of J. D. Barrow, *Impossibility: The Limits of Science and the Science of Limits*. *Science* 280 (29 May): 1396–97.

——2000a. *The Governance of Science: Ideology and the Future of the Open Society*. Milton Keynes: Open University Press.

——2000b. *Thomas Kuhn: A Philosophical History for Our Times*. Chicago, IL: University of Chicago Press.

——2001. Review of Friedman 2000. *British Journal for the History of Science* 34: 457–58.

——2002. *Knowledge Management Foundations*. Woburn, MA: Butterworth-Heinemann.

——2003. *Kuhn versus Popper: The Struggle for the Soul of Science*. Cambridge: Icon.

——2004. "The Case of Fuller versus Kuhn". *Social Epistemology* 18: 3–49.

——2005. *The Intellectual*. Cambridge: Icon.

——2006a. *The Philosophy of Science and Technology Studies*. London: Routledge.

——2006b. *The New Sociological Imagination*. London: Sage.

——2006c. "The Market: Source or Target of Morality?". In *The Moralization of the Market*, N. Stehr, C. Henning and B. Weiler (eds), 129–53. New Brunswick, NJ: Transaction Books.

——2007a. *The Knowledge Book: Key Concepts in Philosophy, Science, and Culture*. Durham: Acumen Press.

——2007b. *New Frontiers in Science and Technology Studies*. Cambridge: Polity.

——2007c. *Science versus Religion? Intelligent Design and the Problem of Evolution*. Cambridge: Polity Press.

——2008a. *Dissent over Descent: Intelligent Design's Challenge to Darwinism*. Cambridge: Icon.

——2008b. "A Tale of Two Narratives: Prolegomena to an Alternative History of Library and Information Science". In *European Modernity and the Information Society*, W. B. Rayward (ed.), 59–73. Farnham: Ashgate.

——2008c. "Justifying Science: The Need for Macroeconomic Knowledge Policy". In *Knowledge Policy: Challenges for the 21st Century*, G. Hearn and D. Rooney (eds), 120–37. Cheltenham: Edward Elgar.

——2009a. *The Sociology of Intellectual Life: The Career of the Mind In and Around the Academy*. London: Sage.

——2009b. "The Genealogy of Judgement: Towards a Deep History of Academic Freedom". *British Journal of Educational Studies* 57: 164–77.

——2010. *Science: The Art of Living*. Durham: Acumen.

——2011. *Humanity 2.0: What It Means to Be Human Past, Present and Future*. London: Palgrave Macmillan.

——2012. *Preparing for Life in Humanity 2.0*. London: Palgrave Macmillan.

——2013a. "Deviant Interdisciplinarity as Philosophical Practice: Prolegomena to Deep Intellectual History". *Synthese* 190: 1899–1916.

——2013b. "Entertainment as Key to Public Intellectual Agency". *Philosophy and Rhetoric* 46(1): 105–13.

——2014. "Neuroscience, Neurohistory and the History of Science: A Tale of Two Brain Images". *Isis* 105: 100–109.

Bibliography

Fuller, S. and J. Collier 2004. *Philosophy, Rhetoric and the End of Knowledge*, 2nd edn. First published 1993 (by S. Fuller). Mahwah, NJ: Lawrence Erlbaum Associates.

Fuller, S. and D. Gorman 1987. "Burning Libraries: Cultural Creation and the Problem of Historical Consciousness". *Annals of Scholarship* 4: 105–19.

Fuller, S. and V. Lipinska 2014. *The Proactionary Imperative*. London: Palgrave Macmillan.

Fuller, S., M. De Mey, T. Shinn and S. Woolgar (eds) 1989. *The Cognitive Turn: Psychological and Sociological Perspectives on Science*. Dordrecht: Kluwer.

Funkenstein, A. 1986. *Theology and the Scientific Imagination*. Princeton, NJ: Princeton University Press.

Galison, P. 1990. "Aufbau/Bauhaus: Logical Positivism and Architectural Modernism". *Critical Inquiry* 16: 709–52.

——1997. *Image and Logic: A Material Culture of Microphysics*. Chicago, IL: University of Chicago Press.

——2004. "Specific Theory". *Critical Inquiry* 30: 379–83.

Galison, P. and D. Stump (eds) 1996. *The Disunity of Science: Boundaries, Contexts, and Power*. Palo Alto, CA: Stanford University Press.

Garfinkel, H. 1967. *Studies in Ethnomethodology*. Englewood Cliffs, NJ: Prentice Hall.

Garner, S. R. 2006. "Transhumanism and the Imago Dei: Narratives of Apprehension and Hope". PhD dissertation, Faculty of Theology, University of Auckland, New Zealand.

Gattei, S. (ed.) 2003. "The Kuhn Controversy". 40 critical reviews of Fuller 2000b. *Social Epistemology* 17(2–3).

Gellner, E. 1979. *Spectacles and Predicaments*. Cambridge: Cambridge University Press.

——1998. *Language and Solitude: Wittgenstein, Malinowski and the Habsburg Dilemma*. Cambridge: Cambridge University Press.

Gholson, B., W. Shadish, R. Neimeyer and A. Houts (eds) 1989. *Psychology of Science: Contributions to Metascience*. Cambridge: Cambridge University Press.

Gibbons, M., C. Limoges, H. Nowotny, S. Schwartzman, P. Scott and M. Trow 1994. *The New Production of Knowledge*. London: Sage.

Giberson, K. 2008. *Saving Darwin*. New York: HarperCollins.

Giere, R. 2003. "A New Program for Philosophy of Science?". *Philosophy of Science* 70: 15–21.

Gigerenzer, G. and D. Murray 1987. *Cognition as Intuitive Statistics*. Hillsdale, NJ: Lawrence Erlbaum Associates.

Goldman, A. 1999. *Knowledge in a Social World*. Oxford: Oxford University Press.

Goodman, N. 1955. *Fact, Fiction and Forecast*. Cambridge, MA: Harvard University Press.

Gordon, P. 2012. "Forum: Kuhn's *Structure* at Fifty: Introduction". *Modern Intellectual History* 9(1): 73–76.

Bibliography   289

Gorman, M. E. 1992. *Simulating Science: Heuristics, Mental Models and Technoscientific Thinking*. Bloomington, IN: Indiana University Press.

Gould, S. J. 1989. *Wonderful Life*. New York: W. W. Norton.

——1999. *Rocks of Ages*. New York: Vintage Books.

Gouldner, A. 1970. *The Coming Crisis in Western Sociology*. New York: Basic Books.

Grafton, A. 1997. *The Footnote*. Cambridge, MA: Harvard University Press.

Green, T. H. 1968. *Hume and Locke*. First published 1882. New York: Thomas Crowell.

Green.view 2010. "Oblique Strategies: A New Look at the Landscape of Climate Politics Calls for Subtler and More Thoughtful Approaches". *The Economist* (11 May), www.economist.com/node/16099521 (accessed 24 May 2014).

Gunnell, J. 2009. "Ideology and the Philosophy of Science: An American Misunderstanding". *Journal of Political Ideologies* 14: 317–37.

Gutierrez, G. 1988. *A Theology of Liberation: History, Politics, Salvation*. First published 1971. Maryknoll, NY: Orbis Books.

Gutting, G. (ed.) 1980. *Paradigms and Revolutions: Applications and Appraisals of Thomas Kuhn's Philosophy of Science*. South Bend, IN: Notre Dame University Press.

Habermas, J. 1973. *Knowledge and Human Interests*. First published 1968. Boston, MA: Beacon Press.

——1981. *A Theory of Communicative Action*. Boston, MA: Beacon Press.

——2003. *The Future of Human Nature*. Cambridge: Polity Press.

Hacking, I. 1975. *The Emergence of Probability*. Cambridge: Cambridge University Press.

——1990. *The Taming of Chance*. Cambridge: Cambridge University Press.

——1992. "The Self-Vindication of the Laboratory Sciences". In *Science as Practice and Culture*, A. Pickering (ed.), 29–64. Chicago, IL: University of Chicago Press.

——1995. *Rewriting the Soul: Multiple Personality and the Sciences of Memory*. Princeton, NJ: Princeton University Press.

——2002. *Historical Ontology*. Cambridge, MA: Harvard University Press.

Hacohen, M. 2000. *Karl Popper: The Formative Years, 1902–1945*. Cambridge: Cambridge University Press.

Hadamard, J. 1945. *An Essay on the Psychology of Invention in the Mathematical Field*. Princeton, NJ: Princeton University Press.

Hansson, S. O. 2008. "Science and Pseudo-science". *Stanford Encyclopedia of Philosophy* (3 September), http://plato.stanford.edu/entries/pseudo-science (accessed 24 May 2014).

Haraway, D. 1991. *Simians, Cyborgs and Women*. London: Free Association Books.

Harding, S. 1986. *The Science Question in Feminism*. Ithaca, NY: Cornell University Press.

Harman, G. 2009. *Prince of Networks: Bruno Latour and Metaphysics*. Melbourne: Re.Press.

Bibliography

Harrington, Ann 1999. *Reenchanted Science: Holism in German Science from Wilhelm II to Hitler*. Princeton, NJ: Princeton University Press.

Harrington, Austin 2001. "Dilthey, Empathy and Verstehen". *European Journal of Social Theory* 4: 311–29.

Harrison, P. 1998. *The Bible, Protestantism and the Rise of Natural Science*. Cambridge: Cambridge University Press.

——2007. *The Fall of Man and the Foundations of Science*. Cambridge: Cambridge University Press.

Hartley, L. P. 1953. *The Go-Between*. London: Hamish Hamilton.

Harvey-Phillips, M. B. 1984. "Malthus' Theodicy: The Intellectual Background of His Contribution to Political Economy". *History of Political Economy* 16(4): 591–608.

Haskell, T. 1984. "Professionalism versus Capitalism: R. H. Tawney, Emile Durkheim, and C. S. Peirce on the Disinterestedness of Professional Communities". In *The Authority of Experts*, T. Haskell (ed.), 180–225. Bloomington, IN: Indiana University Press.

Hawking, S. 1988. *A Brief History of Time*. Oxford: Oxford University Press.

Hayek, F. 1952. *The Counter-Revolution of Science*. Chicago, IL: University of Chicago Press.

Hedges, L. 1987. "How Hard Is Hard Science, How Soft Is Soft Science?". *American Psychologist* 42: 443–55.

Heelan, P. 1983. *Space-Perception and the Philosophy of Science*. Berkeley, CA: University of California Press.

Heidelberger, M. 2004. *Nature from Within: Gustav Fechner and His Psychophysical Worldview*. Pittsburgh, PA: University of Pittsburgh Press.

Heims, S. 1991. *Constructing a Social Science for America: The Cybernetics Group 1946–1953*. Cambridge, MA: MIT Press.

Hesse, M. B. 1963. *Models and Analogies in Science*. South Bend, IN: University of Notre Dame Press.

Higgins, E. T. 1997. "Beyond Pleasure and Pain". *American Psychologist* 52(12): 1280–1300.

Hirschman, A. 1976. *The Passions and the Interests*. Princeton, NJ: Princeton University Press.

——1991. *The Rhetoric of Reaction*. Cambridge, MA: Harvard University Press.

Holton, G. 1973. *The Thematic Origins of Scientific Thought*. Cambridge, MA: Harvard University Press.

Hookway, C. 2009. "Lotze and the Classical Pragmatists". *European Journal of Pragmatism and American Philosophy* 1(1): 1–9.

Horgan, J. 1996. *The End of Science: Facing the Limits of Knowledge in the Twilight of the Scientific Age*. Reading, MA: Addison-Wesley.

Howard, D. 2009. "Better Red than Dead – Putting an End to the Social Irrelevance of Postwar Philosophy of Science". *Science and Education* 18: 199–220.

Hume, D. 1935. *Dialogues Concerning Natural Religion*, ed. N. K. Smith. First published 1779. Oxford: Clarendon Press.

——1987. "Of Superstition and Enthusiasm". In his *Essays Moral, Political and Literary (1742–1754)*, 75–80. Indianapolis, IN: Liberty Fund.

Husserl, E. 1954. *The Crisis of European Sciences and Transcendental Phenomenology*. First published 1937. Evanston, IL: Northwestern University Press.

Huxley, A. 1932. *Brave New World*. London: Chatto & Windus.

Huxley, T. H. 1893. "Evolution and Ethics". Romanes Lecture, Sheldonian Theatre, Oxford (18 May), http://aleph0.clarku.edu/huxley/CE9/E-E.html (accessed 24 May 2014).

InterAcademy Panel 2006. "Statement on the Teaching of Evolution", 21 June, www.interacademies.net/10878/13901.aspx (accessed 24 May 2014).

Isaac, J. 2011. *Working Knowledge: Making the Human Sciences from Parsons to Kuhn*. Cambridge, MA: Harvard University Press.

Jacob, F. 1977. "Evolution and Tinkering". *Science* 196(4295): 1161–66.

Jacquette, D. (ed.) 2004. *The Cambridge Companion to Brentano*. Cambridge: Cambridge University Press.

James, W. 1884. "On Some Omissions of Introspective Psychology". *Mind* 9: 1–26.

——1960. *The Will to Believe, Human Immortality and Other Essays in Popular Philosophy*. First published 1896. New York: Dover.

——1977. *Essays in Radical Empiricism*. First published 1912. Cambridge, MA: Harvard University Press.

——1983. *The Principles of Psychology*. First published 1890. Cambridge, MA: Harvard University Press.

Jarvie, I. 2001. *The Republic of Science: The Emergence of Popper's Social View of Science*. Amsterdam: Rodopi.

Kadvany, J. 2001. *Imre Lakatos and the Guises of Reason*. Durham, NC: Duke University Press.

Kaiser, D. (ed.) 2005. *Pedagogy and the Practice of Science*. Cambridge, MA: MIT Press.

Kauffman, S. 1995. *At Home in the Universe: The Search for the Laws of Self-Organization and Complexity*. Oxford: Oxford University Press.

Keynes, J. M. 1921. *Treatise on Probability*. London: Macmillan.

King, R. G. 2002. "Mad Archive Disease: Archival Spongiform Encephalopathy, the Loss of Corporate Memory, and the Death of Institutional Archives". Paper delivered at the combined SSA/CIMA annual meeting, Flagstaff, AZ.

Kitcher, P. 1993. *The Advancement of Science*. Oxford: Oxford University Press.

——2001. *Science, Truth and Democracy*. Oxford: Oxford University Press.

——2002. "The Third Way: Reflections on Longino's *The Fate of Knowledge*". *Philosophy of Science* 69: 549–59.

——2007. *Living with Darwin*. Oxford: Oxford University Press.

Knight, D. 2004. *Science and Spirituality: The Volatile Connection*. London: Routledge.

Knobe, J. and S. Nichols (eds) 2008. *Experimental Philosophy*. Oxford: Oxford University Press.

292 Bibliography

Koehler, W. 1938. *The Place of Value in a World of Facts*. New York: Liveright.

Koerner, L. 1999. *Linnaeus: Nature and Nation*. Cambridge, MA: Harvard University Press.

Koestler, A. 1959. *The Sleepwalkers*. London: Hutchinson.

Kourany, J. 2003. "A Philosophy of Science for the 21st Century". *Philosophy of Science* 70: 1–14.

Koyre, A. 1968. *Metaphysics and Measurement*. Cambridge, MA: Harvard University Press.

Kripke, S. 1977. "Speaker's Reference and Semantic Reference". *Midwest Studies in Philosophy* 2: 255–76.

Kruglanski, A. 1989. *Lay Epistemics and Human Knowledge*. New York: Plenum Press.

Kubie, L. 1967. *Neurotic Distortion of the Creative Process*. New York: Farrar, Straus & Giroux.

Kuhn, T. 1957. *The Copernican Revolution*. Chicago, IL: University of Chicago Press.

——1970. *The Structure of Scientific Revolutions*, 2nd edn. First published 1962. Chicago, IL: University of Chicago Press.

——1977. *The Essential Tension*. Chicago, IL: University of Chicago Press.

Kurzweil, R. 1999. *The Age of Spiritual Machines*. New York: Viking.

Kusch, M. 1999. *Psychological Knowledge: A Social History and Philosophy*. London: Routledge.

Kusch, M. and P. Lipton (eds) 2002. *Studies in History and Philosophy of Science* 33: 209–423. Special issue on Testimony.

Lakatos, I. 1970. "Falsification and the Methodology of Scientific Research Programmes". See Lakatos and Musgrave (1970), 91–195.

——1978. *Methodology of Scientific Research Programmes*. Cambridge: Cambridge University Press.

——1981. "History of Science and Its Rational Reconstructions". In *Scientific Revolutions*, I. Hacking (ed.), 107–27. Oxford: Oxford University Press.

Lakatos, I. and A. Musgrave (eds) 1970. *Criticism and the Growth of Knowledge*. Cambridge: Cambridge University Press.

Langholm, O. 1998. *The Economic Legacy of Scholastic Thought: Antecedents of Choice and Power*. Cambridge: Cambridge University Press.

Latour, B. 1987. *Science in Action*. Milton Keynes: Open University Press.

——1988. *The Pasteurization of France*. Cambridge, MA: Harvard University Press.

——1993. *We Have Never Been Modern*. First published 1991. Cambridge, MA: Harvard University Press.

——1999. *Pandora's Hope*. Cambridge, MA: Harvard University Press.

——2004. "Why Has Critique Run Out of Steam? From Matters of Fact to Matters of Concern". *Critical Inquiry* 30: 225–48.

Latour, B. and S. Woolgar 1979. *Laboratory Life: The Social Construction of Scientific Facts*. London: Sage.

Laudan, L. 1981. *Science and Hypothesis*. Dordrecht: D. Reidel.

——1984. *Science and Values*. Berkeley, CA: University of California Press.

Leff, G. 1967. *Heresy in the Later Middle Ages*. 2 vols. Manchester: Manchester University Press.

Lehrer, J. 2010. "The Truth Wears Off". *The New Yorker* (13 December): 52–57.

Lepenies, W. 1988. *Between Literature and Science: The Rise of Sociology*. Cambridge: Cambridge University Press.

Lévi-Strauss, C. 1966. *The Savage Mind*. First published 1962. London: Weidenfeld & Nicolson.

Lindberg, D. 1982. "On the Applicability of Mathematics to Nature: Roger Bacon and His Predecessors". *British Journal for the History of Science* 15: 3–25.

Longino, H. 2002a. *The Fate of Knowledge*. Princeton, NJ: Princeton University Press.

——2002b. "Science and the Common Good: Reflections on Kitcher's *Science, Truth and Democracy*". *Philosophy of Science* 69: 560–68.

Löwith, K. 1949. *Meaning in History: The Theological Implications of Philosophy of History*. Chicago, IL: University of Chicago Press.

Lynch, M. 1994. *Scientific Practice and Ordinary Action: Ethnomethodology and Social Studies of Science*. Cambridge: Cambridge University Press.

Lynch, W. 2001. *Solomon's Child: Method in the Early Royal Society of London*. Palo Alto, CA: Stanford University Press.

Lyotard, J.-F. 1983. *The Postmodern Condition*. First published 1979. Minneapolis, MN: University of Minnesota Press.

Mach, E. 1960. *The Science of Mechanics: A Critical and Historical Account of Its Development*, 6th US edn (based on 9th German edn of 1933). First published 1883. LaSalle, IL: Open Court Press.

Machlup, F. 1978. *Methodology of Economics and Other Social Sciences*. New York: Academic Press.

MacIntyre, A. 1981. *After Virtue*. South Bend, IN: University of Notre Dame Press.

——1999. *Dependent Rational Animals*. LaSalle, IL: Open Court Press.

MacKenzie, D. 2006. *An Engine, Not a Camera: How Financial Models Shape Markets*. Cambridge, MA: MIT Press.

Mahoney, M. J. 2004. *Scientist as Subject: The Psychological Imperative*, 2nd edn. First published 1976. Clinton Corners, NY: Percheron Press.

Mannheim, K. 1936. *Ideology and Utopia*. First published 1929. New York: Harcourt Brace & World.

Manuel, F. 1963. *Isaac Newton, Historian*. Cambridge, MA: Harvard University Press.

Marcuse, H. 1964. *One-Dimensional Man*. Boston, MA: Beacon Press.

Maslow, A. 1966. *The Psychology of Science*. New York: Harper & Row.

——1998. *Maslow on Management*. New York: John Wiley & Sons.

Masuzawa, T. 2005. *The Invention of the World-Religions*. Chicago, IL: University of Chicago Press.

294 Bibliography

Mayoral, J. V. 2012. "Five Decades of *Structure*: A Retrospective View". *Theoria* 75: 261–80.

McCalman, I. and P. Pickering (eds) 2010. *Historical Re-enactment: From Realism to Affect*. London: Palgrave Macmillan.

McClelland, D. 1962. "On the Psychodynamics of Creative Physical Scientists". In *Contemporary Approaches to Creative Thinking*, H. Gruber, G. Terrel and M. Wertheimer (eds), 141–74. New York: Atherton.

McConkey, J. 2004. "Knowledge and Acknowledgement: 'Epistemic Injustice' as a Problem of Recognition". *Politics* 24(3): 198–205.

McGrath, A. 2011. *Darwinism and the Divine: Evolutionary Thought and Natural Theology*. Oxford: Wiley-Blackwell.

McNeely, I. and L. Wolverton. 2008. *Reinventing Knowledge: From Alexandria to the Internet*. New York: W. W. Norton.

Meehl, P. 1967. "Theory-Testing in Psychology and Physics: A Methodological Paradox". *Philosophy of Science* 34: 103–15.

Mendelsohn, E. 1989. "Robert K. Merton: The Celebration and Defense of Science". *Science in Context* 3: 269–99.

Merton, R. 1970. *Science, Technology and Society in Seventeenth Century England*. First published 1938. New York: Harper & Row.

——1977. *The Sociology of Science*. Chicago, IL: University of Chicago Press.

Meyer, S. 2009. *Signature in the Cell*. New York: HarperOne.

Micklethwait, J. and A. Wooldridge 2009. *God Is Back: How the Global Revival of Faith Is Changing the World*. London: Penguin.

Milbank, J. 1990. *Theology and Social Theory*. Oxford: Blackwell.

Mirowski, P. 1989. *More Heat than Light*. Cambridge: Cambridge University Press.

——2002. *Machine Dreams: How Economics Became a Cyborg Science*. Cambridge: Cambridge University Press.

Mitroff, I. 1974. *The Subjective Side of Science*. Amsterdam: Elsevier.

Moody, C. 2005. *The Republican War on Science*. New York: Basic Books.

Mulkay, M. and N. Gilbert 1981. "Putting Philosophy to Work: Karl Popper's Influence on Scientific Practice". *Philosophy of the Social Sciences* 11: 389–407.

Nadler, S. 2008. *The Best of All Possible Worlds*. New York: Farrar, Straus & Giroux.

Næss, A. 1965. "Science as Behavior". In *Scientific Psychology*, B. Wolman and E. Nagel (eds), 50–67. New York: Basic Books.

Nagel, T. 1986. *The View from Nowhere*. Oxford: Oxford University Press.

Needham, J. 1963. "Poverties and Triumphs of the Chinese Scientific Tradition". In *Scientific Change*, A. Crombie (ed.), 117–53. New York: Basic Books.

Neiman, S. 2002. *Evil in Modern Thought*. Princeton, NJ: Princeton University Press.

Newberg, A. 2010. *Principles of Neurotheology*. Farnham: Ashgate.

Noble, D. F. 1997. *The Religion of Technology: The Divinity of Man and the Spirit of Invention*. New York: Alfred Knopf.

Nozick, R. 1981. *Philosophical Explanations*. Cambridge, MA: Harvard University Press.

Numbers, R. 2006. *The Creationists: From Scientific Creationism to Intelligent Design*, 2nd edn. First published 1992. Cambridge, MA: Harvard University Press.

Nye, M. J. 2011. *Michael Polanyi and His Generation: Origins of the Social Construction of Science*. Chicago, IL: University of Chicago Press.

Offer, J. 2006. *An Intellectual History of British Social Policy: Idealism versus Non-Idealism*. Bristol: Policy Press.

Paley, W. 1802. *Natural Theology: or, Evidences of the Existence and Attributes of the Deity, Collected from the Appearances of Nature*. London: R. Faulder.

Parfit, D. 1984. *Reasons and Persons*. Oxford: Oxford University Press.

Passmore, J. 1951. *Ralph Cudworth*. Cambridge: Cambridge University Press.

——1966. *A Hundred Years of Philosophy*, 2nd edn. Harmondsworth: Penguin.

——1970. *The Perfectibility of Man*. London: Duckworth.

Pepper, S. 1942. *World Hypotheses: A Study in Evidence*. Berkeley, CA: University of California Press.

Petersen, A. 1984. "The Role of Problems and Problem Solving in Popper's Early Work on Psychology". *Philosophy of the Social Sciences* 14: 239–50.

Plehwe, D. and P. Mirowski (eds) 2009. *The Road from Mount Pelerin: The Making of the Neo-Liberal Thought Collective*. Cambridge, MA: Harvard University Press.

Polanyi, K. 1944. *The Great Transformation*. Boston, MA: Beacon Press.

Polanyi, M. 1957. *Personal Knowledge*. Chicago, IL: University of Chicago Press.

——1963. "Commentary by Michael Polanyi". First published 1961. In *Scientific Change*, A. Crombie (ed.), 375–80. London: Heinemann.

Popper, K. 1945. *The Open Society and Its Enemies*. 2 vols. New York: Harper & Row.

——1957. *The Poverty of Historicism*. New York: Harper & Row.

——1959. *The Logic of Scientific Discovery*. First published 1935. New York: Harper & Row.

——1963. *Conjectures and Refutations*. New York: Harper & Row.

——1972. *Objective Knowledge*. Oxford: Oxford University Press.

——1981. "The Rationality of Scientific Revolutions". In *Scientific Revolutions*, I. Hacking (ed.), 80–106. Oxford: Oxford University Press.

Price, D. de S. 1986. *Little Science, Big Science … and Beyond*, 2nd edn. First published 1963. New York: Columbia University Press.

Proctor, R. 1988. *Racial Hygiene*. Cambridge, MA: Harvard University Press.

——1991. *Value-Free Science?* Cambridge, MA: Harvard University Press.

——2000. *The Nazi War on Cancer*. Princeton, NJ: Princeton University Press.

Putnam, H. 1978. *Meaning and the Moral Sciences*. London: Routledge & Kegan Paul.

——1979. *Mind, Language and Reality*. Cambridge: Cambridge University Press.

Pyle, A. 2003. *Malebranche*. London: Routledge.

Quine, W. V. O. 1953. *From a Logical Point of View*. New York: Harper & Row.

Bibliography

——1960. *Word and Object*. Cambridge, MA: MIT Press.

——1969. *Ontological Relativity and Other Essays*. New York: Columbia University Press.

Quine, W. V. O. and J. S. Ullian 1970. *The Web of Belief*. New York: Random House.

Rabinbach, A. 1990. *The Human Motor: Energy, Fatigue, and the Origins of Modernity*. New York: HarperCollins.

Rasmussen, N. 1997. "The Mid-Century Biophysics Bubble: Hiroshima and the Biological Revolution in America, Revisited". *History of Science* 35: 245–91.

Ravetz, J. 1971. *Scientific Knowledge and Its Social Problems*. Oxford: Oxford University Press.

Reisch, G. 2005. *How the Cold War Transformed the Philosophy of Science*. Cambridge: Cambridge University Press.

——2012. "The Paranoid Style in American History of Science". *Theoria* 75: 323–42

Renwick, C. 2011. *British Sociology's Lost Biological Roots: A History of Futures Past*. London: Palgrave Macmillan.

Rescher, N. 1978. *Peirce's Philosophy of Science*. South Bend, IN: University of Notre Dame Press.

——1998. *Predicting the Future*. Albany, NY: SUNY Press.

——1999. *The Limits of Science*. Pittsburgh, PA: University of Pittsburgh Press.

Ringer, F. 1969. *The Decline of the German Mandarins*. Cambridge, MA: Harvard University Press.

Roco, M. and W. S. Bainbridge (eds) 2002. *Converging Technologies for Improving Human Performance: Nanotechnology, Biotechnology, Information Technology, and Cognitive Science*. Arlington, VA: US National Science Foundation.

Romanell, P. 1984. *John Locke and Medicine*. Buffalo, NY: Prometheus.

Rorty, R. 1979. *Philosophy and the Mirror of Nature*. Princeton, NJ: Princeton University Press.

Rose, H. and S. Rose 1999. "The Red Scientist". See Swann and Aprahamian (1999), 132–59.

Rosen, R. 1999. *Essays on Life Itself*. New York: Columbia University Press.

Ross, A. (ed.) 1996. *Science Wars*. Durham, NC: Duke University Press.

Rothschild, E. 2001. *Economic Sentiments: Adam Smith, Condorcet and the Enlightenment*. Cambridge, MA: Harvard University Press.

Rouse, J. 1987. *Knowledge and Power*. Ithaca, NY: Cornell University Press.

Runyan, W. M. 2006. "Psychobiography and the Psychology of Science". *Review of General Psychology* 10(2): 147–62.

Russell, B. 1912. *The Problems of Philosophy*. Oxford: Oxford University Press.

——1927. *An Outline of Philosophy*. London: George Allen & Unwin.

Safranski, R. 2000. *Martin Heidegger: Between Good and Evil*. Cambridge, MA: Harvard University Press.

Sassower, R. 1993. *Knowledge without Expertise: On the Status of Scientists*. Albany, NY: SUNY Press.

Bibliography   297

——1995. *Cultural Collisions: Postmodern Technoscience*. London: Routledge.

——2006. *Popper's Legacy: Rethinking Politics, Economics and Science*. Durham: Acumen.

Schaefer, W. (ed.) 1984. *Finalization in Science*. Dordrecht: Reidel.

Schilpp, P. A. (ed.) 1974. *The Philosophy of Karl Popper*, vol. 2. LaSalle, IL: Open Court Press.

Schmidt, J. (ed.) 1996. *What Is Enlightenment?: Eighteenth-Century Answers and Twentieth-Century Questions*. Berkeley, CA: University of California Press.

Schnädelbach, H. 1984. *Philosophy in Germany, 1831–1933*. Cambridge: Cambridge University Press.

Schneewind, J. 1997. *The Invention of Autonomy*. Cambridge: Cambridge University Press.

Schrödinger, E. 1955. *What Is Life? The Physical Aspects of the Living Cell*. First published 1944. Cambridge: Cambridge University Press.

Schumacher, E. F. 1973. *Small Is Beautiful*. London: Blond & Briggs.

Schumpeter, J. 1942. *Capitalism, Socialism and Democracy*. London: Allen & Unwin.

Schwartz, S. (ed.) 1977. *Naming, Necessity and Natural Kinds*. Ithaca, NY: Cornell University Press.

Segerstrale, U. 2000. *Defenders of the Truth*. Oxford: Oxford University Press.

Sellars, W. 1963. *Science, Perception and Reality*. London: Routledge & Kegan Paul.

Shadish, W. and S. Fuller (eds) 1994. *Social Psychology of Science*. New York: Guilford Press.

Shapin, S. 1988. "Understanding the Merton Thesis". *Isis* 79: 594–605.

——1992. "Discipline and Bounding: The History and Sociology of Science as Seen Through the Externalism–Internalism Debate". *History of Science* 30: 333–69.

——1994. *A Social Theory of Truth*. Chicago, IL: University of Chicago Press.

——2005. "Hyperprofessionalism and the Crisis of Readership in the History of Science". *Isis* 96: 238–43.

——2008. *The Scientific Life: A Moral History of a Late Modern Vocation*. Chicago, IL: University of Chicago Press.

Shapin, S. and S. Schaffer 1985. *Leviathan and the Air-Pump*. Princeton, NJ: Princeton University Press.

Sharrock, W. 1974. "On Owning Knowledge". In *Ethnomethodology*, R. Turner (ed.), 45–53. Harmondsworth: Penguin.

Sharrock, W. and I. Leudar 2002. "Indeterminacy in the Past?". *History of the Human Sciences* 15(3): 95–115.

Sharrock, W. and R. Read 2002. *Kuhn: Philosopher of Scientific Revolution*. Cambridge: Polity.

Shearmur, J. and P. Norris (eds) 2008. *After the Open Society: Selected Social and Political Writings*. London: Routledge.

298 Bibliography

Shera, J. 1983. "Librarianship and Information Science". In *The Study of Information: Interdisciplinary Messages*, F. Machlup and U. Mansfield (eds), 379–88. New York: John Wiley & Sons.

Siedentop, L. 2000. *Democracy in Europe*. London: Penguin.

Simon, H. A. 1977. *The Sciences of the Artificial*, 2nd edn. First published 1972. Cambridge, MA: MIT Press.

Simonton, D. K. 1988. *Scientific Genius: A Psychology of Science*. Cambridge: Cambridge University Press.

Singer, P. 1975. *Animal Liberation*. New York: Random House.

——1999. *A Darwinian Left*. London: Weidenfeld & Nicolson.

Skinner, B. F. 1948. *Walden Two*. Indianapolis, IN: Hackett.

Skinner, Q. 1969. "Meaning and Understanding in the History of Ideas". *History and Theory* 8(1): 3–53.

Smail, D. L. 2007. *Deep History and the Brain*. Berkeley, CA: University of California Press.

Smart, J. J. C. and B. Williams 1973. *Utilitarianism: For and Against*. Cambridge: Cambridge University Press.

Smith, B. 1994. *Austrian Philosophy: The Legacy of Franz Brentano*. LaSalle, IL: Open Court.

Smith, L. 1986. *Behaviorism and Logical Positivism: A Reassessment of the Alliance*. Palo Alto, CA: Stanford University Press.

Sober, E. 2008. *Evidence and Evolution*. Cambridge: Cambridge University Press.

Sohn-Rethel, A. 1977. *Intellectual and Manual Labour: A Critique of Epistemology*. Atlantic Highlands, NJ: Humanities Press.

Sokal, A. 1996. "Transgressing the Boundaries: Towards a Transformative Hermeneutics of Quantum Gravity". *Social Text* 46–47: 217–52.

——2008. *Beyond the Hoax: Science, Philosophy and Culture*. Oxford: Oxford University Press.

Sokal, A. and J. Bricmont 1998. *Fashionable Nonsense: Postmodern Intellectuals' Abuse of Science*. New York: Picador.

Southgate, C. 2008. *The Groaning of Creation: God, Evolution and the Problem of Evil*. London: Westminster John Knox Press.

Spengler, O. 1926–28. *The Decline of the West*, 2 vols. First published in German 1918–22. New York: Alfred E. Knopf.

Stanford, P. K. 2006. *Exceeding Our Grasp*. Oxford: Oxford University Press.

Stigler, S. 1986. "John Craig and the Probability of History: From the Death of Christ to the Birth of LaPlace". *Journal of the American Statistical Association* 81: 879–87.

Stokes, D. 1997. *Pasteur's Quadrant*. Washington, DC: Brookings Institution.

Sullivan, K. 2011. *The Inner Lives of the Medieval Inquisitors*. Chicago, IL: University of Chicago Press.

Suppe, F. (ed.) 1977. *The Structure of Scientific Theories*. Urbana, IL: University of Illinois Press.

Swann, B. and F. Aprahamian (eds) 1999. *J. D. Bernal: A Life in Science and Politics*. London: Verso.

Swanson, D. 1986. "Undiscovered Public Knowledge". *Library Quarterly* 56(2): 103–18.

Taleb, N. N. 2007. *The Black Swan: The Impact of Highly Improbable Events*. London: Allen Lane.

——2012. *Antifragile: How to Live in a World We Don't Understand*. London: Allen Lane.

Teilhard de Chardin, P. 1955. *The Phenomenon of Man*. New York: Harper & Row.

Ter Hark, M. 2009. "Popper's Theory of the Searchlight: A Historical Assessment of Its Significance". In *Rethinking Popper*, Z. Parusniková and R. Cohen (eds), 175–84. Dordrecht: Springer.

Tetlock, P. 2005. *Expert Political Judgement*. Princeton, NJ: Princeton University Press.

Tetlock, P. and A. Belkin (eds) 1996. *Counterfactual Thought Experiments in World Politics*. Princeton, NJ: Princeton University Press.

Thomasson, B. A. 2011. "Arguing from the Evidence: The Correct Approach to Intelligent Design's Challenge in the US Courts". *Philosophy of the Social Sciences* 41: 495–534.

Tolman, E. C. 1932. *Purposive Behavior in Animals and Men*. New York: Appleton-Century-Crofts.

Turner, S. 1994. "Making Scientific Knowledge a Social Psychological Problem". In *Social Psychology of Science*, W. Shadish and S. Fuller (eds), 345–51. New York: Guilford.

——2007. "Social Theory as Cognitive Neuroscience". *European Journal of Social Theory* 10: 357–74.

——2010. *Explaining the Normative*. Cambridge: Polity.

Tversky, A. and D. Kahneman 1974. "Judgment under Uncertainty: Heuristics and Biases". *Science* 185: 1124–31.

Tweney, R., M. Doherty and C. Mynatt (eds) 1981. *On Scientific Thinking*. New York: Columbia University Press.

Van Fraassen, B. 1980. *The Scientific Image*. Oxford: Oxford University Press.

Voegelin, E. 1952. *The New Science of Politics*. Chicago, IL: University of Chicago Press.

Von Bertalanffy, L. 1950. "An Outline of General System Theory". *British Journal for the Philosophy of Science* 1950(1): 134–65.

Wason, P. and P. Johnson-Laird 1972. *Psychology of Reasoning: Structure and Content*. Cambridge, MA: Harvard University Press.

Weber, M. 1958a. *The Protestant Ethic and the Spirit of Capitalism*. First published 1904. New York: Scribner's.

——1958b. "Science as a Vocation". First published 1918. In *From Max Weber*, H. Gerth and C. W. Mills (eds), 129–58. Oxford: Oxford University Press.

——1963. *The Sociology of Religion*. First published 1922. Boston, MA: Beacon Press.

Weingart, P. 1997. "From Finalization to Mode 2: Old Wine in New Bottles?". *Social Science Information* 36(4): 591–613.

Wernick, A. 2001. *Auguste Comte and the Religion of Humanity: The Post-Theistic Program of French Social Theory*. Cambridge: Cambridge University Press.

Werskey, G. 1988. *The Visible College: Scientists and Socialists in the 1930s*, 2nd edn. First published 1978. London: Free Association Press.

——2007. "The Marxist Critique of Capitalist Science: A History in Three Movements?". *Science as Culture* 16: 397–461.

Wertheimer, M. 1945. *Productive Thinking*. New York: Harper & Row

Wettersten, J. 1985. "The Road through Würzburg, Vienna and Göttingen". *Philosophy of the Social Sciences* 15: 487–505.

White, A. D. 1896. *A History of the Warfare of Science with Theology in Christendom*. New York: D. Appleton & Company.

White, H. 1972. *Metahistory*. Baltimore, MD: Johns Hopkins University Press.

Wiener, N. 1950. *The Human Use of Human Beings*. Boston, MA: Houghton Mifflin.

——1964. *God and Golem, Inc*. Cambridge, MA: MIT Press.

Will, F. 1988. *Beyond Deduction: Ampliative Aspects of Philosophical Reflection*. London: Routledge & Kegan Paul.

Wilson, E. O. 2007. *The Creation: An Appeal to Save Life on Earth*. New York: W. W. Norton.

Winter, A. 2011. *Memory: Fragments of a Modern History*. Chicago, IL: University of Chicago Press.

Wissner-Gross, A. D. and C. E. Freer 2013. "Causal Entropic Forces". *Physical Letters* 110: 168702.

Wolpert, L. 1992. *The Unnatural Nature of Science*. London: Faber & Faber.

Wootton, D. 2006. *Bad Medicine*. Oxford: Oxford University Press.

Wuthnow, R. 1989. *Communities of Discourse: Ideology and Social Structure in the Reformation, the Enlightenment, and European Socialism*. Cambridge, MA: Harvard University Press.

Yates, F. 1966. *The Art of Memory*. London: Routledge & Kegan Paul.

Zagzebski, L. 1996. *Virtues of the Mind*. Cambridge: Cambridge University Press.

Zea, L. 1963. *The Latin American Mind*. Norman, OK: University of Oklahoma Press.

Zijderveld, A. C. 2006. *Rickert's Relevance: The Ontological Nature and Epistemological Functions of Values*. Leiden: Brill.

Ziliak, S. T. and D. N. McCloskey 2008. *The Cult of Statistical Significance: How the Standard Error Costs Us Jobs, Justice, and Lives*. Ann Arbor, MI: University of Michigan Press.

Index

Adaptive preference formation. 11, 23, 29, 97

Adorno, Theodor (see also Frankfurt School). 13, 155

Aquinas, Thomas. 38, 44, 54, 84, 86, 88, 178, 250

Arius (Arian). 42, 48

Aristotle (Aristotelian). 10, 25–27, 38, 60, 124, 142–43, 182, 226, 229, 258, 252–53, 272

Augustine of Hippo (Augustinian). 3, 20–22, 34, 42, 213, 240

Authoritarianism. 54, 154–55, 267, 273

Bacon, Francis. 38, 58, 60, 67, 77–78, 103, 112, 132, 149, 156–57, 160, 170–71, 216, 233, 236

Bacon, Roger. 43, 218, 250–51, 255–60

Behaviourism. 104, 118–22, 259

Behe, Michael. 75, 79–80, 88

Bernal, J.D. 185, 196–202, 207

Bloor, David. 29, 191, 275

Blumenberg, Hans. 46, 56–57, 112

Bonaventure. 41, 45, 73–74, 250

Brentano, Franz. 26–27, 108–9

Campbell, Donald. 33, 103, 111, 114–16, 119, 128

Carnap, Rudolf. 140, 148, 191

Chisholm, Roderick. 11–12, 108

Chomsky, Noam. 229

Clifford, W.K. 28–29, 32, 38

Collingwood, Robin. 252

Collins, Harry. 189–91, 206, 256

Collins, Randall. 10, 36–37, 56, 102, 172, 179

Comte, Auguste (Comtean). 5, 10, 14, 36, 54–56, 58, 107, 145, 159, 216, 242, 261

Conant, James Bryant. 120, 130–32, 202, 205–6

Condorcet, Marquis de. 20, 107, 162

Counterfactuals. 13, 16, 138, 142–43, 165, 210–61, 273–74, 276, 278

Creationist Left (Left Creationism). 15–16, 45, 86–87, 89, 92–93, 96–98

Cudworth, Ralph. 8, 65

Darwin, Charles (Darwinian). 1–2, 10, 15, 35, 44, 48–49, 51, 61–64, 71–73, 76–83, 87, 89–93, 95–96, 99, 107, 113, 121–22, 128–29, 150, 152–53, 159, 169, 178, 193, 195, 197–98, 204, 210, 214, 223, 225, 253–55, 263, 266, 268, 274, 277

Dawkins, Richard. 65, 67, 72, 81–83, 129

Deism. 43, 77

Dembski, William. 70, 87

Dennett, Daniel. 2, 65, 212

Derrida, Jacques. 7, 14, 188, 265

Descartes, René (Cartesian). 4, 11, 19, 26, 46–47, 50, 75–76, 103, 179, 222, 226, 276

Determinism (see also Overdeterminism, Underdeterminism). 100, 208, 210–11, 213, 220, 224, 232, 236, 256

Dewey, John. 7, 61, 102, 121, 140, 154, 158, 194

Diderot, Denis. 12, 171, 179

Dilthey, Wilhelm. 252

Dobzhansky, Theodosius. 73, 153

Dominicans. 15, 25–26, 43–44, 53

Duhem, Pierre. 70, 78–79, 137, 160, 185–86, 193–95, 226

Duns Scotus, John (Scotist). 43–44, 88, 98, 110, 112, 213, 229, 232

Durkheim, Emile. 5, 54–55, 57, 59, 204

Egalitarianism. 122, 163, 185

Einstein, Albert. 36, 47, 56, 76, 91, 102–3, 106, 117, 119, 121, 132, 158, 170, 227, 231–32, 241, 245–46, 276

Elster, Jon. 23, 139, 236

Enlightenment. 27–28, 36–38, 45, 51, 55, 57, 68, 140, 171, 179–80, 206, 208, 212–14, 217–19, 222, 226, 249–50

302 Index

Epicurus (Epicurean). 25–26, 51, 62, 64, 69, 94, 166, 170–71, 210

Ethnomethodology. 156, 164, 187–88, 230, 259

Ferrier, James. 6–8, 34, 65, 110

Feuerbach, Ludwig. 37, 56, 69, 110

Feyerabend, Paul. 61, 136, 145–46, 159, 167, 185, 196, 223

Fichte, Johann von. 26, 55, 65, 182, 243

Finalization (in science). 21, 133, 185, 203–4, 219, 221

Fogel, Robert. 233–34, 238–42

Foucault, Michel (Foucaultian). 6–7, 188, 227, 269–70, 277

Frankfurt School (see also Adorno, Finalization, Habermas). 155, 185

Franciscans. 15, 25–26, 41, 43–46, 53, 62, 88, 98, 250, 258–59

Freud, Sigmund. 27, 108–9, 119, 121, 125–27, 162–63, 262

Free will. 84, 100, 213, 216, 221, 232, 240

Galileo. 10, 61, 160, 179, 226

Galton, Francis. 9, 128, 254

Gestalt Psychology. 34, 102–4, 109, 119, 148, 150, 161

Goldman, Alvin. 10–12, 21, 33

Gould, Stephen Jay. 44, 72, 81–83, 85, 99

Gouldner, Alvin. 13, 187

Grosseteste, Robert. 42–43

Habermas, Jürgen (Habermasian). 14, 21, 111, 133, 149, 155, 185, 203, 214, 219

Hayek, Friedrich. 38, 113, 155, 164, 207

Hegel, G.W.F. (Hegelian). 4–5, 7–10, 14, 36–37, 42, 47, 55–56, 60, 63, 65–66, 107, 146, 153, 182, 191–92, 196–97, 213–18, 221, 236, 242–43, 249, 256–57, 259, 270, 277

Heidegger, Martin (Heideggerian). 7, 13, 38, 109–10, 154

Hobbes, Thomas (Hobbesian). 45, 217–18, 222

Humanism (see also Transhumanism) 31, 43, 56, 90, 121, 127, 127, 175, 188, 190, 205, 252, 267, 269, 278

Hume, David (Humean). 1, 4, 11, 26–27, 32, 62–69, 112, 141, 160, 277

Humboldt, Wilhelm von (Humboldtian). 176, 179–80, 182

Husserl, Edmund. 13–14, 27, 108–9, 184

Huxley, Thomas Henry. 1, 64, 90–92, 122

Intelligent Design (ID). 8, 45–46, 48–50, 57, 60, 67, 71, 74–77, 80, 86–87, 89, 95, 137, 150, 254, 265, 274

James, William. 28–29, 32, 34, 38, 102, 111–12, 117–20, 130, 156, 205, 210–11, 213

Jaspers, Karl. 13

Jesus Christ. 41–42, 45, 73, 223, 253, 263

Kant, Immanuel (Kantian). 3–4, 10–11, 13, 25–27, 34–35, 45, 50, 55, 64, 76, 88, 90, 95, 99, 108–10, 112–13, 117, 157, 210, 212–14, 243, 249–50, 254, 276–77.

Keynes, John Maynard (Keynesian). 38, 63, 69, 113

Kitcher, Philip. 5, 10, 21, 181–84, 186–87, 192

Koyré, Alexandre. 61, 143

Kripke, Saul. 8, 161, 236–37

Kuhn, Thomas (Kuhnian). 5–6, 11, 21, 26, 32, 34–35, 56, 59, 63, 80, 107, 118, 120, 122–23, 130–51, 154, 157–58, 168–69, 171, 173–75, 178, 185, 191–94, 197–98, 202–6, 208, 219, 227, 244, 246, 250–51, 255–57, 273

Lakatos, Imre. 103, 130, 135–38, 144, 146, 167, 191, 194, 196, 227, 246, 248, 260, 275

Lamarck, Jean-Baptiste (Lamarckian). 65, 82, 147, 197–98, 223, 225, 260

Latour, Bruno. 5, 178, 180, 188–89, 191, 202–8, 243–46, 267

Laudan, Larry. 9, 68, 100, 103, 107–8, 146, 160, 185, 275

Left Creationism. See Creationist Left.

Leibniz, Gottfried von (Leibnizian). 23, 26–27, 30, 46–48, 50, 76, 92–93, 95, 100, 222, 276

Lewis, C.I. 34, 205

Lewis, David. 236–37, 242

Liberalism. 38, 53, 55, 59, 66, 110, 125, 127, 140, 154–55, 182, 185, 194, 199, 203–4, 208–9, 239, 269

Libertarianism. 85, 113, 126, 164, 212, 217

Locke, John (Lockean). 26–27, 64–65, 154, 167, 183, 211–13

Logical positivism. See Positivism

Longino, Helen. 185–86

Lotze, Hermann. 108–11, 127

Löwith, Karl. 56–57, 197, 259, 278

Lyotard, Jean-François. 180–81, 191

Mach, Ernst (Machian). 28, 38, 56, 137–38, 193–95, 221, 232–33

Machiavelli, Niccolo (Machiavellian). 5, 133, 217

MacIntyre, Alasdair. 50, 146, 207, 243, 247–49

Malebranche, Nicolas. 50, 75, 93, 100, 276

Malthus, Thomas (Malthusian). 48, 51, 82, 95–96, 240

Mannheim, Karl. 105, 248

Index   303

Marx, Karl (Marxist). 2, 4, 7, 9, 14, 36, 38, 43, 51, 56–59, 63, 69–70, 74, 82, 127–28, 133, 138, 178, 180, 182, 185, 188, 193, 196, 200–201, 207, 213, 217, 239, 259, 261, 269, 278
Maslow, Abraham (Maslovian). 119, 121–29
Merton, Robert. 30, 128, 169–72, 197, 199, 204
Mill, John Stuart. 36, 91, 233, 240, 253
Milton, John. 45

Natural Theology. 59, 62, 74, 76–77, 79, 83, 85–86, 112, 277
Naturalism. 2, 7, 29, 46, 49, 59–64, 69, 72, 78–79, 83–84, 108–9, 112, 114, 135, 147, 170, 177–78, 212, 214, 163, 275, 277
Neo-liberalism. See Liberalism.
Needham, Joseph. 222
Neurath, Otto. 128, 136, 159, 168, 193–95, 217
Newton, Isaac (Newtonian). 2, 36–37, 46–47, 49, 65, 67–68, 73, 76, 91–92, 94, 99–100, 103, 106, 113, 121–22, 125, 131–32, 138, 142, 146, 156, 169–71, 176–77, 179–80, 191, 211–12, 214, 217, 219–20, 222, 226, 232, 235–36, 253–55, 260, 276–77
Nietzsche, Friedrich (Nietzschean). 23, 121, 221, 257
Nozick, Robert. 126

Ockham, William of. 39, 44, 88
Optimism. 48, 51, 55, 92–97, 125, 169–70, 247–48, 250
Oresme, Nicole. 223, 225–28
Original Sin. 7, 84, 92, 97, 240
Otlet, Paul. 37, 136
Overdeterminsm (see also Determinism, Underdeterminism). 211, 213, 220–25, 227, 235, 247–48, 250, 276

Paley, William. 77, 95
Pareto, Vilfredo. 29–30, 59, 133, 171
Parsons, Talcott. 13
Paul of Tarsus (Pauline). 3, 41–43, 45, 63
Peirce, Charles Sanders (Peircean). 9, 21, 28, 103, 107–8, 110, 138, 149–50, 156
Pelagius (Pelagian). 42
Planck, Max. 21, 102, 106–7, 110, 120, 137, 203, 219, 221, 232
Plato (Platonist). 5, 7–8, 10, 25–27, 45, 60, 65, 101, 128, 137, 139, 144, 178, 182, 200, 217–19, 224, 229, 258, 262–63, 275
Polanyi, Michael. 123–24, 206–7, 229
Popper, Karl (Popperian). 5, 7, 9–10, 60, 63, 78, 83–84, 102–4, 106, 109, 117–18, 123–24, 130, 137–38, 140–50, 154–68, 179, 185, 191,

195, 201–2, 204, 207, 209, 213–15, 217, 226–27, 229, 243, 247–48, 250, 269, 278
Positivism. 5–6, 8, 11–12, 37, 43, 54, 58, 83, 103, 110, 118, 120–21, 128, 130, 136–37, 140–41, 155–56, 158–59, 168, 184, 194, 201, 214–15, 217, 236, 272, 274
Postmodernism. 1, 14, 16, 135, 154, 168, 178, 180–81, 200, 224, 249, 256–57, 262–78
Pragmatism. 4, 21, 34–35, 61, 103, 110, 156, 194, 206, 214
Precautionary principle. 28–29, 40, 91, 97, 123, 129, 166, 210, 273
Priestley, Joseph. 43, 68–69, 95, 100, 120
Proactionary principle. 29, 38, 40, 123, 129, 166, 210, 263, 269
Putnam, Hilary. 150, 153, 161, 181–82, 192

Quine, W.V.O. 2, 60–61, 78, 111–12, 118–20, 158, 185

Ravetz, Jerome. 185, 202
Rickert, Heinrich. 110
Rorty, Richard. 17, 154, 250
Rousseau, Jean-Jacques. 8
Russell, Bertrand. 12, 104, 118–20, 146, 155

Schopenhauer, Arthur. 92–94, 97
Schrödinger, Erwin. 47–48, 99, 153
Schumpeter, Joseph. 97
Science Wars. 188–90, 265–66, 268–69
Scientific Revolution. 11, 34, 43–45, 60, 62, 71, 87, 94, 98–99, 107, 130–31, 133, 138–39, 142, 144, 147, 149–50, 165–66, 169–71, 202, 221–23, 225–27, 235–37, 246
Science and Technology Studies (STS). 19, 105, 127, 135, 137, 151, 164, 177–78, 180–81, 183, 185, 187–92, 197, 199–200, 203–6, 208–9, 242–43, 261, 267
Sellars, Wilfrid. 14, 107
Simon, Herbert. 15, 48, 94, 103
Singer, Peter. 90–91
Skinner, B.F. 119, 216
Skinner, Quentin. 258
Smith, Adam. 12, 20, 188
Socialism. 20, 27, 70, 140, 164, 180, 219, 262
Socrates (Socratic). 108, 159, 178, 263
Spencer, Herbert. 36, 68, 122, 240, 261
Spengler, Oswald. 12
Spinoza, Baruch. 170
Stoicism (Stoic). 3, 25–26, 101
Strauss, Leo. 139, 209, 234, 258
STS. See Science and Technology Studies.
Swanson, Don. 10, 30–31, 33–35, 173–74

304 Index

Taleb, Nicholas. 23–25, 35, 129, 279
Theistic Evolution. 44, 88
Theodicy. 7–8, 15–16, 45–46, 48–52, 59, 74–76, 90, 93–96, 249–50, 265, 277
Tolman, Edward Chace. 118–21
Totalitarianism. 164, 197, 202
Transhumanism (see also Humanism). 4, 16, 48, 51, 86, 101, 197, 209, 263

Underdeterminism (see also Determinism, Overdeterminism). 211, 213, 220–25, 227, 235, 247–49, 276
Unitarianism. 43, 47–48, 95

Utilitarianism. 39, 50, 65, 69, 95, 232

Voltaire. 23

Weber, Max (Weberian). 13, 35, 38, 48, 51–53, 55–57, 59, 101, 110, 135, 145, 169, 172, 203–4, 248, 263
Whewell, William. 37, 77, 113, 137, 180, 244, 253
Wiener, Norbert. 48, 70, 146
Wittgenstein, Ludwig. 64, 143, 154, 164, 258
Würzburg School of Psychology. 102–4, 117, 161